English-Swahili-French Dictionary

Kiswahili-Kifaransa-Kiingereza

Français-Kiswahili-Anglais

first edition 2010

ISBN is 144997127X and
EAN-13 is 9781449971274

by A.H. Zemback

Contents

Subject	English	French	swahili
month	January	janvier	mwezi wa kwanza
month	February	février	mwezi wa pili
month	March	mars	mwezi wa tatu
month	April	avril	mwezi wa nne
month	May	mai	mwezi wa tano
month	June	juin	mwezi wa sita
month	July	juillet	mwezi wa saba
month	August	août	mwezi wa nane
month	September	septembre	mwezi wa tisa
month	October	octobre	mwezi wa kumi
month	November	novembre	mwezi wa kumi na moja
month	December	décembre	mwezi wa kumi na mbili
day of week	Sunday	dimanche	siku ya mungu (Jumapili)
day of week	Monday	lundi	siku ya kwanza (Jamatatu)
day of week	Tuesday	mardi	siku ya pili (Jumanne)
day of week	Wednesday	mercredi	siku ya tatu (Jumatano)
day of week	Thursday	jeudi	siku ya ine (Alhamisi)
day of week	Friday	vendredi	siku ya tano (Ijumaa)
day of week	Saturday	samedi	siku ya sita (Jumamosi)
numbers	0 (zero)	zéro	sifuri
numbers	1 one	un, une	moja
numbers	2 two	deux	mbili
numbers	3 three	trois	tatu
numbers	4 four	quatre	nne
numbers	5 five	cinq	tano
numbers	6 six	six	sita
numbers	7 seven	sept	saba
numbers	8 eight	huit	nane
numbers	9 nine	neuf	tisa (kenda)
numbers	10 ten	dix	kumi
numbers	11 eleven	onze	kumi na moja
numbers	12 twelve	douze	kumi na mbili
numbers	13 thirteen	treize	kumi na tatu
numbers	14 fourteen	quatorze	kumi na nne
numbers	15 fifteen	quinze	kumi na tano
numbers	16 sixteen	seize	kumi na sita

Subject	English	French	swahili
numbers	17 seventeen	dix-sept	kumi na saba
numbers	18 eighteen	dix-huit	kumi na nane
numbers	19 nineteen	dix-neuf	kumi na tisa
numbers	20 twenty	vingt	makumi mbili (ishirini)
numbers	21 twenty-one	vingt et un	ishirini na moja
numbers	30 thirty	trente	makumi tatu (thelathini)
numbers	31 thirty-one	trente et un	thelathini na moja
numbers	40 forty	quarante	makumi ine (arobaini)
numbers	50 fifty	cinquante	makumi tano (hamsini)
numbers	60 sixty	soixante	makumi sita (sitini)
numbers	70 seventy	soixante-dix	makumi saba (sabini)
numbers	71 seventy-one	soixante et onze	sabini na moja
numbers	72 seventy-two	soixante-douze	sabini na mbili
numbers	73 seventy-three	soixante-treize	sabini na tatu
numbers	74 seventy-four	soixante-quatorze	sabini na nne
numbers	75 seventy-five	soixante-quinze	sabini na tano
numbers	76 seventy-six	soixante-seize	sabini na sita
numbers	77 seventy-seven	soixante-dix-sept	sabini na saba
numbers	78 seventy-eight	soixante-dix-huit	sabini na nane
numbers	79 seventy-nine	soixante-dix-neuf	sabini na kenda
numbers	80 eighty	quatre-vingts	makumi nane (themanini)
numbers	81 eighty-one	quatre-vingt-un	themanini na moja
numbers	82 eighty-two	quatre-vingt-deux	themanini na mbili
numbers	90 ninety	quatre-vingt-dix	makumi tisa (tisini)
numbers	91 ninety-one	quatre-vingt-onze	tisini na moja
numbers	92 ninety-two	quatre-vingt-douze	tisini na mbili
numbers	100 one hundred	cent	mia moja
numbers	200 two hundred	deux cents	mia mbili
numbers	300 three hundred	trois cents	mia tatu
numbers	400 four hundred	quatre cents	mia nne
numbers	500 five hundred	cinq cents	mia tano
numbers	600 six hundred	six cents	mia sita
numbers	700 seven hundred	sept cents	mia saba
numbers	800 eight hundred	huit cents	mia nane
numbers	900 nine hundred	neuf cents	mia kenda
numbers	1000 one thousand	mille	elfu
numbers	1500 one thousand five hundred	mille cinq cents	elfu moja mia tano
numbers	2000 two thousand	deux mille	elfu mbili
numbers	2500 two thousand five hundred	deux mille cinq cents	elfu mbili mia tano

Subject	English	French	swahili
numbers	5000 five thousand	cinq mille	elfu tano
time	When is the meeting?	À quelle heure est la réunion?	Mkutano ni saa gapi?
time	What time does this plane leave?	À quelle heure parti cet avion?	Ndege hili litaondoka saa ngapi?
time	What time is it?	Quelle heure est-il?	Ni saa ngapi?
time	At what time?	À quelle heure?	Saa ngapi?
time	At 8p.m. (this evening)	À huit heures (du soir).	Saa mbili usiku.
time	At noon.	À midi.	Saa sita mchana.
time	It is 9 a.m.	Il est neuf heures.	Ni saa tatu asubuhi.
time	It is 2:30 p.m.	Il est deux heures et demie (de l'après midi) ou quatorze heures.	Ni saa nane na nusu mchana.
time	It is 7:15 a.m.	Il est sept heures et quart.	Ni saa moja na robo asubuhi.
time	It is 10:45 a.m.	Il est dix heures moins le quart.	Ni saa tano kasarobo.
time	today	aujourd'hui	leo
time	tomorrow	demain	kesho
time	yesterday	hier	jana
time	soon	bientôt	karibu
time	now	maintenant	sasa
time	morning	matin	asubuhi
time	afternoon	après-midi	alasiri
time	evening	soir	jioni
time	night	nuit	usiku
time	last week	la semaine passée	juma jana
time	this week	cette semaine	wiki hii
time	next week	la semaine prochaine	juma kesho
time	last year	an passé	mwaka jana
time	this year	cet an	mwaka huu
time	next year	an prochain	mwaka kesho
greeting	Good morning.	Bonjour.	Subalkheri.
greeting	Good afternoon.	Bon après-midi.	Habari za mchana.
greeting	Sweet dreams.	Dormi bien.	Lala salama.
greeting	Good night.	Bonsoir.	Usiku mwema.
greeting	Hello! (when it has been a while)	Bonjour!	Jambo! or Habari!
greeting	Hello to you.	Et vous, bonjour.	Jambo sana.
greeting	madam	madame	bibi
greeting	sir	monsieur	bwana

Subject	English	French	swahili
greeting	How are you?	Comment ça va?	Hujambo? (singular); Hamjambo? (plural
greeting	How are you? ("news what?")	Comment ça va?	Habari gani?
greeting	All is well.	Très bien.	Habari nzuri.
greeting	I am fine.	Ça va bien.	Sijambo.
greeting	We are fine.	Nous sommes bien portants.	Hatujambo.
greeting	How are you doing?	Comment fait-tu?	Tutafanya nini?
greeting	What's up?	Qu'est-ce qu'il y a?	Vipi?
greeting	I'm fine.	Ça va bien.	Sijambo.
greeting	Please.	S'il vous plaît.	Tafadhali.
greeting	Thank you.	Merci.	Asante.
greeting	Thank you very much.	Merci beaucoup.	Asante shida.
greeting	Good evening.	Bonsoir.	Masalkheri.
greeting	See you tomorrow.	À demain.	Tutaonana kesho.
greeting	See you next time/ soon.	À bientôt.	Tutaonana.
greeting	Good bye.	Au revoir.	Kwa heri. (singular); Kwa herini. (plural)
greeting	yes	oui	ndiyo
greeting	no	non	hapana
greeting	Not at all!	Pas du tout!	Hata kidogo!
greeting	What is your name?	Comment vous appelez-vous?	Jina lako nani?
greeting	My name is...	Je m'appelle...	Jina langu ni...
greeting	Nice to meet you.	Enchanté de rencontrer avec toi.	Nafurahi kukufahamu.
greeting	Is anyone home?	Il y a quelqu'un à la maison?	Hodi?
greeting	Welcome.	Bienvenu.	Ingia.
greeting	Come on in!	Entrez donc!	Karibu! (singular); Karibuni! (plural)
greeting	Feel at home.	Faites comme chez vous.	Starehe.
greeting	Please sit down.	Veuillez vous asseoir.	Tafadhali, unataka kukaa.
greeting	Would you like a fanta; cold or warm?	Voudrez-vous le fanta, froid ou chaud?	Unataka fanta; baridi au ya joto?
greeting	The restroom is over there.	La toilette est là bas.	Ni choo kiko iko hapo.
greeting	I'm pleased to meet you.	Enchanté.	Nafurahi kukufahamu.

7

Subject	English	French	swahili
greeting	Have a good day.	Ayez la bonne journée	Muchana muzuli.
greeting	Have a good evening.	Ayez la bonne soirée.	Magalibi mzuli.
greeting	Have a good night.	Ayez la bonne nuit.	Usiku muzuli.
greeting	Have a good trip.	Ayez la bon voyage.	Safari njema.
greeting	Excuse me.	Pardonne moi.	Samahani.
conversation	What is your profession?	Quelle est ton (votre) profession?	Unafanya kazi gani?
conversation	How is your family?	Comment est votre famille?	Habari za nyumbani?
conversation	No problem.	Pas de problème.	Hamna shida.
conversation	I work for (at)...	Je travaille pour...	Nafanya kazi kwenye...
conversation	I speak a little Swahili.	Je parle un peu le kiswahili.	Nasema kidogo Kiswahili.
conversation	I'm trying.	J'essaye.	Ninajaribu.
	Do you understand?	Comprenez-vous?	Unasikia?
conversation	I don't understand.	Je ne comprends pas.	Sielewi.
conversation	I understand.	Je comprends.	Naelewa.
conversation	I don't know.	Je ne connais pas (or) Je ne sais pas.	Sikujua.
conversation	I know.	Je sais (or) Je connais.	Ninajua.
conversation	Sorry. (pity)	Pardonne.	Pole.
conversation	Sorry. (sympathy)	Désolé.	Pole na msiba wako.
conversation	Me, too.	Moi aussi.	Mimi pia.
conversation	Are you married?	Êtes-vous marié?	Umeoa? (male); Umeolewa (female)
conversation	I am married.	Je suis marié.	Nimeoa. (male); Nimeolewa. (female)
conversation	I am single.	Je suis célibataire.	Mima sina mpenzi.
conversation	Do you have children?	Est-ce que tu as des enfants?	Una watoto?
at the hotel	I want a room with two beds for one night.	Je veux une chambre à deux lit pour une nuit.	Nataka chumba kwa vitanda viwili kwa moja siku.
at the hotel	How much is the room for one night?	Combien est-ce que ça coûte pour une nuit?	Ni bei gani kwa siku?
at the hotel	Does the cost of the room include breakfast?	Le petit déjeuner est-il compris?	Inazingati chakula cha asubuhi.
at the hotel	Is there an internet cafe nearby?	Y a-t-il le cybercafé près?	Intanet Kafe iko wapi?

Subject	English	French	swahili
at the market	I am going to the grocery store.	Je vais au magasin des provisions.	Naenda duka lenye vitu mbalimbali.
at the market	I am looking for...	Je veux...	Nataka...
at the market	Do you have...	Avez-vous...	Una...
at the market	How much does this cost?	Combien est ceci?	Ni bei gani?
at the market	That is too expensive (service)	C'est trop cher.	Ni ghali mno.
at the market	I will not pay that much.	Je ne paye pas ce prix.	Punguza bei, tafadhali.
at the market	I don't have money.	Je n'ai pas de l'argent.	Sina hela.
at the market	I want 2 kilos of...	J'ai besoin deux kilos...	Nataka kilo mbili...
at the market	Where can I buy fabric?	Ou peux-je acheter le tissu?	Naweza kununua nguo wapi?
at the market	I need a mosquito net.	J'ai besoin un filet de moustique.	Naomba chandarua afadhali.
at the market	I want this.	J'ai besoin de ce-ci.	Nataka hicho.
drinks	drink (pl. drinks)	boisson	kinyweo (pl. vinyweo)
drinks	drinking milk	lait frais	maziwa
drinks	water	l'eau	maji
drinks	cold water	l'eau froid	maji ya baridi
drinks	beer	bière	bia (pombe: local beer)
drinks	tea	thé	chai
drinks	coffee	café	kahawa
drinks	fruit juice	jus de fruit	maji ya matunda
food	food	nourriture	maakuli mema
food	fruit	fruit	tunda (pl. matunda)
food	vegetable	légume	mgoba
food	avocado	avocat	embe mafuta
food	banana	banane	ndizi
food	bean	haricot	haragwe (pl. maharagwe)
food	bread	pain	mkate (pl. mikate)
food	butter	beurre	siagi
food	cabbage	chou	kabichi
food	carrot	carotte	karoti
food	cassava	manioc	muhogo (pl. mihogo)
food	chicken	poulet	kinda la kuku
food	clove	girofle	karafuu
food	corn	maïs	mhindi (pl. mihindi)
food	egg	œuf	yai (pl. mayai)
food	fish	poisson	samaki

Subject	English	French	swahili
food	garlic	ail	kitunguu saumu
food	goat	chèvre	mbuzi
food	hot chili	piment	pilipili
food	meat	viande	nyama
food	onion	oignon	kitunguu (pl. vitunguu)
food	passionfruit	maracuja	pasheni
food	pea, peas	petit pois	mbaazi (pl. mibaazi)
food	pineapple	ananas	nanasi (pl. mananasi)
food	potato	pomme de terre	kiazi (pl. viazi)
food	sweet potato	patate douce	viazi vitamu
food	pumpkin	potiron	boga
food	rice	riz	mchele (pl. michele)
food	salt	sel	chumvi
food	sheep	mouton	kondoo
food	sorghum	sorgho	mtami (pl. mitami)
food	soup	soupe	mchuzi (pl. michuzi)
food	spinach	épinards	mchicha
food	sugar	sucre	sukari
food	tomato	tomate	nyanya
restaurant	I do not want the smoking section!	Je n'ai pas besoin la section de fumer!	Sitaka eneo kwa kuvuta sigara!
restaurant	Is the internet available here?	Il y a internet disponible ici?	Naombo kutimia intaneti?
restaurant	We need a table for four.	Nous avons besoin un table pour quatre.	Nataka kuhfadhi meza kwa wanne.
restaurant	How long will the wait be?	Combien de temps j'attends pour un table?	Inabidi kusubiri kwa muda gani?
restaurant	Where is the restroom?	Où est les toilettes?	Vyoo viko wapi?
restaurant	May I have a menu?	Est-ce que je pourrais avoir le menu, s'il vous plaît?	Nataka menyu?
restaurant	I would like a cold fanta.	J'ai besoin de fanta froid.	Nipi fanta ya baridi.
restaurant	I would like a bottle of water.	J'ai besoin une bouteille d'eau.	Nipi kwenye chupa maji.
restaurant	I would like rice, beans and goat meat.	J'ai besoin le riz, les haricots, et la viande de chèvre.	Nipi wali, maharagwe, na nyama mbuzi.
restaurant	What does this mean in english?	Qu'est-ce que ce-ci veut dire en anglais?	Neno hii lina maana gani kwa Kiingereza?

Subject	English	French	swahili
restaurant	Enjoy your meal!	Bon appétit!	Karibu chakula!
restaurant	The food is good.	Aliment, repas est bon.	Chakula kitamu sana.
restaurant	Can we have the bill?	La facture, s'il vous plaît?	Naomba risiti afadhali?
restaurant	Are you thirsty?	Etes-vous soif?	Unasikia kiu?
restaurant	I am not thirsty.	Je n'ai pas soif.	Sisikii kiu.
restaurant	I am thirsty.	J'ai soif.	Nasikia kiu.
restaurant	Are you hungry?	Avez-vous faim?	Unasikia njaa?
restaurant	I am not hungry.	J'ai ne pas faim.	Sisikii njaa.
restaurant	I am full.	Je suis rassasié.	Nimeshiba.
restaurant	I am hungry.	J'ai faim.	Nina njaa.
restaurant	I would like more...	J'ai besoin en plus...	Nataka zaidi...
restaurant	a little, slowly	lentement	kidogo tu
restaurant	a lot	beaucoup	kingi
restaurant	I would like cold tea.	J'ai besoin le thé froid.	Nataka chai ya baridi.
restaurant	I would like hot tea.	J'ai besoin le thé chaud.	Nataka chai ya moto.
money	money	argent	pesa
money	Where is the currency exchange?	Où puis-je changer de l'argent?	Foreks Iko wapi?
money	I would like to exchange money.	J'ai besoin changer de l'argent.	Nataka kubadilisha hela.
money	Where is the bank?	Où est la banque?	Banki iko wapi?
people	man	homme	mwanamume
people	woman	femme	mwanamke
people	girl	fille	msichana
people	boy	garçon	mvulana
people	I would like to introduce...	Permettez-moi de vous présenter...	Huyu ni...
people	my friend	mon amie	rafiki yangu
people	family	famille	familia
people	my mama	ma mère	mamangu
people	your mother	ta mère	mamako
people	his/her mother	sa mère	mamake
people	my papa	mon père	babangu
people	your father	ton père	babako
people	his/her father	son père	babake
people	my wife	mon épouse	mke wangu
people	my husband	mon époux	mume wangu
people	sister	sœur	dada
people	brother	frère	ndugu

Subject	English	French	swahili
people	my child	mon enfant	mwana wangu
people	my children	mes enfants	wana wangu
people	your child	ton enfant	mwana wako
people	his/her child	son enfant	mwana wake
expressions	What did he say?	Que dit-il?	Alisema nini?
expressions	Why?	Pourquoi?	Kwa nini?
expressions	Who?	Qui?	Nani?
expressions	When?	Quand?	Wakati gani?
expressions	What is this?	Qu'est-ce que c'est?	Hapa ni gani?
expressions	Where is...?	Où est...?	...iko wapi?
expressions	but	mais	lakini
expressions	or	ou	au
expressions	both	tous les deux	vyote viwili
expressions	because	parce que	kwani
expressions	very	très	kabisa
expressions	and	et	na
expressions	also	aussi	pia
expressions	always	toujours	daima
expressions	never	jamais	kamwe
expressions	I am...	Je suis...	Mimi...
expressions	I want...	Je voudrais..., Je veux...	Nataka...
expressions	I do not want..	Je ne veux pas...	Sitaka...
expressions	I need...	J'ai besoin...	Nahitaji...
expressions	I have...	J'ai...	Nina...
expressions	I don't have...	Je n'ai pas...	Sina...
expressions	I like...	J'aime...	Ninapenda...
expressions	I do not like...	Je n'aime pas...	Sipendi...
expressions	It is true!	C'est vrai!	Kweli!
expressions	Where is the bathroom?	Où est la salle de bain?	Choo kiko wapi?
expressions	Bless you.	À tes souhaits.	Heri zote.
expressions	It is good.	C'est bien.	Nzuri kabisa.
expressions	What are you saying?	Qu'est-ce que vous dites?	Uko nasema nini?
expressions	Talk slowly please.	Dis lentement s'il vous plaît.	Tafadhali, sema pole pole.
expressions	What are you doing?	Qu'est-ce que vous faites?	Unafanya nini?
expressions	Who are you looking for?	Qu'est-ce qui tu cherches?	Unatafuta nini?
expressions	No one.	Personne.	Hapana mtu.
expressions	This is difficult.	C'est difficile.	Ni viguma.

Subject	English	French	swahili
expressions	This is easy.	C'est facile.	Ni rahisi.
expressions	I love...	J'aime de...	Napenda...
expressions	I am tired.	Je suis fatigué.	Nasikia hafifu.
expressions	I am happy.	Je suis heureux.	Nasikia furaha.
expressions	Are you happy?	Êtes-vous heureux?	Unasikia furaha?
expressions	Happy birthday.	Joyeux anniversaire.	Heri za siku kuu ya kuzaliwa.
Getting there	Where can I find a taxi?	Où peux-je trouver un taxi?	Nataka tekse?
Getting there	Where can I find a bus?	Où peux-je trouver le bus?	Matatu iko wapi?
Getting there	I do not want to ride a motorcycle.	Je n'ai pas besoin de faire du tour de moto.	Sitaka kukaa pikipiki yako.
Getting there	Does this bus go to...?	Ce bus va à...?	Hii hi basi kwenda...?
Getting there	When is the next bus to...?	Quand est le bus prochain à...?	Basi ijayo itaondoka lini...?
Getting there	How much is the fare to...?	Combien est le prix de billet à...?	Ni bei gani...?
Getting there	Where is this bus going?	Que est-ce que la destination pour ce bus?	Basi itaenda iko wapi?
Getting there	I need a map of...	J'ai besoin le carte de...	Nataka ramani kwa...
Getting there	I want to go to this address...	J'ai besoin aller cette l'adresse...	Tafadhali niendeshe mpaka anwani hii...
Getting there	Where are you going?	Où allez-vous?	Unakwenda wapi?
Getting there	Where are you coming from?	Où viens-tu?	Umetoka wapi?
Getting there	Where do you live?	Où habitez-vous?	Unatoka wapi?
Getting there	I live... (I am from)	J'habite...	Natoka...
Getting there	I want to go.	Je veux aller.	Nataka kwenda.
Getting there	Where is...?	Où est...?	...iko wapi?
Getting there	Is it close?	C'est près?	Ni karibu?
Getting there	Is it far?	C'est loin?	Ni mbali?
Getting there	Go straight.	Avancer.	Moja kwa moja.
Getting there	Left.	A gauche.	Kushoto.
Getting there	Right.	A droite.	Kulia.
Getting there	It is there.	C'est là bas.	Iko hapo.
Getting there	Stop!	Arrêtez!	Basi!
Getting there	Wait!	Attendre!	Suburi hapa!
Getting there	I am lost.	Je me suis égaré.	Nimejipotea.
Getting there	Where can I buy a bicycle?	Où je peux acheter un vélo?	Nataka kukodisha baisikeli.

Subject	English	French	swahili
Getting there	Where can I rent a car?	Où je peux louer une voiture?	Naweza kukondi gari wapi?
Getting there	I want to go to the airport.	J'ai besoin d'aller à l'aéroport.	Nataka kwenda kwenye uwanja wa ndege.
Getting there	I am going to...	J'ai vais...	Naenda...
tourism	Where is the travel agency?	Oû est l'agence de voyages?	Uwakala wa safari kiko wapi?
tourism	I want to go to...	J'ai besoin d'aller à...	Nataka kwenda...
tourism	I would like a guide who speaks english.	J'ai besoin le guide qui parle l'anglais.	Nahitaji kiongozi anayesema Kiingereza.
tourism	How do I get there?	Comment est-ce qu'on là bas?	Nifikaje?
tourism	Do you have information on...	Pourriez-vous me renseigner sur...	Mna maarifa kuhusu...
tourism	How much does it cost to see...	Combien de l'argent pour à visiter...	Ni bei gani kwenda...
tourism	Is there a guided tour...?	Il y a un voyage organisé à...?	Kuna safari kwa miguu kwenye viongozi...?
tourism	Please stop the car, I want to take a picture.	S'il vous plaît, arrête la voiture, j'ai besoin prendre la photo.	Tafadhali simama hapa, nataka nikipiga picha.
medical phrases	I am sick.	Je suis malade.	Mimi ni mgonjwa.
medical phrases	I need a nurse right away.	J'ai besoin une infirmière tout de suite.	Nahitaji mwuguzi sasa.
medical phrases	Take me to the hospital.	Emmenez-moi à l'hôpital.	Niendeshe mpaka hospitali.
medical phrases	I've got a headache.	J'ai mal à la tête.	Nina maumiva ya kichwa.
medical phrases	I've have a stomach ache.	J'ai mal au ventre.	Tumbo yangu inauma.
medical phrases	Here is a prescription for my medicine.	Voici une ordonnance de mon médecin.	Nina agizo la daktari.
medical phrases	I want something to treat diarrhea.	J'ai besoin de quelque chose contre la diarrhée.	Nahitaji dawa kwa kuhara.
medical phrases	Where is the pharmacy?	Où est la pharmacie?	Duka la madawa hapo karibuni iko wapi?
medical phrases	Do you have any cipro?	Avez-vous cipro?	Mna cipro?
medical phrases	Can you stop the bus, I think I need to vomit.	Pouvez-vous arrête le bus, j'ai besoin de vomir?	Tafadhali simama hapa, nataka kutapika.

parts of speech	english	swahili	french
adj.	a lot	-inga	beaucoup
verb	abandon, to	kuacha	abandonner
verb	abate, to	kupungua, kupunguza	s'apaiser
verb	abbreviate, to	kufupisha	abréger
n.	abdomen	tumbo (pl. matumbo)	abdomen (m)
verb	abduct, to	kutorosha	enlever
verb	abide by, to	kushika	se conformer à
n.	ability, (to have)	akili, ustadi, uwezo	capable
verb	able, to be	kuweza	pouvoir
adv.	aboard	melini, chomboni	a' bord de
adv.	about (approximately); news	habari za, yapata	à peu près, environ
adv.	about to, to be	tayari	être sur le point de
adv.	above	juu (ya)	ci-dessus, sur
adv.	above; on top of	juu ya	au-dessus de, sur
n.	abrasion	chubuko (pl. machubuko)	écorchure (f)
verb	abridge, to; abbreviate, to	kufupisha	abréger
n.	abscess	jipu (pl. majipu)	abcès (m)
n.	absence	ughaibu	absence (f)
verb	absent, to be	kutokuwapo	s'absenter
adj.	absent-minded	-sahaulifu	distrait
adv.	absolutely	kabisa	absolument, tout à fait
interj.	Absolutely not!	Hasha!	Absolument pas!
verb	absorb, to	kunywa	absorber
verb	abstain, to	kujinyima	s'abstenir de,
n.	abundance	ujazi, wingi	abondance (f)
adj.	abundant	sana, tele	abondant
verb	abuse, to (verbal)	kutumia vibaya, kutukana	s'insulter
verb	accelerate, to	kuhimiza	accélérer
verb	accept, to	kukubalia, kupokea	accepter
n.	access	njia ya kufikia	accès (m)
n.	accident	tukio (pl.matukio), ajali	accident (m)
verb	accommodate, to	mahali pa kukaa	loger
verb	accompany, to	kufuatana na, kusindikiza	accompagner
verb	accompany, to (part of the way)	kusindikiza	accompagner
verb	accomplish, to	kutimiza	accomplir
adv.	according to	kadiri ya	selon
adv.	accordingly	kwa hiyo	en conséquence
n.	account (finance)	hesabu, masimulizi	compte (m)

parts of speech	english	swahili	french
verb	accumulate, to	kuongezeka kwa kulimbikwa	accumuler
adj.	accurate	sahihi	exact
n.	accusation	mashtaka	accusation (f)
n.	accusation	shtaka (pl. mashtaka)	accusation (f)
verb	accuse, to	kushtaki	accuser
verb	accustomed, to be	kuzoea	accoutumé, être
n.	ache	maumivu	souffrance (f)
verb	ache, to	kuuma	faire mal
verb	achieve, to; finish, to	kufaulu	achever
n.	achievement	tendo bora, utimizo	exploit (m)
adj.	acid	-chungu, -kali	acide
verb	acknowledge, to	kukiri	reconnaître
n.	acquaintance	ujuzi maarifa, mtu umjuaye	connaissance (f)
verb	acquainted, to be	kujuana	connaître
verb	acquire, to	kujipatia	acquérir
prep.	across (valley)	toka upande mmoja mpaka upande wa pili	à travers
verb	act, to	kutenda, kuigiza hadithi	agir
n.	action	tendo (pl. matendo)	action (f)
n.	actor	mtenda (pl. watenda)	acteur (m)
adj.	adamant	-gumu	inflexible
verb	add up, to	kujumlisha	additionner
verb	address, to 1. letter 2. speech	1. kuandika anwani (2) kuhutubu	adresser
n., med	adenoids	tezi la nyuma ya pua	ganglion engorgé
adj.	adequate	-a kutosha	suffisant
verb	adhere, to	kuambatana, kushika	adhérer à
adj.	adjacent	-a kupakana	voisin
n.	adjustment	kulinganisha, kusawazisha	rajustement (m)
n.	administration	serkali, usimamizi	administration (f)
verb	admit, to (confess)	kukiri	admettre
verb	admit, to (into a place)	kuingiza	permettre (admit)
verb	adopt (child)	kupokea kama mwana	adopter
verb	adopt (habit)	kupokea na kufuata	choisir
verb	adore, to	kuabudu	adorer
n.	adultery	uasherati	adultère (m)
verb	adultery, to commit	kuzini	commettre l'adultère
verb	advance, to	kuenda au kuendesha mbele	avancer
n.	adversity	msiba	adversité (f)
n.	advice	shauri (pl. mashauri)	conseil (m)
verb	advise, to	kutoa shauri, kuonya	conseiller

16

parts of speech	english	swahili	french
n.	advocate	mteteaji	défenseur (m)
verb	aerate, to	kutia hewa ya	aérer une plantation
n.	affair	jambo (mambo)	affaire (f)
verb	affect	kugeuza, kujifanya	affecter
n.	affection	kipendo (pl. vipendo)	affection (f)
verb	afraid, to be	kuogopa	avoir peur de
n.	African continent	nchi ya Africa	continent africain (m)
adv.	after	baada ya, nyuma ya	après
n.	afternoon	alasiri, mangaribi	après-midi (m or f)
adv.	afterward	baadaye, halafu, kisha	ensuite
adv.	again	tena	de nouveau
adv.	again and again	mara kwa mara	maintes et maintes fois
n.	age (How old are you?)	umri, maisha, miaka (Una miaka mingapi?)	âge (m) (Quel âge avez-vous?)
n.	age, old	uzee	vieillesse (f)
verb	aggravate, to	kuudhi, kuongeza ubaya	aggraver
n.	aggression	shambilio	agression (f)
adj.	aghast, to be	kushikwa na fadhaa	atterré
adv.	ago, long	zamani sana	il y a longtemps
phrase	ago?, How long	Tangu lini?	Il y a combien de temps?
n.	agony	maumivu makali	angoisse (f)
verb	agree on, to	kukubali	convenir de
verb	agree, to	kupatana	d'accord, être
n.	agreement	mapatano	accord (m)
n.	agriculture	kilimo, ukulima	agriculture (f)
adv.	ahead	mbele	devant
phrase	aid, financial	msaada (pl. misaada)	secours financier
verb	aid, to	kusaidia	aider à
n., med	AIDS	ukimwi	sida (m)
verb	aim, to take	kupiga shabaha	braquer
n.	air	hewa	air (m)
n.	airplane	ndege	avion (m)
n.	alarm	mshtuko, kamsa	alarme (f)
n.	albinos	mazeru (pl.)	albinos (m,f)
n.	alcohol	kileo	alcool (m)
verb	alert, to be	kuwa macho	alerte, être
adv.	alias	jina la pili la kificho	alias
n.	alibi	dai la kuwapo mahali pengine	alibi (m)
verb	alienate, to	kufarakisha	aliéner
n.	alignment	msafa (pl. misafa)	alignement (m)

17

parts of speech	english	swahili	french
adj.	alike	-a kufanana	semblable
adj.	alive	hai, -zima	vivant
adv.	all the time	siku zote	tout le temps
adj.	all, everything	-ote	tout
n.	allegation	ushuhuda	allégation (f)
n.	allergy	mzio	allergie (f)
n.	alliance	mwungano	alliance (f)
n.	alligator	mamba wa (Amerika)	alligator (m)
verb	allocate, to	kugawanyia	allouer
verb	allow, to	kuruhusu	permettre (admit)
verb	allude, to	kutaja	faire allusion
adv.	almost	karibu	presque
adj.	alone	peke yake	seul
prep.	along	kwa mbele	le long de
adv.	alongside	kando	à côté de
adj.	aloof	mbali	distant
adv.	already	tayari	déjà
adv.	also, again	tena, pia	aussi, encore
adv.	also, too	tena	aussi
n.	altar	mazabahu	autel (m)
verb	alter, to	kubadili	modifier
n. & adj.	alternative	njia ya pili	choix (m); autre
conj.	although	ingawa	bien que
adv.	altogether	kabisa	en tout
adv.	always; everyday	sikuzote	toujours
verb	amass, to	kukusanya	amasser
verb	amaze, to	kushangaza	étonner
n.	ambassador	balozi (pl. malozi)	ambassadeur (m)
adj.	ambiguous	-enye maana mbili	ambigu
adj.	ambitious	-enye kutaka makuu	ambitieux
n.	ambulance	gari au namna ya machela ya kuchukulia wagonjwa	ambulance (f)
n.	ambush	oteo	embuscade (f)
verb	ambush, to	kuotea njiani	tendre une embuscade à
verb	ameliorate, to	kutengeneza	améliorer
verb	amend, to	kutengeneza ifae zaidi	amender
n.	amendment	matengenezo	amendement (m)
verb	amends, make	kuridhisha	faire amende honorable
n.	America, US of	nchi ya Amerika	États-Unis du Amérique (f)
prep.	among	katikati ya	parmi, entre
verb	amputate, to	kukata	amputer

18

parts of speech	english	swahili	french
verb	amuse, to	kuchekesha	amuser
n.	amusement	furaha	amusement (m)
n.	analogy	mfano (pl. mifano)	analogie (f)
n.	ancestor	mkale	ancêtre (m)
n.	anchor	nanga	ancre (f)
adj.	ancient	-a kale	ancien
conj.	and, also	na	et
n.	anecdote	hekaya	anecdote (f)
n.	anemia	upungufu wa damu	anémie (f)
n.	angel	malaika	ange (m)
n	anger	gazabu, kasirani	colère (f)
verb	angry, to get	kukasirika	fâcher, se
n.	anguish	huzuni kuu	angoisse (f)
n.	animal	mnyama (pl. wanyama)	animal (m)
n., med	ankle	kifundo cha muguu (pl, vifundo cha muguu)	cheville (f)
verb	annihilate, to	kuangamiza kabisa	anéantir
n.	anniversary	ukumbusho wa kila mwaka	anniversaire (m)
verb	announce, to	kutangaza	communiquer
n.	announcement	tangazo	annonce (f)
verb	annoy, to	kuudhi	ennuyer
verb	annul, to	kutangua	annuler
verb	anoint, to	kupaka mafuta	oindre
adj.	another (another man)	-ingine	un autre (m), une autre (f) (un autre homme)
n.	answer	jibu (pl. majibu)	réponse (f)
imper.	Answer!	Jibu!	Répondre!
verb	answer, to	kujiba	répondre
n.	ant	chungu	fourmi (f)
verb	antagonize	kufanya adui	provoquer
n.	antelope	paa	antilope (f)
adj.	anterior	-a kabla	antérieur
verb	anticipate, to	kutazamia mbele	prévoir
n.	anus	mkundu	anus (m)
n.	anxiety	hofu, fadhaa	anxiété (f)
verb	anxious, to be	kuhofu, kufadhaika	être anxieux
phrase	any time	wakati wo wote	n'importe quelle heure
pronoun	anybody (somebody)	ye yote	quelqu'un
phrase	anyhow	vyo vyote	n'importe comment
pronoun	anything (something)	cho chote	quelque chose
phrase	anywhere	po pote	n'importe où

parts of speech	english	swahili	french
adv.	**apart**	mbali	à part
n.	**ape**	nyani	singe (m)
verb	**apologize, to**	kuomba radhi	s'excuser de
n.	**apostle**	mtume (pl. mitume)	apôtre (m)
adj.	**apparent**	dhahiri	apparent
verb	**appeal, to**	kuomba	faire appeler
verb	**appear, to**	kutokea	paraître
verb	**appear, to**	kuonekana	apparaître
n.	**appearance**	tokeo	apparence (f)
n.	**appetite**	tamaa ya chakula	appétit (m)
verb	**applaud, to**	kupiga makofi	applaudir
n.	**apple**	tunda a kizungu	pomme (f)
n.	**application**	tendo la kutia	application (f)
phrase	**apply oneself, to**	kupeleka maombi kwa	s'appliquer
n.	**appointment**	mapatano ya kukutana	rendez-vous (m)
verb	**appreciate, to**	kuthamini	se rendre compte de
n.	**apprehension**	tendo la kukamatwa	appréhension (f)
adj.	**apprehensive**	-enye akili	appréhensif
n.	**apprentice**	mwanafunzi wa kazi	apprenti (m,f)
verb	**approach, to**	kukaribia	s'approcher de
z	**approval**	kibali	adoption
verb	**approve, to**	kukubali, kupokea	d'accord, être
n.	**approximation**	kisio	approximation (f)
n.	**April**	Aprili, mwezi wa nne wa mwaka wa kizungu	avril (m)
n.	**Arab**	Mwarabu	Arabe (m, f)
adj.	**arbitrary**	-geugeu	arbitraire
phrase	**Are you happy?**	Unasikia furaha?	Êtes-vous heureux?
phrase	**Are you hungry?**	Unasikia njaa?	Avez-vous faim?
n.	**area; surface**	eneo (pl. maeneo)	étendue (f)
verb	**argue, to**	kubishana	se disputer
n.	**argument (dispute)**	mabishano	dispute (f)
verb	**arise, to**	kuinuka	s'élever
n.	**arm**	mkono (pl. mikono)	bras (m)
n.	**armpit**	kwapa	aisselle (f)
n.	**army**	jeshi	armée (f)
verb	**around, to go**	kuzunguka	contourner
verb	**arrange, to (Put all these things in order.)**	kupanga, kutandika	arranger (Arrangez toutes ces choses.)
n.	**arrangement**	mupango, matengenezo	arrangement (m)
verb	**arrest, to**	kusimamisha	arrêter

parts of speech	english	swahili	french
verb	arrive, to	kufika	arriver
n.	arrow	mshale (pl. mishale)	flèche (f)
n.	artery	mshipa mkubwa wa damu	artère (f)
n.	artist	mstadi, (pl. wastadi)	artiste (m)
adv.	as	kama, -vyo, kwa sababu	comme
adv.	as well	pia	aussi
adv.	as well as	kama vile	ainsi que
verb	ascend, to	kupanda	monter
verb	ashamed of, to be	kuona haya	avoir honte
n.	ashes	majivu (pl.)	cendres (f)
verb	ask (question), to	kuuliza	demander à
verb	ask entrance, to	kupiga hodi	demande entrée
verb	ask for, to	kuomba	demander
n.	aspiration	tamaa	aspirée (f)
n.	assault	jeuri	armée en marche, tyrannie
verb	assemble, to	kukusanya	assembler
verb	assert, to	kukaza ukweli	affirmer
n.	assessment	kadiri ipasayo	évaluation (f)
verb	assign, to	kugawanyia	assigner
verb	assist, to	kusaidia	aider à
n.	assistant	msaidizi (pl. wasaidizi)	assistant (m), assistante (f)
n.	associate	mwenzi (pl. wenzi)	camarade (m,f)
n.	asthma	ugonjwa wa pumu	asthme (m)
verb	astonish, to	kushangaza	émerveiller
phrase	astounded, to be	kushangaa	stupéfier, être
verb	astray, to go	kupotea	s'égarer
prep.	at	penye, kwa	à
adv.	at first	kwanza	d'abord
adv.	at last	mwisho	enfin
n.	atheist	mkana Mungu	athée (m,f)
n.	atmosphere	hewa	atmosphère (f)
verb	atone, to	kupfanya upatanisho	expier
n.	atonement	malipo	expiation
n.	attack	mashambulio	attaque (f)
verb	attack, to	kushambulia	attaquer
verb	attain, to	kufikia	atteindre
verb	attempt, to	kujaribu	essayer
interj.	Attention!	Ange!	Écouter!
verb	attention, to pay	kuangalia	faire attention
verb	attest, to	kushuhudia	attester
n.	attic	1. chumba cha juu 2. ghala	grenier (m)

parts of speech	english	swahili	french
n.	attitudes	hali ya myo au mwili	tournure (f)
verb	attract, to	kuvuta	attirer
adj.	audacious	-jasiri	audacieux
verb	audit, to	kukagua hesabu	vérifier
verb	augment, to	kuongeza	augmenter
n.	August	Ogusti, mwezi wa nane wa mwaka wa kizungu	août
n.	aunt (father's sister)	shangazi (pl. mashangzi)	tante paternelle
n.	aunt (mother's sister)	mama mdogo	tante maternelle
n.	authority	amri, mamlaka	autorité (f)
n.	automobile	motakaa	automobile (f)
n.	autonomy	ihtiari	liberté (f)
verb	avenge, to	kulipiza kisasi	venger
n.	aversion	machukio	aversion (f)
verb	avoid, to	kuepuka	éviter
phrase	aware, to be	kufahamu	conscient, être
adj.,adv.	away	mahali pengine	absent
adj.	awful	-baya sana	affreux
adv.	awkward	-enye matata	délicat
n.	ax	shoka (pl. mashoka)	hache (f)
verb	babble, to	kupayuka	babiller
n.	baby (newborn)	mtoto muchanga	nouveau né
n.	bachelor	mtu asiyeoa	célibataire (m)
n., med	back (of a person)	mgongo	dos, (m)
n	backing (support)	msaada (pl. misaada)	soutien (m)
adv.	backwards	nyuma	en arrière
adj.	bad	-baya, -bovu	mauvais
adv.	badly	vibaya	méchamment
n.	badness	ubaya	méchanceté (f)
verb	baffle, to	kutatiza	déconcerter
n.	bag	mfuko (pl. mifuko)	sac (m)
n.	bait	chambo	leurre (m)
verb	bake, to	kuoka	faire cuire
verb	balance, to	kusawazisha	tenir en équilibre
n.	baldness	upaa	calvitie (f)
n.	ball	mpira (pl. mipira)	balle (m)
n.	bamboo	mwanzi (pl. mianzi)	bambou (m)
n	banana	ndizi	banane (f)
n.	bandage	kitambaa cha kufungia dawa	pansement (m)
verb	banish, to	kuhamisha	exiler

22

parts of speech	english	swahili	french
n.	bank (for money)	benki ya fedha	banque (f)
n.	bank of river	kando	bord relevé
n.	bankruptcy	ufilisi	faillite (f)
n.	baptism	ubatizo	baptême (m)
verb	baptize, to	kuabatiza	baptiser
n.	barber	kinyozi (pl. vinyozi)	barbier (m)
adj.	bare	-tupu	pelé
adv.	barely	kwa shida	à peine
n.	bargain	mapatano	marché (m)
verb	bargain, to	kupiga bei	marchander
n.	bark (tree)	gome	écorce (f)
verb	bark, to	kubweka	aboyer
n.	barley	shayiri	orge (f)
n.	barn	banda	grange (f)
verb	barter, to	kubadilishana	troquer
adj.	bashful	-enye haya	timide
n.	basin (wash)	bakuli	cuvette (f)
verb	bask (in the sun), to	kuota jua	se dorer
n.	basket	kitunga (pl. vitunga)	panier (m)
n.	basket, large	kapu (pl. makapu)	panier, grand
n.	bat	popo	chauve-souris (f)
n.	bath	chombo cha kuogea	bain (m)
verb	bathe, to (oneself)	kuoga	se baigner
n.	bathroom	choo	salle de bain (f)
n.	battle	pigano (pl. mapigano)	bataille (f)
n.	bay	ghuba	baie (f)
phrase	Be strong! (stay well)	Bakia vizuri!	Soie courage!
verb	be, to	kuwa	être
n.	beach	pwani	plage (f)
n.	bean	haragwe (pl. maharagwe)	haricot (m)
n.	bear (animal)	dubu	ours (m)
phrase	bear in mind, to	kukumbuka	se rappeler
verb	bear, to (child)	kuzaa	donner naissance à
n.	beard	ndevu (poil de barbe = udevu)	barbe (f)
verb	beat, to	kupiga	battre
adj.	beautiful	-zuri	beau (m), belle (f)
n.	beauty	uzuri	beauté (f)
conj.	because	kwa kuwa, kwa maana, kwa sababu	parce que
conj.	because	kwani, maana, kwa sababu	car

23

parts of speech	english	swahili	french
conj.	because of	kwa sababu hii	à cause de
verb	become, to	kuwa, kufaa	devenir
n.	bed	kitanda (pl. vitanda)	lit (m)
n.	bed sheet	shuka (pl. mashuka)	drap (m) de lit
verb	bed, to make a (with grass)	kutandika kitanda	faire un lit (de l'herbe)
n.	bee	nyuki	abeille (f)
n.	beehive (empty)	mzinga (pl. mizinga)	ruche (f)
n.	beer	pombe	bière (f)
verb	beer, to brew	kupika pombe	brasser de la bière
n.	beetle	nyenje	coléoptère (m)
adv.,prep	before	mbele ya, kabla ya	avant de (place) avant (time)
prep.	before	kabla	avant que
verb	befriend, to	kufadhili	donner son amitié à
verb	beg, to	kuomba	mendier
n.	beggar	mwombaji (pl. waombaji)	mendiant (m)
adv.	begin with, to	kwanza	d'abord
verb	begin, to	kuanza	débuter, commencer
n.	beginning	mwanzo (pl. mianzo)	1. début (m) 2. commencement (m)
verb	behave, to	kutenda	se conduire
n.	behavior	mwenendo (pl. mienendo)	conduite (f), comportement (m)
adv, n. prep.	behind	nyuma ya	derrière (m)
verb	behold, to; notice, to	kutazama	apercevoir
adj.	belated	chelea	tardif
n.	Belgium	Mbelgiji	Belgique (f)
n.	beliefs (confidence)	imani	confiance (f)
verb	believe, to	1. kusadiki 2. kuamini	croire
n.	bell	kengele	cloche (m)
n.	bell	njuga	grelot (m)
verb	belong to, to	kuwa mali yake	appartenir à
adv. prep.	below	chini ya	en bas (adv), au-dessous de (prep)
n.	belt	mshipi (pl. mishipi)	ceinture (f)
n.	bench	ubao wa kukalia	banc (m)
verb	bend over, to	kuinama	se pencher
verb	bend, to; to fold	kukunja	plier
adv. prep.	beneath, under	chini ya	sous
adj.	beneficial	-enye manufaa	salutaire

parts of speech	english	swahili	french
verb	beseech, to	kusihi	supplier
prep.	beside	kando ya, karibu na	à côté de
adj.	best	bora kabisa	meilleur
verb	bet, to	kubahatisha fedha	parier
verb	betray, to	kusaliti	trahir
adv.	better	afazali	mieux
verb	better (after illness) to be; to be improved physically	kupata nafuu, kuponya	guérir
prep.	between	katikati ya	entre
verb	beware, to	kujihadhari	prendre garde à
verb	bewilder, to	kutia wasiwasi	ahurir
verb	bewitch, to	kuloga	ensorceler
adv.	beyond	kupita	au delà
n.	Bible	Biblia	Bible (f)
n.	bicycle	baisikeli	bicyclette (f)
verb	bid farewell, to	kuaga	faire ses adieux à
adj.	big	-kubwa	grand
n., med	bile	nyongo	bile (f)
n., med	bilharzia (schistosomiasis)	kichocho	bilharzia
n.	bill	hesabu ya fedha	facture (f)
verb	bind, to	kufunga	lier
n.	bird (small)	ndege	oiseau (m)
n.	birth	uzazi	naissance (f)
verb	birth, to give	kuzaa	accoucher
n.	birthday	sikukuu ya kuzaliza	anniversaire (m)
verb	bite, to	kuuma	mordre
adj.	bitter	-chungu	amer
n.	bitterness	uchungu	amertume (f)
adj.	black	-eusi, -a giza	noir
n. & adj.	black (for person)	mweusi	Noir (m), Noire (f)
n.	black {color}	weusi	noir (m) {couleur}
n.	blackboard	ubao wa skuli	tableau noir (m)
n.	blackmail	mrungula	chantage (m)
n.	blacksmith	mhunzi	forgeron (m)
n., med	bladder	kibofu	vessie (f)
n.	blade (grass)	jani	brin (m)
n.	blade (knife)	ubaba	lame (f)
n.	blame	hatia	responsabilité (f)
verb	blame, to	kulaumu	rejeter la responsabilité
n.	blanket	balangiti	couverture (f)
verb	bleed, to	kutoka damu	saigner

parts of speech	english	swahili	french
verb	**blend, to**	kuchanganya	mélanger
phrase	**Bless you.**	Akuweke.	À tes souhaits.
verb	**bless, to**	kubariki	bénir
n.	**blessing**	baraka	bénédiction (f)
adj.	**blind**	-pofu	aveugle
n	**blind person**	kipofu (pl. vipofu)	personne aveugle
adv.	**blindly**	kipofu	aveuglément
n.	**blindness**	upofu	cécité (f)
verb	**blink, to**	kupepesa macho	cligner des yeux
verb	**block, to**	kuziba njia	boucher
n.	**blood**	damu	sang (m)
n., med	**blood vessel**	mushipa wa damu	vaisseau sanguin
verb	**blow a whistle, to**	kupiga filimbi	siffler avec un sifflet
verb	**blow, to**	kuvuma	souffler
adj.	**blue**	buluu, samawati	bleu, couleur
verb	**blush, to**	kugeuka rangi	rougir
n.	**board (plank)**	ubao (pl. mbao)	planche (f)
verb	**boast, to**	kujivuna	se vanter de
n.	**boasting**	majivuno	arrogance
n.	**boat**	chombo (pl. vyombo)	bateau (m)
n.	**body**	mwili (pl. miili)	corps (m)
n.	**bodyguard**	askari wafuasi	gardes du corps (m)
n., med	**boil (medical)**	jipu (pl. majipu)	furoncle (m)
verb	**boil, to**	kuchmuka, kutokosa	bouillir
n.	**boldness**	ujasiri	hardiesse (f)
n.	**bolt (of door)**	komeo	targette (f)
verb	**bolt, to**	kukomea	boulonner
n.	**bomb**	kombora	bombe (f)
n	**bonds**	kifungo	lien (m)
n.	**bone**	mfupa (pl. mifupa)	os (m)
n., med	**bone marrow**	uboho	moelle (des os)
n.	**bonus**	ziada	prime (f)
verb	**boo, to**	kuzomea	huer
n.	**book**	kitabu (pl. vitabu)	livre (m)
n.	**boot**	kiatu kirefu	botte (f)
n.	**boredom**	uchovu	ennui (m)
verb	**born, to be**	kuzaliwa	naître
verb	**borrow, to (money)**	kukopa	emprunter
n.	**boss**	msimamizi (pl. wasimamizi)	patron (m), patronne (f)

parts of speech	english	swahili	french
adj & pr	both	vyote viwili	tous (les) deux (m); toutes (les) deux (f)
n.	bottle	chupa (pl. machupa)	bouteille (f)
n.	bottle-opener	kifungua chupa	ouvre-bouteille (m)
n.	bottom	upande wa chini	fond (m)
verb	bounce, to	kuruka kama mpira	rebondir
n.	bow (as in arrow)	upinde (pl. pinde)	arc (m)
n.	bowl	bakuli	bol (m)
n.	box	sanduku (pl. masanduku)	boîte (f)
n.	boxer shorts (or slip)	chupi	caleçon (m)
n.	boy	mtoto wa kiume	garçon (m)
n.	boyfriend	mpenzi (pl. wapenzi)	copain (m)
n.	bra	sidiria	soutien-gorge (m)
n.	bracelet	kikuku	bracelet (m)
verb	brag, to	kujigamba	se vanter
n.	braid	utepe	tresse (f)
verb	braid, to	kusokota	tresser
n.	brain	ubongo	cerveau (m)
n.	branch	tawi (pl. matawi)	branche (f)
phrase	brand new	-pya kabisa	flambant neuf
n.	brass	shaba	cuivre jaune (m)
adj.	brave	hodari	brave
n.	bravery	ujasiri	courage (m)
n.	bread	mkate (pl. mikate)	pain (m)
verb	break, to	kuvunja	casser
n.	breakfast	chakula cha asubuhi	petit déjeuner (m)
n.	breast	kifua, maziwa	sein (m)
n.	breast milk	maziwa ya mama	lait (m) de femme
verb	breast-feed, to	kunyonyesha	allaiter
n.	breastbone	kidari (pl. vidari)	poitrail
n.	breath	pumzi	haleine (f)
verb	breathe	kuvuta pumzi	respirer
phrase	breathless, to be	kutwetatweta	essoufflé, être
n.	bribe	rushwa	pot-de-vin
verb	bribe, to	kutoa rushwa	soudoyer
verb	bribe, to take	kula rushwa	accepter soudoyer
n.	brick	tofali (pl. matofali)	brique (f)
n.	bricklayer	mwashi aakaye kwa matofali	ouvrier-maçon (m)
n.	bride	bibi arusi	mariée (f)
n.	bride-groom	bwana arusi	marié (m)

parts of speech	english	swahili	french
n.	bridge	daraja (pl. madaraja)	pont (m)
adj.	brief	-fupi	bref
adj.	bright	-enye kung'aa, -enye akili	vif
n.	brim	ukingo	bord (m) (d'un pot en argile)
verb	bring in, to	kuingiza	faire entrer
verb	bring to	kuleta	amener
adj.	broad, wide, spacious	-pana	large, spacieux
verb	broil, to	kuchoma	griller
n., med	bronchitis	ugonjwa wa kifua	bronchite
n.	bronze	shaba nyeusi	bronze (m)
n.	broom	ufagio (pl. fagio)	balai (m)
n.	brother	ndugu, kaka	frère (m)
n.	brother-in-law	shemeji	beau-frère
adj.	brown	rangi ya kunde	brun
n.	brush	ufagio (pl. fagio)	balai (m)
n.	brush (paintbrush) {hair brush}	burashi (hair or paint brush)	brosse (f) (la brosse due peintre) {la brosse à cheveux}
verb	brush teeth, to	kusukula meno	se laver les dents
verb	brush, to	kupangusa	brosser
n.	bubble	povu	bulle (f)
n.	bucket	ndoo	seau (m)
n.	budget	taarifa ya gharama	budget (m)
n.	buffalo	1. nyati 2. mbogo	buffle (m)
n.	bug	kunguni	insecte (m)
verb	build, to	kujenga	bâtir
n.	builder	mjengaji (pl. wajengaji)	constructeur (m)
n.	building (construction)	jengo (pl. majengo)	bâtiment (m)
n.	bull	ng'ombe dume	taureau (m)
n.	bullet	risasi ya bunduki	balle (f)
n.	bunch (of fruit)	kichala (pl. vichala)	botte (f)
n.	bundle	bunda	liasse (f)
n.	burden	mzigo (pl. mizigo)	fardeau (m)
n.	burlap	gunia (pl. magunia)	gros canevas (m)
n	burn	umizo la moto	brûlure (f)
verb	burn, to	kuchoma, kuwaka	brûler
verb	burst, to	kupasuka ghafula	éclater
verb	bury, to	kuzika	1. enterrer 2. enfouir
n.	bus	motakaa ya abiria	autobus (m)
n.	bush	kichaka (pl. vichaka)	brousse (f)
n.	business	shughuli, kazi	affaire (f)

parts of speech	english	swahili	french
verb	bustle about, to	kutaharuki	s'affairer
conj.	but	lakini	mais
n.	butcher	mwuza nyama	boucher (m)
n.	butter	siagi	beurre (m)
n.	butterfly	kipepeo (pl. vipepeo)	papillon (m)
n.	buttock	tako (pl. matako)	fesse (f)
n.	button	kifungo (pl. vifungo)	bouton (m)
n.	buttonhole	kitanzi (pl. vitanzi)	boutonnière (f)
verb	buy, to	kununua	acheter
prep.	by (through)/ (near)	kwa, na	par / près de
n.	bystander	mwenye kuwapo	spectateur (m), spectatrice (f)
n.	cabin	kijumba melini	cabane (f)
n.	café	mkahawa (pl. mikahawa)	café (m) {endroit où l'on boit le café}
n.	cage	tundu (pl. matundu), kizimba (pl. vizimba)	cage (f)
n.	calamity	maafa	calamité (f)
n.	calendar	takwimu	calendrier (m)
n.	calf {calf - lower leg}	ndama {shavu la mguu}	veau (m) {mollet}
n.	call	mwito (pl. miito)	appel (m)
verb	call on, to	kwenda kuamkia	rendre visite à
verb	call, to	kuita	appeler
verb	calm down, to	kutulia	calme, se
n.	calm, quiet	shwari	calme (m)
n.	camel	ngamia	chameau (m)
n.	camp	kambi (pl. makambi)	campement (m)
verb	camp, to	kupiga kambi	camper
verb	can	kuweza	pouvoir
n.	can, tin	kopo (pl. makopo)	boîte (f)
n.	Canadian	mwenyeji wa Canada	Canadien (m)
n.	cancer	jamii moja ya nyota	cancer (m)
n.	candidate	mtaka kazi au cheo fulani	candidat (m)
n.	candle	mshumaa	bougie (f)
n.	candlestick	kinara (pl. vinara)	bougeoir (m)
n.	candy	tamutamu	bonbon (m)
n.	cane	fimbo	canne (f)
n.	canoe (dugout)	mtumbwi (pl. mitumbwi)	pirogue (f)
adj.	capable, able	-enye kuweza	capable
n.	capacity	ujazo, nafasi	capacité (f)
n.	capital (city)	mji mkuu	capitale (f)
n.	capital (letter)	herufi kubwa	capitale (f)

29

parts of speech	english	swahili	french
n.	captivity	utumwa	captivité (f)
verb	capture, to	kukamata	capturer
n.	car	motakaa	voiture (f), véhicule
n.	car	gari (pl. magari)	voiture (f)
verb	care for, to (the sick)	kutunza	soigner
adj.	careful	-angalifu	prudent
adv.	carefully	taratibu	soigneusement
adj.	careless	-zembe	qui manque de soin
verb	caress, to	kukumbatia kwa upendo	caresser
n.	caretaker	mwangalizi	gardien (m), gardienne (f)
n.	carpenter	seremala (pl. maseremala)	menuisier (m)
n.	carpentry	usermala	menuiserie (f)
n.	carrot	karoti	carotte (f)
verb	carry on one's back, to	kubeba	porter sur le dos
verb	carry on one's hip, to	kueleka	porter sur la hanche
verb	carry on, to	kuendelea	continuer
verb	carry, to	kuchukua	porter
verb	carve, to	kuchora	découper
n.	case	jambo, kesi	cas (m)
n.	cash	fedha taslimu	argent (m)
n.	cashew	korosho	noix de cajou
n.	cashier	karani wa fedha	cassier (m)
n.	cassava	muhogo, (pl. mihogo)	manioc
verb	cast lots, to	kupiga kura	jouer un tour à, le tromper
verb	cast, to; to fling	kutupa	jeter
verb	castigate, to	kuadhibu	châtier
n.	castle	ngome	château (m)
verb	castrate, to	kuhasi	châtrer
n.	cat	paka	chat (m), chatte (f)
n.	catastrophe	msiba mkuu	catastrophe (f)
verb	catch fire, to	kuwaka	prendre feu
verb	catch, to	kukamata	attraper
n.	category	aina, jamii	catégorie (f)
n.	caterpillar	kiwavi (pl. viwavi)	chenille (f)
n.	caterpillar	mtoto wa kipepeo	chenille (f)
n.	catholic	katoliko	catholique (m,f)
n.	cattle	mifugo	bétail (m)
n.	cause	sababu	cause (f)
verb	cause, to	kufanyiza	être cause de
adj.	cautious	-enye hadhari	prudent
n.	cave	pango (pl. mapango)	galerie souterraine

parts of speech	english	swahili	french
n.	cavity	shimo (pl. mashimo)	cavité (f)
verb	cease, to	kukoma	cesser
n.	ceiling	upande wa juu wa chumba	plafond (m)
verb	celebrate, to	kushangilia	célébrer
n.	celebration	mwadhimisho	célébration (f)
n.	cellar	ghala ya chini	cave (f)
n.	cement	udongo ulaya	ciment (m)
n.	cemetery	makaburini	cimetière (m)
n.	censer	chetezo	encensoir (m)
n.	census	hesabu ya watu wa nchi	recensement (m)
n.	center, in the	palipo katikati hasa	centre (f)
n.	centipede	tandu	mille pattes
n.	century	karne	siècle (m)
n.	ceremony	ibada au sherehe ya heshima	cérémonie (f)
adj.	certain	fulani	certain
adv.	certainly	hakika	certainement
n.	cessation	ukomo	cessation (f)
n.	chain	mnyororo (pl. minyororo)	chaîne (f)
n.	chair	kiti (pl. viti)	chaise (f)
n.	chairman	mwenye-kiti	président (m)
n.	chalk	chaki	craie (f)
n.	challenge	kutaka thibitisho	défi (m)
n.	chameleon	kinyonga (pl. vinyonga)	caméléon (m)
n.	change (coins)	senti	monnaie (f)
verb	change money, to	kuvunga	changer de l'argent
verb	change one's mind, to	kughairi	changer d'avis
verb	change, to	kubadilisha	changer de
n.	channel	mfereji (pl. mifereji)	canal (m)
n.	chaos	machafuko makubwa	chaos (m)
n.	chapter	sura	chapitre (m)
n.	character	tabia	caractère (m)
n.	charcoal	makaa ya miti	charbon de bois (m)
n.	charcoal, ember	kaa (pl. makaa)	charbon, braise
n.	charge (in battle)	shambulio	charge (f)
verb	charge, to be in	kuwa mwangilizi	s'occuper de
n.	charm	hirizi	charme (m) (amulette)
verb	chase, to	kukimbiza	poursuivre
n.	chat	maongezi	causerie (f)
verb	chat, to	kuzungumza	causer
n.	chauffeur	dreva wa motakaa	chauffeur (m)

parts of speech	english	swahili	french
adj.	cheap	rahisi	bon marché
verb	cheat, to	kudanganya	tromper
n.	cheater	mdanganyifu (pl. wadanganyifu)	escroc (m)
n.	cheek	shavu la uso	joue (f)
adj.	cheerful	-kunjufu	joyeux
n.	cheese	jibini	fromage (m)
n.	cheetah	duma	guépard (m)
n.	chest (body)	kifua (pl. vifua)	poitrine (f)
n.	chest (crate)	sanduku (pl. masanduku)	caisse (f)
verb	chew, to	kutafuna	1. mâcher 2. mastiquer
n.	chicken	kinda la kuku	poulet (m)
n.	chicken pox	tetewanga	varicelle (f)
verb	chide, to	kukaripia	gronder
n.	chief	sultani	chef (m)
n.	child	mtoto (pl. watoto); mwana (pl. wana)	enfant (m,f); fils; fille
n.	childhood	utoto	enfance (f)
n.	chills (tremor)	homa ya baridi	tremblement (m)
n.	chimpanzee	sokwe	chimpanzé (m)
n.	chin	kidevu (pl. videvu)	menton (m)
n.	choice	hiari	choix (m)
n.	choir	jamii ya waimbaji	chœur (m)
verb	choke, to	kukaba au kukabwa roho	étouffer
n., med	cholera	kipindupindu	choléra
verb	choose, to	kuchagua	choisir
n.	Christ	Kristo	le Christ (m)
n.	Christian	Mkristo	Chrétien (m) {person}
n.	Christmas {Merry Christmas}	Krismas {Heri za Krismas.}	Noël (m) {Bonne fête de Noël.}
adj.	chronic	-a kusedeka	chronique
n.	church (building)	kanisa	église (f)
n.	cigar	sigara	cigare (m)
n.	cigarette	sigareti	cigarette (f)
n.	circle	mviringo (pl. miviringo), duara	cercle (m)
verb	circulate, to	kuzunguka	circuler
verb	circumcise, to	kutahiri	circoncire
n.	circumcision	tohara	circoncision (f)
n.	circumference	mzingo	circonférence (f)
n.	circumstance	jambo, maneno	circonstance (f)
n.	citizen	raia	citoyen (m)

parts of speech	english	swahili	french
n.	city	mji (pl. miji)	ville (f), cité (f)
adj.	civilized	-staarabu	civilisé
verb	claim, to	kudai	revendiquer
n.	clan	ukoo (pl. koo)	clan (m)
verb	clap, to	kupiga makofi	applaudir
verb	clarify, to	kubainisha	clarifier
n.	class (students)	darasa (pl. madarasa)	classe (f)
n.	clatter (of voices)	kishindo	bruit (m)
n., med	clavicle	mtulinga	clavicule
n.	claw	kucha	griffe (f)
n.	clay	udongo	argile (f), glaise (f)
adj.	clean	safi	propre
verb	clean, to	kusafisha	nettoyer
n.	cleanliness	usafi	propreté
verb	cleanse, to	kutakasa	nettoyer, purifier
adj.	clear	wazi	clair
verb	clear, to be (2) swim, to	kuelea	intelligible, être (2) nager
adv.	clearly	kwa dhahiri	clairement
n.	clemency	huruma	clémence (f)
verb	clench, to	kukaza	serrer
n.	clerk	karani (pl. makarani)	employé(e) {m,(f)}
adj.	clever	-enye akili	intelligent
n.	cliff	jabali	falaise (f)
verb	climb down, (tree), to	kutelemka	descendre (l'arbre)
verb	climb, to	kupanda	gravir
n.	cloak	kifuniko (pl. vifuniko)	manteau (m)
n.	clock	saa	horloge (f)
verb	close the eyes, to	fumba macho	fermer les yeux
adv.	close to	karibu na	près de
verb	close, to	kufunga, kufumba	fermer
n.	closet	kijumba	placard (m)
verb	clothe, to	kuvika	vêtir
n.	clothes	nguo	vêtements (m)
n.	cloud	wingu (mawingu)	nuage (m)
n.	club (stick)	fimbo	massue (f)
n.	cluck	mwito wa kuku kwa watoto wake	bruit (m)
n.	cluster	kichala (pl. vichala)	grappe (f)
verb	coagulate, to	kuganda	coaguler, se
n.	coast (of river)	pwani	plage (f)
n.	coat (clothing), {of paint}	koti {mpako}	manteau (m) {couche} (f)

33

parts of speech	english	swahili	french
verb	**coax, to**	kubembeleza	amadouer
n.	**cobra**	nyoka	cobra (m)
n.	**cobweb**	utando wa buibui	toile d'araignée (f)
n., med	**coccyx**	kifandugu	coccyx (os du bassin)
n.	**cock-crowing**	kuwika jogoo	chant (m) du coq
n.	**cockroach**	mende	cancrelat (m)
n.	**coconut**	dafu (pl. madafu)	noix (f) de coco
verb	**coerce, to**	kushurutisha	contraindre
n.	**coffee**	kahawa	café (m)
n.	**coffee bean**	buni	grain (m) de café
n.	**coffee plant**	mbuni (pl. mibuni)	caféier (m)
n.	**coffin**	sanduku la maiti	cercueil (m)
verb	**cogitate, to**	kufikiri	méditer
n.	**coin**	sarafu	pièce (f) de monnaie
verb	**coincide, to**	kulingana	coïncider
adj.	**cold**	-a baridi	froid
n.	**cold in head**	baridi	rhume (m)
n.	**cold season**	kipupwe	saison froide (juin-juillet)
verb	**cold, to be**	kupoa	froid, être
verb	**collaborate, to**	kushirikiana katika kazi	collaborer
verb	**collapse, to**	kuanguka	s'effondrer
verb	**collect, to**	kuchanga, kukusanya	ramasser
n., med	**colon**	sehemu ya chini ya tumbo kubwa	gros intestin
n.	**color**	rangi	couleur (f)
n.	**comb**	kitana (pl. vitana)	peigne (m)
verb	**comb, to**	kuchana	peigner
verb	**come across, to**	kukuta	traverser
verb	**come back, to; to return**	kurudi	revenir
interj.	**Come here!**	Uje hapa!	Viens ici!
phrase	**Come in!**	Karibu!	Entrez!
verb	**come out of, to**	kutokea wazi	sortir de
verb	**come, to**	kuja	venir
n.	**comfort**	faraja	confort (m)
verb	**comfort, to**	kufariji	réconforter
adj.	**comfortable**	-enye raha	confortable
n.	**command**	amri (pl. amri)	commandement (m)
verb	**command, to**	kuamuru	commander
n.	**commander**	mwenye amri	chef (m)
verb	**commence, to**	kuanza	commencer
verb	**commit an error, to**	kukosa	commettre une faute

parts of speech	english	swahili	french
verb	commit oneself, to	kuweka ahadi	s'engager
n.	committee	halmashauri	comité (m)
adj.	common	-a kawaida	commun
verb	communicate, to	kupelekeana habari	communiquer
n.	companion	mwenzi (pl. wenzi)	compagnon (m), compagne (f)
verb	compare, to	kulinganisha	comparer
n.	comparison	mfano (pl. mifano)	comparaison (f)
n.	compensation	fidia	dédommagement (m)
verb	compete, to	kushariki	participer
n.	competition	shindano (pl. mashindano)	compétition (f)
verb	complain, to	kunung'unika	se plaindre
n.	complaint (illness)	ugonjwa	maladie (f)
adj.	complete	-timilifu	complet
adv.	completely, totally	pia	complètement, tout à fait
n.	complication	matata	complication (f)
verb	compose, to	kutunga	composer
verb	comprehend, to	kufahamu	comprendre
n.	comprehension	ufahamu	compréhension (f)
verb	conceal, to	kuficha	dissimuler
verb	concede, to	kukubali	concéder
n.	conceit	kiburi	vanité (f)
verb	conceive, to	kufahamu	concevoir
n.	concern	shughuli	inquiétude (f)
verb	conclude, to	kumaliza	conclure
n.	conclusion	mwisho	conclusion (f)
verb	concur, to	kupatana	être d'accord
verb	condemn, to	kupatiliza	condamner
n.	condemnation	lawama	condamnation (f)
n.	condition	hali	condition (f)
n.	conduct	mwenendo (pl. mienendo)	conduite (f)
verb	confess, to	kukiri	1. confesser 2. avouer
n.	confession	maungamo	confession (f)
verb	confirm, to	kuthibitisha	confirmer
n.	conflict	mapigano	conflit (m)
verb	confront, to	kukabili	se mesurer à
verb	confuse, to	kuchafua	confondre
n.	confusion	chafuko	confusion (f)
verb	congratulate, to (graduate)	kupongeza	féliciter (en ce qui concerne obtention du diplôme)
interj.	Congratulations.	Hongera.	Félicitations.

parts of speech	english	swahili	french
verb	conjecture about, to	kudhani tu	conjecturer
n., med	conjunctivitis	uvimbe wa mboni	conjonctivite
verb	connect, to	kuunga	relier
verb	conquer, to	kushinda	conquérir
n.	conscience	dhamiri	conscience (f)
verb	consent, to	kukubali	consentir
n.	consequence (without repercussions)	jambo litokealo kwa sababu fulani	conséquence (sans conséquence)
verb	consider, to	kufikili	considérer
n.	consideration	uangalifu	considération (f)
verb	console, to	kufariji	consoler
adv.	constantly	daima	constamment
n.	constitution	sheria ya serkali	constitution (f)
verb	construct, to	kufanyiza	construire
verb	consult, to	kushauri	consulter
adj.	contagious	-a kuambukiza	contagieux
verb	contemplate, to	kutafakari	contempler
n.	contempt	dharau	mépris (m)
n.	continuation	mfulizo	continuation (f)
verb	continue, to	kudumu	continuer
adj.	continuous	bila kukoma	continu
verb	contradict, to	kubisha	contredire
verb	contribute, to	kutoa fedha au msaada	contribuer
n.	contribution	kitu kilichotolewa	contribution (f)
verb	control, to (govern)	kutawala	contrôler
n.	controversy	mabishano	controverse (f)
n.	contusion	chubuo	contusion (f)
n.	conversation	mazungumzo	conversation (f)
verb	converse with, to	kusemezana, kuzungumza	converser
verb	convince, to	kusadikisha	convaincre
n.	convulsion	kifafa	convulsion (f)
n.	cook	mpishi (pl. wapishi)	cuisinier (m)
verb	cook, to	kupika	cuire
phrase	cooked, to be well (to be done)	kuiva	cuit, être
n.	cooking stone	figa (pl. mafiga)	pierre servant de chenet
adj.	cool	-a baridi	frais (m), fraîche (f)
verb	cool, to become	kupoa	frais, devenir
verb	cooperate, to	kusaidiana	coopérer
n.	cooperation	shirika	coopération (f)
adj.	copious	tele	copieux

parts of speech	english	swahili	french
n.	copper	shaba	cuivre (m)
n.	cord	kamba	corde (f)
n.	corkscrew	kizibuo	tire-bouchon (m)
n.	corn	muhindi (pl. mihindi)	maïs (m)
n.	corner	pembe	coin (m)
n.	corpse	maiti	cadavre (m)
adj.	correct	safi	exact
verb	correct, to	kusahihisha	corriger
verb	correspond with, to	kufanana	s'entendre avec (quelqu'un)
n.	cost	bei, gharama	coût (m)
n.	cottage	nyumba ndogo	gîte (m)
n.	cotton	pamba	coton (m)
n.	cough	kikohozi (pl. vikohozi)	toux (f)
verb	cough, to	kukohoa	tousser
n.	council, advice	baraza	conseil (m)
verb	counsel, to	kuonya	conseiller
verb	count, to	kuhesabu	compter
verb	counteract, to	kubatilisha	neutraliser
adj.	countless	bila idadi	innombrable
adj.	country	nchi	campagnard
n.	couple	jozi	couple (m)
n.	couple	jozi	paire (f)
n.	courage	uhodari	courage (m)
adj.	courageous	-jasiri	courageux
n.	court	nyumba ya mfaime	cour (f)
n.	courtesy	jamala	courtoisie (f)
n.	cover	kifuniko (pl. vifuniko)	couvercle (m)
verb	cover oneself, to	kuvaa nguo	couvrir, se
verb	cover, to	kufunika, kutamani	couvrir
verb	covet, to	kutamani	convoiter
n.	cow	ngombe	vache (f)
n.	coward	mwoga	lâche (m,f)
n.	crack (fissure)	ufa (pl. nyufa)	fente (f)
verb	crack, to	kualika	casser
n.	cracker	biskuti	biscuit (m)
n.	craftsman	fundi (pl. mafundi)	artisan (m)
adj.	crafty	-erevu	roublard
verb	cram, to	kushindilia	tasser
verb	crash into, to	kudunda	percuter contre
adj.	crazy	-enye kichaa	fou
n.	cream	maziwa ya mtindi	crème (f)

37

parts of speech	english	swahili	french
verb	create, to	kuumba	créer
n.	creature	kiumbe (pl. viumbe)	créature (f)
verb	creep, to	kutambaa	ramper
n.	crevice	ufa (pl. nyufa)	fissure (f)
n.	crime	hatia	crime (m)
n.	criminal	mhalifu	criminel (m), criminelle (f)
n.	cripple	kiwete	estropié (m)
n.	crocodile	mamba	crocodile (m)
adj.	crooked	-a kupotoka	courbé
n.	crop (farming)	mavuno (pl.)	récolte (f)
n.	cross	msalaba (pl. misalaba)	croix (f)
verb	cross,to	kuvuka	croiser
n.	crossroads	njia panda	carrefour (m)
adv.	crosswise	-a kukingama	en travers
verb	crouch, to	kujinyata	s'accroupir
verb	crow, to	kuwika	chanter
n.	crowd	mkutano (pl. mikutano)	foule (f)
n.	crown	taji	couronne (f)
verb	crucify, to	kusulibi	crucifier
n.	cruelty	ukatili	cruauté (f)
n.	crumb	kombo	miette (f)
verb	crumble, to	kufikicha	s'ébouler
verb	crush, to	kuponda	écraser
verb	cry, to	kulia	pleurer
verb	cultivate, to	kulima	cultiver
n.	cultivator	mkulima (pl. wakulima)	cultivateur (m)
n.	cunning	hila	ruse
n.	cup	kikombe (pl. vikombe)	tasse (f)
n.	cupboard	kabati	armoire (f)
n.	cure	dawa	remède (m)
n.	cure	tibu	guérison
verb	cure, to	kuponya	guérir
n.	curiosity	kitu cha shani	curiosité (f)
verb	curse, to	kulaani, kutukana	maudire
n.	curtain	pazia (pl. mapazia)	rideau (m)
n.	cushion	takia (pl. matakia)	coussin (m)
n.	custom	desturi	coutume (f)
verb	cut lengthwise, to	kupasua	fendre en long
verb	cut, to	kukata	couper
n.	cyclone	kimbunga; tufani	cyclone (m)
adv.	daily	kila siku	tous les jours

parts of speech	english	swahili	french
n.	dairy	duka la maziwa	laiterie (f)
n.	dam	boma la kuzuia maji	digue (f)
verb	damage, to	kutia hasara	endommager
adj.	damp	majimaji	humide
n.	dance	dansi	danse (f)
verb	dance, to	kucheza ngoma	danser
n.	danger	hatari	danger (m)
adj.	dangerous	-a hatari	dangereux
verb	dare, to	kuthubutu	oser
adj.	dark	-eusi	foncé
n.	dark	giza	noir (m)
phrase	dark., It is getting	Magalibi imefika.	La nuit tombe.
n.	date (fruit)	tende	datte
n.	date (in month)	tarehe	date (f)
n.	daughter	binti	fille (f)
verb	dawdle, to	kutangatanga	flâner
n.	dawn	pambazuko	aube (f)
n.	day	siku	jour (m)
phrase	day after tomorrow, the	kesho kutwa	après-demain
adv.	day before yesterday	juzi	avant-hier
n.	day laborer	kibarua (pl. vibarua)	journalier
n.	day long, all	mchana kutwa	toute la journée
n.	daytime	mchana	journée (f)
n.	dazzle	kutia kiwi	éblouissement (m)
adj.	dead	amekufa	mort
n.	dead person	mfu (pl. wafu)	les morts
n.	deadline	muda	délai (m)
n., med	deadlock	mgogoro	l'impasse
n.	deaf person	kiziwi (pl. viziwi)	personne sourd
adj., n	dear	-penzi, ghali	cher (m), chère (f)
n.	death	kufa (pl. kufa), mauti	mort (f)
n.	debate	jadiliano	débat (m)
verb	debate, to	kujadiliana	débattre
n.	debauchery	utongozi	débauche (f)
n.	debris	kifusi	débris (m)
n.	debt	deni	dette (f)
verb	decay, to	kuoza	se détériorer
n.	deceit	udanganyifu	tromperie (f)
verb	deceive, to	kudanganya	1. tromper 2. décevoir

parts of speech	english	swahili	french
n.	December	Desemba; mwezi wa kumi na mbili wa mwaka wa kizungu	décembre (m)
verb	decide, to	kuamua	décider
n.	decision (final)	maamuzi	décision (f)
verb	decline, to	kukataa	décliner
verb	decorate, to	kupamba	décorer
n.	decoy	kutega kwa hila	compère (m)
n.	decrease	upunguo	diminution (f)
verb	decrease, to	kupunguka	diminuer
verb	deduce, to	kutambua maana	déduire
verb	defame, to	kusengenya	diffamer
verb	defeat, to	kushinda	vaincre
verb	defend, to	kulinda	défendre
n.	defense	ulinzi	défense
verb	defile, to	kunajisi	violer d'un objet sacré
verb	define, to	kubainisha	définir
n.	definition	ubainisho	définition (f)
verb	deflate, to	kupwesha	dégonfler
verb	delay, to	kukawa	tarder
n.	deliberation	shauri (pl. mashauri)	délibération (f)
adj.	delicious	-tamu	délicieux
adj.	delightful	-a kupendeza	charmant
verb	delude oneself	kudanganya	se leurrer
verb	demand, to	kudai	exiger
n.	democracy	utawala wa raia	démocratie (f)
verb	demolish, to	kubomoa	démolir
n.	demon	pepo mbaya	démon (m)
n.	den	pango la mnyama	antre (m)
verb	denigrate, to	kuchongea	dénigrer
adj.	dense	-zito	épais
n.	dentist	daktari wa meno	dentiste (m,f)
verb	deny, to	kukana	1. démentir 2. nier
verb	depart, to	kuondoka	partir
verb	depend on, to	kutegemea	dépendre de
verb	deposit, to	kuweka	déposer
n.	depravity	ufisadi	dépravation (f)
verb	depreciate, to	kupungua thamani	déprécier
n.	deprivation	kutwaliwa	privation (f)
verb	deprive, to	kunyima	priver
n.	depth	urefu	profondeur

40

parts of speech	english	swahili	french
verb	descend, to; go down, to	kushuka, kutelemuka	descendre
verb	describe, to	kuwasifu	décrire
n.	desert (ie. Sahara desert)	jangwa	désert
verb	deserve, to	kustahili	mériter
n.	design (sketch)	kielelezo	dessein (m)
n.	desire	hamu	désir (m)
verb	desire, to	kutaka	désirer
n.	desk	meza	bureau (m)
verb	despair, to	kukata tamaa	désespérer
verb	despise, to	kutweza	mépriser
n.	dessert	matunda	dessert (m)
n.	destiny	ajali	destin (m)
n.	destitution	ufukara	destitution (f)
verb	destroy, to	kuangamiza, kuharibu	détruire
n.	destruction	uharibifu	destruction (f)
verb	detach, to	kutenga	détacher
verb	deteriorate, to	kupotewa na uzuri	dégrader, se
verb	determine, to	kukaza nia	déterminer
verb	detest, to	kuchukia sana	détester
verb	deviate, to	kuenda upande	dévier
n.	devil	ibilisi	diable (m); satan
n.	dew	umande	rosée(f)
n., med	diabetes	kisukari	diabète
n.	dialogue	mazungumzo	causerie (f)
n., med	diaphragm	kiwambo	diaphragme (m)
verb	diarrhea, to have	kuhara	avoir la diarrhée
verb	dicker, to	kubadili	troquer
n.	dictionary	kamusi	dictionnaire (m)
verb	die, to	kufa	mourir
n.	difference	tofauti	différence (f)
adj.	different	mbali mbali	différent
verb	different, to be	kuhitilafiana	différent, être
adj.	difficult	-gumu	difficile
n.	difficulty	mashaka, taabu	difficulté (f)
verb	dig, to	kuchimba	fouiller
n.	dignity	heshima na upendo	dignité (f)
verb	diminish the quantity, to	kupunguza	diminuer quantité
n.	dinner (night)	chakula kikuu cha siku	dîner (m)
n.	dinner (noon)	chakula kikubwa cha kutwa	déjeuner (f)
n.	diploma	hati ya sifa	diplôme (m)
verb	direct, to	kuagiza, kuongoza	diriger

parts of speech	english	swahili	french
n.	direction	upande	direction (f)
n.	director	msimamizi (pl. wasimamizi)	directeur (m)
n.	dirt	takataka, uchafu	saleté (f)
adj.	dirty	-chafu	sale
verb	disagree, to	kutopatana	ne pas être d'accord
verb	disappear, to	kutoweka	disparaître
verb	disapprove, to	kutoridhia	désapprouver
n.	disaster	baa, msiba	désastre (m)
verb	discard, to	kutupa	jeter
verb	discern, to	kutambua	discerner
n.	discipline	nidhamu	discipline (f)
verb	disconnect, to	kutenga	se désunir
verb	discourage, to	kuvunja moyo	décourager
verb	discover, to	kufumbua, kuvumbua	découvrir
verb	discuss, to	kuzungumzia habari	discuter
n.	discussion	mazungumzo	discussion (f)
n.	disdain	dharau	dédain (m)
n.	disease	ugonjwa (pl. maogonjwa)	maladie (f)
n.	disgrace	aibu	honte (f)
n.	disgust	karaha	dégoût (m)
n.	dish	sahani	plat (m)
adj.	dishonest	-danganyifu	malhonnête
n.	dishonesty	uwongo	malhonnêteté (f)
verb	dislike, to	kuchukia	ne pas tolérer
verb	dislocate, to (one's joint)	kushtua	se désarticuler (ie. bras)
n.	disobedience	ukaidi	désobéissance (f)
verb	disobey, to	kuasi	désobéir
n.	disorder	fujo (pl. mafujo)	désordre (m)
verb	disperse, to	kusambaa	se disperser
n.	dispute	ugomvi	dispute (f)
adj.	disrespectful	-tovu wa heshima	irrespectueux
n.	dissension	faraka	dissension (f)
verb	dissolve, to	kuyeyuka	dissoudre
verb	dissuade, to	kujaribu	dissuader
n.	distance	umbali	distance (f)
adj.	distinct	dhahiri	distinct
verb	distinguish between, to	kupambanua	distinguer
verb	distract, to	kuvuta mawazo pengine	distraire
n.	distress	huzuni, dhiki	détresse (f)
n.	disturbance	ghasia, fujo	troubles (m)

parts of speech	english	swahili	french
n.	ditch	mfereji (pl. mifereji)	fossé (m)
adv.	ditto	vile vile	idem
verb	diverge, to	kuachana	diverger
n.	divergence	tofauti	divergence
verb	divide, to	kugawa	diviser
n.	division	mgawo	division (f)
verb	divorce, to	kuvunja ndoa	divorcer
n.	dizziness	kizunguzungu	vertiges (m)
phrase	Do you have children?	Una watoto?	Est-ce que tu as des enfants?
phrase	Do you have...	Ukonayo...	Avez-vous...
phrase	Do you live here?	Unakaa hapa?	Habitez-vous ici?
verb	do, to	kufanya, kutenda	faire
n.	doctor (academic, medicine)	1. tabibu (pl. matabibu) 2. mganga (pl. waganga	docteur (m), médecin (m)
n.	document	hati	document (m)
n.	dog	mbwa	chien (m)
n.	doll	mtoto wa bandia	poupée (f)
verb	dominate, to	kushinda	dominer
n.	donkey	punda	âne (m)
n.	donut	kitumbua, (pl. vitumbua)	beignet
n.	door	mlango (pl. milango)	porte (f)
n.	dormitory	chumba cha kulala	maison (f) d'étudiants
n.	dose	kipimo cha dawa	dose (f)
verb	double, to	kurudufya	doubler
n.	doubt	shaka	doute (m)
verb	doubt, to	kushuku	douter (de)
n.	dove	hua	colombe (f)
adv.	down	chini	en bas
n.	dowry	mahari	dot (f)
verb	drag, to	kukokota	traîner
verb	draw a line, to	kupiga mustari	fixer les limites
verb	draw near, to	kukaribia	tirer; s'approcher
verb	draw, to	kuandika sanamu	dessiner
verb	dread, to	kuogopa	appréhender
n.	dream	ndoto	rêve (m)
verb	dream, to	kuota ndoto	rêver
n.	dress	gauni (pl. magauni)	robe (f)
verb	dress another, to	kuvika	mettre à (quelqu'un) un vêtement
verb	dress, to	kuvalia	vêtir
n.	dresser	kabati	commode (f)

parts of speech	english	swahili	french
verb	**drill, to (a hole)**	kutoboa	percer
n.	**drink**	kinyweo (pl. vinyweo)	boisson (f)
verb	**drink, to (What would you like to drink?)**	kunywa (Unataka kunywa nini?)	boire (Que voulez-vous boire?)
n.	**drinking glass**	bilauri	verre (m)
verb	**drip, to**	kudondoka	dégoutter
verb	**drive away, to**	kufukuza	chasser
verb	**drive, to**	kuendesha	conduire
n.	**driver**	dereva	chauffeur (m)
verb	**drop, to**	kuangusha	laisser tomber
n.	**drought**	ukosefu wa mvua	sécheresse (f)
verb	**drown, to**	kufa maji	noyer
n.	**drug (medication)**	dawa	drogue (f)
n.	**drum**	ngoma	tambour (m)
verb	**drunk, to be**	kulewa	ivre, être
n.	**drunkard**	mlevi (pl. walevi)	ivrogne (m)
adj.	**dry**	-kavu	sec
n.	**dry skin (dandruff)**	ganda (pl. maganda)	pellicules (f)
verb	**dry, to**	kukausha	sécher
verb	**dry, to become; to wither**	kunyauka	faner, se
n.	**duck**	bata (pl. mabata)	canard (m)
adj.	**dull**	-pumbavu	ignorant
n.	**dungeon**	kifungo	cachot (m)
n.	**duration**	muda	durée (f)
prep.	**during**	wakati wa	pendant
n.	**dusk**	giza la jioni	crépuscule (m)
n.	**dust**	mavumbi	poussière (f)
verb	**dust, to**	kupangusa	épousseter
n.	**duty**	wajibu	devoir (m)
adj. & n.	**dwarf**	kibeti	nain (m)
verb	**dwell, to**	kukaa	demeurer
n.	**dwelling place, house**	nyumba	maison (f)
n	**dynamite**	baruti ya kupasulia mwamba	dynamite (f)
verb	**dysentery, to have**	kuhara damu	dysenterie, avoir la
adj & pr	**each**	kila	1. chaque 2. chacun
adj.	**eager**	-enye bidii	désireux
n.	**eagle**	tai (pl. matai)	aigle (m)
n.	**ear**	sikio (pl. masikio)	oreille (f)
n.	**ear (of sorghum)**	suke	épi (m)
adv.	**early**	mapema	de bonne heure , tôt

parts of speech	english	swahili	french
verb	earn, to; to gain	kuchuma kwa kazi	gagner
n.	earth	dunia	terre (f); univers
n.	earth (ground)	udongo	sol (m)
n.	earthquake	tetemeko la nchi	grande tremblement (m) (de terre)
n.	ease	raha	aise (f)
verb	ease, to be at	kustarehe	à l'aise, être
adv.	easily	polepole	facilement
n.	east	mashariki	est (m)
n.	Easter	Pasaka	Pâques (m)
adj.	easy	-epesi	facile
verb	eat, to	kula	manger
verb	eavesdrop, to	kudukiza	écouter en cachette
n., med	ecchymosis	chubuko (pl. machubuko)	ecchymose
phrase	eclipse of the sun	kupatwa jua	éclipse de soleil
adj.	economical	-wekevu	économique
verb	economize, to	kupunguza gharama	économiser
n.	edge	ukingo	bord (m)
verb	educate, to	kuelimisha	instruire
n.	education	mafunzo	éducation (f)
n.	education (learning)	elimu	instruction (f)
n.	effect	tokeo (pl. matokeo)	effet (m)
verb	effort, to make an	kujitahidi	s'efforcer
n.	egg	yai (pl. mayai)	œuf (m)
n.	eggplant	mubilingani (pl. mibilingani)	aubergine (f)
n.	eggshell	ganda la yai	coquille (f)
adj. & n.	eight	nane	huit (m)
n.	eighteen	kumi na nane	dix-huit
adj.	eighth	-a nane	huitième
n.	eighty	themanini; makumi manane	quatre-vingts
conj.	either...or	ama...ama	soit...soit
n.	elbow	kiko cha mkono; kivi	coude (m)
n.	election	mchaguo	élection (f)
n.	electricity	umeme	électricité (f)
n.	elephant	tembo	éléphant (m)
n., med	elephantiasis of legs	ugonjwa wa matende	éléphantiasis des jambes
n.	eleven	kumi na moja	onze
adv.	elsewhere	pengine	ailleurs
verb	embarrass, to	kutahayarisha	embarrasser
n.	embassy	jumba la balozi	ambassade (f)

parts of speech	english	swahili	french
verb	embellish, to	kupamba	embellir
n.	embers	makaa ya moto	braise (f)
verb	embrace, to	kukumbatia	entourer de ses bras
n.	embryo	mimba	embryon (m)
n.	employee	mtu wa kazi	employé (m)
n.	employer	bwana wa kazi	patron (m), patronne (f)
adj.	empty	-tupu	vide
verb	empty, to	kumwaga	vider
adv.	empty-handed, (to be)	mikono bule	avoir les mains vides
verb	enable, to	kuwezesha	permettre
verb	encircle, to	kuzingira	entourer
n.	enclosure	kitalu	enclos (m)
verb	encourage, to	kutia moyo	encourager
n.	end	mwisho (pl. miisho)	1. fin (f) 2. terme (m)
verb	end, to	kukomesha	terminer
n.	endorsement	sahihi	approbation (f)
n.	endurance	ustahimilivu	endurance (f)
verb	endure, to	kudumu, kuvumilia	supporter
adj. & n.	enemy	adui	ennemi (m)
n.	energy (strength)	nguvu; bidii	forces, vigueur (f)
n.	English (people)	Waingereza	Anglais (m)
n.	English {language} (Do you speak English?)	Kiingereza (Umasema Kiingereza?)	anglais (Parlez-vous anglais?)
phrase	enjoy your meal	karibu chakula	bon appétit.
verb	enjoy, to	kufurahia	aimer, trouver agréable
adj.	enough	-a kutosha	assez de
interj.	Enough!	Basi!	Assez!
verb	enrich, to	kutajirisha	enrichir
verb	enter, to	kuingia	entrer
verb	entertain, to	kufurahisha	égayer
verb	entice, to	kuvuta kwa werevu	amadouer
adj.	entire	-zima, -ote	entier, tout
adv.	entirely	kabisa	entièrement
n.	entrance	mlango (pl. milango)	entrée (f)
n.	entrance; hall	sebule	parloir (m)
n.	envelope	bahasha	enveloppe (f)
n.	environment	mazingira	milieu (m)
n.	envy	wivu	envie (f)
n.	epidemic	maradhi ya pukupuku	épidémie (f)
n., med	epilepsy	kifafa	épilepsie (f)
adj.	equal	sawa	égal

parts of speech	english	swahili	french
adv.	**equally**	sawa	également
n.	**equivalent**	sawa; badala	équivalent (m)
verb	**erase, to**	kufuta	effacer
verb	**erect, to**	kusimamisha	ériger
n.	**erection**	msimiko	érection (f)
n.	**erosion**	momonyoko wa ardhi	érosion (f)
n.	**error**	kosa (pl. makosa)	erreur (f)
verb	**escape, to**	kuponyoka	échapper
verb	**escort, to**	kufuatana na	escorter
adj.	**especially**	hasa	surtout
adj.	**essential**	-a asili	essentiel
verb	**establish, to**	kuweka imara	instaurer
n.	**esteem**	heshima	estime (f)
verb	**estimate, to**	kukiasi	estimer
n.	**Europe**	Ulaya	Europe (f)
adj.	**European**	Mzungu (pl. Wazungu)	européen
verb	**evade, to**	kuepuka	éviter
adv.	**even**	hata, sawa	même
adv.	**even if**	hata ikiwa	même si
conj.	**even though, although**	ijapo	bien que
adv. n.	**evening**	jioni	soir (m)
n.	**event**	jambo	événement (m)
adj.	**every, whole (always)**	kila (daima)	chaque, entier (toujours)
adj.	**everyday**	-a kila siku	tous les jours
pronoun	**everyone**	kila mtu	tout le monde
n.	**everything**	kila kitu	tout
adv.	**everywhere, throughout**	po pote, kila mahali	partout
adj.	**evident**	wazi	évident
adj.	**evil**	-ovu	mauvais
verb	**exaggerate, to**	kutia chumvi	exagérer
verb	**exalt, to**	kutukuza	exalter
n.	**examination**	ukaguzi	examen (m)
verb	**examine, to**	kupima	examiner
n.	**examiner**	mkaguaji	examinateur (m)
n.	**example**	mfano (pl. mifano)	exemple (m)
verb	**exceed, to**	kuzidi	dépasser
adv.	**exceedingly**	muno	extrêmement
adj.	**excellent**	bora	excellent
conj.	**except**	ila	excepté
n.	**excess, surplus**	wingi kupita kiasi	excédent (m)
adj.	**excessive**	-a kupita kiasi	excessif

47

parts of speech	english	swahili	french
adv.	excessively	muno	avec excès
verb	exchange, to	kubadilisha	échanger
verb	exclude, to	kukataa	exclure
verb	excommunicate, to	kuharimisha	excommunier
n.	excrement	mavi (pl.)	excréments (m)
n.	excursion	matembezi ugenini	excursion (f)
n.	excuse	udhuru	excuse (f)
phrase	Excuse me.	Niwie radhi.	Je m'excuse. Pardon!
verb	exercise, to	kuzoea	exercer
verb	exhaust, to	kumaliza	épuiser
verb	exhausted, to be	kuchoka kabisa	épuisé, être
n.	exhaustion	état de faiblesse	accablement (m)
verb	exhibit, to	kuonyesha	exhiber
verb	exhume, to	kufukua	exhumer
verb	exile, to be in	kuhamisha	fuir à
verb	exist, to	kuwako	exister
n.	existence	maisha	existence (f)
verb	expand, to	kutanua	dilater
verb	expect, to	kutazamia	s'attendre à
verb	expectorate, to	kutema mate	cracher
verb	expedite, to	kuhimiza	faire exécuter rapidement
adj.	expensive	ghali	cher (m), chère (f)
verb	experience, to	kupatwa na	éprouver
verb	expire, to; to die	kufa, kuisha	expirer, décéder
verb	explain, to	kueleza	expliquer
n.	explanation	maelezo	explication (f)
n.	exploration	uvumbuzi	exploration (f)
verb	explore, to	kuvumbua	explorer
n.	explosive	baruti	explosif (m)
verb	extend, to	kuenea	tendre
adj.	exterior	-nje	extérieur
verb	exterminate, to	kukomesha kabisa	exterminer
verb	extinguish, to	kuzima	éteindre
verb	extort, to	kutoza kwa nguvu	extorquer
adj.	extra	zaidi	de plus
adj.	extraordinary	-a ajabu	extraordinaire
adv.	extremely	mno	extrêmement
n.	eye	jicho (pl. macho)	œil (m)
n.	eyebrow	nyushi	sourcil (m)
n.	eyelash	ukope	cil (m)
n.	eyelid	ukope	paupière (f)

parts of speech	english	swahili	french
n.	fable	hadithi fupi	fable (f)
n.	fabrication	uongo	fabrication (f)
n.	face	uso (pl. nyuso)	visage (m)
verb	face (someone), to	kukabili	se tenir l'un face de l'autre
verb	facilitate, to	kufanya rahisi	faciliter
n.	facsimile	mwigo sawasawa	fac-similé (m)
n.	fact	jambo la hakika	fait (m)
n.	fad	kinyongo	marotte (f)
verb	fade, to	kufifia	se faner
verb	fail, to	kukosa	échouer; négliger
verb	faint, to	kuzimia	s'évanouir
adj.	fair	-a haki	juste
adv.	fairly	sana kidogo	honnêtement
n.	faith	imani	foi (f)
adj.	faithful	-aminifu	fidèle
n.	faithfulness	uaminifu	fidélité (f)
verb	fall on, to	kuangukia	tomber sur
verb	fall, to	kuanguka	tomber
adj.	FALSE	-a uongo	faux (m), fausse (f)
verb	falsify, to	kugeuza kwa uongo	falsifier
n.	fame	sifa	renommée (f)
n.	family	jamaa	famille (f)
n.	famine	njaa kuu	famine (f)
adj.	famous	mashuhuri	célèbre
adv.	far	mbali	loin
prep.	far from	mbali na	loin de
n.	fare, price	nauli	prix (m)
verb	farewell, to bid	kuaga	saleur au départ
n.	farmer	mlimaji (pl. walimaji)	fermier (m)
adv.	farther	mbali zaide	plus loin
adj.	fast	upesi	rapide
verb	fast, to	kufunga chakula	jeûner
n. & adj.	fat	1. -nene 2. mafuta	gras (m), grasse (f)
n.	father	baba	père (m)
n.	father (my)	babangu	père (m), mon
n.	fatigue	uchovu	fatigue (f)
n.	fault	hatia	faute (f)
n.	favorite	kipenzi	favori (m), favorite (f)
n.	fear	woga	crainte (f)
verb	fear, to	kuogopa	craindre
adj.	fearful	-a hofu	peureux

49

parts of speech	english	swahili	french
adj.	fearless	-a jasiri	intrépide
verb	feasible, to be	kuwezekana	faisable, être
n.	feast	karamu	festin (m)
n.	feather	nyoya	plume (f)
n.	February	Februari; mwezi wa pili wa mwaka wa kizungu	février (m)
adj.	feeble	dhaifu	faible
verb	feed, to	kulisha	nourrir
phrase	Feel at home.	Starehe.	Faites comme chez vous.
verb	feel, to	kupapasa	sentir; palper
n.	feelings	maono	sentiment (m)
n.	fellowship	ushirika	union (f)
n.	female	mwanamke (pl. wanawake)	genre féminin
adj.	feminine	-a kike	féminin
n.	fence	ugo (pl. nyugo)	clôture (f)
adj.	fertile	-enye rutuba	fertile
n.	fertilizer	mbolea	engrais (m)
n.	fetus	mimba	foetus
n.	feud	uadui	hostilité
n.	fever {He has a high fever.}	homa {Ana homa.}	fièvre (f) {Il a beaucoup de fièvre.}
adj.	few	-chache	peu de
n.	fiancé	mchumba	fiancé (m)
n.	fiction	hadithi tu	romans (m)
n.	field	shamba (pl. mashamba)	champ (m)
n.	fifteen	kumi na tano	quinze
adj.	fifth	-a tano	cinquième
adj. & n.	fifty	hamsini	cinquante (m)
n.	fig	tini	figue (f)
n.	fig tree	mtini	figuier (m)
verb	fight, to	kupigana	combattre
verb	fill, to	kujaza	remplir
verb	filter, to	kuchuja	filtrer
n.	filth	uchafu	saleté (f)
adv.	final	-a mwisho	définitivement
adv.	finally	mwisho	finalement, enfin
verb	find, to	kukuta	trouver
adj.,adv.	fine	-zuri	excellent
n.	fine (i.e. to pay a)	faini	amende (f)
n.	finger	kidole (pl. vidole)	doigt (m)
n.	finger, index	kidole cha shahada	doigt (m) index

parts of speech	english	swahili	french
n.	finger, little	kidole cha mwisho	petit doigt (m)
n.	finger, middle	kidole cha kati	doigt (m) du milieu
n.	finger, ring	kidole cha pete	doigt (m) anneau
n.	fingernail	ukucha (pl. kucha)	ongle (m)
verb	finish, to	kumaliza	finir
n.	fire	moto (pl. mioto)	feu (m)
n.	fireplace	mahali nyumbani pa kukokea moto	cheminée (f)
n.	firewood	ukini (pl. kuni)	bois (m) de chauffage
adv.	firmly	imara	fermement
adj.	first	-a kwanza	premier (m), première (f)
n.	fish	samaki	poisson (m)
verb	fish, to	kuvua	pêcher
n.	fish-hook	ndoana	hameçon (m)
n.	fisherman	mvuvi (pl. wavuvi)	pêcheur (m)
n.	fist	ngumi	poing (m)
adj. & n.	five	tano	cinq (m)
n.	five hundred	mia tano	cinq cents
n.	five thousand	elfu tano	cinq mille
verb	fix, to	kukaza	fixer
adj.	flabby	-tepetevu	flasque
n.	flag	bendera	drapeau (m)
n.	flank, waist, hip	kiuno (pl. viuno)	flanc (m)
verb	flap wings, to	kupiga mabawa	battre des ailes
verb	flash, to	kumulika ghafula	clignoter
adj.	flat	-pana; sawa	plat
verb	flatter, to	kubembeleza	flatter
n.	flavor	ladha	goût (m)
verb	flavor, to	kukoleza	donner du goût à
n.	flaw	kombo	défaut (m)
n.	flea	kiroboto (pl. viroboto)	puce (f)
verb	flee, to	kukimbia	fuir/s'enfuir
n.	flesh (to have goose bumps)	nyama (kimbibi)	chair (f) (avoir la chair de poule)
n.	flimsy	hafifu	léger
verb	float, to	kuelea	flotter
n.	flock (of sheep)	kundi (pl. makundi)	troupeau (m)
n.	flood	1. gharika 2. mafuriko	inondation (f)
n.	floor	sakafu ya chini	plancher (m)
n.	flour	unga	farine (f)
verb	flourish, to	kusitawi	prospérer

parts of speech	english	swahili	french
verb	**flow, to**	kutiririka	couler
n.	**flower**	ua (pl. maua)	fleur (f)
n.	**flu**	fluu	grippe (f)
verb	**fluctuate, to**	kupanda na kushuka	fluctuer
n.	**fly**	inzi (pl. mainzi)	mouche (f)
verb	**fly, to**	kuruka	voler
n.	**foam**	povu	mousse (f)
n.	**fog**	umande	brouillard (m)
verb	**fold, to**	kukunja	plier
verb	**follow, to**	kufuata	suivre
n.	**folly**	ujinga	folie (f)
verb	**fond of, to be**	kupenda	aimer beaucoup
n.	**food**	chakula (pl. vyakula)	nourriture (f)
n.	**fool**	mpumbavu (pl. wapumbavu)	bouffon (m)
verb	**fool, to**	kudanganya	duper
adj.	**foolish**	-jinga	bête
n.	**foot**	mguu (pl. miguu)	pied (m)
n.	**football (U.S. soccer ball)**	mpira (wa miguu)	ballon (m)
n.	**footstep**	hatua	pas (m)
interj.	**For pity's sake!**	Wapi!	De grâce!
prep.	**for, by, with**	kwa	pour, pendant, depuis
verb	**forbid entry, to**	Kujitafutiya kuingiya.	défendre à d'entrer
verb	**forbid, to**	kukataza	défendre
n.	**forbidden**	marufuku	défendu
verb	**force, to**	kushurutisha	forcer
n.	**ford**	kivuko (pl. vivuko)	gué (m)
n.	**forehead**	paji la uso	front (m)
n.	**foreigner**	mgeni (pl. wageni)	étranger (m)
n.	**forerunner**	mtangulizi (pl. watangulizi)	précurseur
verb	**foresee, to**	kutazama mbele	prévoir
n.	**forest**	mwitu	forêt (f)
verb	**foretell, to**	kutabiri	prédire
adv.	**forever**	milele	pour toujours
verb	**forget, to**	kusahau	oublier
adj.	**forgetful**	-sahaulifu	oublieux
verb	**forgive, to**	kusamehe	pardonner
n.	**forgiveness**	masamaha	pardon (m)
n.	**fork**	uma (pl. nyuma)	fourchette (f)
adv.	**formerly**	zamani	jadis
verb	**forsake, to**	kuacha	abandonner

parts of speech	english	swahili	french
verb	**fortify, to**	kuongeza nguvu	fortifier
adj.	**fortunate**	-a heri	avoir de la chance
n.	**fortune, good**	bahati	fortune (f) bien
n.	**fortune, luck**	bahati	chance (f)
adj. & n.	**forty**	arobaini	quarante (m)
n.	**foundation**	msingi (pl. misingi)	fondation (f)
n.	**fountain**	bomba la kurushia maji juu	fontaine (f)
adj. & n.	**four**	nne	quatre (m)
n.	**four hundred**	mia nne	quatre cents
n.	**fourteen**	kumi na nne	quatorze
adj.	**fourth**	-a nne	quatrième
n.	**fowl**	kuku	volaille (f)
n.	**fox**	mbweha	renard (m)
n.	**fracture**	mvunjo	fracture (f)
adj.	**fragile**	dhaifu	fragile
n.	**fragment**	kipande kidogo	tesson (m)
n.	**fragrance**	harufu tamu	parfum (m)
n.	**franc**	sarafu ya kifaransa	franc (m)
adj.	**free**	huru	libre
adj.	**free (no charge)**	bure	gratuit
n.	**freedom**	uhuru	liberté (f)
adv.	**freely**	bila sharti	libéralement
n.	**French**	Wafaransa (people, Kifaransa (language)	français (m)
n.	**French person**	mfaransa (pl. wafaransa)	français
adj.	**frequent**	-a mara nyingi	fréquent
adv.	**frequently**	mara kwa mara	fréquemment
adj.	**fresh, cool**	-bichi	frais
n.	**Friday**	Ijumaa	vendredi (m)
n.	**friend**	rafiki (pl. marafiki)	ami (m), amie (f)
adj.	**friendly**	-zuri	gentil (m), gentille (f)
n.	**friendship**	urafiki	amitié (f)
verb	**frighten, to**	kuogofya	faire peur à
n.	**fringe**	matamvua	frange (f)
adj.	**frivolous**	pasipo maana	frivole
n.	**frog**	chura (pl. vyura)	grenouille (f)
prep.	**from, (time)**	toka	de, (depuis)
prep.	**from...to (place)**	toka...hata	de...à
prep.	**from...to (time)**	tangu...hata	de...à
adv.	**front of, in**	mbele	devant
n.	**frontier (border)**	mpaka (pl. mipaka)	frontière

53

parts of speech	english	swahili	french
n.	froth, foam	povu	écume (f)
verb	frown, to	kukunja uso	froncer les sourcils
adj.	frugal	-wekevu	frugal
n.	fruit	tunda (pl. matunda)	fruit (m)
verb	fry, to	kukaanga	frire
verb	fulfill, to	kutimiza	accomplir
verb	full, to be (not hungry)	kujaa	ne plus avoir faim; s'emplir
adv.	fully	kabisa	pleinement
n.	fun	furaha	bonheur
n.	funeral	maziko	enterrement (m)
n.	funnel	mrija	entonnoir (m)
adj.	funny	-a kuchekesha	drôle
n.	fur	ngozi laini ya manyoya	fourrure (f)
adj.	furious	-enye hasira nyingi	furieux
verb	furnish, to	kupamba nyumba	fournir
adv.	further	mbele zaidi	plus
adv.	furthermore	zaidi	en outre
verb	fuss, to	kujisumbua bure	faire des histoires
adj.	futile	bure	futile
n.	future	wakati ujao	avenir (m)
n.	gain	faida	gain (m)
verb	gain, to	kupata faida	gagner
n., med	gallbladder	nyongo	vésicule biliaire
verb	gamble, to	kuchezea fedha	jouer
n.	game	mchezo (pl. michezo)	jeu (f)
n.	game, wild	mawindo	gibier (m)
n.	gap	mwanya	ouverture (f)
n.	garbage	takataka	ordures (m)
n.	garden	shamba (pl. mashamba)	jardin (m)
n.	gardener	mtunza bustani	jardinier (m)
verb	gargle, to	kusukutua kooni	gargariser
n.	garlic	kitunguu saumu	ail (m)
n.	garment	nguo	vêtement (m)
n.	gas	mvuke kama hewa	gaz (m)
verb	gasp, to	kutweta	avoir le souffle coupé
n.	gastritis	ugonjwa mmojawapo wa tumbo	gastrite (f)
n.	gate	mlango wa nje	porte (f)/barrière (f)
verb	gather, to	kuchuma	rassembler
n.	gathering	mkutano	rassemblement (m)
n.	gazelle	1. mpala 2. paa	gazelle (f)

parts of speech	english	swahili	french
adj. & n.	general	mkuu wa jeshi	général (m)
adv.	generally	kwa kawaida	généralement
n.	generation	kizazi (pl. vizazi)	génération (f)
n.	generosity	ukarimu	générosité (f)
adj.	generous	-karimu	généreux
n.	genius	mwenye akili maalum	génie (m)
adj.	gentle	-pole	doux
n.	gentleman	mwungwana (waungwana)	monsieur (m)
adv.	gently	polepole	tout doucement
adj.	genuine	hasilia	véritable
n.	German	Mjeremani (person), Kidachi	allemand (m)
verb	germinate, to	kuchipuka	germer
verb	get off, to	kushuka	débarquer
verb	get up, to	kusimama	lever, se
verb	get, to; to be given	kupata	recevoir
n.	ghost	roho, kizuka	fantôme (m)
n.	giant	jitu (pl. majitu)	géant (m)
n.	gift	zawadi	don (m)
n.	ginger	tangawizi	gingembre (m)
n.	giraffe	twiga	girafe (f)
n.	girl	msichana (pl. wasichana)	jeune fille (f)
n.	girlfriend	mpenzi (pl. wapenzi)	copine (f)
verb	give back, to	kurudisha	rendre
verb	give birth, to	kuzaa	enfanter
verb	give in, to	kushindwa	renoncer
verb	give, to	kupa	donner
verb	give, to	kutoa	donner
verb	glad, to be	kufurahi	heureux, être
n.	glance	kutupa jicho	coup d'oeil
n.	glass	kioo (pl. vioo)	verre (m)
n.	glasses (eye)	miwani	lunettes (f)
n.	glucose	sukari	glucose (f)
n.	glue	gundi	colle (f)
n.	glue	sherizi	résine (f)
n.	glutton	mlafi (pl. walafi)	goinfre (m)
verb	go away, to	kuondoka	partir
verb	go before, to	kutangulia	précéder
phrase	go out (fire) , to	kuzimika	s'éteindre
verb	go, to	kwenda	aller
verb	go, to; to leave	kwenda; kuondoka	partir

parts of speech	english	swahili	french
n.	goal	kikomo	objectif (m)
n.	goal (as in football)	mlango (pl. milango)	but (m)
n.	goat	mbuzi	chèvre (f)
n.	God	Mungu	Dieu (m)
n.	gold	dhahabu	or (m)
n. med	gonorrhea	kisonono	blennorragie (f)
adj.	good	-ema	1. bon (m), bonne (f) 2. bien
phrase	Good-bye.	Kwa heri.	Au revoir.
adj.	good-for-nothing	-a bure	vaurien
n.	good-night	kwa heri	bonsoir (m)
n.	goodness	wema	bonté (f)
n.	gorilla	maheshe	gorille (m)
n.	Gospel	Injili	évangile (m)
n.	gossip	porojo	bavardage (m)
n.	gourd	buyu (pl. mabuyu)	gourde (f)
verb	govern, to	kutawala	gouverner
n.	government	serkali	gouvernement (m)
n.	gown	kanzu	robe (f)
verb	grab, to	kunyakua	empoigner
n.	grace	neema	grâce (f)
n.	grain	nafaka	grain (m)
n.	grandchild	mjukuu (pl. wajukuu)	petit-fils (m),petit-fille (f)
n.	grandfather	babu	grand-père (m)
n.	grandmother	mama mkuu; nyanya	grand-mère (f)
verb	grant, to	kujalia	accorder
n.	grape	zabibu (pl.)	du raisin (m)
n.	grass	majani (pl.)	herbe (f)
n.	grasshopper	panzi (pl. mapanzi)	sauterelle (f)
n.	grave	kaburi (pl. makaburi)	tombe (f)
n.	gravel	changarawe	gravier (m)
n.	gravity	uzito	pesanteur (f)
n.	gravy	mchuzi (pl. michuzi)	jus (m) de viande
verb	graze, to	kulisha	brouter
n.	grease	mafuta	graisse (f)
adj.	great	-kubwa	grand
n.	greatness	ukubwa	grandeur (f)
n.	greed	choyo	avidité (f)
adj.	greedy	-lafi	cupide
adj.	green (color)	-a rangi ya majani; kijani	vert
adj.	green (unripe)	-bichi	pas mûr
verb	greet, to	kusalimu	accueillir

56

parts of speech	english	swahili	french
n.	greetings	salamu	salutation (f)
adj.	grey	kijivu	gris
n.	grief	huzuni	chagrin (m)
verb	grieve, to	kusikitika	peiner
verb	grind, to	kusaga	moudre
n.	groan	mauguzi	gémissement (m)
verb	groan, to; to wail	kuugua	gémir
n.	groceries	vyakula	provisions (f)
n.	groin	mamena	aine (f)
n.	ground	ardhi	terre (f)
n.	ground nut, peanut	karanga	arachide (f)
n.	group	kundi (pl. makundi)	groupe (m) de personnes
verb	grow, to	kuota	croître
verb	growl, to	kunguruma	gronder
verb	grumble, to	kunungunika	bougonner
n.	guarantee	rahani	garantie (f)
n.	guard	mlinzi (pl. walinzi), zamu	1. garde (f) 2. gardien (m)
verb	guard, to	kuchunga, kulinda	garder
n.	guava	pera	goyave
verb	guess, to	kukisi	deviner
n.	guest	mgeni (pl. wageni)	invité (f)
n.	guest room	chomba cha mgeni	chambre d'amis (f)
n.	guide	kiongozi (pl. viongozi)	guide (m)
n.	guilt	hatia	culpabilité (f)
adj.	gullible	-jinga	crédule
n.	gun	bunduki	arme à feu (f)
n.	gurgling (sound made when drinking water)	guru	glouglou (m)
n.	gutter	mchirizi	caniveau (m)
n.	habit	desturi, mazoea	habitude (f)
n.	hail	mvua ya mawe	grêle (f)
n.	hair (of human) {I want a haircut.}	unywele (pl. nywele) {Nataka kutaka nywele.}	cheveu(m) {J'ai besoin me faire couper les cheveux.}
n.	hairbrush	burashi ya nywele	brosse à cheveux (f)
n.	half	nusu	1. moitié (f) 2. demi (adv.)
n.	hallucination	mazigazi	hallucination (f)
n.	halo	uzingo	auréole (f)
n.	hammer	nyundo	marteau (m)
n.	hammock	machila	hamac (m)
n.	hand	mkono (pl. mikono)	main (f)
n.	hand, left	mukono wa kushoto	main gauche

parts of speech	english	swahili	french
n.	hand, right	mukono wa kuume	main droit
n.	handcuffs	pinga ya mikono	menotte (f)
n.	handkerchief	kitambaa	mouchoir (m)
n.	handle	mpini, shikio	anse (f)
adj.	handsome	-zuri	beau
verb	hang up, to	kutundika	raccrocher
verb	hang, to	kutungika	suspendre, être pendant
verb	happen, to	kupita	passer, se
n.	happiness	heri	bonheur (m)
adj.	happy	-a furaha	heureux
phrase	Happy birthday.	Heri za siku kuu ya kuzaliwa.	Joyeux anniversaire.
verb	happy, to be	kufurahi	heureux, être
verb	happy, to make	kufurahisha	faire heureux
verb	harass, to	kutesa	harceler
adj.	hard	-gumu	dur
n.	hardness, severity	ugumu	dureté (f)
n.	hardship	mashaka	épreuves (f) privations
n.	hare	sungura	lièvre (m)
verb	harm, to	kudhuru	faire du mal
adj.	harmless	si -a shari	inoffensif
n.	harp	kinubi (pl. vinubi)	harpe (f)
adj.	harsh	-kali	sévère
n.	harvest	mavuno (pl.)	moisson (f)
verb	harvest, to	kuvuna	récolter
n.	hat	kofia	chapeau (m)
verb	hate, to	kuchukia	haïr
phrase	Have a good evening.	Magalibi mzuli.	Ayez la bonne soirée.
phrase	Have a good morning.	Muchana muzuli.	Ayez la bonne journée
phrase	Have a good night.	Usiku muzuli.	Ayez la bonne nuit.
phrase	Have a good trip.	Safari njema.	Ayez la bon voyage.
verb	have a stool (bowel movement), to	kunya; kuenda choo	déféquer
verb	have, to	kuwa na	avoir
adj.	hazardous	-a hatari	hasardeux
n.	haze	unyenyezi	brume (f)
pronoun	he	yeye	il
n.	head	kichwa (pl. vichwa)	tête (f)
n.	headache	maumivu ya kichwa	mal de tête (m)
phrase	headache., I have a	Nina maumiva ya kichwa.	J'ai mal à la tête.
verb	heal, to; to cure	kupona	guérir

parts of speech	english	swahili	french
n.	health	afya	santé (f)
n.	health center	kituo cha afya	centre de santé (f)
adj.	healthy	-enye afya	sain
n.	heap	chungu	tas (m)
verb	hear, to	kusikia	entendre
n.	heart	moyo (pl. mioyo)	cœur (m)
n.	heart attack	kushambuliwa na maradhi	crise cardiaque (f)
n.	heartburn	kiungulia	brûlures d'estomac
n.	heat	joto, moto	chaleur (f)
verb	heat, to	kupasha moto	chauffer
adj. & n.	heathen	mshenzi (pl. washenzi)	païen (m), païenne (f)
n.	heaven	mbinguni	ciel (m)
adj.	heavy	-zito	lourd
n.	hedge	ugo (pl. nyugo)	haie (f)
n.	heel	kisingino (pl. visingino)	talon (m)
n.	height	kimo, urefu	taille (f)
n.	hell	gehena	enfer (m)
interj.	Hello.	Jambo.	Allô.
n.	help	musaada	aide (f)
verb	help, to	kusaidia	aider à
adj.	helpful	-a kusaidia	obligeant
adj.	helpless	hoi	impotent
n.	hemorrhage	kutoa damu	hémorragie (f)
n.	hen	kuku	poule (f)
adv.	henceforth	tangu sasa	dorénavant
n.	hepatitis	uvimbi wa ini	hépatite (f)
adj & pr	her	yeye, -ake	son (m), sa (f), ses (pl)
n.	herd	kundi (pl. makundi)	troupeau (m)
adv.	here	hapa, huko	ici
adv.	here (Here and there.)	hapa, huko (huko na huko)	ci (Par ci, part là.)
adv.	here is	ndi	voici
phrase	Here is my prescription for medicine.	Nina agizo la daktari.	Voici une ordonnance de mon médecin.
adv.	hereafter	baadaye	après cela
phrase	hereditary trait	ufananaji wa mtoto na wazazi wake	caractère héréditaire
n.	hero	shujaa	héros (m)
pronoun	herself	yeye mwenyewe	elle-même
verb	hesitate, to	kusita	hésiter
n.	hiccup	kwikwi	hoquet (m)
verb	hide, to	kuficha	cacher

parts of speech	english	swahili	french
adj.	hideous	-enye sura ya kuchukiza	hideux
adj.	high	-refu, -kuu	haut
phrase	hiking, to go	kutembea parini	faire une randonnée
n.	hill	mlima (pl. milima)	colline (f)
pronoun	him	yeye	le, lui
verb	hinder, to	kuzuia	gêner
n.	hinderance	kizuio (pl. vizuio)	empêchement (m)
n.	Hindu	hindi	Hindou (m)
n.	hinge	pata (pl. mapata)	gond (m)
n.	hippopotamus	kiboko (pl. viboko)	hippopotame (m)
verb	hire, to	kuajiri	louer
adj.	his	-ake	son (m), sa (f), ses (pl)
n.	history	hadisi	histoire (f)
verb	hit, to	kupiga	frapper
phrase	hither and yon	mpaka sasa	ici et y là
n.	hoe	jembe (pl. majembe)	houe (f)
verb	hoe, to	kulima	biner
verb	hold, to	kushika	tenir
n.	hole	tundu (pl. matundu)	trou (m)
verb	hollow out, to	kukomba	évider
adj.	holy	-takatifu	saint
n.	Holy Spirit	Roho Mtakatifu	Saint-Esprit (m)
prep.	home	nyumba	chez
n	homeless	msikwao	sans abri
adj.	homesick	hamu ya kwao	nostalgique
adj.	honest	-nyofu	honnête
n.	honesty	uaminifu	honnêteté (f)
n.	honey	asali	miel (m)
n.	honor	heshima	honneur (m)
verb	honor, to	kuheshimu	honorer
n.	hoof	ukwato (pl. kwato)	sabot (m)
n.	hook	ndobani, kulabu	hameçon (m)
n.	hope	matumaini	espérance (f), espoir (m)
verb	hope, to	kutumaini	espérer
n.	horizon	upeo wa macho	horizon (m)
n.	horn (of animal)	pembe (pl. mapembe)	corne (f)
n.	horse	farasi	cheval (m)
n.	hospital	hospitali	hôpital (m)
n.	hostility	uadui	hostilité
adj.	hot	-a moto	chaud
n.	hot dry season	kiangazi	saison sèche

parts of speech	english	swahili	french
n.	hour	saa	heure (f)
n.	house (traditional)	nyumba	maison (f) (traditionnelle)
adv.	how	namna gani	comment
phrase	How are you doing?	Mambo?	Comment fait-tu?
phrase	How are you?	Hujambo? (singular); Hamjambo? (plural)	Comment ça va?
phrase	How is your family?	Habari za nyumbani?	Comment est votre famille?
phrase	how long	kwa muda gani	combien de temps
phrase	How long have you been ill?	Umekuwa hivyo kwa muda gani?	Il y a combien de temps que tu es malade?
phrase	how many	-ngapi	combien de
phrase	How many times?	Malangapi?	Combien de fois?
adv.	how much	-ngapi	combien
phrase	How much does this cost?	Ni bei gani?	Combien est ceci?
adv.	however	walakini	1. pourtant 2. cependant
verb	hug, to	kukumbatia	serrer dans ses bras
adj.	human	-a mtu	humain (m)
adj.	humane	-enye huruma	humain
verb	humble, to be	kunyenyekea	humble, être
n., med	humerus	mfupa wa mkono katkati ya kiko na bega	humérus
n.	humility	unyenyekevu	humilité (f)
adj. & n.	hundred (one hundred)	mia (mia moja)	cent (m)
n. & adj.	hundred thousand	laki	cent mille
n.	hunger	njaa	faim (f)
adj.	hungry	-enye njaa	affamé
verb	hunt, to	kuwinda	chasser
n.	hunter	mwindaji (pl. waindaji)	chausseur (m)
n.	hurricane	zoruba	ouragan (m)
adv.	hurriedly	haraka	précipitamment
n.	hurry, haste	haraka	hâte (f)
verb	hurry, to	kufanya haraka	marcher vite
n.	husband	mume (pl. waume)	mari (m)
n.	hyena	fisi	hyène
n.	hymn	wimbo (pl. nyimbo)	hymne (m)
n.	hypocrisy	unafiki	hypocrisie (f)
n.	hysteria	ugonjwa wa akili	hystérie (f)
pronoun	I	mimi	Je
phrase	I am full.	Nimeshiba.	Je suis rassasié.
phrase	I am going to the airport.	Ninakwenda uwanja wa ndege.	Je vais à l'aéroport.
phrase	I am going to...	Ninakwenda...	Je vais à...

parts of speech	english	swahili	french
phrase	**I am happy.**	Nisikia furaha.	Je suis heureux.
phrase	**I am hungry.**	Nina njaa.	J'ai faim.
phrase	**I am ill.**	Mimi ni mgonjwa.	Je suis malade.
phrase	**I am looking for...**	Nataka...	Je veux...
phrase	**I am not hungry.**	Sisikii njaa.	J'ai ne pas faim.
phrase	**I am thirsty.**	Nasikia kiu.	J'ai soif.
phrase	**I am tired.**	Nasikia hafifu.	Je suis fatigué.
phrase	**I cannot.**	Siwezi.	Je ne puis pas.
phrase	**I do not like...**	Sipenda...	Je n'aime pas...
phrase	**I do not want...**	Sitaki...	Je ne veux pas...
phrase	**I don't have money.**	Sina pesa.	Je n'ai pas de l'argent.
phrase	**I don't have...**	Sina...	Je n'ai pas...
phrase	**I don't know.**	Sijui.	Je ne connais pas (ou) Je ne sais pas.
phrase	**I don't mind.**	Ni mamoja kwangu.	Pas de problème.
phrase	**I don't understand.**	Naelewa.	Je ne comprends pas.
phrase	**I know.**	Ninajua.	Je sais (or) Je connais.
phrase	**I like...**	Ninapenda...	J'aime...
phrase	**I need a nurse right away.**	Nahitaji mwuguzi sasa.	J'ai besoin une infirmière tout de suite.
phrase	**I need...**	Nahitaji...	J'ai besoin...
interj.	**I say... (look here)**	Ati...	Dis donc...
phrase	**I speak a little Swahili.**	Nasema kidogo Kiswahili.	Je parle un peu le kiswahili.
phrase	**I want something to treat diarrhea.**	Nataka dawa kwa kuhara.	J'ai besoin de quelque chose contre la diarrhée.
phrase	**I want...**	Nataka...	Je voudrais..., Je veux...
n.	**ice**	barafu	glace (f)
n.	**idea**	wazo	idée (f)
n.	**idiot**	juha	idiot (m)
adj.	**idle**	-vivu	fainéant
n.	**idleness**	uvivu	oisiveté (f)
n.	**idol**	sanamu ya kuabudiwa	idole (f)
conj.	**if**	kama	si
n.	**ignoramus**	mjinga (pl. wajinga)	ignare (m,f)
n.	**ignorance**	ujinga	ignorance (f)
verb	**ignore someone to**	kutoangalia	négliger
verb	**ill, to be**	1. kuwa mgonjwa 2. kuugua	malade, être
n.	**ill-will**	husuda	rancune (f)
adj.	**illiterate**	asiyefundishwa	illettré
n.	**illness, disease, sickness, malady**	ugonjwa (pl. maogonjwa)	maladie (f)
n.	**image**	sura	image (f)

parts of speech	english	swahili	french
verb	imitate, to	kuiga	imiter
adv.	immediately, right now	mara moja	immédiatement
verb	immerse, to	kuchovya	plonger
adj.	impartial	bila upendeleo	impartial
verb	impasse, to be at an	kutopitika	se trouver dans une impasse
adj.	impatient	-enye haraka	impatient
verb	implore, to	kusihi	implorer
adj.	impolite	-sio adabu	impoli
n.	importance	maana	importance (f)
adj.	important	muhimu	important
verb	impossible to do, to be	kutowezekana	impossible à faire, être
adj.	impotent	pasipo nguvu	impotent
verb	improve, to	kukuza hali	améliorer
n.	improvement	maendeleo mazuri	amélioration (f)
adj.	impulsive	-enye haraka	impulsif
prep.	in, into	katika	en, dans
n.	in-laws	semeki	beaux-parents (m)
adj.	incapable	-sioweza	incapable
n.	inception	mwanzo (pl. mianzo)	commencement (m)
n.	inch	inchi	pouce (m)
n.	incident	tukio (pl. matukio)	incident (m)
verb	incise, to	kukata	inciser
n.	income	mpato	revenu (m)
verb	increase, to	kuzidi	augmenter
verb	inculcate, to	kufundisha	inculquer
n.	indecision	kusita moyoni	indécision (f)
adv.	indeed; in fact	kweli	en effet
verb	independent, to be	kujiangalia	indépendant, être
n.	Indian	Mhindi	Indien (m)
adj.	indiscreet	-a kukosa busara	indiscret
adj.	inert	-tepetevu	inerte
n.	infancy	utoto	toute petite enfance (f)
n.	infant	mtoto mdogo	un nouveau-né
n., med	infection	ambukizo	infection (f)
adj. & n.	inferior to	duni	inférieur (m)
n.	influence	mvuto	influence (f)
verb	inform, to	kufahamisha	instruire, notifier
adj.	infrequent	si mara nyingi	peu fréquent
verb	inhabit, to	kukaa	habiter
verb	inherit, to	kurisi	hériter
n.	inheritance	uriti	héritage (m)

63

parts of speech	english	swahili	french
n.	injection	dawa ya sindano	injection (f)
verb	injure, to	kudhuru	blesser
n.	injury	madhara	blessure (f)
n.	ink	wino	encre (f)
n.	innocence	usafi	innocence (f)
adj.	innocent	bila hatia	innocent
n.	inquiry	swali (pl. maswali)	enquête (f)
adj.	insatiable	isiyotosheleka	insatiable
n.	insect	mdudu (pl. wadudu)	insecte (m)
verb	insert, to	kuingiza ndani	insérer
adv. prep.	inside	ndani ya	dedans (m)
adj.	insignificant	duni	insignifiant
verb	insist, to	kushurutisha	insister
n.	insolence	ufidhuli	insolence (f)
verb	inspire, to	kutia moyoni	inspirer
phrase	instance, for	kwa mfano	exemple, par
adj.	instantaneous	pale pale	instantané
adv.	instantly	mara moja	immédiatement
adv.	instead	badalya ya	au lieu de cela
verb	instruct, to	kufundisha	instruire
adj.	insubordinate	-ate	insubordonné
adj.	insufficient	haba	insuffisant
n.	insult	matusi (pl.)	insulte (f)
verb	insult, to	kuzarau	1. calomnier 2. insulter
n.	insurgent	mwasi	insurgé (m)
n.	intelligence	akili	intelligence (f)
adj.	intelligent	-enye akili	intelligent
verb	intend, to	kukusudi	avoir l'intention
n.	intention	kusudi (pl. makusudi)	intention (f)
adv.	intentionally	kwa kusudi	intentionnellement
n.	interim	muda wa kati	intérim (m)
n.	interior	upande wa ndani	intérieur (m)
adj.	interminable	-a daima	interminable
verb	interpret, to ask to	kufasiri	demander des explications
n.	interpreter	mkalimani	interprète (m,f)
verb	interrogate, to	kuulizauliza	interroger
verb	interrupt, to	kudakiza	interrompre
n.	interruption	madakizo	interruption (f)
n., med	intestinal worms	minyoo	vers (ascaris)
n., med	intestines	matumbo (pl.)	intestins
verb	intimidate, to	kutisha	intimider

parts of speech	english	swahili	french
n.	intimidation	kitisho	intimidation (f)
verb	intoxicated, to be	kulewa	s'enivrer
verb	introduce (something new), to	kuingiza	introduire
verb	invade, to	kushambulia	envahir
adj. & n.	invalid	mgonjwa (pl. wagonjwa)	infirme (m,f)
verb	invent, to	kuvumbua	inventer
n.	inventor	mtungaji (pl. watungaji)	inventeur (m)
verb	investigate, to	kupeleleza	scruter
n.	investigation	kuchungua	investigation (f)
verb	invigorate, to	kutia nguvu	fortifier
verb	invite, to	kualika	inviter
n.	iron (for clothes)	pasi	fer (m) à repasser
n.	iron (ore)	chuma	fer (m)
verb	iron, to	kupiga pagi	repasser
adj.	irrational	isiyo na maana	déraisonnable
adj.	irregular	si ya kawaida	irrégulier
adj.	irrelevant	isiyohusu	sans rapport
verb	irritate, to	kuudhi	irriter
n.	irritation	kuwasho	irritation (f)
verb	is (to be)	ni	être
phrase	Is it close?	Ni karibu?	C'est près?
phrase	Is it far?	Ni mbali?	C'est loin?
n.	island	kisiwa (pl. visiwa)	île (f)
phrase	It does not matter.	Hamna shida. Hapana maneno.	Ça ne fait rien.
phrase	It is good.	Nzuri kabisa.	C'est bien.
pronoun	it, that (That is right.)	ile, kile, vile (Ndivyo.)	cela (C'est cela.)
n	itch	upele	démangeaison (f)
verb	itch, to	kuwasha	démanger
pronoun	itself	-enyewe	lui-même (m), elle-même (f)
phrase	I'm fine.	Sijambo	Ça va bien.
phrase	I've got a headache.	Nina maumiva ya kichwa.	J'ai mal à la tête.
phrase	I've have a stomach ache.	Tumbo yangu inauma.	J'ai mal au ventre.
n.	jackal	mbweha	chacal
n.	jacket	koti (pl. makoti)	veston (m), jaquette (f)
n.	jail	kifungo (pl. vifungo), gereza	prison (f)
n.	January	Januari; mwezi wa kwanza wa mwaka wa kizungu	janvier (m)
n.	jar (container/shock)	chupa	pot (m), petit
n.	jaundice	safura	jaunisse (f)

65

parts of speech	english	swahili	french
n.	jaw	taya (pl. mataya)	mâchoire (f)
adj.	jealous	-wivu	jaloux
n.	jealousy	wivu	jalousie (f)
n.	Jesus	Yesu	Jésus (m)
n.	jewel	johari	bijou (m)
n.	job	kazi	travail (m)
verb	join, to (things, group)	kuunga	joindre, se
n.	joint (anatomy), articulation	kiungo (pl. viungo)	articulation (f)
n.	joint (anatomy), articulation	ungo (pl. maungo)	articulation (f)
n.	joint, link	kiungo (pl. viungo)	rapport (m)
n.	joke	neno la kuchekesha	plaisanterie (f)
verb	joke, to (I'm only joking.)	kucheka (Natania tu.)	badiner (Je plaisante.)
verb	jostle, to	kusukumana	bousculer
n.	journal	gazeti (pl. magazeti)	journal (m)
n.	joy	furaha	joie (f)
n.	judge	mwamuzi (pl. waamuzi)	juge (m)
verb	judge, to	kuhukumu	rendre un jugement
n.	judgement	hukumu	jugement (m)
n.	jug	mtungi (pl. mitungi)	cruche (f)
n.	July	Julai; mwezi wa saba wa mwaka wa kizungu	juillet (m)
verb	jump, to	kuruka	sauter
n.	June	Juni; mwezi wa sita wa mwaka kizungu	juin (m)
n.	jungle	mwitu	jungle (f), brousse (f)
n.	justice	haki	justice (f)
verb	keep on, to	kuendelea	continuer à
verb	keep, to	kuweka	garder
n.	ketchup	mchuzi wa nyanya	ketchup (m)
n.	key {I lost my keys.}	ufunguo (pl. funguo) {Nilipoteza funguo.)	clé (f) {J'ai perdu mes clefs.}
phrase	kick	teke (pl. mateke)	coup de pied
verb	kick, to	kupiga teke	donner un coup de pied
n., med	kidney	figo (pl. mafigo)	rein (m)
verb	kill, to	kuua	tuer
n.	kiln	tanuu	four (m)
n.	kin	jamaa	famille (f)
n.	kind (species)	namna	genre (m)
n.	kindness	fadhili	bienfait (m)
n.	king	mfalme (pl. wafalme)	roi (m)

parts of speech	english	swahili	french
n.	kingdom	ufalme	royaume (m)
verb	kiss, to	kubusu	embrasser
n.	kitchen	jiko	cuisine (f)
n.	kite	tiara	cerf-volant (m)
verb	knead (as in bread), to	kukanda	malaxer, pétrir
n	knee	goti (pl. magoti)	genou (m)
n.	knee cap	pia ya goti	rotule (du genou)
verb	kneel, to	kupiga magoti	s'agenouiller
n.	knife	kisu (pl. visu)	couteau (m)
verb	knit, to	kusuka	tricoter
verb	knock, to	kugonga	frapper
n.	knot	fundo (pl. mafundo)	nœud (m)
verb	knot, to tie a	kupiga fundo	nouer
verb	know, to	kujua	1. savoir 2. connaître
n.	knowledge	maarifa	1. science (f) 2. connaissance (f)
n.	knuckles	konzi	articulation (f) du doigt
n.	laboratory	nyumba ya sayansi	laboratoire (m)
n.	lace	nguo ya kimia	lacet (m)
adj.	lacking	-tovu	simplet
n.	ladder	ngazi	échelle (f)
n.	lady	bibi	dame (f)
n.	lair	malalo ya mnyama wa mwitu	tanière (f)
n.	lake	ziwa (pl. maziwa)	lac (m)
n.	lamp	taa	lampe (f)
n	land	nchi	terre (f)
n.	language	lugha	langage (m)
adj.	large	-kubwa	grande, gros
n., med	laryngitis	ugonjwa wa kuumia kikoromeo	laryngite (f)
n., med	larynx	kikoromeo	larynx
adj.	last	-a mwisho	dernier
phrase	last year	mwaka wa jana	an passé
verb	late, to be	kuchelewa	être en retard
adv.	lately	siku hizi	dernièrement
adv.	later	baadaye	plus retard
verb	laugh, to	kucheka	rire
n.	laughter	kicheko	rires (m)
n.	laundry	kiwanda cha dobi	linge (m)
n.	law	sheria	loi (f)
adj.	lawful	halali	légal

parts of speech	english	swahili	french
n	lawsuit	kesi	intenter un procès
n.	lawyer	mwana sheria	juriste (m)
verb	lay, to	kuweka, kulaza	poser
n.	laziness	uvivu	paresse (f)
adj.	lazy	-vivu	paresseux
n.	lazy person	mvivu (pl. wavivu)	fainéant (m), fainéante (f)
verb	lead, to	kuongoza	mener
n.	leader	kiongozi (pl. viongozi)	chef (m)
n.	leaf	jani	feuille (f)
verb	leak, to	kuvuja	fuir
verb	lean on, to	kuegemea, kutegemea	s'appuyer contre
verb	leap, to	kuruka	bondir
verb	learn, to	kufundishwa, kujifunza	apprendre
adj.	learned	-enye elimu	savant
adj.	least	-dogo kabisa	moindre
phrase	least, at	lakini	au moindre
verb	leave of, to take	kuaga	prendre congé
verb	leave, to	kuacha	laisser
n.	leaven	chachu	levain (m)
n., adj.	left	upande wa kushuto; -a kushoto	gauche (f)
n.	leg	mguu (pl. miguu)	jambe (f)
verb	legalize, to	kuhalalisha	légaliser
n.	legend	hekaya	légende (f)
n.	lemon	limau (pl. malimau)	citron (m)
verb	lend, to	kukopesha	prêter
n.	length (dimension, time)	urefu	longueur (f)/durée (f)
verb	lengthen, to	kuongeza urefu	allonger
n.	leniency	huruma	indulgence (f)
n.	leopard	chui	léopard (m)
n.	leper	mwenye ukoma	lépreux (m)
n.	leprosy	ukoma	lèpre (f)
n.	lesson	somo (pl. masomo)	leçon (f)
verb	let, to	kuacha	laisser
n.	letter (as in, I wrote a letter to a friend.)	barua	lettre (f)
n.	letter (of alphabet)	herufi	lettre (f)
n.	lettuce	saladi	laitue (f)
phrase	Let's go!	Basi, safari!	Allons-y!
adj.	level	sawa	plat
n.	liability	madaraka	responsabilité (f)

parts of speech	english	swahili	french
n.	liar	mwongo (pl. waongo)	menteur (m), menteuse (f)
verb	liberate, to	kufanya huru	libérer
n.	liberty, freedom	uhuru	liberté (f)
n.	library	jamii ya vitabu	bibliothèque (f)
n.	lice	chawa	pou (m)
n.	license	ruhusu	patente (f)
verb	lick, to	kulamba	lécher
n.	lid	kifuniko (pl. vifuniko)	couvercle (m)
verb	lie down, to	kulala	s'étendre
n.	lie, falsehood	uwongo	mensonge (m)
verb	lie, to	kusema uongo	mentir
n.	life	maisha, udogo	vie (f)
verb	lift, to	kuinua	1. lever 2. soulever
adj.	light	-epesi	léger
n.	light	nuru	lumière (f)
verb	light (kindle), to	kuwasha	allumer
n.	lightning	umeme	éclair (m)
prep.	like	kama	pareil
verb	like, to	kupenda	aimer
verb	like, to be	kufanana na	ressembler à
n.	likeness	mfano (pl. mifano)	ressemblance (f)
n.	lime (fruit)	ndimu	citron (m) vert
n.	lime (substance)	chokaa	terra blanche
n.	limit, boundary	mpaka (pl. mipaka)	borne (f)
verb	limit, to	kuweka mpaka	limiter
n.	limitation	mpaka (pl. mipaka)	limitation (f)
n.	line	mstari (pl. mistari)	ligne (f)
n.	lion	simba	lion (m)
n.	lip	mdomo (pl. midomo)	lèvre (f)
verb	listen, to	kusikiliza	écouter
n. & adv	little	-dogo	peu (m)
phrase	little by little	kidogo kwa kidogo	petit à petit
verb	live to	kuishi	vivre
n.	livelihood	maishilio	moyens (m) d'existence
n.	liver	ini (pl. maini)	foie
n.	liver	maini	foie (m)
n.	lizard	mjusi	lézard (m)
n.	load	mzigo (pl. mizigo)	charge (f)
verb	load, to	kupakiza	charger
n.	loan (borrowing)	mkopo	fardeau (m)
verb	loan, to	kukopesha	prêter

69

parts of speech	english	swahili	french
n.	locality	mahali fulani	localité (f)
verb	lock, to	kufunga	fermer à clef
n.	locust	nzige	sauterelle (f)
n.	lodging place	mahali pa kukaa	logement (m)
n.	log	gogo (pl. magogo)	bûche (f)
n.	loneliness	upweke	solitude (f)
adj.	long	-refu	long (m), longue (f)
adv.	long ago	zamani sana	longtemps, il y a
verb	long for, to	kutamani	désirer ardemment
verb	look after, to	kutunza	s'occuper de
verb	look for, to	kutafuta	chercher
interj.	Look!	Lino!	Attention!
verb	look, to	kutazama	regarder
n.	lord	maulana	seigneur (m)
verb	lose weight, to	kukondesha	faire maigrir
verb	lose, to	kupoteza	perdre
n.	loss	hasara	perte (f)
verb	lost, to be	kupotea	perdre, se
n.	love	mapendo	amour (m)
verb	love, to	kupenda	aimer
adj.	low	-fupi	bas (f. basse)
adj.	lower	chini zaidi	inférieur
verb	lower, to	kushusha	1. baisser 2. abaisser
n.	lozenge	kidonge cha kufyonza	pastille (f)
n.	lubricant	mafuta	lubrifiant (m)
adj.	lucky	-a bahati njema	chance, avoir de la
n.	luggage	mizigo	bagages (m pl.)
adj.	lukewarm	uvuguvugu	tiède
n.	lullaby	kitumbuizo	berceuse (f)
n., med	lumbago	maumivu ya viunoni	lumbago
n.	lump	bonge	morceau (m)
n.	lunatic	mkichaa	fou (m), folle (f)
n.	lunch	chakula cha mchana	déjeuner
n.	lung	pafu	poumon (m)
n.	lust	tamaa	luxure (f)
n.	luxury	anasa	luxe (m)
n.	machete	panga (pl. mapanga)	machette
n.	machine	mashini	machine (f)
adj.	mad (insane)	-enye wazimu	fou (f. folle)
n.	maggot	buu (pl. mabuu)	ver (m)
n.	magic	uganga	magie (f)

parts of speech	english	swahili	french
verb	**magnify, to**	kukuza	grossir
n.	**magnitude**	ukubwa	grandeur (f)
n.	**mahogany**	mkangazi	acajou (f)
n.	**maid**	mwanamwali	bonne (f)
n.	**mail**	posta	poste (f)
verb	**maintain, to**	kushika	maintenir
n.	**maintenance**	msaada (pl. misaada)	maintien (m)
n.	**maize, corn**	muhindi (pl. mihindi)	maïs (m)
n.	**majesty**	enzi	majesté (f)
n.	**majority**	wingi	majorité (f)
verb	**make believe, to**	kujifanya	faire semblant
verb	**make good, to**	kufaulu	se tirer d'affaire
verb	**make sure, to**	kuhakikisha	certifier
verb	**make up, to**	kubuni	rattraper
verb	**make, to**	1. kufanya 2. kufanyiza	fabriquer
n.	**malaria**	homa ya mbu	malaria (f)
adj. & n.	**male**	mwanamume (pl. wanaume)	mâle (m)
n.	**malice**	kijicho	méchanceté (f)
verb	**malign, to**	kusingizia	calomnier
n.	**malnutrition**	ukosefu wa chakula chema	sous-alimentation (f)
n.	**mama**	mama mzazi	mère (f)
n.	**man**	1. mwanadamu (pl. wanadamu) 2. mwanaume (pl. wanaume)	homme (m)
verb	**manage, to**	kuamuru	gérer
n.	**manager**	msimamizi (pl. wasimamizi)	directeur (m)
n.	**mange**	upele wa mbwa	gale (f)
n.	**mango (fruit)**	embe (pl. maembe)	mangue (f)
n.	**manifestation**	ufunuo	manifestation (f)
n.	**manner**	jinsi	manière (f)
n.	**manners, good**	adabu	bonnes manières (f)
adj.	**many**	-ingi	beaucoup
n.	**map**	ramani	carte (f) géographique
n.	**March**	Machi; mwezi wa tatu wa mwaka wa kizungu	mars (m)
n.	**mark**	alama	marque (f)
verb	**mark, to**	kutia alama	marquer
n.	**market**	soko (pl. masoko)	marché (m)
n.	**marriage**	ndoa	mariage (m)
phrase	**marriage proposal**	kuposa	demande en mariage

parts of speech	english	swahili	french
verb	**marry, to**	1. kuoa (man) 2. kuolewa (woman)	marier, se
n.	**martyr**	shahidi	martyr (m), martyre (f)
verb	**mash, to**	kuseta	faire de la purée
n.	**mason**	mwashi	maçon (m)
n.	**master**	mwalimu (pl. walimu)	maître (m)
verb	**master, to**	kushinda	maîtriser
n.	**mat**	jamvi	paillasson (m)
n.	**mat, grass woven**	mkeka (pl. mikeka)	paillasson (m), herbe
n.	**match**	kiberiti (pl. viberiti)	allumette (f)
n.	**mate (a pair of things), companion**	mwenzi (pl. wenzi)	compagnon (m), compagne (f)
n.	**math**	elimu ya hesabu	mathématiques (f)
n.	**mattress**	godoro (pl. magodoro)	matelas (m)
adj. & n.	**maximum**	kipeo	maximum (m)
n.	**May**	Mei; mwezi wa tano wa mwaka wa kizingu	mai (m)
adv.	**maybe**	labda	peut-être
pronoun	**me**	mimi	moi
n.	**meal**	chakula (pl. vyakula)	repas (m)
verb	**meal, to have (to eat)**	kula	manger
n.	**meaning**	maana	sens (m)
adj.	**meaningless**	bila maana	dénué de sens
n.	**means (of doing something)**	njia	moyen (m)
n.	**measles**	surua	rougeole (f)
verb	**measure, to**	kupima	mesurer
n.	**measurement**	kipimo (pl. vipimo)	mesure (f)
n.	**meat**	nyama	viande (f)
n.	**mechanic**	fundi wa mashine	mécanicien (m)
phrase	**meddler**	mdukizi	touche-à-tout
n.	**medication; medicine**	dawa	médicament (m)
phrase	**medicine, practice of**	uganga	l'art de guérir
verb	**meditate, to**	kutafakari	méditer
adj.	**medium**	-a kadiri	moyen
adj.	**meek**	-pole	doux
verb	**meet, to**	kukutana	rencontrer
n.	**meeting**	mkutano (pl. mikutano)	réunion (f)
phrase	**meeting place**	kiagano	rendez-vous (m)
verb	**melt, to (sugar)**	kuyeyusha	fondre
n.	**member**	kiungo (pl. viungo)	membre (m)
verb	**memorize, to**	kujifunza kwa moyo	retenir

parts of speech	english	swahili	french
n.	memory	uwezo wa kukumbuka	mémoire (f)
verb	mend, to	kutengeneza	raccommoder
n., med	meningitis	ugonjwa wa ngozi inayufunika ubongo	méningite
n., med	menopause	wakati wa mwanamke kuingia ugumba	ménopause
verb	menstruate, to	kuingia mwezini	avoir ses règles
n.	menstruation	hedhi	menstruation (f)
verb	mention, to	kutaja	mentionner
n.	menu	orodha ya vyakula	menu (m)
adj. & n.	mercenary	askari mgeni wa mshahara	mercenaire (m)
n.	mercy	rehema	miséricorde (f)
adv.	merely	tu	simplement
verb	merit, to	kustahili	mériter
n.	message	maneno	message (m)
n	messenger	mjumbe (pl. wajumbe)	messager (m)
n.	metal	madini	métal (m)
n.	meter	meta	compteur (m)
n.	method	kawaida	méthode (f)
n.	middle	kati	milieu (m)
n.	midnight	saa sita usika	minuit (m)
n.	midwife	mkunga	sage-femme (f)
adj.	mild	-pole	doux
n.	mildew	kawa	rouille (f)
n.	mile	maili	mile (m)
n.	milk	maziwa (pl.)	lait (m)
verb	milk, to	kukama	traire
n.	millet	mtama (pl. mitama)	grain (m)
verb	mimic, to	kuiga	imiter
n.	mind	akili	esprit (m)
n.	minute	dakika	minute (f)
phrase	minute., Just a	Ngo jasaa kidogo.	Attends une minute.
n.	miracle	mwujiza	miracle (m)
n.	mirror	kioo (pl. vioo)	miroir (m)
verb	misbehave, to	kukosa adabu	conduire mal, se
verb	miscalculate, to	kufikiri yasivyo	mal calculer
n.	miscarriage	kuharibika mimba	échec (m)
adj.	miscellaneous	-a namna nyingi	divers
n.	mischief	fitina	espièglerie (f)
n.	miser	bahili	avare (m,f)
n.	misery	huzuni	misère

parts of speech	english	swahili	french
n.	misfortune	bahati mbaya	malheur (m)
n.	misgiving	shaka	appréhension
verb	misjudge, to	kupima visivyo	mal évaluer
n.	Miss	mwali	mademoiselle (f)
verb	miss, to	kukosa	manquer
n.	mist	ukungu	brume (f)
n.	mistake	kosa (pl. makosa)	faute (f)
verb	mistrust, to	kushuku	se méfier de
verb	mix, to	kuchanganya	1. malaxer 2. mélanger
n.	mixture	mchanganyiko (pl. michanganyiko)	mélange (m)
verb	moan, to	kuugua	gémir
verb	mock, to	kudhihaki	se moquer de
n.	mockery	dhihaka	raillerie (f)
adv.	moderately	si sana	avec modération
verb	modify, to	kugeuza kidogo	faire changer de forme
n.	moisture	rutuba	humidité (f)
n.	mole	fuko	taupe (f)
n.	moment	nukta	moment (m)
n.	Monday	Jamatatu	lundi (m)
n.	money	feza	argent (m)
n.	money	pesa	monnaie (m)
n.	monitor lizard	kenge	lézard, grand
verb	monitor, to	kuhakiki	assurer
n.	monk	mtawa mwanamume	moine (m)
n.	monkey	kima	singe (m)
verb	monopolize, to	kujishikia yote	monopoliser
n.	monotony	kuchosha	monotonie (f)
n.	month	mwezi (pl. miezi)	mois (m)
n.	moon	mwezi (pl. miezi)	lune (f)
adv.	more	zaidi	plus
adv.	moreover	zaidi ya hayo	de plus, d'ailleurs
adj.	moribund	-a kufani	moribond
adv. n.	morning	asubuhi	matin (m)
n.	mosquito	mbu	moustique (m)
n.	mosquito net	chandalua (pl. vyandalua)	moustiquaire (m)
adj.	most	kupita yote	le plus
adv.	mostly	zaidi	pour la plupart
n.	moth	nondo	papillon (m) de nuit
n.	mother	mama mzazi	mère
adj.	motionless	kimya	immobile

74

parts of speech	english	swahili	french
n.	motive	kusudi (pl. makusudi)	motif (m)
adv.	motorcycle	pikipiki	motocyclette (f)
n.	mound	chungu	monceau (m)
n.	mountain	mlima (pl. milima)	montagne (f)
adj.	mountainous	-enye milima mingi	montagneux
verb	mourn, to	kuomboleza	1. se lamenter 2. pleurer
n.	mourning	kilio	deuil (m)
n.	mouse	panya mdogo	souris (f)
n.	mouth	kinywa (pl. vinywa)	bouche (f)
verb	move, to	kujongea	déplacer; s'avancer
verb	move, to	kusukuma	mouvoir
verb	move, to (dwelling)	kuhama	déménager
n.	movement	mwendo (pl. miendo)	mouvement (m)
n.	movie theater	filamu	cinéma (m)
verb	mow, to	kukata majani	faucher
n.	Mr.	bwana	M. (m) (for Monsieur)
n.	Mrs.	bibi	Mme. (f) (for madame)
adj & pr	much	-ingi	beaucoup
n.	mud	matope	boue (f)
verb	multiply, to	kuzidisha	multiplier
verb	mumble, to	kumumunya maneno	marmotter
n.	mumps	matubwitubwi	oreillons (m)
n.	murder	uuaji	meurtre (m)
n.	murderer	mwuaji (pl. waji)	assassin (m)
n.	muscle	mshipa	muscle (m)
n.	mushroom	kiyoga (pl. viyoga)	champignon (m)
n.	music	muziki	musique (f)
verb	must	lazima	devoir; il faut que
adj.	mute (without speech)	bila sauti	muet
adj.	my (my children)	-angu (wana wangu)	mon (m), ma (f), mes (pl) (mes enfants)
phrase	My name is...	Jina langu ni...	Je m'appelle...
pronoun	myself	mimi mwenyewe	moi-même
n.	mystery	siri, fumbo	mystère (m)
n.	nail (metal)	msumari (pl. misumari)	clou (m)
verb	nail, to	kupiga musumari	clouer
n.	nakedness	uchi	nudité (f)
n.	name	jina (pl. majina)	nom (m)
n.	name, first	jina la kupanga	surnom
verb	name, to	kutaja	nommer
n.	nap	usingizi mfupi	petit somme (m)

parts of speech	english	swahili	french
n.	napkin	kitambaa	serviette (de table)
verb	narrate, to	kusimulia	raconter
n.	narrative	masimulizi	récit (m)
adj.	narrow	-embamba	étroit
adv.	narrowly	kwa shida	de justesse
n.	nasal mucous	makamasi	morve (f)
adj.	nasty	-a kuchukiza	désagréable
n	nation	taifa (pl. mataifa)	nation (f)
n.	nationality	taifa la mtu fulani	nationalité (f)
n.	native	mwenyeji (pl. wenyeji)	indigène (m,f)
adv.	naturally	bila shaka	naturellement
n.	nature	maumbile	nature (f)
n., med	nausea	ugagazi	nausée
adv. prep.	near	karibu na	près
adj.	nearby	karibu	proche
n.	necessity	lazimu	nécessité (f)
n.	neck	shingo (mashingo)	cou (m)
n.	need	haja	besoin (m)
verb	need, to	kuhitaji	avoir besoin de
n.	needle	sindano	aiguille (f)
verb	neglect, to	kutoangalia	négliger
n.	negligence	uzembe	négligence
n.	neighbor	jirani	voisin (m), voisine (f)
n.	neighborhood	ujirani	voisinage (m)
conj.	neither...nor	wala...wala	ni...ni
n.	nephew	mpwa (pl. wapwa)	neveu (m)
n.	nerve	mshipa (pl. mishipa)	nerf (m)
n.	nest	kioto (pl. vioto)	nid (m)
n.	net	wavu (pl. nyavu)	filet (m)
adv.	never	kamwe	jamais
phrase	never mind	haidhuru	ça ne fait rien
interj.	Never!	Kamwe!	Jamais!
adv.	nevertheless	walakini	néanmoins
adj.	new	-pya	neuf
n.	New Testament	Agano Jipya	le Nouveau Testament (m)
n.	news	habari	nouvelles (f)
adj.	next	-a kufuata	prochain, suivant
phrase	next month	mwezi kesho	mois prochain
adv.	next to	kando	à côté de
phrase	next week	juma kesho	semaine prochain
phrase	next year	mwaka wa kesho	an prochain

parts of speech	english	swahili	french
verb	**nibble, to**	kumega	grignoter
adj.	**nice**	-ema	gentil
phrase	**Nice to meet you. (one person)**	Nafurahi kukufahamu.	Enchanté de rencontrer avec toi.
n.	**nickname**	jina la utani	surnom (m)
n.	**niece**	mpwa wa kike	nièce (f)
n.	**night**	usiku	nuit (f)
n.	**night, all**	usiku kucha	tout la nuit
adv.	**night, last**	usiku wa leo	nuit dernière, la
adj.	**nine**	tisa; kenda	neuf
n.	**nine hundred**	mia kenda	neuf cents
n.	**nineteen**	kumi na tisa	dix-neuf
n.	**ninety**	tisini	quatre-vingt-dix (m)
n.	**ninety-one**	tisini na moja	quatre-vingt-onze
n.	**ninety-two**	tisini na mbili	quatre-vingt-douze
adj.	**ninth**	-a kenda	neuvième
adj., adv.	**no**	hapana, siyo	pas de, non
pronoun	**no one**	si mtu	personne, ne...personne
phrase	**No problem.**	Hamna shida.	Pas de problème.
n.	**noise**	makelele	bruit (m)
verb	**noise, to make**	kupiga kelele	faire du bruit
adj.	**noisy**	-enye makelele	bruyant
pronoun	**none**	hata moja	aucun
n.	**nonsense**	upuzi	bêtises (f)
n.	**noon**	adhuhuri	midi (m)
adv.	**normally**	kwa kawaida	généralement
n.	**north**	kaskazini	nord (m)
n.	**nose**	pua	nez (m)
n.	**nostril**	tunda la pua	narine (f)
adv.	**not (am not, are not, is not)**	si	pas, non
phrase	**Not at all!**	Hata kidogo!	Pas du tout!
interj.	**Not possible!**	Haiwezekani!	Pas possible!
adv.	**not so; (that is not so)**	sivyo	ça n'est pas le cas
phrase	**not the same**	wala	pas même
adv.	**not yet**	bado	pas encore
n.	**note**	barua fupi	note (f)
verb	**note, to**	kuangalia	remarquer
pronoun	**nothing**	si kitu	rien
n.	**notice**	tangazo (pl. matangazo)	avis (m)
verb	**notice, to**	kuangalia	remarquer

77

parts of speech	english	swahili	french
verb	notify, to	kujulisha	signaler
verb	nourish, to	kulisha vema	nourrir
n	nourishment	maakuli mema	nourriture (f)
n.	November	Novemba	novembre (m)
adv.	now	sasa	maintenant
phrase	now and then, occasionally	mara kwa mara	de temps en temps
adv.	now, right	sasa hivi	en ce moment
adv.	nowhere	si mahali po pote	nulle part
adj.	nude	-tupu	nu
n.	nuisance	udhia	ennui (m)
phrase	numb, to be	kufa ganzi	engourdi, être
n.	number	1. idadi 2. hesabu	nombre (m)
n.	numbness	ganzi	engourdissement (m)
adj.	numerous	-ingi	nombreux
n.	nun	mtawa wa kike	bonne sœur (f)
n.	nurse	mwuguzi	infirmière (f), infirmier (m); garde malade
verb	nurse, to (suckle)	kunyonyesha	allaiter
interj.	O.K!	Haya!	Allons!
interj.	O.K.	Nakubali.	D'accord.
n.	oar	kasia (pl. makasia)	rame (f)
n.	oath	kiapo (pl. viapo)	serment (m)
adj.	obedient	-sikivu	obéissant
verb	obese, to become	kunenepa	devenir obèse
verb	obey, to	kutii	obéir à
n.	objection	pingamizi	objection (f)
n.	obligation	wajibu	devoir
adj.	obnoxious	kuchukiza	odieux
n.	obscenity	upujufu	obscénité (f)
verb	observe, to	kutazama	observer
n.	obstacle	kizuio (pl. vizuio)	entrave (f)
adj.	obstinate	-kaidi	obstiné
verb	obstruct, to	kupinga	obstruer
n.	obstruction	zuio (pl. mazuio)	obstacle (m)
verb	obtain, to	kupata	obtenir
adj.	obvious	dhahiri	évident
n.	occasion	mara	occasion (f)
n.	occiput	kogo	occiput
verb	occupy, to	kukalia	occuper
verb	occur, to	kutukia	lieu, avoir

parts of speech	english	swahili	french
n.	occurrence	matukio	événement (m)
n.	ocean	bahari kuu	océan (m)
n.	October	Oktoba	octobre (m)
n.	octopus	pweza	pieuvre (f)
prep.	off	katika	éteint, annulé
interj.	Off with you!	Toka!	Va-t'en!
verb	offend, to	kuchukiza	offenser
verb	offer, to	kutolea	offrir
n.	offering	kipaji	offre (f)
n.	office	afisi	office (m)
n.	offspring	mzao (pl. wazao)	progéniture (f)
adv.	often	mara nyingi	souvent
n.	oil	mafuta	huile (f)
n.	ointment	marhamu	pommade (f)
adj.	old	-zee	vieux
n.	old man	mzee (pl. wazee)	vieillard (m)
n.	old woman	kizee	femme vieux
n.	omen, bad	ndege mbaya	augure (m), mauvais
n.	omen, good	ndege njema	augure (m), bon
n.	omission	jambo lililoachwa	omission (f)
verb	omit, to	kukosa kutia	omettre
prep.	on	juu ya	sur
adv.	once	mara moja tu	une fois
phrase	Once upon a time there was...	Hapo kale...	Il était une fois...
adj. & n.	one	moja	un, une
n.	one million	elfu mara elfu	un million
n.	onion	kitunguu (pl. vitunguu)	oignon (m)
adv.	only	tu	seul (seulement)
adj.	open	wazi	ouvert
verb	open, to {Open the door.}	kufungua (Fungua mlango.)	ouvrir {Ouvre la porte.}
adv.	openly	waziwazi	ouvertement
verb	operate (medical), to	kupasua mgonjwa	opérer
n.	operation (surgery)	utabibu wa kupasua	opérer
n.	opinion	rai	opinion (f)
n.	opportunity	nafasi	occasion (f)
adv.	opposite	kuelekeana	en face de
verb	oppress, to	kudhulumu	opprimer
prep.	or	ama	ou
n.	orange (fruit)	chungwa (pl. machungwa)	orange (f)
verb	ordain, to	kuagiza	ordonner

79

parts of speech	english	swahili	french
n.	ordeal	jaribio kali	épreuve (f)
n.	order	amri (pl. amri)	ordre (m)
verb	order, to	kuamuru	ordonner
adv.	orderly	taratibu	méthodique
adj.	ordinary	-a kawaida	ordinaire
n	organization	matengenezo	organisation (f)
verb	organize	kutengeneza	organiser
n.	origin	asili	origine (f)
n.	orphan	yatima	orphelin (m)
adj & pr	other	-ingine	autre
adv.	other side	ngambo	de l'autre côté
conj.	otherwise	ama sivyo	sinon
verb	ought (to have to), must	kupaswa	devoir
adj.	our (our children)	-etu (wana wetu)	notre (sg), nos (pl) (nos enfants)
pronoun	ourselves	sisi wenyewe	elles-même
adv.	out	nje	dehors
n.	outcast	msikwao	proscrit (m), proscrite (f)
n.	outcome	tokeo	issue (f)
n.	outhouse	kibanda cha nje	appentis (m)
adv.	outside	nje	dehors
prep.	outside of	nje ya	en dehors de
adj.	outstanding	-a ajabu	remarquable
prep.	over	juu ya	sur
adv.	over there	pale	là-bas
verb	overcharge, to	taka bei kubwa kuliko haki	demander un prix exagéré
verb	overcome, to; to defeat	kushinda	vaincre
verb	overflow, to	kufurika	déborder
verb	overturn, to	kupinduka	répandre
n.	owl	bundi	hibou (m)
verb	own, to	kumiliki	posséder
n.	pace	hatua	pas (m)
verb	pack, to	kufunganya	emballer
n.	packet	bahasha	paquet (m)
n.	paddle	kafi	pagaie (f)
verb	paddle, to	kupiga kafi	pagayer
n.	padlock	kufuli	cadenas (m)
adj. & n.	pagan	mtu asiye Mkristo	païen (m)
n.	page	ukurasa (pl. kurasa)	page (f)
n.	pail	ndoo	seau (m)
n.	pain	maumivu (pl.)	douleur (f)

parts of speech	english	swahili	french
verb	pain, to have; to suffer	kuuma	souffrir
n.	paint	rangi	peinture (f)
verb	paint, to	kupakaa	peindre
n.	palm of hand	kitanga cha mkono	paume (f)
n.	palm oil	mawese	huile de palmier (m)
n.	palm tree	mti wa jamii ya mnazi	palmier
verb	palpate, to	kugusa	palper
n.	palpitation	papo la moyo	palpitation (f)
verb	pamper, to	kudekeza	se bichonner
n.	pan, cooking	sufuria (pl. masufuria)	casserole (f)
n., med	pancreas	kongosho	pancréas (m)
n.	pandemonium	makelele mengi	tohu-bohu (m)
n.	panic	woga mkuu	panique (f)
verb	pant, to	kutweta	haleter
n.	pants	suruali	pantalon (m)
n.	papa	baba	père (m)
n.	papaya	papai	papaye
n.	paper	karatasi	papier (m)
n.	parable	mfano wenye mafundisho	parabole (f)
n.	parallel	sambamba	parallèle (m)
n.	paralysis	kipooza	paralysie (f)
n.	parasite	kimelea	parasite (m)
n.	pardon, forgiveness	usamehe	pardon (m)
verb	pardon, to	kusamehe	pardonner
n.	parent	mzazi (pl. wazazi)	père (m), mère (f)
phrase	parliament	halmashauri kuu	l'assemblée nationale
n.	parrot	kasuku	perroquet (m)
n.	part	kipande (pl. vipande)	partie (f)
verb	participate, to	kushiriki	participer
n.	participation	ushirika	participation (f)
adv.	partly	kwa nusu	en partie
n.	partner	mshiriki katika kazi	associé (m), associée (f)
n.	partnership	shirika	association (f)
n.	party (entertainment)	karamu	fête (f)
verb	pass, to	kufaulu	passer
n.	passenger	abiria	passager (m), passagère (f)
n.	passerby	mpitaji	passant (m)
n.	passport	ruhusa ya kupita	passeport (m)
n.	past	-a zamani	passé (m)
verb	past, to go	kupita	passer avant
n.	pastor	mchungaji wa roho	pasteur (m)

parts of speech	english	swahili	french
n.	pasture	malisho	pâturage (m)
n.	patch	kiraka (pl. viraka)	pièce (f)
n.	path	njia ya kufikia	sentier (m)
n.	patience	saburi	patience (f)
n.	patience	subira	patience (f)
adj.	patient	-vumilivu	patient
adv.	patiently	kwa saburi	patiemment
n.	patrimony	urithi	patrimoine (m)
verb	patronize, to	kufadhili	traiter avec condescendance
n.	pattern	kilezo	motif (m)
n.	pause	kituo (pl. vituo)	repos (m)
verb	pause, to	kutua	hésiter
n.	pay (noun)	ujira	récompense (f)
verb	pay attention, to	kuangalia	faire attention à
verb	pay, to	kulipa	payer
n.	payment	malipo	paiement (m)
n.	pea	mbaazi (pl. mibaazi)	pois (m)
n.	peace	amani, salama	paix (f)
adj.	peaceful	-pole	tranquille
n.	peak (mountain)	kilele (pl. vilele)	sommet (m)
n.	peanut	karanga	arachide (f)
n.	pearl	lulu (pl. malulu)	perle (f)
n.	peasant	mkulima (pl. wakulima)	paysan (m), paysanne (f)
n.	pebble	makokoto (pl.)	caillou (m)
verb	peddle, to	kuchuuza	mettre en vente
verb	peel, to	kumenya	1. peler 2. éplucher
n.	peelings	maganda (pl.)	épluchures (f)
n.	pencil	kalamu	crayon (m)
verb	penetrate, to	kupenya	pénétrer
n.	penis	mboo	pénis
n.	penis	uume	pénis (m)
n.	pension	malipo ya uzeeni	pension (f)
n.	pepper	pilipili manga	poivre (m)
adj.	perfect	kamili	parfait
n.	perfection	ukamilifu	perfection (f)
n.	perfume	manukato	parfum (m)
adv.	perhaps	labda	peut-être
n.	period (of time)	kipindi (pl. vipindi)	espace temps
n.	period (of time)	muda	période (f)
n.	period, to have (female)	hedhi	menstruation (f)
verb	perish, to	kuharibika	périr

parts of speech	english	swahili	french
n.	permission	ruhusa	permission (f)
verb	permit, to	kuruhusu	permettre
n.	perplexity	mashaka	perplexité (f)
verb	persecute, to	kutesa	persécuter
n.	persecution	mateso	persécution (f)
n.	persecutor	mtesi (pl. watesi)	persécuteur (m)
n.	perseverance	udumu	persévérance (f)
n.	person	mtu (pl. watu)	personne (f)
n.	perspiration	jasho	transpiration (f)
verb	persuade, to	kushawishi	persuader
verb	pester, to	kuudhi	importuner
n.	petroleum	mafuta ya motakaa	pétrole (m)
n.	pharmacy	duka la mwuza dawa	pharmacie (f)
n.	phlegm	kohozi	flegme (m)
n.	photograph	picha iliyopigwa kwa kamera	photographie (f)
verb	photograph, to	kupiga sanamu	photographier
n.	phrase	fungu la maneno machache	expression (f)
n.	piano	kinanda (pl. vinanda)	piano (m)
verb	pick up, to	kuokota	ramasser
verb	pick, to	kuchuma	cueillir
n.	picture	picha, sanamu	tableau (m)
n.	piece	kipande (pl. vipande)	morceau (m)
n.	piece of cloth used to carry baby on one's back	mbeleko	linge pour porter un enfant sur le dos
verb	pierce, to	kuchoma	percer
n.	pig	nguruwe	cochon (m)
n.	pigeon	njiwa	pigeon (m)
verb	pile, to	kupanganya	s'entasser
n.	pill	kidonge (pl. vidonge)	pilule (f)
n.	pillar	nguzo	pilier (m)
n.	pillow	mto (pl. mito)	oreiller (m)
n.	pimple	kipele (pl. vipele)	bouton (m)
n.	pin	msumari (pl. misumari)	épingle (f)
n.	pineapple	nanasi (pl. mananasi)	ananas (m)
n.	pipe (hose)	bomba (pl. mabomba	tuyau (f)
n.	pipe (tobacco)	kiko (pl. viko)	pipe (f)
n.	pit	shimo (pl. mashimo)	fosse (f)
n.	pitcher	gudulia	cruche (f)
n.	pity	huruma	pitié (f)
verb	pity, to	kurehemu	plaindre

83

parts of speech	english	swahili	french
n.	place	pahali (pl. pahali)	endroit (m)
adv.	place of, in	badala ya	au lieu de
n., med	placenta	kondo la nyuma	placenta
n.	plain (near river)	tambarare	plaine (f)
n.	plaintiff	mshitaki (pl. washitaki)	plaignant (m,f)
verb	plan, to	kuazimu	prévoir
n.	planet	sayari	planète (f)
n.	plant	mmea (pl. mimea)	plante (f)
verb	plant, to	kupanda	planter
n.	plantain	matoke	banane plantain
n.	plantation	shamba (pl. mashamba)	plantation (f)
verb	plaster, to	kukandika	plâtre
n.	plate	sahani	assiette (f)
verb	play an instrument, to	sikuya vyombo vya nyimbo	jouer d'un instrument
verb	play, to	kucheza	jouer
n.	playground	kiwanja	terrain (m) de jeu
verb	plead, to (court)	kuleta hoja	plaider
verb	please, to	kupendeza	plaire à
phrase	Please.	Tafadhali.	S'il vous plaît.
n.	pleasure	anasa	plaisir (m)
n.	plenty	wingi	abondance (f)
verb	plow, to	kulima	labourer
verb	plunder, to	kunyanganya	piller
n.	poet	mshairi	poète (m)
n.	poetry	shairi (pl. mashairi)	poésie (f)
n.	point	ncha	pointe (f)
n.	poison	sumu	poison (m)
verb	poison, to	kutia sumu	empoisonner
n.	police agent	polisi (pl. mapolisi)	agent (m) de police
verb	polish, to	kung'arisha	polir
n.	politeness	adabu	politesse (f)
n.	pollution	uchafu	pollution (f)
n.	pond	kiziwa (pl. viziwa)	mare (f)
verb	ponder, to	kufikiri	réfléchir
n.	pool	kidimbwi	mare (f)
adj.	poor	masikini	pauvre
phrase	poor person	masikini	mendiant (m)
adj.	poorly	-gonjwa	souffrant
n.	porch	baraza	porche (m)
n.	pork, hog	nyama ya nguruwe	porc (m)
n.	porridge	uji mzito	bouillie (f)

parts of speech	english	swahili	french
n.	porter	mchukuzi	porteur (m)
n.	portion	sehemu	portion (f)
n.	portrait	picha ya mtu	portrait (m)
n.	Portuguese (language)	kireno	portugais (m)
verb	possess, to	kuwa na	posséder
verb	possible, to be	kuwezekana	possible, être
adv.	possibly	labda	il est possible que, peut-être
n.	post (mail)	posta	poste (f)
n.	post office	barua za posta	bureau (m) de poste
n.	postage stamp	ada ya posta	timbre-poste (m)
n.	pot (clay)	chombo (pl. vyombo)	marmite (f) de argile
n.	pouch, pocket	mfuko (pl. mifuko)	poche (f)
verb	pound, to; to crush	kutwanga	piler, broyer
verb	pour, to	kumimina	verser
n.	poverty	umasikini	pauvreté (f)
n.	powder	unga	poudre (f)
phrase	powdered milk	maziwa ya unga	lait en poudre
n.	power (authority)	mamlaka	pouvoir (m)
n.	power (strength)	uwezo	puissance (f)
verb	practice, to	kuzoea	pratiquer
n.	praise	sifa	éloge (m)
verb	praise, to	kusifu	louer
verb	pray, to	kusali	prier
n.	prayer	1. maombi 2. sala	prière (f)
verb	preach, to	kuhubiri	prêcher
n.	preacher	mhubiri (pl. wahubiri)	prédicateur (m)
adj.	precarious	-a hatari	précaire
verb	precede, to	kutangulia	précéder
adv.	precisely	sawasawa	naturellement
n.	precursor	mjumbe (pl. wajumbe)	prédécesseur (m)
verb	predict, to	kutabiri	prédire
n.	preference	upendeleo	préférence (f)
n.	pregnancy	mimba	grossesse (f)
verb	pregnant, to be	kuwa na mimba	enceinte, être
n.	preparation	matengenezo	préparation (f)
verb	prepare, to	kutayarisha	1. apprêter 2. préparer
n.	present (gift)	zawadi	cadeau (m)
verb	preserve, to	kuhifadhi	conserver
verb	press, to	kubana, kusonga	appuyer
n.	presumption	ujuvi	présomption (f)
adj.	pretentious	-a fahari	prétentieux

85

parts of speech	english	swahili	french
adj.	pretty	-zuri	joli
verb	prevent, to	kuzuia	empêcher
n.	price	bei	prix (m)
n.	pride	kiburi, majivuno	fierté (f)
n.	priest	kasisi (pl. makasisi)	prêtre (m)
n.	prince	mwana wa mfalme	prince (m)
adj.	principal (important)	-kuu	principal
verb	print, to	kuchapa, kupiga chapa	imprimer
adj.	prior to	-a kwanza	antérieur
n.	priority	haki ya kutangulia	priorité (f)
n.	prison	kifungo (pl. vifungo)	prison (f)
n.	prisoner	mfungwa (pl. wafungwa)	prisonnier (m)
verb	probe, to	kuchungua	sonder
n.	problem?	matatizo?	introduire une requête
n.	problems	hoja	ennuis (m)
n.	procrastination	kuahirisha	procrastination (f)
adj.	prodigal	-a potevu wa mali	prodigue
verb	produce, to (fruit)	kutoa	produire
n.	profession	kazi ya elimu	profession (f)
n.	professor	mwalimu mkuu	professeur (m)
n.	profit (increase)	faida	profit (m)
adj.	profound	-refu	profond
n.	progeny	wazao	progéniture (f)
n.	program	azimio la mambo ya kufanyika	programme (m)
n.	progress	maendeleo	progrès (m)
verb	progress, to	kuendelea	s'avancer
verb	prohibit, to	kukataza	défendre
n.	project	azimio (pl. mazimio)	projet (m)
n.	promise	ahandi	promesse (f)
verb	promise, to	kuahidi	promettre
adv.	prone position	kifudifudi	étendu face contre terre
n.	proof	ushahidi	preuve (f)
verb	propagate, to	kuzalisha	se propager
adv.	properly	vema	convenablement, correctement
n.	property	mali	propriété (f)
verb	prophesy	kutabiri	prophétiser
n.	prophet, seer	nabii (pl. manabii)	prophète (m)
verb	prosecute, to	kuendesha	interroger avec insistance
n.	prosperity	usitawi	prospérité (f)

parts of speech	english	swahili	french
n.	prostitute	malaya	prostituée (f)
verb	protect, to	kulinda	protéger
adj.	proud	-enye kiburi	fier
n.	proverb	methali	proverbe (m)
adj.	provisional	-a kitambo	provisoire
n.	provisions	riziki	subsistance (f)
n	provocation	uchokozi	provocation (f)
verb	provoke, to	kuchokoza	provoquer
n.	pruritus, itch	kiwasho	démangeaison (f)
n.	psalm	zaburi	psaume (m)
adj.	public	waziwazi	public (m); publique (f)
verb	publish, to	kutangaza	publier
verb	pull down, to	kuangusha	rabattre
verb	pull out, to	kuchopoa	déboîter
verb	pull, to	kuvuta	tirer
n.	pumpkin	boga (pl. maboga)	potiron (m)
phrase	punch	kupiga ngumi	coup de poing
n.	punctuation	vituo	ponctuation (f)
verb	punish, to	kuadhibu, kuazibu	punir
n.	punishment	azabu	peine (f)
adj.	puny	-dogo	chétif
n.	pupil (student)	mwanafunzi (pl. wanafunzi)	élève (m,f)
n., med	pupil, (eye)	mboni ya jicho	pupille (f) de l'oeil
n.	purity	usafi	pureté (f)
adj. & n.	purple	rangi ya zambarau bivu	violet (m)
n.	purpose	kusudi (pl. makusudi)	but (m)
n.	purse	kifuko cha kutilia fedha	bourse (f)
n., med	pus	usaha	pus (m)
verb	push away, to	piga kikumbo	pousser pour déplacer
verb	push, to	kusukuma	pousser
n.	pustule	kipele (pl. vipele)	pustule (f)
verb	put an end to, to	kukomesha	mettre fin à; terminer
verb	put back, to	kurudisha	remettre
verb	put in, to	kuingiza	faire escale
verb	put, to	kuweka	mettre
n.	pygmy	mmbuti (pl. wabuti)	batwa
n.	python	chatu	python (m)
n.	quality	tabia	qualité (f)
n.	quantity	kiasi	quantité (f)
verb	quarrel, to	kugomba	quereller
n.	quarrels	maugomvi (pl.)	querelles (f)

87

parts of speech	english	swahili	french
n.	queen	malkia	reine (f)
n.	question	swali (pl. maswali)	question (f)
adv.	quickly	mbio, upesi	rapidement
verb	quiet, to make	kunyamazisha	faire tranquille
adv.	quietly	kimya, polepole	silencieusement
adv.	quite	halisi	tout à fait
verb	quote or cite, to	kutaja	citer
n.	rabbit	sungura	lapin (m)
n.	rabies	kalab	rage (f)
n.	race (people)	ujamaa	race (f)
n.	racket (noise)	ghasia	vacarme (m)
adj.	radiant	-a angavu	épanoui
n.	radio	kupeleka simu	radio (f)
n.	raft	chelezo	radeau (m)
n.	rag	kitambaa (pl. vitambaa)	chiffon (m)
n., med	rage	gazabu	folie, rage
n.	rain	mvua	pluie (f)
verb	rain, to	kunyesha, kunya	pleuvoir
n.	rainbow	upindi wa mvua	arc-en-ciel (m)
verb	raise the voice, to	kupaza sauti	élever la voix
verb	raise voice, to	kupaza sauti	faire voix fort
verb	raise, to	kuinua	lever
n.	rake	jembe la meno	râteau (m)
verb	ramble, to	kutembea	divaguer
n.	ransom	ukombozi	rançon (f)
verb	rape, to	kuanjisi mwanamke kwa jeuri	violer
n.	rash	upele	éruption (f)
n.	rat	panya	rat (m)
adv.	rather (but rather)	afazali	plutôt
n.	ravine	genge (pl. magenge)	ravin (m)
adj.	raw	-bichi	cru
n.	razor	wembe (pl. nyembe)	rasoir (m)
verb	reach, to	kufika	parvenir à
verb	reach, to	kuwasili	atteindre
verb	read, to	kusoma	lire
adj.	ready	tayari	prêt
adv.	really	kweli	vraiment
n.	reason	akili	raison (f)
verb	reason, to	kutimia	raisonner
adj. & n.	rebel	mwasi (pl. wawasi)	rebelle (m,f)

parts of speech	english	swahili	french
verb	**rebel, to**	kuasi	se rebeller
n	**rebellion**	futina	rébellion (f)
verb	**rebuke, to**	kugombeza	réprimander
verb	**receive, to**	kupokea	recevoir
adj.	**recent**	-pya	récent
adv.	**recently**	juzi juzi	récemment
adj.	**reckless**	-jasiri	téméraire
verb	**reclaim, to**	kuomba	réclamer
verb	**recognize, to**	kutambua	reconnaître
verb	**recoil, to (through fear)**	kurudi nyuma	reculer (par peur)
verb	**reconcile, to**	kupatanisha	réconcilier
verb	**record, to**	kuandika	enregistrer
verb	**recount, to**	kuhadisi	raconter
verb	**recover, to**	kusimama	se redresser
verb	**recover, to (from illness)**	kupata afya tena	se remettre
verb	**recover, to (find again)**	kujipatia tena	retrouver
verb	**rectify, to**	kusahihisha	rectifier
adj. & n.	**red**	-ekundu	rouge (f)
verb	**redeem, to**	kukomboa	racheter
n.	**redeemer**	mkombozi	racheterier
n.	**redemption**	ukombozi	rédemption (f)
verb	**reduce, to; diminish, to**	kupunguza	diminuer
n.	**reeds**	unyasi (pl. nyasi)	rousseau
n.	**reel**	kijiti cha kukunjia uzi	bobine (f) de fil à coudre
verb	**reflect light, to**	kuangaza	briller
verb	**reflect, to**	kufikiri	réfléchir
n.	**reflection**	fikira	réflexion (f)
verb	**refrain from, to**	kujizuia	se retenir de
n.	**refuge**	kimbilio	asile (m)
n.	**refugee**	mkimbizi	réfugié (m)
verb	**refuse, to**	kukataa	refuser
verb	**regain, to**	kupata tena	rentrer en possession de
n.	**region**	upande (pl. pande)	région (f)
n.	**region, area (locality)**	jimbo (pl. majimbo)	région (f)
n.	**reign**	utawala	règne (m)
verb	**reimburse, to**	kulipa	rembourser
verb	**reinforce, to**	kuleta msaada	renforcer
verb	**reject, to**	kukataa	rejeter
verb	**rejoice, to**	kufuahisha	réjouir
verb	**rekindle, to**	kuwasha	se ranimer
phrase	**related, to be**	-wa ndugu ya	avoir un lien de famille

parts of speech	english	swahili	french
n.	**relationship**	ufungu	rapport (m)
n.	**relative**	ndugu	relatif (m)
verb	**relax, to**	kulegea	se détendre
verb	**release, to**	kufanya huru	libérer
n	**religion**	dini	religion (f)
n.	**reluctance**	kutotaka	réticence (f)
verb	**rely on, to**	kutegemea	compter sur
verb	**remain, to**	kubaki	demeurer
n.	**remedy**	uganga	remède (m)
verb	**remember, to**	kukumbuka	1. se rappeler 2. se souvenir de
verb	**remind, to**	kukumbusha	rappeler
verb	**remove, to**	kuondosha	ôter
verb	**repair, to**	kutengeneza	réparer
verb	**repel, to**	kufukuza	repousser
verb	**repent, to**	kutubu	repentir, se
verb	**replace, to**	kurudishia hali	remplacer
n.	**replacement**	mkombozi (pl. wakombozi)	remplaçant (m,f)
n.	**reprimand**	magombezi	réprimande (f)
verb	**reprimand, to**	kuhamakia	réprimander
n.	**reputation**	sifa	réputation (f)
phrase	**reputation, to have a bad**	sifa mbaya	avoir mauvaise réputation
verb	**rescue, to**	kuponya	délivrer
n.	**rescuer**	mwokozi	libérateur (m)
verb	**resemble, to**	kufanana	se ressembler
n.	**resentment**	uchungu	ressentiment (m)
n.	**reserve**	akiba	réserver
n.	**resolution**	kusudi (pl. makusudi)	résolution (f)
n.	**respect**	heshima	respect (m)
verb	**respect, to**	kuheshimu	respecter
n.	**respite**	nafasi	relâche (m)
n.	**response**	jibu (pl. majibu)	réponse (f)
n.	**responsibility**	daraka (pl. madaraka)	responsabilité (f)
verb	**rest, to**	kupumzika	se reposer
verb	**resume, to**	kutwaa	reprendre
n.	**resurrection**	ufufuko	résurrection (f)
verb	**retch, to**	kokomoka	avoir des haut-le-cœur
verb	**retrace the path**	kufuasa nyuma	rebrousser chemin
verb	**return something, to**	kurudisha kitu	rendre quelque chose
verb	**return, to**	kurudi	1. revenir 2. retourner
verb	**reunite, to**	kutanisha	réunir

parts of speech	english	swahili	french
verb	reveal, to	kufunua	dévoiler
n.	revelation	ufunuo	révélation (f)
n.	revenge	kisasi (pl. visasi)	vengeance (f)
verb	revive, to	kufufua	1. revivre 2. remettre en état
n.	revolt	maasi (pl.)	révolte (f)
verb	revolt against, to	kufitini	se révolter contra
n.	reward	zawabu	récompense (f)
verb	reward, to	kutuza	récompenser
n.	rhinoceros	kifaru (pl. vifaru)	rhinocéros (m)
n.	rhythm	mwendo (pl. miendo)	rythme (m)
n.	rib, shore (side by side)	ubavu	côte (f) (côte à côte)
n.	rice	mchele (pl. michele)	riz (m)
adj.	rich	tajiri (pl. matajiri)	riche
adj.	rich (person)	-enye mali	riche
n.	riddle	kitandawili (pl. vitandawili)	crible (m)
verb	ridicule, to	kufanya mzaha	se moquer de
adj.	right	-a upande wa kuume	droit
n.	right (civil, legal)	haki	droit (m)
n.	right (correct)	usawa	correct
prep.	right (direction)	kulia	droit
phrase	right now; right away	sasa hivi	tout de suite
phrase	right, on the	kwa upande wa kuume	à droit
phrase	right., All	Vema.	C'est bien.
n.	ring	pete	anneau (m)
verb	ring a bell, to	kupiga kengele	sonner à la porte
n.	ringworm	baka	teigne (f)
verb	rinse, to	kuosha	rincer
n.	riot	ghasia	émeute (f)
verb	rip, to	kupasua	fendre
adj.	ripe	-bivu	mûr
verb	rise (from lying position); to get up	kusimama	se lever
verb	rise, to (sun)	kucha	lever, se
n. & adj.	ritual	kawaida za dini	rituel
n.	river	mto (pl. mito)	fleuve (m)
n.	road	barabara, njia	route (f)
verb	roar, to (bellow)	kunguruma	mugir
verb	roar, to (like a storm)	kugombeza	gronder (orage)
verb	roast, to	kuoka	rôtir
n.	robber	mnyanganyi (pl. wanyanganyi)	voleur (m)

parts of speech	english	swahili	french
n.	**robe, dress**	vazi la kike	robe (f)
adj.	**robust**	-a afya	robuste
n.	**rock**	mwamba (pl. miamba)	roche (f)
verb	**rock, to**	kupembeza	bercer
verb	**roll along, to**	kufingirisha	rouler
verb	**roll around, to**	kusukasuka	ballotter
phrase	**roof, to put on**	kutia mapaa	couvrir un toit
n.	**room (in house)**	chumba	chambre (f)
n.	**rooster, cock (fowl)**	jogoo	coq (m)
n.	**root**	mzizi (pl. mizizi)	racine (f)
n.	**rope**	kamba	corde (f)
n.	**rosary**	tasbihi	chapelet (f)
verb	**rot, to; to deteriorate**	kuoza	pourrir
adj.	**rotten**	-bovu	pourri
n.	**row**	msafa (pl. misafa)	rang (m)
verb	**row, to (boat)**	kuvuta makasia	ramer
adj.	**royal**	-a kifalme	royal
n.	**rubber**	mpira (pl. mipira)	caoutchouc (m)
n.	**rug**	zulia (pl. mazulia)	tapis (m)
n.	**rule**	mamlaka	règle (f)
verb	**rule, to**	kutawala	gouverner
n.	**ruler (person)**	mutawala (pl. watawala)	chef (m)
n.	**rumor**	uvumi	rumeur (f)
verb	**run, to**	kupiga mbio	courir
n.	**rural**	shamba (pl. mashamba)	campagne (f)
verb	**rush, to**	kuboromoka	se précipiter
n.	**rust**	kutu	rouille (f)
n.	**sack, bag**	mfuko (pl. mifuko)	sac (m)
n.	**sacrifice**	zabihu	sacrifice (m)
verb	**sacrifice, to**	kutoa sadaka	sacrifier
adj.	**sad**	-a huzuni	triste
verb	**sad, to be**	kuhuzunika	triste, être
n.	**sadness**	huzuni	tristesse (f)
n.	**safe (to hold valuables)**	kilindo (pl. vilindo)	coffre-fort (m)
adj.	**safe and sound**	thabiti madhubuti	sain et sauf
adj.	**saint**	-takatifu	saint
n.	**saint**	mutakatifu (pl. watakatifu)	saint (m), sainte (f)
phrase	**sake of, for the**	ili kusaidia au kupendeza	pour l'amour de
n.	**salary**	mshahara (pl. mishahara)	appointements (m)
n.	**saliva**	mate	salive (f)
n	**salt**	chumvi	sel (m)

92

parts of speech	english	swahili	french
n.	salvation	wokovu	salut (m)
adj & pr	same	-moja, yule yule	même
n.	sand	mchanga (pl. michanga)	sable (m)
n.	sandal	kiatu (pl. viatu)	sandale (f)
n.	sarcasm	uchokozi	sarcasme (m)
n.	sardine	dagaa	sardine (f)
adj.	satisfactory	-a kuridhisha	satisfaisant
phrase	satisfied, to be (ate enough)	-enye kushiba	être rassasié
verb	satisfy, to	kupendezwa	contenter
verb	satisfy, to	kushibisha	rassasier
n.	Saturday	Jumamosi	samedi (m)
n.	sauce	mchuzi (pl. michuzi)	sauce (f)
verb	save, to	kuokoa	sauver
verb	save, to	kuweka akiba	épargner
verb	save, to	kukabidhi	mettre de côté
n.	savior	mwokozi	sauveur (m)
n.	saw	msumeno (pl. misumeno)	scie (f)
verb	saw, to	kupasua kwa msumeno	scier
n.	sawdust	unga wa mbao	sciure (f)
verb	say to, to	kusema na	dire à
verb	say, to	kusema	dire
n.	scales (fish)	gamba (pl. magamba)	écailles (f)
n., med	scapula	mtulinga	omoplate
n.	scar	kovu (pl. makovu)	cicatrice (f)
n.	scarecrow	kuamia shamba	épouvantail (m)
n.	scarf	kitambaa (pl. vitambaa)	foulard (m)
verb	scatter, to	kusambaa, kutawanya	se disperser
n.	school	1. chuo (pl. vyuo) 2. shule	école (f)
n.	scissors	makasi	ciseaux (m)
verb	scold, to	kuhamakia	réprimander
verb	scorn, to; to despise	kuchukia	mépriser
n.	scorpion	nge	scorpion
verb	scour, to, to clean	kusafisha	nettoyer
verb	scrape, to	kuparuza	racler
n.	scratch	mtai (pl. mitai)	égratignure (f)
verb	scratch oneself, to	kujukuna	gratter, se
verb	scratch, to	kuparua	égratigner
verb	scream, to	kupiga kiyowe	vociférer
phrase	scribe	mwahdishi ovyo	texte rédigé
n. med	scrotum	mfuko wa pumbu	scrotum

parts of speech	english	swahili	french
verb	scrub, to	kusugua	frotter
verb	scrutinize, to	kuchunguza	scruter
n.	sea	bahari	mer (f)
n.	seal	muhuri (pl. mihuri)	cachet (m)
verb	search, to	kutufata	fouiller
phrase	seasoned, to be well	kukolea	assaisonné, être
n.	seat	kiti (pl. viti)	siège (m)
verb	seat, to	kutetisha	asseoir
adj.	second	-a pili	deuxième
n.	second	dakika	seconde (f)
n.	secret	siri	secret (m)
n.	secretary	mwandishi (pl. wandishi)	secrétaire (m,f)
n.	section	mkato	section (f)
phrase	See you next time/soon.	Tutaonana baadaye.	À bientôt.
phrase	See you tomorrow.	Tutaonana kesho.	À demain.
phrase	See you...	Tutaonana...	Au revoir...
verb	see, to	kuona	voir
n.	seed	mbegu	semence (f)
verb	seek, to; search, to	kutafuta	chercher
verb	seize, to	kukamata	saisir
verb	select, to	kuchagua	sélectionner
n.	self	moyo, nafasi	moi (m), personne (f)
phrase	self-love	kujipenda nafsi	aimer-se
n.	self-respect	kujistahi nafsi	amour-propre (m)
adj.	selfish	-a choyo	égoïste
n.	selfishness	choyo	égoïsme (m)
verb	sell, to	kuuza	vendre
verb	send, to	kutuma	envoyer
verb	separate, to	kutenga	séparer
n.	September	Septemba	septembre (m)
n.	servant (male or female)	mtumishi (pl. watumishi)	domestique (m,f)
verb	serve, to (food)	kutumikia	servir
n.	session	baraza	session (f)
verb	set, to	kutia, kuweka	poser
verb	set, to (sun)	kuchwa	coucher, se
adj. & n.	seven	saba	sept (m)
n.	seven hundred	mia saba	sept cents
n.	seventeen	kumi na saba	dix-sept
adj.	seventh	-a saba	septième
adj. & n.	seventy	sabini	soixante-dix (m)
n.	seventy-eight	sabini na nane	soixante-dix-huit

parts of speech	english	swahili	french
n.	seventy-five	sabini na tano	soixante-quinze
n.	seventy-four	sabini na nne	soixante-quatorze
n.	seventy-nine	sabini na kenda	soixante-dix-neuf
n.	seventy-one	sabini na moja	soixante et onze
n.	seventy-seven	sabini na saba	soixante-dix-sept
n.	seventy-six	sabini na sita	soixante-seize
n.	seventy-three	sabini na tatu	soixante-treize
n.	seventy-two	sabini na mbili	soixante-douze
verb	sever, to	kukata	séparer
n.	severity	ukali	sévérité (f)
verb	sew, to	kushona	coudre
n.	sex (gender)	jinsi	sexe (m)
n.	shadow, shade	kivuli (pl. vivuli)	ombre (f)
verb	shake (object) hard, to	kutikisa	secouer/agiter
verb	shake hands, to	kupana mikono	serrer la main à
verb	shake, to	kusukusuka	secouer
verb	shake, to (as rug)	kukunguta	secouer
n.	shame	aibu, haya	honte (f)
n.	shape, form	umbo	forme (f)
verb	share with others, to	kushiriki	partager entre plusieurs
adj.	sharp	-a kali	aiguise
adj.	sharp (fierce)	-kali	féroce
verb	sharpen, to	kunoa	aiguiser
verb	shave, to	kunyoa	raser
pronoun	she	yeye	elle
verb	shed, to	kutoka	reprendre, verser
n.	sheep	kondoo	1. lustre (m) 2. mouton (m)
n.	sheet	nguo ya kutandika kitandani	drap (m) de lit
phrase	sheet of paper	ukurasa	feuille de papier
verb	shell, to	kupua	écosser
n.	shepherd	mchungaji (pl. wachungaji)	berger (m)
verb	shepherd, to	kuchunga	faire le berger
n.	shield	ngabo	bouclier (m)
verb	shield, to	kulinda	protéger
verb	shine, to	kungaa, kuwaka	briller, faire reluire
n.	shipwreck	kuvunjika meli	navire (m) naufragé
n.	shirt	shati (pl. mashati)	chemise (f)
n.	shiver	kitapo	frisson (m)
verb	shiver, to	kutetemeka	grelotter
n.	shoe	kiatu (pl. viatu)	chaussure (f)
verb	shoot, to (gun)	kupiga bunduki	tirer

parts of speech	english	swahili	french
n.	shop	duka (pl. maduka)	boutique (f)
adj.	short	-fupi	court
n.	short cut	njia ya kukatiliza	raccourci (m)
verb	shorten, to	kufupisha	raccourcir
verb	should; to be obligated	kuwa na lazima	devoir
n.	shoulder	bega (pl. mabega)	épaule (f)
phrase	show oneself, to	kuonekana	montrer se
verb	show, to	kuonyesha	montrer
n.	shred	kidogo	lambeau (m)
verb	shrink, to	kunywea	rétrécir
verb	shut, to; to close	kufunga	fermer
adj.	shy	-enye haya	peureux
n.	sick person	mgonjwa (pl. wagonjwa)	malade (f)
verb	sick, to be	kugua	malade, être
phrase	sick, to care for the	kuuguza	soigner
n.	side (next to)	upande (karibu na)	côté (m) (à côté de)
prep.	side of, on the	kando ya	à côté de
adj.	side, on this	hali moja na	au bord de
n.	sieve	kiyongela (pl. viyongela)	tamis (m)
verb	sift, to	kuchekecha	tamiser
verb	sigh, to	kupiga kite	soupirer
n.	sign	alama	signe (m)
n.	significance	maana	importance (f)
interj.	Silence!	Makelele!	Taisez-vous!
verb	silence, to	kunyamazisha	faire taire
adj.	silent	-a nyamavu	silencieux
verb	silent, to be	kunyamaza	se taire
adv.	silently	kimya	silencieusement
n.	silver	feza	argent (m)
n.	sin	zambi	péché (m)
verb	sin, to	kufanya dhambi	pécher
adv.	since	tangu	depuis
verb	sing, to	kuimba	chanter
verb	sink, to	kuzama	enfoncer
n.	sir	bwana	monsieur (m)
n.	sister	dada; ndugu mke; (if spoken of by brother: umbu)	sœur (f)
n.	sister-in-law	shemeji	belle-sœur
verb	sit, to	kukaa, kuketi	s'asseoir
adj. & n.	six	sita	six (m)

parts of speech	english	swahili	french
n.	six hundred	mia sita	six cents
n.	sixteen	kumi na sita	seize
adj.	sixth	-a sita	sixième
adj. & n.	sixty	sitini	soixante (m)
n.	size	ukubwa	grandeur (f)
n.	skim milk	maziwa yaliyoenguliwa	lait (m) écrémé
n.	skin	ngozi	peau (f)
n.	skin, pelt	ngozi	peau (f)
verb	skirt around, to	kupakana na	contourner
n.	sky	anga, mbingu	ciel (m)
verb	slacken, to	kupungua	se détendre
n.	slander	masingizio	calomnie (f)
verb	slander, to	kusingizia	1. calomnier 2. proférer des imprécations
n.	slap	kofi	claque (f)
verb	slap, to	kupiga kofi	gifler
n.	slate (to write on)	kibao cha jiwe	ardoise (f)
n.	slave	mtumwa (pl. watumwa)	esclave (m,f)
n.	slavery	utumwa	esclavage (m)
n.	slay, to	kuchinja	tuer
n.	sleep	usingizi	sommeil (m)
verb	sleep, to	kulala	dormir
n.	slice	kipasu (pl. vipasu)	tranche (f)
n.	slide	kuteleza	glissade (f)
verb	slide, to	kuteleza	se glisser
adv.	slightly	kidogo	légèrement
n.	sling	kombeo (pl. makombeo)	fronde (f)
verb	sling, to; to throw	kutupa	lancer
verb	slip out, to	kupitia	se détacher
adv.	slowly	polepole	lentement
adj.	small	-dogo	petit
verb	smash up, to	kutomoa	défoncer
verb	smear, to	kupakaa	salir
verb	smell, to	kunusa	sentir
verb	smile, to	kucheka	sourire
n.	smoke	moshi	fumée (f)
verb	smoke, to	kuvuta tumbako	fumer du tabac
adj.	smooth	laini	lisse
verb	smooth out, to	adoucir	défroisser
n.	snail	konokono	escargot (m)
n.	snake	nyoka	serpent (m)

97

parts of speech	english	swahili	french
verb	**sneeze, to**	kupiga chafya	éternuer
verb	**snivel, to**	kutoka kamasi	pleurnicher
verb	**snore, to**	kukoroma	ronfler
n.	**snow**	seluji	neige (f)
adv., conj.	**so**	vile, vivyo, basi	alors, ainsi
conj.	**so that, in order to**	ili, kusudi	afin que
phrase	**so, so that**	hata	de sorte que
verb	**soak, to**	kubambika	tremper, faire
n.	**soap**	sabuni	savon (m)
n.	**sock**	kama mfuko wa kuvaa mguuni	chaussette (f)
adj.	**soft**	laini	uni, souple
n.	**soil**	udongo	terroir (m)
verb	**soil, to**	kuchafua	salir
n.	**solder, to**	kutia pua	souder
n.	**soldier**	askari	soldat (m)
adj.	**sole**	-a peke	unique
adj.	**some**	chache	quelque
adv.	**sometimes**	mara na mara	quelquefois
adv.	**sometimes**	pengine	parfois
adv.	**somewhat**	kidogo	un peu
adv.	**somewhere else**	pengine	ailleurs
adv.	**somewhere, anywhere**	po pote	quelque part
n.	**son**	mwana (pl. wana)	fils (m)
n.	**song**	wimbo (pl. nyimbo)	chanson (f), chant (m)
adv.	**soon**	bado kidogo	1. bientôt 2. vite
n.	**soot**	masizi	1. noir de fumée 2. suie (f)
adj.	**sore (painful)**	kuuma	douloureux
n.	**sore (ulcer)**	jeraha, kidonda (pl. vidonda)	ulcère (m)
n.	**sorghum**	mtama (pl. mitama)	sorgho
n.	**sorrow**	huzuni	tristesse (f)
n.	**sorrow, deep**	sikitiko	chagrin (m)
n.	**sort**	namna	sorte (f)
n.	**soul**	moyo nafsi	âme (f)
n.	**sound**	kapi (pl. makapi)	son (m)
n.	**soup**	mchuzi (pl. michuzi)	soupe (f)
adj.	**sour**	-kali	aigre
n.	**south**	kusini	sud (m)
n.	**souvenir**	ukumbuko	souvenir (m)
verb	**sow, to**	kupanda	ensemencer

parts of speech	english	swahili	french
n	space	nafasi	espace (m)
adj.	spacious	-pana	spacieux
n.	spade	jembe (pl. majembe)	bêche (f)
verb	sparkle, to	kungariza	miroiter
n.	spatula	kisu kipana cha kufanyia dawa	spatule (f)
verb	speak frankly, to	-a kwenda sawa, être	dire franchement
verb	speak indistinctly, to	kunongona	ne parler pas clairement
verb	speak to, to	kusema na	parler à
verb	speak, to	kusema	parler
n.	spear	mkuki (pl. mikuki)	lance (f)
adj.	special	-a peke yake	spécial
n.	speech	usemi	manière de parler
n.	speed	upesi	vitesse (f)
verb	speed, to	kupeleka	expédier
verb	spend, to	kutoa	dépenser
n.	spider	buibui	araignée (f)
verb	spill, to	kumwanga	1. renverser 2. répandre
verb	spill, to be	kumwangika	se répandre
n.	spine	uti wa mgongo	épine (f) dorsal
n.	spirit	roho	esprit (m)
phrase	spirit, harmful	pepo	toute poésie moderne
n.	spit	mate	crachat (m)
verb	spit, to	kutema mate	cracher
verb	split, to	kupasuka	fendre
verb	spoil, to	kuharibu	abîmer
verb	spoil, to (food)	kuoza	gâter, se
n.	sponge	sifongo	éponge (f)
n.	spoon	kijiko (pl. vijiko)	cuiller (f)
verb	spread out, to	kuenea	espacer
n	spring (of water)	chemchemi	source (f)
verb	spring up, to	kufika	surgir
verb	sprinkle, to	kunyunyizia	saupoudrer
n.	spy	mpelelezi (pl. wapelelezi)	espion (m)
verb	spy on, to	kupeleleza	espionner
verb	squander, to	kuharibu	gaspiller
n.	squash (botanical)	mboga	courge (f)
verb	squeak, to	kusaga	grincer
verb	squeeze, to	kubana, kukamua	serrer
verb	squint, to	kuwa na upogo	loucher
n.	squirrel	kidiri	écureuil (m)

parts of speech	english	swahili	french
verb	stabilize, to	kuimarisha	stabiliser
n.	staircase	ngazi	escalier (m)
verb	stammer, to	kubabaika	bégayer
verb	stammer, to	kuwa na kigugumizi	bredouiller
verb	stamp one's feet	kukanyaga	piétiner
verb	stand up straight, to	kuondoka	se tenir droit
verb	stand up, to	kusimama	se tenir debout
n.	star	nyota	étoile (f)
verb	stare at, to; to gaze at	kukodolea	regarder fixement
verb	stare wide-eyed, to	kukodoa	écarquiller les yeux
verb	start, to	kuanza	entamer
verb	startle, to	kuogofya	effrayer
adj.	startling	-a kushtusha	surprenant
n.	statistics	habari zinazoonyeshwa kwa hesabu	statistique (f)
n.	statue	sanamu	statue (f)
verb	stay, to; to remain	kukaa	rester
verb	steal, to	kuiba	voler
n.	steam	mvuke (pl. mivuke)	vapeur (f)
n.	steel	pua	acier
verb	step over, to	kukiuka	enjamber
verb	step, to	kupima kwa hatua	poser le pied en marchant
n.	steward	msimamizi (pl. wasimamizi)	steward (m)
n.	stick	fimbo	bâton (m)
phrase	stick of firewood	ukuni	le feu de bois
verb	stick to, to	kukamatisha	coller à
verb	stick together, to	kuambatanisha	agglutiner
adj.	still	kimya	tranquille
verb	sting, to	kuchoma	piquer
n.	stinginess	ubahili	avarice (f)
verb	stink, to	kunuka	puer, sentir mauvais
verb	stir, to; shake, to	kukoroga	agiter (un liquide)
n.	stock	akiba	réserve (f)
n., med	stomach	tumbo (pl. matumbo)	estomac (m)
n.	stomach cramp	tumbo linanyonga	crampe (f) d'estomac
n.	stone	jiwe (pl. mawe)	pierre (f)
n., med	stool (excrement)	choo	selles
phrase	stool., Go to	Kuenda chooni.	Va à la selle.
verb	stoop down, to	kuinama	se pencher
n.	stop	kituo (pl. vituo)	arrêt

parts of speech	english	swahili	french
verb	stop talking, to	kunyamaa	taire, se
verb	stop up, to	kuziba	boucher
interj.	Stop!	Basi!	Arrêtez!
verb	stop, to	kusimamisha	cesser
n.	stopper (in bottle), cork	kizibo (pl. vizibo)	bouchon (m)
n.	store (shop)	duka	magasin (m)
n.	storehouse	gala	entrepôt (m)
n.	stork	korongo	cigogne
n.	storm	tufani, zoruba	déluge (m)
n.	storm on lake	zoruba	orage (m)
n	story	kisa (pl. visa)	histoire (f)
n	story (floor)	dari	étage (m)
adj.	stout	-nene	solide
n.	stoutness	unene	embonpoint (m)
adj.	straight	sawa	droit
verb	straight, to be (as in line)	kunyoloka	droit, être
verb	straighten that which is bent, to	kukeua	redresser ce qui est courbé
verb	straighten, to	kunyolosha	redresser
verb	strain, to (filter)	kung'uta chuja	passer
verb	strained, to become	kunyosha	se tendre
n.	strainer	kifumbu	tamis (m)
adj.	strange	-geni	étranger
n.	straw (to cover a roof)	kuezeka	paille (pour couvrir un toit de paille)
verb	stray, to	kutangatanga	vagabonder
n.	stream (small river)	kijito (pl. vijito)	ruisseau (m)
n.	street	njia	rue (f)
n.	strength	nguvu	force (f)
n.	stretcher	machela	brancard (m)
n.	strife	upigano (pl. maupigano)	lutte (f)
verb	strike, to (hit)	kupiga, kugonga	frapper
n.	string	ugwe (pl. nyugwe)	ficelle (f)
verb	strive for, to	kujaribu	s'efforcer d'obtenir
verb	stroke, to	kupapasa	palper
adj.	strong	hodari, -enye nguvu	fort
adv.	strongly	sana	fortement
adj.	stubborn	-kaidi	entêtée
n.	stubbornness	uthabiti	entêtement (m)
verb	stuck, to be	kukwama	bloqué, être
n.	student	mwanafunzi (pl. wanafunzi)	étudiant (m)

parts of speech	english	swahili	french
verb	study, to	kujifunza	1. faire des études 2. étudier
verb	stumble, to	kukwaa	trébucher
n.	stump	kisiki (pl. visiki)	souche (f)
n.	stupidity	upumbavu	stupidité (f)
verb	stutter, to	kubabaika	bégayer
verb	stutter, to	kugugumiza	balbutier
verb	submerge, to	kuzamisha	submerger
verb	subtract, to	kutoa	soustraire
verb	succeed, to	kushinda	surmonter
verb	successful, to be	kustawi	réussir
n.	successor	halifa	successeur (m)
verb	suck, to	kunyonya	téter
adj.	sudden, abrupt	-a ghafula	brusque
adv.	suddenly	gafula	brusquement
phrase	suffering from?, What are you	Kuna shida gani?	De quoi souffres-tu?
verb	suffice, to	kufaa	suffire
verb	sufficient, to be	kutosha	suffire
n.	sugar	sukari	sucre (m)
n.	sugar cane	muwa (pl. miwa)	canne à sucre
adj.	suitable	-ema	convenable
verb	sulk, to	kununa	bouder
verb	sum up, to	kujumlisha	résumer
n.	summary	muhtasari	œuvre (f)
n.	sun	jua (pl. majua)	soleil (m)
n.	Sunday	Jumapili	dimanche (m)
adj.	sunny	-a jua	ensoleillé
n.	sunset	magharibi	coucher du soleil (m)
adj.	superior (chief)	-a juu	supérieur
verb	supervise, to	kusimamia	surveiller
adv.	supine position	chalichali	sur le dos
n.	supper	chakula cha usika	repas du soir
adj.	supplementary	-a kuongeza	charge supplémentaire
verb	support, to	kutegemeza	soutenir
verb	suppose, to	kuzani	supposer, imaginer
adv.	surely	hakika	certitude
n.	surgery	udaktari, kazi ya surgeon	chirurgie (f)
verb	surpass, to	kupita	surpasser
n.	surplus	baki	surplus (m)
verb	surprise, to	kushangaza	surprendre
phrase	surprised, to be	kustaajabu	étonné, être

parts of speech	english	swahili	french
phrase	surrender to, to	kusalimisha	se rendre à
verb	surround, to	kuzunguka	entourer
verb	surround, to (To have rings under one's eyes.)	kuzungusha	cerner (Avoir les yeux cernés.)
verb	survive, to	kuishi baada ya kufiwa	survivre à
verb	suspect, to	kushuku	soupçonner
verb	suspend, to	kutundika	suspendre
n.	suspicion	zana	soupçon (m)
verb	swallow, to	kumeza	avaler
n.	swamp, marsh	bwawa	marais (m)
n.	swarm	kundi (pl. makundi)	essaim (m)
verb	sway, to	kuyumbayumba	vaciller
n.	sweat	jasho	sueur (f)
verb	sweat, to	kutoka jasho	transpirer
n.	sweater	namna ya fulana nzito	pull-over (m)
verb	sweep, to	kufagia	balayer
adj.	sweet	-tamu	agréable
n.	sweet potatoes	kiazi (pl. viazi)	patates, douce
verb	swell, to	kuvimba	1. gonfler 2. enfler
n.	swelling	kivimbe (pl. vivimbe)	enflure (f)
verb	swim, to	kuogolea	nager
n.	swing (for child to use)	pembea	balançoire (f)
verb	swing, to	kupembea	se balancer
verb	swollen with air	kupuliza	gonfler avec l'air
n.	sword	upanga (pl. panga)	épée (f)
n.	symbol	mfano (pl. mifano)	symbole (m)
n.	sympathy	mapatano	1. sympathie (f) 2. compassion (f)
n., med	syphilis	sekeneko	syphilis
n.	Syria	Sham	Syrie (f)
n., med	syringe	bomba ndogo	seringue
n.	system	utaratibu	système (m)
n.	table	meza	table (f)
n.	tablet (pill)	kibonge	comprimé (m)
n.	taboo	mwiko	tabou (m)
n.	tactics	maarifa ya vita	tactiques (f)
n.	tail	mkia (pl. mikia)	queue (f)
verb	take away, to	kuchukua	emporter
verb	take back, to	kurudisha	ramener
verb	take from, to	kutwalia	emporter
verb	take hold of, to	kushika	saisir

parts of speech	english	swahili	french
verb	**take out, to; pull out, to**	kungoa	arracher
verb	**take out, to; to go out; to exit**	kutoka	sortir
verb	**take part in, to**	kushariki	participer à
verb	**take place, to**	kufanyika	avoir lieu
verb	**take, to**	kutwaa; kushika	prendre
verb	**take, to**	kutwaa	emporter
n.	**talk**	mazungumzo	conversation (f)
verb	**talk against, to**	kuhukumu au pima	critiquer
verb	**talk, to**	kusema	parler
adj.	**talkative**	-a maneno mengi	bavard
adj.	**tall**	-refu	grand
verb	**tangle, to (ensnare)**	kutatiza	enchevêtrer
verb	**tangled up, to get**	kujitatiza	s'enchevêtrer
adj.	**tardy**	-zembe	tardif
n.	**target**	shabaha	cible (f)
n.	**tarpaulin**	turubali	bâche (f)
n.	**task**	kazi	tâche (f)
verb	**taste, to**	kuonja	goûter
n.	**tattoo**	chale	tatouage (m)
verb	**taunt, to**	kusuta	se moquer
n.	**tax**	kodi	impôt (m)
n	**tea**	chai	thé (m)
verb	**teach, to**	kufundisha	enseigner
n.	**teacher**	mwalimu (pl. walimu)	1. instituteur (m) 2. enseignant (m)
n.	**teaching, (lesson)**	mafundisho; somo (pl. masomo)	leçon (f)
verb	**tear down, to**	kubomoa	démolir
verb	**tear, to**	kupasua	déchirer
n.	**tears**	machozi	larmes (f)
verb	**tease, to**	kuuzi	taquiner
n.	**technique**	ufundi	technique (f)
phrase	**teeth, lacking**	-siye na meno	dépourvue de dents
n.	**telephone**	simu	téléphone (m)
n.	**telescope, microscope**	darubini	microscope, télescope
phrase	**tell a lie, to**	kusema uwongo	dire de mensonge
verb	**tell the news, to**	kupasha habari	annoncer les nouvelles
verb	**tell, to**	kuambia	dire à
n.	**temperament**	tabia	tempérament (m)
n.	**temperance**	kiasi	tempérance (f)
n.	**temple**	panja	temple (m)

parts of speech	english	swahili	french
adj.	temporary	-a wakati	intérimaire
verb	tempt, to	kujaribu	tenter
n.	temptation	jaribu	tentation (f)
n. & adj.	ten	kumi	dix (m)
n.	tenacity	nguvu ya kushika	ténacité (f)
n.	tendency	maelekeo	tendance (f)
n.	tenderness	wembamba	tendresse (f)
n.	tent	hema	tente (f)
adj.	tenth	-a kumi	dixième
n.	terror	hofu kuu	terreur (f)
n.	test	jaribu	épreuve (f)
verb	test, to	kupima	mettre l'épreuve
n.	Testament, Old	Agano la Kale	Ancien Testament
n., med	testicle	pumbu (pl. mapumbu)	testicule (m)
verb	testify, to	kuhakiki	affirmer
phrase	Thank you very much.	Asante sana.	Merci beaucoup.
phrase	Thank you.	Asante.	Merci.
verb	thank, to	kushukuru	remercier
adj.,pro.	that	yule (sing. person); ile (sing. thing)	ce, cet, cette
x	That is too expensive. (service)	Nibeyisana.	C'est trop cher.
pronoun	that one	hiyo	celui-là, celle-là
phrase	That's right.	Wakaligani.	C'est ça.
phrase	That's too expensive. (thing)	Ni ghali mno.	C'est trop cher.
phrase	The food is good.	Chakula kitamu sana.	Aliment, repas est bon.
n.	theft	wizi	vol (m)
adj.	their (their children)	-ao (wana wao)	leur (sg), leurs (pl) (leurs enfants)
pronoun	them	wao, hao, wale	eux (m), elles (f)
adv.	then	kisha	1. alors 2. ensuite
prep.	then; afterwards	halafu	ensuite; puis; après
adv.	there	kule	là-bas
phrase	There is...	Kuna...	Il y a...
adj & pr	these	hawa (pl. person); hizi (pl. things)	ces, ceux-ci (m), celles-ci (f)
pronoun	they (and they)	wao	ils (m), elles (f) (et eux)
pronoun	they are	kuna	ce sont, ils sont, elles sont
n.	thief	mnyanganyi (pl. wanyanganyi)	voleur (m)
adj.	thieving	mwivi	voleur

parts of speech	english	swahili	french
n.	thigh	paja (pl. mapaja)	cuisse (f)
adj.	thin	-embamba	svelte
verb	thin, to become	kukonda	maigrir
n.	thing	kitu (pl. vitu)	chose (f)
verb	think about, to	kufikiri	réfléchir à
verb	think of, to	kuwaza; kufikiri	penser à
phrase	think that..., I	Nafikiri...	Je pense que...
verb	think, to	kuwaza	penser
adj.	third	-a tatu	troisième
n.	thirst	kiu	soif (f)
phrase	thirsty, to be	-a enye kiu	avoir soif
n.	thirteen	kumi na tatu	treize
adj. & n.	thirty	thelathini (makumi matatu)	trente (m)
n.	thirty-one	thelathini na moja	trente et un
adj.,pro.	this	huyu (person, sing.); hii (thing, sing.)	ce, cet, cette
phrase	this week	wiki hii	cette semaine
phrase	this year	mwaka huu	cette an
n.	thorn	mwiba (pl. miiba)	épine (f)
adj & pr	those	wale (pl. person); zile (pl. thing)	ces, ceux-là (m), celles-là (f)
n.	thought	wazo	pensée (f)
adj.	thoughtless	-a si ahgalifu	étourdi
adj. & n.	thousand	elfu	mille (m)
verb	thrash around, to	kujipigapiga	se débattre
n.	thread	uzi (pl. nyuzi)	fil (m)
n.	three	tatu	trois
n.	three hundred	mia tatu	trois cents
verb	thrive, to	kupata mali	se multiplier
n.	throat	koo (pl. makoo)	gorge (f)
verb	throw away, to	kutupa	jeter
n.	thumb	kidole cha gumba	pouce (m)
n.	thunder	radi	tonnerre (m)
n.	thunder	nguruwe	tonnerre (m)
verb	thunder, to	kunguruma	tonner
n.	Thursday	siku ya nne; alhamisi	jeudi (m)
adv.	thus (and so on)	hivi, vile (na vingine vivyo hivyo)	ainsi (et ainsi de suite)
n., med	tibia	muundi wa mguu	tibia (os de la jambe)
n.	tick	kimputu (pl. vimputu)	tique
n.	tick	kupe	tique des animaux
n.	ticket	cheti (pl. vyeti)	billet (m)

parts of speech	english	swahili	french
verb	tickle, to	kutekenya	chatouiller
verb	tie up, to	kufunga	lier
verb	tie, to	kufunga	attacher
verb	tighten, to	kukaza	serrer
n.	tile (roof)	kigae (pl. vigae)	tuile (f)
adv., n.	time	mara, wakati (pl. nyakati)	fois, une fois
n.	time	wakati	temps (m)
adv.	time ago, long	kale	autrefois
n.	time off	ruhusa	vacances (m)
adv.	time to time, from	mara kwa mara	de temps en temps
phrase	time, on	kuwahi	à l'heure
phrase	time?, At what	Saa ngapi?	Que est-ce que temps?
adj.	timid	-oga	craintif
n.	tin (holds one gallon)	debe (pl. madebe)	tine (un gallon)
n.	tip (gratuity)	zawadi	pourboire (m)
n.	tire	mpira (pl. mipira)	pneu (m)
verb	tired, to be	kuchoka	avoir fatigué
n.	tithe	zaka	offrande
adv.	to and fro	huko na huko	de long en large
prep.	to, at	hadi, kwenye, kwa	à
n.	toad	chura (pl. vyura)	crapaud (m)
n.	tobacco	tumbako	tabac (m)
adv.	today	leo	aujourd'hui
n.	toe	kidole cha mguu	orteil (m)
n.	toenail	ukucha (pl. kucha)	ongle (m)
adv.	together	pamoja	ensemble
n.	together, a get	kikoa	soirée (f)
n.	toilet	choo (pl. vyoo)	cabinet (m)
n.	tomato	nyanya	tomate (f)
adv.	tomorrow	kesho	demain
phrase	tomorrow, day after	kesho kutwa	après-demain
n.	tongue	ulimi (pl. ndimi)	langue (f)
adv.	tonight	usiku huu	cette nuit
n., med	tonsillitis	ugonjwa wa umio	angine (f)
n.	tool (metal)	madini	outil (m)
n.	tooth {I have a toothache.}	jino (pl. meno) {Nina maumivu ya jino.}	dent (f) {J'ai mal aux dents.}
n.	toothbrush	mswaki (pl. miswaki)	brosse (f) à dents
n.	top (on the top)	urefu	haut (m)
n.	torch	mwenge	torche (f)
n.	torment	adhabu	tourment (m)

parts of speech	english	swahili	french
n.	torrent	mvo	torrent (m)
n.	tortoise	kobe (pl. makobe)	tortue (f)
verb	torture, to	kutesa	affliger
verb	touch, to	kugusa	toucher
n.	tower	mnara (pl. minara)	tour (f)
n.	town	mji (pl. miji)	agglomération (f)
n., med	trachea	umio wa pumzi	trachée
n.	trade	biashara	métier (m)
verb	trade, to	kufanya biashara	faire du commerce
n.	trader	mfanyi biashara	commerçant (m)
n.	tradition	mapokeo	tradition (f)
n.	train	gari la moshe	locomotive (f)
verb	train, to (child)	kuvuta	entraîner
n.	trait	tofauti	trait (m)
verb	trample on, to	kukanyaga	piétiner
verb	transcribe, to	kufuatisha	transcrire
verb	translate, to	kufasiri, kutafsiri	traduire
verb	transmit, to	kupisha	transmettre à
n.	trap, snare	mtego (pl. mitego)	piège (m)
verb	trap, to	kunasa, kutega	piéger
z	travel, to	kusafiri	voyager
n.	traveler	msafiri (pl. wasafiri)	voyageur (m), voyageuse (f)
n.	traveller	kusafiri	voyageur (m)
verb	traverse, to	kuvuka	traverser
verb	tread on, to	kukanyaga	marcher
n.	treasury	hazina	trésor (m)
verb	treat (medical), to	kutendea	traiter
n.	tree	mti (pl. miti)	arbre (m)
n.	tremble (earthquake)	tetemeko	tremblement (m) de terre
verb	tremble, to	kutetemeka	trembler
n.	trial	mashtaka	procès (m)
n.	tribe	kabila (pl. makabila)	tribu (f)
n.	tribunal	baraza ya hukumu	le tribunal de la tribu
verb	trick, to	kupunja	duper
adj.	trickery	werevu	astucieux
verb	trickle, to	kutirika	dégouliner
verb	trickle, to	kutiririka	couler goutte à goutte
n.	trip; journey	1. mwendo (pl. miendo) 2. safari	voyage (m)
verb	triumph, to	kupindua	renverser
n.	troop, company	kikosi (pl. vikosi)	troupe (f)

parts of speech	english	swahili	french
n.	trouble, problem	taabu	problème (m)
verb	trouble, to	kuondoa	déranger
verb	troubled, to be	kufazaika	troubler, se
n.	trowel	mwiko (pl. miiko)	truelle (f)
n.	truck	gari doga	camion (m)
adj.	true {You speak the truth.}	kweli {Kweli.}	vrai {Tu dis vrai.}
adv.	truly	hakika, kweli	vraiment
n.	trunk (of body)	kiwiliwili (pl. viwiliwili)	tronc (m)
n.	trunk (of elephant)	mkono (pl. mikono)	trompe (de l'éléphant) (f)
n.	trust (I trust him.)	tumaini	confiance (f) (J'ai confiance en lui.)
n.	truth	kweli	vérité (f)
verb	try, to	kujaribu	essayer
n.	tuberculosis	ugonjwa fulani	tuberculose (f)
n.	Tuesday	Jumanne	mardi (m)
n., med	tumor	kivimbe (pl. vivimbe)	tumeur (f)
n.	tunnel	shimo (pl. mashimo)	tunnel (m)
n.	turban	kilemba (pl. vilemba)	turban
n.	turkey	bata mzinga	dindon (m)
n.	turmoil	kelele (pl. makelele)	tumulte (m)
verb	turn around, to	kugeuka	se retourner
verb	turn over, to	kupindua	intervertir
verb	turn upside down, to	kufudikiza	reverser
n.	twelve	kumi na mbili	douze
n. & adj.	twenty	makumi mawili; ishirini	vingt (m)
n.	twenty-one	ishirini na moja	vingt et un
adv.	twice	mara mbili	deux fois
n.	twilight	ukungu wa ijioni	crépuscule (m)
adj. & n.	twin	pacha (pl. mapacha)	jumeau (m), jumelle (f)
verb	twist, to	kusokota	tordre
n. & adj.	two	mbili	deux (m)
n.	two hundred	mia mbili	deux cents
n.	two thousand	elfu mbili	deux mille
n.	type	mtindo	type (m)
n., med	typhoid	homa mbaya matumboni	typhus
n., med	typhoid fever	homa ya matumbo	typhoïde fièvre
n., med	ulcer (wound)	jeraha	blessure (f)
n.	umbilicus; navel	kitovu (pl. vitovu)	nombril (m)
n.	umbrella	mwavuli (pl. miavuli)	parapluie (m)
phrase	unable to find	sikupata	ne pas trouver

parts of speech	english	swahili	french
n.	uncle (father's older brother)	baba mukubwa	oncle paternel (aîné)
n.	uncle (father's younger brother)	baba mudogo	oncle paternel (plus jeune)
n.	uncle, maternal	mjomba (pl. wajomba)	oncle (m) maternel
adj.	unconscious	bila kufahamu	inconscient
adj.	uncouth	-jinga	rustre
adv.	under	chini ya	dessous
verb	underestimate, to	kuhesabu	sous-estimer
adv.	underneath	china	en-dessous
verb	understand, to {Do you understand?} [I did not understand.]	kufahamu {Unaelewa?} [Sielewi.]	comprendre {Comprends-tu?} [Je n'ai pas compris.]
n.	understanding	ufahamu	compréhension (f)
verb	undo, to	kutangua	se défaire
verb	unfold, to	kunjua	déplier
adj.	unique	-a namna ya peke yake	unique
verb	unite, to	kuunga	unir
n.	unity	umoja	unité (f)
conj.	unless	ila	sauf
verb	unload, to	kushusha	décharger
verb	unlock, to	kufungua	ouvrir
adj. & n.	unmarried person	mtawa (pl. watawa)	célibataire (m, f)
adj.	unripe	-bichi	sans mûr
adj.	unsatisfactory	-sioridhisha	insatisfaisant
verb	untie, to	kufungua	dénouer
prep.	until	hata, mpaka	jusqu'à
verb	unveil, to	kufunua	dévoiler
adv.	upright	wima	position debout
verb	upset, to	kupindua	peiner
verb	urgent, to be	kusihi sana	urgent, être
verb	urinate, to	kukojoa, kunya	uriner
n., med	urine	mkojo	urine
n.	use	matumizi	usage (m)
verb	use, to	kutumia	se servir de
adj.	useless	-a bure	inutile
adv.	usually	desturi	d'ordinaire
n., med	uterus	mji wa mimba	utérus
n.	vacation	kuacha	congé (m)
n.	vagina	kuma	vagin (m)
adj.	vain, in	-tupu	vain
n.	valley	bonde	vallée (f)

parts of speech	english	swahili	french
adj.	valuable	-a thamani	de valeur
n.	value	thamani	valeur (f)
verb	vanquish, to	kushinda	vaincre
n.	vapor	mvuke (pl. mivuke)	vapeur (f)
n.	vegetable	mboga	légume (m)
n.	veil	utaji	voile (m)
n.	vendor	mwuza (pl. wauza)	vendeur (m), vendeuse (f)
n.	verb	kiarifu	verbe (m)
verb	verify, to	kuhakiki	contrôler
n.	verse	aya	vers (m)
n.	vertigo	kizunguzungu	vertige (m)
adv.	very	sana; kabisa	très
adv.	very much	muno	beaucoup
n.	vicinity	ujirani	voisinage (m)
n.	village	boma, kijiji, (pl. vijiji)	village (m)
n.	vine	mzabibu (pl. mizabibu)	vigne (f)
n.	vinegar	siki	vinaigre (m)
n.	vineyard	shamba la mizabibu	vigne (f)
n.	violence	jeuri	violence (f)
n.	virtue	nguvu	vertu (f)
adj.	visible	-a kuonekana	visible
verb	visible, to be	kuonekana	visible, être
verb	visit, to	kuzuru	visiter
n.	visitor (guest)	mgeni (pl. wageni)	invité (m), invitée (f)
n.	voice	sauti	voix (f)
n.	volcano	mlima wa moto	volcan (m)
verb	vomit, to {I am vomiting worms.}	kutapika {Ninatapita minyoo.)	vomir {Je vomis des vers.}
verb	vow, to, to swear (oath)	kuweka nadhiri	jurer
n.	vulture	tai (pl. matai)	vautour (m)
n.	wages	mshahara (pl. mishahara)	salarie (m)
verb	wait for, to	kungoja	attendre
interj.	Wait!	Ngoja!	Attends!
verb	wait, to	kungoja	1. attendre 2. patienter
verb	wake up, to	kuamsha	réveiller
verb	walk, to	kwenda	marcher
verb	walk, to go for a	kutembea	se promener
n.	walking stick	fimbo	canne (f)
n.	wall	kiambaza (pl. viambaza)	mur (m)
verb	want, to	kutaka	vouloir
n.	war	vita	guerre (f)

parts of speech	english	swahili	french
adj.	warm	-a moto	chaud
verb	warn, to	kupasha habari	prévenir
n.	warthog	ngiri	phacochère
verb	wash hands and feet, to	kunawa	laver mains ou pieds, se
verb	wash, to	kuosha	laver
verb	wash, to (body-self)	kunawa	laver se
verb	wash, to (clothes)	kufua	laver les vêtements
verb	waste, to	kuharibu	gaspiller
n.	watch (clock)	saa	montre (f)
n.	watchman	mngoje	gardien (m)
n.	water	maji	eau (f)
n.	water pot	mtungi (pl. mitungi)	pot (m) de l'eau
n.	waterfall	anguko la maji	cascade (f)
n.	wave (of water)	wimbi (pl. mawimbe)	vague (f)
n.	wax	nta	cire (f)
n.	way (road)	njia	chemin (m)
pronoun	we, us	sisi, siye	nous
adj.	weak	1. teketeke 2. zaifu 3. -regevu	faible
n.	weakness	uzaifu	faiblesse (f)
n.	wealth	mali, utajiri	richesse (f)
n.	weapon	silaha	arme (f)
verb	wear, to	kuvaa; kuchukua	porter
n.	wedding	arusi	noces (f)
n.	wedding	harusi	mariage (m)
n.	Wednesday	Jumatano	mercredi (m)
verb	weed, to	kupalia magugu	sarcler
n.	week	juma	semaine (f)
n.	week, last	juma jana	après-semaine (f); semaine (f) dernière
n.	weekday	siku yo yote ya juma isipokuwa Jumapili	jour (m) de semaine
verb	weep, to	kulia	pleurer
verb	weigh, to	kupima	peser
verb	weighed down, to be	kuelemea	accabler
n.	weight	uzito	poids (m)
verb	weight, to gain	kuvimbisha	grossir
verb	weight, to lose	kukonda	maigrir
verb	welcome, to	kukaribisha	accueillir
phrase	Welcome.	Karibu.	Bienvenu.
adv.	well	vema, vizuri	bien
n.	well (ie. for water)	kisima (pl. visima)	puits (m)

112

parts of speech	english	swahili	french
verb	**well, to get**	kupona	remets-toi
adj., adv.	**well, very**	vizuri	bien
n. & adj.	**west**	magharibi	ouest (m)
adj.	**wet**	majimaji	mouillé
verb	**wet, to**	kuloweka	mouiller
adj.	**what**	gani, nini	quoi
phrase	**What are you doing?**	Uko nafanya nini?	Qu'est-ce que vous faites?
phrase	**What are you looking for?**	Unatafuta nini?	Qu'est-ce que tu-veux?
phrase	**What are you saying?**	Uko nasema nini?	Qu'est-ce que vous dites?
phrase	**what is more**	kutambusha	en plus
phrase	**What is new?**	Habari?	Quoi de neuf?
phrase	**What is this?**	Hapa ni gani?	Qu'est-ce que c'est?
phrase	**What is your name?**	Jina lako nani?	Quel est ton nom?
phrase	**What is your profession?**	Unafanya kazi gani?	Quelle est ton (votre) profession?
phrase	**What!**	Kumbe!	Quoi!
phrase	**What's up? (familiar person)**	Vipi?	Qu'est-ce qu'il y a?
n.	**wheat**	ngano	blé (m)
n.	**wheel**	duara	roue (f)
conj.	**when**	wakati gani	quand
conj.	**When?**	Wakati gani?	Quand est-ce que?
conj.	**whenever**	kila mara	toutes les fois que
conj.	**where**	wapi	où
phrase	**Where are you coming from?**	Umeyok wapi?	Où viens-tu?
phrase	**Where are you going?**	Unakwenda wapi?	Où allez-vous?
phrase	**Where is the bathroom?**	Choo kiko wapi?	Où est la salle de bain?
phrase	**Where is...?**	Wapi ni...?	Où est...?
conj.	**whereas**	kwa maana	tandis que
conj.	**whether**	kama	soit que
adj.	**which**	gani	quel (m), quelle (f)
n.	**whip**	fimbo	fouet (m)
verb	**whip, to**	kuchapa	fouetter
n.	**whirlpool**	kizingia cha maji	tourbillon (m)
verb	**whisper, to**	nong'ona	chuchoter
n.	**whistle**	1. filimbi 2. mluzi	sifflet (m)
adj.	**white**	-eupe	blanc
phrase	**white people**	wazungu	les blancs
n.	**white person**	mzungu (pl. wazungu)	le blanc
verb	**whiten, to**	kufanya -eupe	blanchir
phrase	**whiteness, dazzling**	weupe	blancheur éclatante

parts of speech	english	swahili	french
phrase	who (Who are you looking for?)	nani (Unatafuta nani?)	qui (Qu'est-ce qui tu cherches?)
adj.	whole (good healthy)	-zima	bien portant
adv.	why	1. kwa maana gani 2. kwa nini 3. kwa ajilini gani	pourquoi
n.	wick	utambi	mèche de lampe
adj.	wicked	-ovu	méchant
n.	widow	mjane (pl. wajane)	veuve (f)
n.	widower	mjane (pl. wajane)	veuf (m)
n.	width	upana	largeur (f)
n.	wife	bibi; mke (pl. wake)	femme (f), épouse
n.	wilderness	jangwa	désert (m)
n.	will	kusudi (pl. makusudi)	volonté (f)
verb	wilt, to	kufifia	flétrir
verb	win, to	kushinda	gagner
n.	wind	upepo (pl. pepo)	vent (m)
verb	wind, to	kuupepo	enrouler
n.	window	dirisha (pl. madirisha)	fenêtre (f)
n.	wine	divai	vin (m)
n.	wing	bawa (pl. mabawa)	aile (f)
n.	winner	mshinda (pl. washinda)	vainqueur (m)
verb	wipe away, to	kufuta	effacer
verb	wipe, to	kupangusa	essuyer
n.	wisdom	1. akili 2. hekima	sagesse (f)
adj.	wise	-a busara	sage
n.	wish	mapenzi	désir (m)
n.	witch	mchawi (pl. wachawi)	sorcier (m)
n.	witch doctor	mfumu (pl. wafumu)	docteur (m) de sorcière
phrase	witchcraft	uchawi	métier de sorcière
prep.	with	kwa, na, pamoja na	avec, de
prep.	with	na	avec, par
verb	withhold, to	kunyima	refuser
prep.	without	bila, pasipo	sans
verb	withstand, to	kusimamia	résister à
n.	witness	mshuhuda (pl. washuhuda)	témoin (m)
verb	witness, to	kushuhuda	témoin de, être
n.	wolf	mbwa mwitu	loup
n.	woman (married)	bibi; mwanamke (pl. wanawake)	madame (f)
n.	woman (old)	kizee	madame (f) vieille
n.	wonder	mshangao (pl. mishangao)	merveille (f)
verb	woo, to	kuposa	faire la cour à

parts of speech	english	swahili	french
n.	wood (for fire)	kuni	bois (m)
n.	word	neno (pl. maneno)	mot (m)
phrase	word mean?, What does this	Neno...lina maana gani?	Que signifie ce mot?
n.	work	kazi	travail (m)
verb	work with zeal, to	kufanya bidii	s'efforcer
verb	work, to	kutumika	travailler
n.	worker	mfanya kazi	travailleur
n.	workshop	kibanda (pl. vibanda)	atelier (m)
n.	world	ulimwengu	monde (m)
verb	worried, to be	kuuzi	tracasser
n.	worry	taabu	souci (m)
verb	worship, to	kuabudu	rendre un culte à Dieu
n.	worth	thamani	valeur (f)
n.	wound, injury	jeraha	blessure (f)
n.	wound, sore	kidonda (pl. vidonda)	blessure (f)
verb	wounded, to be	kuumwa	être blesser
verb	wrap, to	kufunika	envelopper
verb	wring out to	kukamua	essorer
n.	wrinkle	kunjo (pl. makunjo)	ride (m)
verb	wrinkle, to	kufanya vifinyo	rider
n.	wrist	kiwiko (pl. viwiko)	poignet (m)
verb	write, to	kuandika	écrire
n.	yam	kiazi kikuu	igname
n.	yawn	mwayo (pl. miayo)	bâillement
verb	yawn, to	kupiga miayo	bâiller
n.	year	mwaka, (pl. miaka)	an (m), année (f)
adv.	year after year	mwaka kwa mwaka	an après an
n.	yeast	chachu	levure (f)
verb	yell, to (pain, sorrow); to howl	kulia	hurler
adj. & n.	yellow	-a kimanjano	jaune (m)
adv.	yes	ndiyo; ndivyo; naam	oui
adv.	yesterday	jana	hier
adv.	yet	bado; hata sasa	encore
pronoun	you (plural)	ninyi	vous
pronoun	you (singular)	wewe	tu, vous
phrase	You don't really mean that!	Haiwezekani!	Allons donc!
phrase	You know.	Unajua.	Vous savez, vous connaissez.
n.	young lady (unmarried)	mwali; kibibi (pl. vibibi)	mademoiselle (f)

parts of speech	english	swahili	french
n.	**young man, (unmarried)**	mvulana (pl. wavulana)	jeune homme pubère
n.	**young person**	kijana mwanaume	jeune homme
adj.	**your (plural) (your children)**	-enu (wana wenu)	vos, votre (vos enfants)
adj.	**your (singular) (your child)**	-ako (mwana wako)	votre, ton, ta, tes (ton enfant)
n.	**youth**	kijana (pl. vijana) (boy or girl)	enfant, entre 10 et 12 ans
n.	**youth**	ujana	jeunesse (f)
n.	**zeal**	bidii	zèle (m)
adj.	**zealous**	-enye bidii	zélé
n.	**zebra**	punda milia	zèbre (m)
n.	**zero**	sifuri	zéro (m)

parts of speech	swahili	french	english
adj.	-a afya	robuste	robust
adj.	-a ajabu	extraordinaire	extraordinary
adj.	-a ajabu	remarquable	outstanding
adj.	-a angavu	épanoui	radiant
adj.	-a asili	essentiel	essential
adj.	-a bahati njema	chance, avoir de la	lucky
adj.	-a baridi	froid	cold
adj.	-a baridi	frais (m), fraîche (f)	cool
adj.	-a bure	vaurien	good-for-nothing
adj.	-a bure	inutile	useless
adj.	-a busara	sage	wise
adj.	-a choyo	égoïste	selfish
adj.	-a daima	interminable	interminable
verb	-a enye kiu	avoir soif	thirsty, to be
adj.	-a fahari	prétentieux	pretentious
adj.	-a furaha	heureux	happy
adj.	-a ghafula	brusque	sudden, abrupt
adj.	-a haki	juste	fair
adj.	-a hatari	1. dangereux 2. hasardeux 3. précaire	1. dangerous 2. hazardous 3. precarious
adj.	-a heri	avoir de la chance	fortunate
adj.	-a hofu	peureux	fearful
adj.	-a huzuni	triste	sad
adj.	-a jasiri	intrépide	fearless
adj.	-a jua	ensoleillé	sunny
adj.	-a juu	supérieur	superior (chief)
adj.	-a kabla	antérieur	anterior
adj.	-a kadiri	moyen	medium
adj.	-a kale	ancien	ancient
adj.	-a kali	aiguise	sharp
n.	kati	milieu (m)	middle
adj.	-a kawaida	1. commun 2. ordinaire	1. common 2. ordinary
adj.	-a kenda	neuvième	ninth
adj.	-a kifalme	royal	royal
adj.	-a kike	féminin	feminine
adj.	-a kila siku	tous les jours	everyday
adj. & n.	-a kimanjano	jaune (m)	yellow
adj.	-a kitambo	provisoire	provisional
adj.	-a kuambukiza	contagieux	contagious

parts of speech	swahili	french	english
adj.	-a kuchekesha	drôle	funny
adj.	-a kuchukiza	désagréable	nasty
adj.	-a kufanana	semblable	alike
adj.	-a kufani	moribond	moribund
adj.	-a kufuata	prochain, suivant	next
adv.	-a kukingama	en travers	crosswise
adj.	-a kukosa busara	indiscret	indiscreet
adj.	-a kumi	dixième	tenth
adj.	-a kuonekana	visible	visible
adj.	-a kuongeza	charge supplémentaire	supplementary
adj.	-a kupakana	voisin	adjacent
adj.	-a kupendeza	charmant	delightful
adj.	-a kupita kiasi	excessif	excessive
adj.	-a kupotoka	courbé	crooked
adj.	-a kuridhisha	satisfaisant	satisfactory
adj.	-a kusaidia	obligeant	helpful
adj.	-a kusedeka	chronique	chronic
adj.	-a kushoto	gauche	left
adj.	-a kushtusha	surprenant	startling
adj.	-a kutosha	suffisant	adequate
adj.	-a kutosha	assez de	enough
adj.	-a kwanza	premier (m), première (f)	first
adj.	-a kwanza	antérieur	prior to
verb	-a kwenda sawa, être	dire franchement	speak frankly, to
adj.	-a maneno mengi	bavard	talkative
adj.	-a mara nyingi	fréquent	frequent
adj.	-a moto	chaud	hot
adj.	-a moto	chaud	warm
adj.	-a mtu	humain (m)	human
adv.	-a mwisho	définitivement	final
adj.	-a mwisho	dernier	last
adj.	-a namna nyingi	divers	miscellaneous
adj.	-a namna ya peke yake	unique	unique
adj.	-a nane	huitième	eighth
adj.	-a nne	quatrième	fourth
adj.	-a nyamavu	silencieux	silent
adj.	-a peke	unique	sole
adj.	-a peke yake	spécial	special
adj.	-a pili	deuxième	second
adj.	-a potevu wa mali	prodigue	prodigal
adj.	-a rangi ya majani; kijani	vert	green (color)

parts of speech	swahili	french	english
adj.	-a saba	septième	seventh
adj.	-a si ahgalifu	étourdi	thoughtless
adj.	-a sita	sixième	sixth
adj.	-a tano	cinquième	fifth
adj.	-a tatu	troisième	third
adj.	-a thamani	de valeur	valuable
adj.	-a uongo	faux (m), fausse (f)	FALSE
adj.	-a upande wa kuume	droit	right
adj.	-a wakati	intérimaire	temporary
n.	-a zamani	passé (m)	past
adj.	-ake	son (m), sa (f), ses (pl)	his
adj.	-ako (mwana wako)	votre, ton, ta, tes (ton enfant)	your (singular) (your child)
adj.	-aminifu	fidèle	faithful
adj.	-angalifu	prudent	careful
adj.	-angu (wana wangu)	mon (m), ma (f), mes (pl) (mes enfants)	my (my children)
adj.	-ao (wana wao)	leur (sg), leurs (pl) (leurs enfants)	their (their children)
adj.	-ate	insubordonné	insubordinate
adj.	-baya sana	affreux	awful
adj.	-baya, -bovu	mauvais	bad
adj.	-bichi	frais	fresh, cool
adj.	-bichi	1. pas mûr 2. sans mûr	1. green 2. unripe
adj.	-bichi	cru	raw
adj.	-bivu	mûr	ripe
adj.	-bovu	pourri	rotten
adj.	-chache	peu de	few
adj.	-chafu	sale	dirty
adj.	-chungu	amer	bitter
adj.	-chungu, -kali	acide	acid
adj.	-danganyifu	malhonnête	dishonest
adj.	-dogo	petit	small
n. & adv	-dogo	peu (m)	little
adj.	-dogo	chétif	puny
adj.	-dogo kabisa	moindre	least
adj. & n.	-ekundu	rouge (f)	red
adj.	-ema	bon (m), bonne (f)	good
adj.	-ema	bien	good
adj.	-ema	gentil	nice
adj.	-ema	convenable	suitable
adj.	-embamba	1. étroit 2. svelte	1. narrow 2. thin

parts of speech	swahili	french	english
adj.	-enu (wana wenu)	vos, votre (vos enfants)	your (plural) (your children)
adj.	-enye afya	sain	healthy
adj.	-enye akili	1. appréhensif 2. intelligent	1. apprehensive 2. clever 3. intelligent
adj.	-enye bidii	1. désireux 2. zélé	1. eager 2. zealous
adj.	-enye elimu	savant	learned
adj.	-enye hadhari	prudent	cautious
adj.	-enye haraka	1. impatient 2. impulsif	1. impatient 2. impulsive
adj.	-enye hasira nyingi	furieux	furious
adj.	-enye haya	1. timide 2. peureux	1. bashful 2. shy
adj.	-enye huruma	humain	humane
adj.	-enye kiburi	fier	proud
adj.	-enye kichaa	fou	crazy
adj.	-enye kung'aa, -enye akili	vif	bright
phrase	-enye kushiba	être rassasié	satisfied, to be (ate enough)
adj.	-enye kutaka makuu	ambitieux	ambitious
adj.	-enye kuweza	capable	capable, able
adj.	-enye maana mbili	ambigu	ambiguous
adj.	-enye makelele	bruyant	noisy
adj.	-enye mali	riche	rich (person)
adj.	-enye manufaa	salutaire	beneficial
adv.	-enye matata	délicat	awkward
adj.	-enye milima mingi	montagneux	mountainous
adj.	-enye njaa	affamé	hungry
adj.	-enye raha	confortable	comfortable
adj.	-enye rutuba	fertile	fertile
adj.	-enye sura ya kuchukiza	hideux	hideous
adj.	-enye wazimu	fou (f. folle)	mad (insane)
pronoun	-enyewe	lui-même (m), elle-même (f)	itself
adj.	-epesi	1. facile 2. léger	1. easy 2. light
adj.	-erevu	roublard	crafty
adj.	-etu (wana wetu)	notre (sg), nos (pl) (nos enfants)	our (our children)
adj.	-eupe	blanc	white
adj.	-eusi	foncé	dark
adj.	-eusi, -a giza	noir	black
adj.	-fupi	1. bref 2. bas (f. basse) 3. court	1. brief 2. low 3. short
adj.	-geni	étranger	strange
adj.	-geugeu	arbitraire	arbitrary

parts of speech	swahili	french	english
adj.	-gonjwa	souffrant	poorly
adj.	-gumu	1. inflexible 2. difficile 3. dur	1. adamant 2. difficult 3. hard
adj.	-ingi	1. beaucoup 2. nombreux	1. a lot 2. many 3. much 4. numerous
adj.	-ingine	un autre (m), une autre (f) (un autre homme)	another (another man)
adj & pr	-ingine	autre	other
adj.	-jasiri	1. audacieux 2. courageux 3. téméraire	1. audacious 2. courageous 3. reckless
adj.	-jinga	1. bête 2. crédule 3. rustre	1. foolish 2. gullible 3. uncouth
adj.	-kaidi	1. obstiné 2. entêtée	1. obstinate 2. stubborn
adj.	-kali	1. sévère 2. féroce 3. aigre	1. harsh 2. sharp (fierce) 3. sour
adj.	-karimu	généreux	generous
adj.	-kavu	sec	dry
adj.	-kubwa	1. grand 2. gros	1. big 2. great 3. large
adj.	-kunjufu	joyeux	cheerful
adj.	-kuu	principal	principal (important)
adj.	-lafi	cupide	greedy
adj & pr	-moja, yule yule	même	same
n. & adj.	-nene	1. gras (m), grasse (f) 2. solide	1. fat 2. stout
adv.	-ngapi	1. combien de 2. combien	1. how many 2. how much
adj.	-nje	extérieur	exterior
adj.	-nyofu	honnête	honest
adj.	-oga	craintif	timid
adj.	-ote	tout	all, everything
adj.	-ovu	1. mauvais 2. méchant	1. evil 2. wicked
adj.	-pana	1. large 2. spacieux	1. broad 2. wide 3. spacious
adj.	-pana; sawa	plat	flat
adj.	-penzi	cher (m), chère (f)	dear
adj.	-pofu	aveugle	blind
adj.	-pole	1. doux 2. tranquille	1. gentle 2. meek 3. mild 4. peaceful
adj.	-pumbavu	ignorant	dull
adj.	-pya	1. neuf 2. récent	1. new 2. recent
phrase	-pya kabisa	flambant neuf	brand new
adj.	-refu	1. long (m), longue (f) 2. grand 3. profond	1. long 2. tall 3. profound
adj.	-refu, -kuu	haut	high

parts of speech	swahili	french	english
adj.	-regevu	faible	weak
adj.	-sahaulifu	1. distrait 2. oublieux	1. absent-minded 2. forgetful
adj.	-sikivu	obéissant	obedient
adj.	-sio adabu	impoli	impolite
adj.	-sioridhisha	insatisfaisant	unsatisfactory
adj.	-sioweza	incapable	incapable
phrase	-siye na meno	dépourvue de dents	teeth, lacking
adj.	-staarabu	civilisé	civilized
adj.	-takatifu	saint	1. holy 2. saint
adj.	-tamu	1. délicieux 2. agréable	1. delicious 2. sweet
adj.	-tepetevu	1. flasque 2. inerte	1. flabby 2. inert
adj.	-timilifu	complet	complete
adj.	-tovu	simplet	lacking
adj.	-tovu wa heshima	irrespectueux	disrespectful
adj.	-tupu	1. pelé 2. vide 3. nu 4. vain	1. bare 2. empty 3. nude 4. in vain
adj.	-vivu	1. fainéant 2. paresseux	1. idle 2. lazy
adj.	-vumilivu	patient	patient
phrase	-wa ndugu ya	avoir un lien de famille	related, to be
adj.	-wekevu	1. économique 2. frugal	1. economical 2. frugal
adj.	-wivu	jaloux	jealous
adj.	-zee	vieux	old
adj.	-zembe	1. qui manque de soin 2. tardif	1. careless 2. tardy
adj.	-zima	bien portant	whole (good healthy)
adj.	-zima, -ote	entier, tout	entire
adj.	-zito	1. épais 2. lourd	1. dense 2. heavy
adj.	-zuri	1. beau (m), belle (f) 2. excellent 3. gentil (m), gentille (f) 4. beau 5. joli	1. beautiful 2. fine 3. friendly 4. handsome 5. pretty
n.	abiria	passager (m), passagère (f)	passenger
n.	ada ya posta	timbre-poste (m)	postage stamp
n.	adabu	1. bonnes manières (f) 2. politesse (f)	1. good manners 2. politeness
n.	adhabu	tourment (m)	torment
n.	adhuhuri	midi (m)	noon
verb	adoucir	défroisser	smooth out, to
adj. & n.	adui	ennemi (m)	enemy
adv.	afazali	1. mieux 2. plutôt	1. better 2. rather
n.	afisi	office (m)	office
n.	afya	santé (f)	health

parts of speech	swahili	french	english
n.	**Agano Jipya**	le Nouveau Testament (m)	New Testament
n.	**Agano la Kale**	Ancien Testament	Testament, Old
n.	**ahandi**	promesse (f)	promise
n.	**aibu**	honte (f)	disgrace
n.	**aibu, haya**	honte (f)	shame
n.	**aina, jamii**	catégorie (f)	category
n.	**ajali**	destin (m)	destiny
n.	**akiba**	réserve (f)	1. stock 2. reserve
n.	**akili**	1. intelligence (f) 2. esprit (m) 3. raison (f) 4. sagesse (f)	1. intelligence 2. mind 3. reason 4. wisdom
n.	**akili, ustadi, uwezo**	capable	ability, (to have)
phrase	**Akuweke.**	À tes souhaits.	Bless you.
n.	**alama**	1. marque (f) 2. signe (m)	1. mark 2. sign
n.	**alasiri, mangaribi**	après-midi (m or f)	afternoon
prep.	**ama**	ou	or
conj.	**ama sivyo**	sinon	otherwise
conj.	**ama...ama**	soit...soit	either...or
n.	**amani, salama**	paix (f)	peace
n., med	**ambukizo**	infection (f)	infection
adj.	**amekufa**	mort	dead
n.	**amri (pl. amri)**	1. commandement (m) 2. ordre (m)	1. command 2. order
n.	**amri, mamlaka**	autorité (f)	authority
n.	**anasa**	1. luxe (m) 2. plaisir (m)	1. luxury 2. pleasure
n.	**anga, mbingu**	ciel (m)	sky
interj.	**Ange!**	Écouter!	Attention!
n.	**anguko la maji**	cascade (f)	waterfall
n.	**Aprili, mwezi wa nne wa mwaka wa kizungu**	avril (m)	April
n.	**ardhi**	terre (f)	ground
adj. & n.	**arobaini**	quarante (m)	forty
n.	**arusi**	noces (f)	wedding
n.	**asali**	miel (m)	honey
phrase	**Asante sana.**	Merci beaucoup.	Thank you very much.
phrase	**Asante.**	Merci.	Thank you.
n.	**asili**	origine (f)	origin
adj.	**asiyefundishwa**	illettré	illiterate
n.	**askari**	soldat (m)	soldier
adj. & n.	**askari mgeni wa mshahara**	mercenaire (m)	mercenary
n.	**askari wafuasi**	gardes du corps (m)	bodyguard

123

parts of speech	swahili	french	english
adv. n.	asubuhi	matin (m)	morning
interj.	Ati...	Dis donc...	I say... (look here)
n.	aya	vers (m)	verse
n.	azabu	peine (f)	punishment
n.	azimio (pl. mazimio)	projet (m)	project
n.	azimio la mambo ya kufanyika	programme (m)	program
n.	baa, msiba	désastre (m)	disaster
adv.	baada ya, nyuma ya	après	after
adv.	baadaye	1. après cela 2. plus retard	1. hereafter 2. later
adv.	baadaye, halafu, kisha	ensuite	afterward
n.	baba	père (m)	1. father 2. papa
n.	baba mudogo	oncle paternel (plus jeune)	uncle (father's younger brother)
n.	baba mukubwa	oncle paternel (aîné)	uncle (father's older brother)
n.	babangu	père (m), mon	father (my)
n.	babu	grand-père (m)	grandfather
adv.	badala ya	au lieu de	place of, in
adv.	badalya ya	au lieu de cela	instead
adv.	bado	pas encore	not yet
adv.	bado kidogo	1. bientôt 2. vite	soon
adv.	bado; hata sasa	encore	yet
n.	bahari	mer (f)	sea
n.	bahari kuu	océan (m)	ocean
n.	bahasha	1. enveloppe (f) 2. paquet (m)	1. envelope 2. packet
n.	bahati	1. fortune (f) bien 2. chance (f)	good fortune
n.	bahati mbaya	malheur (m)	misfortune
n.	bahili	avare (m,f)	miser
n.	baisikeli	bicyclette (f)	bicycle
n.	baka	teigne (f)	ringworm
n.	baki	surplus (m)	surplus
phrase	Bakia vizuri!	Soie courage!	Be strong! (stay well)
n.	bakuli	1. cuvette (f) 2. bol (m)	1. basin (wash) 2. bowl
n.	balangiti	couverture (f)	blanket
n.	balozi (pl. malozi)	ambassadeur (m)	ambassador
n.	banda	grange (f)	barn
n.	barabara, njia	route (f)	road
n.	barafu	glace (f)	ice
n.	baraka	bénédiction (f)	blessing

parts of speech	swahili	french	english
n.	baraza	1. conseil (m) 2. porche (m) 3. session (f)	1. council, advice 2. porch 3. session
n.	baraza ya hukumu	le tribunal de la tribu	tribunal
n.	baridi	rhume (m)	cold in head
n.	barua	lettre (f)	letter (as in, I wrote a letter to a friend.)
n.	barua fupi	note (f)	note
n.	barua za posta	bureau (m) de poste	post office
n.	baruti	explosif (m)	explosive
n	baruti ya kupasulia mwamba	dynamite (f)	dynamite
interj.	Basi!	1. Assez! 2. Arrêtez!	1. Enough! 2. Stop!
phrase	Basi, safari!	Allons-y!	Let's go!
n.	bata (pl. mabata)	canard (m)	duck
n.	bata mzinga	dindon (m)	turkey
n.	bawa	aile (f)	wing
n.	bega (pl. mabega)	épaule (f)	shoulder
n.	bei	prix (m)	price
n.	bei, gharama	coût (m)	cost
n.	bendera	drapeau (m)	flag
n.	benki ya fedha	banque (f)	bank (for money)
n.	biashara	métier (m)	trade
n.	bibi	1. Mme. (f) (for madame) 2. dame (f)	1. Mrs. 2. lady
n.	bibi arusi	mariée (f)	bride
n.	bibi; mke (pl. wake)	femme (f), épouse	wife
n.	bibi; mwanamke (pl. wanawake)	madame (f)	woman (married)
n.	Biblia	Bible (f)	Bible
n.	bidii	zèle (m)	zeal
adj.	bila hatia	innocent	innocent
adj.	bila idadi	innombrable	countless
adj.	bila kufahamu	inconscient	unconscious
adj.	bila kukoma	continu	continuous
adj.	bila maana	dénué de sens	meaningless
adj.	bila sauti	muet	mute (without speech)
adv.	bila shaka	naturellement	naturally
adv.	bila sharti	libéralement	freely
adj.	bila upendeleo	impartial	impartial
prep.	bila, pasipo	sans	without
n.	bilauri	verre (m)	drinking glass
n.	binti	fille (f)	daughter

parts of speech	swahili	french	english
n.	biskuti	biscuit (m)	cracker
n.	boga (pl. maboga)	potiron (m)	pumpkin
n.	boma la kuzuia maji	digue (f)	dam
n.	boma, kijiji, (pl. vijiji)	village (m)	village
n.	bomba (pl. mabomba)	tuyau (f)	pipe (hose)
n.	bomba la kurushia maji juu	fontaine (f)	fountain
n., med	bomba ndogo	seringue	syringe
n.	bonde	vallée (f)	valley
n.	bonge	morceau (m)	lump
adj.	bora	excellent	excellent
adj.	bora kabisa	meilleur	best
n.	buibui	araignée (f)	spider
adj.	buluu, samawati	bleu, couleur	blue
n.	bunda	liasse (f)	bundle
n.	bundi	hibou (m)	owl
n.	bunduki	arme à feu (f)	gun
n.	buni	grain (m) de café	coffee bean
n.	burashi (hair or paint brush)	brosse (f) (la brosse due peintre) {la brosse à cheveux}	brush (paintbrush) {hair brush}
n.	burashi ya nywele	brosse à cheveux (f)	hairbrush
adj.	bure	1. gratuit 2. futile	1. free (no charge) 2. futile
n.	buu (pl. mabuu)	ver (m)	maggot
n.	buyu (pl. mabuyu)	gourde (f)	gourd
n.	bwana	M. (m) (for Monsieur)	Mr.
n.	bwana	monsieur (m)	sir
n.	bwana arusi	marié (m)	bride-groom
n.	bwana wa kazi	patron (m), patronne (f)	employer
n.	bwawa	marais (m)	swamp, marsh
adj.	chache	quelque	some
n.	chachu	1. levain (m) 2. levure	1. leaven 2. yeast
n.	chafuko	confusion (f)	confusion
n	chai	thé (m)	tea
n.	chaki	craie (f)	chalk
n.	chakula (pl. vyakula)	1. nourriture (f) 2. repas (m)	1. food 2. meal
n.	chakula cha asubuhi	petit déjeuner (m)	breakfast
n.	chakula cha mchana	déjeuner	lunch
n.	chakula cha usika	repas du soir	supper
n.	chakula kikubwa cha kutwa	déjeuner (f)	dinner (noon)
n.	chakula kikuu cha siku	dîner (m)	dinner (night)

126

parts of speech	swahili	french	english
phrase	**Chakula kitamu sana.**	Aliment, repas est bon.	The food is good.
n.	**chale**	tatouage (m)	tattoo
adv.	**chalichali**	sur le dos	supine position
n.	**chambo**	leurre (m)	bait
n.	**chandalua (pl. vyandalua)**	moustiquaire (m)	mosquito net
n.	**changarawe**	gravier (m)	gravel
n.	**chatu**	python (m)	python
n.	**chawa**	pou (m)	lice
adj.	**chelea**	tardif	belated
n.	**chelezo**	radeau (m)	raft
n	**chemchemi**	source (f)	spring (of water)
n.	**chetezo**	encensoir (m)	censer
n.	**cheti (pl. vyeti)**	billet (m)	ticket
adv.	**china**	en-dessous	underneath
adv.	**chini**	en bas	down
adv. prep.	**chini ya**	1. en bas (adv) 2. au-dessous de (prep) 3. sous	1. below 2. beneath 3. under
adj.	**chini zaidi**	inférieur	lower
pronoun	**cho chote**	quelque chose	anything (something)
n.	**chokaa**	terra blanche	lime (substance)
n.	**chomba cha mgeni**	chambre d'amis (f)	guest room
n.	**chombo (pl. vyombo)**	1. bateau (m) 2. marmite (f) de argile	1. boat 2. pot (clay)
n.	**chombo cha kuogea**	bain (m)	bath
n.	**choo**	1. salle de bain (f) 2. selles	1. bathroom 2. stool (excrement)
n.	**choo (pl. vyoo)**	cabinet (m)	toilet
phrase	**Choo kiko wapi?**	Où est la salle de bain?	Where is the bathroom?
n.	**choyo**	1. avidité (f) 2. égoïsme (m)	1. greed 2. selfishness
n.	**chubuko (pl. machubuko)**	1. écorchure (f) 2. ecchymose	1. abrasion 2. ecchymosis
n.	**chubuo**	contusion (f)	contusion
n.	**chui**	léopard (m)	leopard
n.	**chuma**	fer (m)	iron (ore)
n.	**chumba**	chambre (f)	room (in house)
n.	**chumba cha juu**	grenier (m)	attic
n.	**chumba cha kulala**	maison (f) d'étudiants	dormitory
n	**chumvi**	sel (m)	salt
n.	**chungu**	1. fourmi (f) 2. tas (m) 3. monceau (m)	1. ant 2. heap 3. mound
n.	**chungwa (pl. machungwa)**	orange (f)	orange (fruit)
n.	**chuo (pl. vyuo)**	école (f)	school

parts of speech	swahili	french	english
n.	chupa	pot (m), petit	jar (container/shock)
n.	chupa (pl. machupa)	bouteille (f)	bottle
n.	chupi	caleçon (m)	boxer shorts (or slip)
n.	chura (pl. vyura)	1. grenouille (f) 2. crapaud (m)	1. frog 2. toad
n.	dada; ndugu mke; (if spoken of by brother: umbu)	sœur (f)	sister
n.	dafu (pl. madafu)	noix (f) de coco	coconut
n.	dai la kuwapo mahali pengine	alibi (m)	alibi
adv.	daima	constamment	constantly
n.	dakika	1. minute (f) 2. seconde (f)	1. minute 2. second
n.	daktari wa meno	dentiste (m,f)	dentist
n.	damu	sang (m)	blood
n.	dansi	danse (f)	dance
n.	daraja (pl. madaraja)	pont (m)	bridge
n.	daraka (pl. madaraka)	responsabilité (f)	responsibility
n.	darasa	classe (f)	class (students)
n	dari	étage (m)	story (floor)
n.	dawa	1. remède (m) 2. drogue (f) 3. médicament (m)	1. cure 2. drug 3. medication
n.	dawa ya sindano	injection (f)	injection
n.	deni	dette (f)	debt
n.	dereva	chauffeur (m)	driver
n.	Desemba; mwezi wa kumi na mbili wa mwaka wa kizungu	décembre (m)	December
n.	desturi	1. coutume (f) 2. habitude (f)	1. custom 2. habit
adv.	desturi	d'ordinaire	usually
n.	dhahabu	or (m)	gold
adj.	dhahiri	1. apparent 2. distinct 3. évident	1. apparent 2. distinct 3. evident
adj.	dhaifu	1. faible 2. fragile	1. feeble 2. fragile
n.	dhamiri	conscience (f)	conscience
n.	dharau	1. mépris (m) 2. dédain (m)	1 .contempt 2. disdain
n.	dhihaka	raillerie (f)	mockery
n	dini	religion (f)	religion
n.	dirisha (pl. madirisha)	fenêtre (f)	window
n.	divai	vin (m)	wine
n.	dreva wa motakaa	chauffeur (m)	chauffeur
n.	dubu	ours (m)	bear (animal)

128

parts of speech	swahili	french	english
n.	duka (pl. maduka)	1. boutique (f) 2. magasin (m)	1. shop 2. store
n.	duka la maziwa	laiterie (f)	dairy
n.	duka la mwuza dawa	pharmacie (f)	pharmacy
adj. & n.	duni	1. inférieur (m) 2. insignifiant	1. inferior to 2. insignificant
n.	dunia	terre (f); univers	earth
adj. & n.	elfu	mille (m)	thousand
n.	elfu mara elfu	un million	one million
n.	elfu mbili	deux mille	two thousand
n.	elfu tano	cinq mille	five thousand
n.	elimu ya hesabu	mathématiques (f)	math
n.	embe (pl. maembe)	mangue (f)	mango (fruit)
n.	enzi	majesté (f)	majesty
n.	état de faiblesse	accablement (m)	exhaustion
n.	fadhili	bienfait (m)	kindness
n.	faida	1. gain (m) 2. profit (m)	1. gain 2. profit (increase)
n.	faini	amende (f)	fine (i.e. to pay a)
n.	faraja	confort (m)	comfort
n.	faraka	dissension (f)	dissension
n.	farasi	cheval (m)	horse
n.	Februari; mwezi wa pili wa mwaka wa kizungu	février (m)	February
n.	fedha taslimu	argent (m)	cash
n.	feza	argent (m)	1. money 2. silver
n.	fidia	dédommagement (m)	compensation
n., med	figo (pl. mafigo)	rein (m)	kidney
n.	fikira	réflexion (f)	reflection
n.	filamu	cinéma (m)	movie theater
n.	fimbo	1. canne (f) 2. massue (f) 3. bâton (m) 4. fouet (m)	1. cane 2. stick 3. walking stick 4. whip
n.	fitina	espièglerie (f)	mischief
n.	fluu	grippe (f)	flu
n.	fujo (pl. mafujo)	désordre (m)	disorder
n.	fuko	taupe (f)	mole
adj.	fulani	certain	certain
verb	fumba macho	fermer les yeux	close the eyes, to
n.	fundi (pl. mafundi)	artisan (m)	craftsman
n.	fundi wa mashine	mécanicien (m)	mechanic
n.	fundo (pl. mafundo)	nœud (m)	knot
n.	fungu la maneno machache	expression (f)	phrase

parts of speech	swahili	french	english
n.	**furaha**	1. amusement (m) 2. bonheur 3. joie (f)	1. amusement 2. fun 3. joy
n	**futina**	rébellion (f)	rebellion
adv.	**gafula**	brusquement	suddenly
n.	**gala**	entrepôt (m)	storehouse
n.	**gamba (pl. magamba)**	écailles (f)	scales (fish)
n.	**ganda (pl. maganda)**	pellicules (f)	dry skin (dandruff)
n.	**ganda la yai**	coquille (f)	eggshell
adj.	**gani**	quel (m), quelle (f)	which
adj.	**gani, nini**	quoi	what
n.	**ganzi**	engourdissement (m)	numbness
n.	**gari au namna ya machela ya kuchukulia wagonjwa**	ambulance (f)	ambulance
n.	**gari doga**	camion (m)	truck
n.	**gari la moshe**	locomotive (f)	train
n.	**gauni**	robe (f)	dress
n., med	**gazabu**	folie, rage	rage
n	**gazabu, kasirani**	colère (f)	anger
n.	**gazeti**	journal (m)	journal
n.	**gehena**	enfer (m)	hell
n.	**genge (pl. magenge)**	ravin (m)	ravine
n.	**ghala ya chini**	cave (f)	cellar
n.	**ghali**	cher (m,f)	dear
adj.	**ghali**	cher (m), chère (f)	expensive
n.	**ghasia**	1. vacarme (m) 2. émeute (f)	1. racket (noise) 2. riot
n.	**ghasia, fujo**	troubles (m)	disturbance
n.	**ghuba**	baie (f)	bay
n.	**giza**	noir (m)	dark
n.	**giza la jioni**	crépuscule (m)	dusk
n.	**godoro (pl. magodoro)**	matelas (m)	mattress
n.	**gogo (pl. magogo)**	bûche (f)	log
n.	**gome**	écorce (f)	bark (tree)
n	**goti (pl. magoti)**	genou (m)	knee
n.	**gudulia**	cruche (f)	pitcher
n.	**gunia (pl. magunia)**	gros canevas (m)	burlap
adj.	**haba**	insuffisant	insufficient
n.	**habari**	nouvelles (f)	news
phrase	**Habari za nyumbani?**	Comment est votre famille?	How is your family?
adv.	**habari za, yapata**	à peu près, environ	about (approximately)
n.	**habari zinazoonyeshwa kwa hesabu**	statistique (f)	statistics

130

parts of speech	swahili	french	english
prep.	hadi, kwenye	à	to, at
n.	hadisi	histoire (f)	history
n.	hadithi fupi	fable (f)	fable
n.	hadithi tu	romans (m)	fiction
n.	hafifu	léger	flimsy
adj.	hai, -zima	vivant	alive
phrase	haidhuru	ça ne fait rien	never mind
interj.	Haiwezekani!	1. Pas possible! 2. Allons donc!	1. Not possible! 2. You don't really mean that!
n.	haja	besoin (m)	need
n.	haki	justice (f)	justice
n.	haki	droit (m)	right (civil, legal)
n.	haki ya kutangulia	priorité (f)	priority
adv.	hakika	1. certainement 2. certitude	1. certainly 2. surely
adv.	hakika, kweli	vraiment	truly
adj.	halali	légal	lawful
n.	hali	condition (f)	condition
adj.	hali moja na	au bord de	side, on this
n.	hali ya myo au mwili	tournure (f)	attitudes
n.	halifa	successeur (m)	successor
adv.	halisi	tout à fait	quite
n.	halmashauri	comité (m)	committee
phrase	halmashauri kuu	l'assemblée nationale	parliament
phrase	Hamna shida.	Pas de problème.	No problem.
phrase	Hamna shida. Hapana maneno.	Ça ne fait rien.	It does not matter.
adj. & n.	hamsini	cinquante (m)	fifty
n.	hamu	désir (m)	desire
adj.	hamu ya kwao	nostalgique	homesick
phrase	Hapa ni gani?	Qu'est-ce que c'est?	What is this?
adv.	hapa, huko	ici	here
adv.	hapa, huko (huko na huko)	ci (Par ci, part là.)	here (Here and there.)
adj., adv.	hapana, siyo	pas de, non	no
phrase	Hapo kale...	Il était une fois...	Once upon a time there was...
n.	haragwe (pl. maharagwe)	haricot (m)	bean
adv.	haraka	précipitamment	hurriedly
n.	haraka	hâte (f)	hurry, haste
n.	harufu tamu	parfum (m)	fragrance
adj.	hasa	surtout	especially
adj.	hasilia	véritable	genuine

parts of speech	swahili	french	english
phrase	hata	de sorte que	so, so that
adv.	hata ikiwa	même si	even if
phrase	Hata kidogo!	Pas du tout!	Not at all!
pronoun	hata moja	aucun	none
prep.	hata, mpaka	jusqu'à	until
adv.	hata, sawa	même	even
n.	hatari	danger (m)	danger
n.	hati	document (m)	document
n.	hati ya sifa	diplôme (m)	diploma
n.	hatia	1. responsabilité (f) 2. crime (m) 3. faute (f) 4. culpabilité (f)	1. blame 2. crime 3. fault 4. guilt
n.	hatua	pas (m)	1. footstep 2. pace
adj & pr	hawa (pl. person); hizi (pl. things)	ces, ceux-ci (m), celles-ci (f)	these
n.	hazina	trésor (m)	treasury
n.	hedhi	menstruation (f)	menstruation
n.	hekaya	1. anecdote (f) 2. légende (f)	1. anecdote 2. legend
n.	hema	tente (f)	tent
n.	heri	bonheur (m)	happiness
phrase	Heri za siku kuu ya kuzaliwa.	Joyeux anniversaire.	Happy birthday.
n.	herufi	lettre (f)	letter (of alphabet)
n.	herufi kubwa	capitale (f)	capital (letter)
n.	hesabu	nombre (m)	number
n.	hesabu ya fedha	facture (f)	bill
n.	hesabu ya watu wa nchi	recensement (m)	census
n.	hesabu, masimulizi	compte (m)	account (finance)
n.	heshima	1. estime (f) 2. honneur (m) 3. respect (m)	1. esteem 2. honor 3. respect
n.	heshima na upendo	dignité (f)	dignity
n.	hewa	1. atmosphère (f) 2. air (m)	1. atmosphere 2. air
n.	hiari	choix (m)	choice
n.	hila	ruse	cunning
n.	hindi	Hindou (m)	Hindu
n.	hirizi	charme (m) (amulette)	charm
adv.	hivi, vile (na vingine vivyo hivyo)	ainsi (et ainsi de suite)	thus (and so on)
pronoun	hiyo	celui-là, celle-là	that one
adj.	hodari	brave	brave
adj.	hodari, -enye nguvu	fort	strong
n.	hofu kuu	terreur (f)	terror

parts of speech	swahili	french	english
n.	hofu, fadhaa	anxiété (f)	anxiety
adj.	hoi	impotent	helpless
n.	hoja	ennuis (m)	problems
n.	homa {Ana homa.}	fièvre (f) {Il a beaucoup de fièvre.}	fever {He has a high fever.}
n., med	homa mbaya matumboni	typhus	typhoid
n.	homa ya baridi	tremblement (m)	chills (tremor)
n., med	homa ya matumbo	typhoïde fièvre	typhoid fever
n.	homa ya mbu	malaria (f)	malaria
interj.	Hongera.	Félicitations.	Congratulations.
n.	hospitali	hôpital (m)	hospital
n.	hua	colombe (f)	dove
phrase	Hujambo? (singular); Hamjambo? (plural)	Comment ça va?	How are you?
adv.	huko na huko	1. par-ci par-là 2. de long en large	1. here and there 2. to and fro
n.	hukumu	jugement (m)	judgement
adj.	huru	libre	free
n.	huruma	1. clémence (f) 2. indulgence (f) 3. pitié (f)	1. clemency 2. leniency 3. pity
n.	husuda	rancune (f)	ill-will
adj.,pro.	huyu (person, sing.); hii (thing, sing.)	ce, cet, cette	this
n.	huzuni	chagrin (m) 2. tristesse (f) 3. misère	1. grief 2. sadness 3. sorrow 4. misery
n.	huzuni kuu	angoisse (f)	anguish
n.	huzuni, dhiki	détresse (f)	distress
n.	ibada au sherehe ya heshima	cérémonie (f)	ceremony
n.	ibilisi	diable (m)	devil
n.	ihtiari	liberté (f)	autonomy
conj.	ijapo	bien que	even though, although
n.	Ijumaa	vendredi (m)	Friday
conj.	ila	1. excepté 2. sauf	1. except 2. unless
pronoun	ile, kile, vile (Ndivyo.)	cela (C'est cela.)	it, that (That is right.)
phrase	ili kusaidia au kupendeza	pour l'amour de	sake of, for the
conj.	ili, kusudi	afin que	so that, in order to
n.	imani	1. confiance (f) 2. foi (f)	1. beliefs (confidence) 2. faith
adv.	imara	fermement	firmly
n.	inchi	pouce (m)	inch
conj.	ingawa	bien que	although
n.	Injili	évangile (m)	Gospel

parts of speech	swahili	french	english
n.	inzi (pl. mainzi)	mouche (f)	fly
n.	ishirini na moja	vingt et un	twenty-one
adj.	isiyo na maana	déraisonnable	irrational
adj.	isiyohusu	sans rapport	irrelevant
adj.	isiyotosheleka	insatiable	insatiable
n.	jabali	falaise (f)	cliff
n.	jadiliano	débat (m)	debate
n.	jamaa	famille (f)	1. family 2. kin
n.	jamala	courtoisie (f)	courtesy
n.	Jamatatu	lundi (m)	Monday
n.	jambo	événement (m)	event
n.	jambo (mambo)	affaire (f)	affair
n.	jambo la hakika	fait (m)	fact
n.	jambo lililoachwa	omission (f)	omission
n.	jambo litokealo kwa sababu fulani	conséquence (sans conséquence)	consequence (without repercussions)
n.	jambo, kesi	cas (m)	case
n.	jambo, maneno	circonstance (f)	circumstance
interj.	Jambo.	Allô.	Hello.
n.	jamii moja ya nyota	cancer (m)	cancer
n.	jamii ya vitabu	bibliothèque (f)	library
n.	jamii ya waimbaji	chœur (m)	choir
n.	jamvi	paillasson (m)	mat
adv.	jana	hier	yesterday
n.	jangwa	désert (m)	1. desert (ie. Sahara desert) 2. wilderness
n.	jani	1. brin (m) 2. feuille (f)	1. blade (grass) 2. leaf
n.	Januari; mwezi wa kwanza wa mwaka wa kizungu	janvier (m)	January
n.	jaribio kali	épreuve (f)	ordeal
n.	jaribu	1. tentation (f) 2. épreuve (f)	1. temptation 2. test
n.	jasho	transpiration (f)	perspiration
n.	jasho	sueur (f)	sweat
n.	jembe (pl. majembe)	1. bêche (f) 2. houe (f)	1. spade 2. hoe
n.	jembe la meno	râteau (m)	rake
n.	jengo (pl. majengo)	bâtiment (m)	building (construction)
n., med	jeraha	blessure (f)	1. ulcer 2. wound 3. injury
n.	jeraha; kidonda (pl. vidonda)	ulcère (m)	sore (ulcer)
n.	jeshi	armée (f)	army

parts of speech	swahili	french	english
n.	jeuri	1. armée en marche 2. tyrannie 3. violence	1. assault 2. violence
n.	jibini	fromage (m)	cheese
n.	jibu (pl. majibu)	réponse (f)	1. answer 2. response
imper.	Jibu!	Répondre!	Answer!
n.	jicho (pl. macho)	œil (m)	eye
n.	jiko	cuisine (f)	kitchen
n.	jimbo (pl. majimbo)	région (f)	region, area (locality)
n.	jina (pl. majina)	nom (m)	name
n.	jina la kupanga	surnom	first name
adv.	jina la pili la kificho	alias	alias
n.	jina la utani	surnom (m)	nickname
phrase	Jina lako nani?	Quel est ton nom?	What is your name?
phrase	Jina langu ni...	Je m'appelle...	My name is...
n.	jino (pl. meno) {Nina maumivu ya jino.}	dent (f) {J'ai mal aux dents.}	tooth {I have a toothache.}
n.	jinsi	1. manière (f) 2. sexe (m)	1. manner 2. sex (gender)
adv. n.	jioni	soir (m)	evening
n.	jipu (pl. majipu)	1. abcès (m) 2. furoncle (m)	1. abscess 2. boil
n.	jirani	voisin (m), voisine (f)	neighbor
n.	jitu (pl. majitu)	géant (m)	giant
n.	jiwe (pl. mawe)	pierre (f)	stone
n.	jogoo	coq (m)	rooster, cock (fowl)
n.	johari	bijou (m)	jewel
n.	joto, moto	chaleur (f)	heat
n.	jozi	1. couple (m) 2. paire (f)	couple
n.	jua (pl. majua)	soleil (m)	sun
n.	juha	idiot (m)	idiot
n.	Julai; mwezi wa saba wa mwaka wa kizungu	juillet (m)	July
n.	juma	semaine (f)	week
n.	juma jana	après-semaine (f); semaine (f) dernière	week, last
phrase	juma kesho	semaine prochain	next week
n.	Jumamosi	samedi (m)	Saturday
n.	Jumanne	mardi (m)	Tuesday
n.	Jumapili	dimanche (m)	Sunday
n.	Jumatano	mercredi (m)	Wednesday
n.	jumba la balozi	ambassade (f)	embassy
n.	Juni; mwezi wa sita wa mwaka kizungu	juin (m)	June
adv.	juu (ya)	ci-dessus, sur	above

parts of speech	swahili	french	english
adv. prep.	**juu ya**	1. sur 2. au-dessus de	1. on 2. over 3. above 4. on top of
adv.	**juzi**	avant-hier	day before yesterday
adv.	**juzi juzi**	récemment	recently
n.	**kabati**	1. armoire (f) 2. commode (f)	1. cupboard 2. dresser
n.	**kabila (pl. mabila)**	tribu (f)	tribe
adv.	**kabisa**	1. absolument 2. tout à fait 2. en tout 3. entièrement 4. pleinement	1. absolutely 2. altogether 3. entirely 4. fully
n.	**kaburi**	tombe (f)	grave
n.	**kadiri ipasayo**	évaluation (f)	assessment
adv.	**kadiri ya**	selon	according to
n.	**kafi**	pagaie (f)	paddle
n.	**kahawa**	café (m)	coffee
n.	**kalab**	rage (f)	rabies
n.	**kalamu**	crayon (m)	pencil
phrase	**kale**	autrefois	time ago, long
conj.	**kama**	1. si 2. soit que	1. if 2. whether
prep.	**kama**	pareil	like
n.	**kama mfuko wa kuvaa mguuni**	chaussette (f)	sock
adv.	**kama vile**	ainsi que	as well as
adv.	**kama, -vyo, kwa sababu**	comme	as
n.	**kamba**	corde (f)	1. cord 2. rope
n.	**kambi (pl. makambi)**	campement (m)	camp
adj.	**kamili**	parfait	perfect
n.	**kamusi**	dictionnaire (m)	dictionary
adv.	**kamwe**	jamais	never
interj.	**Kamwe!**	Jamais!	Never!
adv.	**kando**	à côté de	1. alongside 2. next to
n.	**kando**	bord relevé	bank of river
prep.	**kando ya**	à côté de	side of, on the
prep.	**kando ya, karibu na**	à côté de	beside
n.	**kanisa**	église (f)	church (building)
n.	**kanzu**	robe (f)	gown
n.	**kapi (pl. makapi)**	son (m)	sound
n.	**karaha**	dégoût (m)	disgust
n.	**karamu**	1. festin (m) 2. fête (f)	1. feast 2. party
n.	**karanga**	arachide (f)	1. ground nut 2. peanut
n.	**karani**	employé(e) {m,(f)}	clerk
n.	**karani wa fedha**	cassier (m)	cashier

parts of speech	swahili	french	english
n.	karatasi	papier (m)	paper
adv.	karibu	1. presque 2. proche	1. almost 2. nearby
phrase	karibu chakula	bon appétit.	enjoy your meal
adv. prep.	karibu na	1. près 2. près de	1. near 2. close to
phrase	Karibu!	1. Entrez! 2. Bienvenu	1. Come in! 2. Welcome.
n.	karne	siècle (m)	century
n.	karoti	carotte (f)	carrot
n.	kasia (pl. makasia)	rame (f)	oar
n.	kasisi (pl. makasisi)	prêtre (m)	priest
n.	kaskazini	nord (m)	north
prep.	katika	en, dans	in, into
prep.	katika	éteint, annulé	off
prep.	katikati ya	1. parmi 2. entre	1. among 2. between
n.	katoliko	catholique (m,f)	catholic
n.	kawa	rouille (f)	mildew
n.	kawaida	méthode (f)	method
n. & adj.	kawaida za dini	rituel	ritual
n.	kazi	1. travail (m) 2. tâche (f)	1. job 2. work 3. task
n.	kazi ya elimu	profession (f)	profession
n.	kelele (pl. makelele)	tumulte (m)	turmoil
n.	kengele	cloche (m)	bell
adv.	kesho	demain	tomorrow
phrase	kesho kutwa	après-demain	day after tomorrow
n	kesi	intenter un procès	lawsuit
phrase	kiagano	rendez-vous (m)	meeting place
n.	kiambaza (pl. viambaza)	mur (m)	wall
n.	kiapo (pl. viapo)	serment (m)	oath
n.	kiarifu	verbe (m)	verb
n.	kiasi	quantité (f)	quantity
n.	kiasi	tempérance (f)	temperance
n.	kiatu (pl. viatu)	1. sandale (f) 2. chaussure (f)	1. sandal 2. shoe
n.	kiatu kirefu	botte (f)	boot
n.	kiazi	patates, douce	sweet potatoes
z	kibali	adoption	approval
n.	kibanda (pl. vibanda)	atelier (m)	workshop
n.	kibanda cha nje	appentis (m)	outhouse
n.	kibao cha jiwe	ardoise (f)	slate (to write on)
n.	kiberiti (pl. viberiti)	allumette (f)	match
adj. & n.	kibeti	nain (m)	dwarf
n., med	kibofu	vessie (f)	bladder

parts of speech	swahili	french	english
n.	kiboko (pl. viboko)	hippopotame (m)	hippopotamus
n.	kibonge	comprimé (m)	tablet (pill)
n.	kiburi	vanité (f)	conceit
n.	kiburi, majivuno	fierté (f)	pride
n.	kichaka (pl. vichaka)	brousse (f)	bush
n.	kichala (pl. vichala)	1. botte (f) 2. grappe (f)	1. bunch (of fruit) 2. cluster
n.	kicheko	rires (m)	laughter
n., med	kichocho	bilharzia	bilharzia (schistosomiasis)
n.	kichwa (pl. vichwa)	tête (f)	head
n.	kidevu	menton (m)	chin
n.	kidimbwi	mare (f)	pool
n.	kidogo	lambeau (m)	shred
adv.	kidogo	1. légèrement 2. un peu	1. slightly 2. somewhat
phrase	kidogo kidogo; kidogo kwa kidogo	petit à petit	little by little
n.	kidole (pl. vidole)	doigt (m)	finger
n.	kidole cha gumba	pouce (m)	thumb
n.	kidole cha kati	doigt (m) du milieu	finger, middle
n.	kidole cha mguu	orteil (m)	toe
n.	kidole cha mwisho	petit doigt (m)	finger, little
n.	kidole cha pete	doigt (m) anneau	finger, ring
n.	kidole cha shahada	doigt (m) index	finger, index
n.	kidonge (pl. vidonge)	pilule (f)	pill
n.	kidonge cha kufyonza	pastille (f)	lozenge
n.	kielelezo	dessein (m)	design (sketch)
n.	kifafa	1. convulsion (f) 2. épilepsie (f)	1. convulsion 2. epilepsy
n., med	kifandugu	coccyx (os du bassin)	coccyx
n.	kifaru (pl. vifaru)	rhinocéros (m)	rhinoceros
n.	kifua (pl. vifua)	poitrine (f)	chest (body)
n.	kifua, maziwa	sein (m)	breast
adv.	kifudifudi	étendu face contre terre	prone position
n.	kifuko cha kutilia fedha	bourse (f)	purse
n.	kifumbu	tamis (m)	strainer
n., med	kifundo cha muguu (pl, vifundo cha muguu)	cheville (f)	ankle
n.	kifungo (pl. vifungo)	bouton (m)	button
n.	kifungo (pl. vifungo), gereza	1. prison (f) 2. cachot (m) 3. lien (m)	1. jail 2. dungeon 3. prison 4. bonds
n.	kifungua chupa	ouvre-bouteille (m)	bottle-opener
n.	kifuniko	manteau (m)	cloak
n.	kifuniko (pl. vifuniko)	couvercle (m)	1. cover 2. lid

parts of speech	swahili	french	english
n.	kifusi	débris (m)	debris
n.	kigae (pl. vigae)	tuile (f)	tile (roof)
n.	Kiingereza (Umasema Kiingereza?)	anglais (Parlez-vous anglais?)	English {language} (Do you speak English?)
n.	kijana (pl. vijana) (boy or girl)	enfant, entre 10 et 12 ans	youth
n.	kijana mwanaume	jeune homme	young person
n.	kijicho	méchanceté (f)	malice
n.	kijiko (pl. vijiko)	cuiller (f)	spoon
n.	kijiti cha kukunjia uzi	bobine (f) de fil à coudre	reel
n.	kijito (pl. vijito)	ruisseau (m)	stream (small river)
adj.	kijivu	gris	grey
n.	kijumba	placard (m)	closet
n.	kijumba melini	cabane (f)	cabin
n.	kiko	pipe (f)	pipe (tobacco)
n.	kiko cha mkono; kivi	coude (m)	elbow
n.	kikoa	soirée (f)	together, a get
n.	kikohozi (pl. vikohozi)	toux (f)	cough
n.	kikombe (pl. vikombe)	tasse (f)	cup
n.	kikomo	objectif (m)	goal
n., med	kikoromeo	larynx	larynx
n.	kikosi (pl. vikosi)	troupe (f)	troop, company
n.	kikuku	bracelet (m)	bracelet
adj.,pro.	kila	1. chaque 2. chacun	each
adj.	kila (daima)	chaque, entier (toujours)	every, whole (always)
n.	kila kitu	tout	everything
conj.	kila mara	toutes les fois que	whenever
pronoun	kila mtu	tout le monde	everyone
adv.	kila siku	tous les jours	daily
n.	kilele (pl. vilele)	sommet (m)	peak (mountain)
n.	kileo	alcool (m)	alcohol
n.	kilezo	motif (m)	pattern
n.	kilimo, ukulima	agriculture (f)	agriculture
n.	kilindo (pl. vilindo)	coffre-fort (m)	safe (to hold valuables)
n.	kilio	deuil (m)	mourning
n.	kima	singe (m)	monkey
n.	kimbilio	asile (m)	refuge
n.	kimbunga; tufani	cyclone (m)	cyclone
n.	kimelea	parasite (m)	parasite
n.	kimo, urefu	taille (f)	height
n.	kimputu (pl. vimputu)	tique	tick

parts of speech	swahili	french	english
adj.	kimya	1. immobile 2. silencieusement 3. tranquille	1. motionless 2. silently 3. still
n.	kinanda (pl. vinanda)	piano (m)	piano
n.	kinara (pl. vinara)	bougeoir (m)	candlestick
n.	kinda la kuku	poulet (m)	chicken
n.	kinubi (pl. vinubi)	harpe (f)	harp
n.	kinyonga (pl. vinyonga)	caméléon (m)	chameleon
n.	kinyongo	marotte (f)	fad
n.	kinyozi	barbier (m)	barber
n.	kinywa (pl. vinywa)	bouche (f)	mouth
n.	kinyweo (pl. vinyweo)	boisson (f)	drink
n.	kiongozi (pl. viongozi)	1. guide (m) 2. chef (m)	1. guide 2. leader
n.	kioo (pl. vioo)	1. miroir (m) 2. verre (m)	1. mirror 2. glass
n.	kioto (pl. vioto)	nid (m)	nest
n.	kipaji	offre (f)	offering
n.	kipande (pl. vipande)	1. morceau (m) 2. partie (f)	1. piece 2. part
n.	kipande kidogo	tesson (m)	fragment
n.	kipasu (pl. vipasu)	tranche (f)	slice
n.	kipele (pl. vipele)	1. bouton (m) 2. pustule	1. pimple 2. pustule
n.	kipenzi	favori (m), favorite (f)	favorite
adj. & n.	kipeo	maximum (m)	maximum
n.	kipepeo (pl. vipepeo)	papillon (m)	butterfly
n.	kipimo	mesure (f)	measurement
n.	kipimo cha dawa	dose (f)	dose
n., med	kipindupindu	choléra	cholera
adv.	kipofu	aveuglément	blindly
n	kipofu (pl. vipofu)	personne aveugle	blind person
n.	kipooza	paralysie (f)	paralysis
n.	kiraka	pièce (f)	patch
n.	kiroboto (pl. viroboto)	puce (f)	flea
n	kisa (pl. visa)	histoire (f)	story
n.	kisasi (pl. visasi)	vengeance (f)	revenge
adv.	kisha	1. alors 2. ensuite	then
n.	kishindo	bruit (m)	clatter (of voices)
n.	kisiki (pl. visiki)	souche (f)	stump
n.	kisima (pl. visima)	puits (m)	well (ie. for water)
n.	kisingino (pl. visingino)	talon (m)	heel
n.	kisio	approximation (f)	approximation
n.	kisiwa (pl. visiwa)	île (f)	island
n. med	kisonono	blennorragie (f)	gonorrhea

parts of speech	swahili	french	english
n.	kisu (pl. visu)	couteau (m)	knife
n.	kisu kipana cha kufanyia dawa	spatule (f)	spatula
n., med	kisukari	diabète	diabetes
n.	kitabu (pl. vitabu)	livre (m)	book
n.	kitalu	enclos (m)	enclosure
n.	kitambaa (pl. vitambaa)	1. chiffon (m) 2. foulard (m) 3. mouchoir (m) 4. serviette (de table)	1. rag 2. scarf 3. handkerchief 4. napkin
n.	kitambaa cha kufungia dawa	pansement (m)	bandage
n.	kitana	peigne (m)	comb
n.	kitanda (pl. vitanda)	lit (m)	bed
n.	kitandawili (pl. vitandawili)	crible (m)	riddle
n.	kitanga cha mkono	paume (f)	palm of hand
n.	kitapo	frisson (m)	shiver
n.	kiti (pl. viti)	1. chaise (f) 2. siège (m)	1. chair 2. seat
n.	kitisho	intimidation (f)	intimidation
n.	kitovu (pl. vitovu)	nombril (m)	umbilicus; navel
n.	kitu (pl. vitu)	chose (f)	thing
n.	kitu cha shani	curiosité (f)	curiosity
n.	kitu kilichotolewa	contribution (f)	contribution
n.	kitumbua, (pl. vitumbua)	beignet	donut
n.	kitumbuizo	berceuse (f)	lullaby
n.	kitunga (pl. vitunga)	panier (m)	basket
n.	kitunguu (pl. vitunguu)	oignon (m)	onion
n.	kitunguu saumu	ail (m)	garlic
n.	kituo	1. repos (m) 2. arrêt	1. pause 2. stop
n.	kituo cha afya	centre de santé (f)	health center
n.	kiu	soif (f)	thirst
n.	kiumbe (pl. viumbe)	créature (f)	creature
n.	kiungo (pl. viungo)	articulation (f)	joint (anatomy), articulation
n.	kiungo (pl. viungo)	rapport (m)	joint, link
n.	kiungo (pl. viungo)	membre (m)	member
n.	kiuno (pl. viuno)	flanc (m)	flank
n.	kivimbe (pl. vivimbe)	1. enflure (f) 2. tumeur (f)	1. swelling 2. tumor
n.	kivuko (pl. vivuko)	gué (m)	ford
n.	kivuli (pl. vivuli)	ombre (f)	shadow, shade
n., med	kiwambo	diaphragme (m)	diaphragm
n.	kiwanda cha dobi	linge (m)	laundry

parts of speech	swahili	french	english
n.	kiwanja	terrain (m) de jeu	playground
n.	kiwasho	démangeaison (f)	pruritus, itch
n.	kiwete	estropié (m)	cripple
n.	kiwiko (pl. viwiko)	poignet (m)	wrist
n.	kiwiliwili (pl. viwiliwili)	tronc (m)	trunk (of body)
n.	kiyoga (pl. viyoga)	champignon (m)	mushroom
n.	kiyongela (pl. viyongela)	tamis (m)	sieve
n.	kizazi (pl. vizazi)	génération (f)	generation
n.	kizee	madame (f) vieille	woman (old)
n.	kizibo (pl. vizibo)	bouchon (m)	stopper (in bottle), cork
n.	kizibuo	tire-bouchon (m)	corkscrew
n.	kizingia cha maji	tourbillon (m)	whirlpool
n.	kiziwa (pl. viziwa)	mare (f)	pond
n.	kiziwi (pl. viziwi)	personne sourd	deaf person
n.	kizuio (pl. vizuio)	1. empêchement (m) 2. entrave (f)	1. hinderance 2. obstacle
n.	kizunguzungu	vertige (m)	1. vertigo 2. dizziness
n.	kobe (pl. makobe)	tortue (f)	tortoise
n.	kodi	impôt (m)	tax
n.	kofi	claque (f)	slap
n.	kofia	chapeau (m)	hat
verb	kokomoka	avoir des haut-le-cœur	retch, to
n.	kombeo (pl. makombeo)	fronde (f)	sling
n.	kombo	1. défaut (m) 2. miette (f)	1. flaw 2. crumb
n.	kombora	bombe (f)	bomb
n.	komeo	targette (f)	bolt (of door)
n., med	kondo la nyuma	placenta	placenta
n.	kondoo	1. lustre (m) 2. mouton (m)	sheep
n., med	kongosho	pancréas (m)	pancreas
n.	konzi	articulation (f) du doigt	knuckles
n.	koo (pl. makoo)	gorge (f)	throat
n.	kopo	boîte (f)	can, tin
n.	korosho	noix de cajou	cashew
n.	kosa (pl. makosa)	erreur (f)	error
n.	kosa (pl. makosa)	faute (f)	mistake
n.	koti	veston (m), jaquette (f)	jacket
n.	koti {mpako}	1. manteau (m) 2. veston (m) 3. jaquette (f) {couche} (f)	1. coat (clothing) 2. coat{of paint}
n.	kovu (pl. makovu)	cicatrice (f)	scar
n.	Krismas {Heri za Krismas.}	Noël (m) {Bonne fête de Noël.}	Christmas {Merry Christmas}

parts of speech	swahili	french	english
n.	**Kristo**	le Christ (m)	Christ
verb	**kuabatiza**	baptiser	baptize, to
verb	**kuabudu**	1. adorer 2. rendre un culte à Dieu	1. adore, to 2. to worship
verb	**kuacha**	1. abandonner 2. laisser	1. to abandon 2. to forsake 3. to leave 4. to let
n.	**kuacha**	congé (m)	vacation
verb	**kuachana**	diverger	diverge, to
verb	**kuadhibu**	châtier	castigate, to
verb	**kuadhibu, kuazibu**	punir	punish, to
verb	**kuaga**	1. faire ses adieux à 2. saleur au départ 3. prendre congé	1. to bid farewell 2. to take leave of
verb	**kuagiza**	ordonner	ordain, to
verb	**kuagiza, kuongoza**	diriger	direct, to
verb	**kuahidi**	promettre	promise, to
n.	**kuahirisha**	procrastination (f)	procrastination
verb	**kuajiri**	louer	hire, to
verb	**kualika**	1. casser 2. inviter	1. to crack 2. to invite
verb	**kuambatana, kushika**	adhérer à	adhere, to
verb	**kuambatanisha**	agglutiner	stick together, to
verb	**kuambia**	dire à	tell, to
n.	**kuamia shamba**	épouvantail (m)	scarecrow
verb	**kuamini**	croire	believe, to
verb	**kuamsha**	réveiller	wake up, to
verb	**kuamua**	décider	decide, to
verb	**kuamuru**	1. commander 2. gérer 3. ordonner	1. to command 2. to manage 3. to order
verb	**kuandika**	1. enregistrer 2. écrire	1. to record 2. to write
verb	**kuandika anwani (1) kuhutubu (2)**	adresser	to address letter (1) speech (2)
verb	**kuandika sanamu**	dessiner	draw, to
verb	**kuangalia**	1. faire attention 2. remarquer	1. to pay attention 2. to note 3. to notice
verb	**kuangamiza kabisa**	anéantir	annihilate, to
verb	**kuangamiza, kuharibu**	détruire	destroy, to
verb	**kuangaza**	briller	reflect light, to
verb	**kuanguka**	1. s'effondrer 2. tomber	1. to collapse 2. to fall
verb	**kuangukia**	tomber sur	fall on, to
verb	**kuangusha**	1. laisser tomber 2. rabattre	1. to drop 2. to pull down
verb	**kuanjisi mwanamke kwa jeuri**	violer	rape, to

143

parts of speech	swahili	french	english
verb	kuanza	1. débuter 2. commencer 3. entamer	1. to begin 2. to commence 3. to start
verb	kuasi	1. désobéir à 2. se rebeller	1. to disobey 2. to rebel
verb	kuazimu	prévoir	plan, to
verb	kubabaika	bégayer	1. to stammer 2. to stutter
verb	kubadili	1. modifier 2. troquer	1. to alter 2. to dicker
verb	kubadilisha	1. changer de 2. échanger	1. to change 2. to exchange
verb	kubadilishana	troquer	barter, to
verb	kubahatisha fedha	parier	bet, to
verb	kubainisha	1. clarifier 2. to définir	1. to clarify 2. to define
verb	kubaki	demeurer	remain, to
verb	kubambika	tremper, faire	soak, to
verb	kubana, kukamua	serrer	squeeze, to
verb	kubana, kusonga	appuyer	press, to
verb	kubariki	bénir	bless, to
verb	kubatilisha	neutraliser	counteract, to
verb	kubeba	porter sur le dos	carry on one's back, to
verb	kubembeleza	1. amadouer 2. flatter	1. to coax 2. to flatter
verb	kubisha	contredire	contradict, to
verb	kubishana	se disputer	argue, to
verb	kubomoa	démolir	1. to demolish 2. to tear down
verb	kuboromoka	se précipiter	rush, to
verb	kubuni	rattraper	make up, to
verb	kubusu	embrasser	kiss, to
verb	kubweka	aboyer	bark, to
n.	kucha	griffe (f)	claw
verb	kucha	lever, se	rise, to (sun)
verb	kuchafua	1. confondre 2. salir	1. to confuse 2. to soil
verb	kuchagua	1. choisir 2. sélectionner	1. to choose 2. to select
verb	kuchana	peigner	comb, to
verb	kuchanga, kukusanya	ramasser	collect, to
verb	kuchanganya	1. mélanger 2. malaxer	1. to blend 2. to mix
verb	kuchapa	fouetter	whip, to
verb	kuchapa, kupiga chapa	imprimer	print, to
verb	kucheka	1. badiner 2. rire 3. sourire	1. to joke 2. to laugh 3. to smile
verb	kuchekecha	tamiser	sift, to
verb	kuchekesha	amuser	amuse, to
verb	kuchelewa	être en retard	late, to be
verb	kucheza	jouer	play, to
verb	kucheza ngoma	danser	dance, to

parts of speech	swahili	french	english
verb	kuchezea fedha	jouer	gamble, to
verb	kuchimba	fouiller	dig, to
n.	kuchinja	tuer	slay, to
verb	kuchipuka	germer	germinate, to
verb	kuchmuka, kutokosa	bouillir	boil, to
verb	kuchoka	avoir fatigué	tired, to be
verb	kuchoka kabisa	épuisé, être	exhausted, to be
verb	kuchokoza	provoquer	provoke, to
verb	kuchoma	1. griller 2. percer 3. piquer	1. to broil 2. to pierce 3. to sting
verb	kuchoma, kuwaka	brûler	burn, to
verb	kuchongea	dénigrer	denigrate, to
verb	kuchopoa	déboîter	pull out, to
verb	kuchora	découper	carve, to
n.	kuchosha	monotonie (f)	monotony
verb	kuchovya	plonger	immerse, to
verb	kuchuja	filtrer	filter, to
verb	kuchukia	1. haïr 2. mépriser 3. ne pas tolérer	1. to hate 2. to scorn 3. to despise 4. to dislike
verb	kuchukia sana	détester	detest, to
adj.	kuchukiza	odieux	obnoxious
verb	kuchukiza	offenser	offend, to
verb	kuchukua	1. porter 2. emporter	1. to carry 2. to take away
verb	kuchuma	1. rassembler 2. cueillir	1. to gather 2. to pick
verb	kuchuma kwa kazi	gagner	earn, to; to gain
verb	kuchunga	faire le berger	shepherd, to
verb	kuchunga, kulinda	garder	guard, to
n.	kuchungua	investigation (f)	investigation
verb	kuchungua	sonder	probe, to
verb	kuchunguza	scruter	scrutinize, to
verb	kuchuuza	mettre en vente	peddle, to
verb	kuchwa	coucher, se	set, to (sun)
verb	kudai	1. revendiquer 2. exiger	1. to claim 2. to demand
verb	kudakiza	interrompre	interrupt, to
verb	kudanganya	1. tromper 2. décevoir 3. se leurrer 4. duper	1. to cheat 2. to deceive 3. to delude oneself 4. to fool
verb	kudekeza	se bichonner	pamper, to
verb	kudhani tu	conjecturer	conjecture about, to
verb	kudhihaki	se moquer de	mock, to
verb	kudhulumu	opprimer	oppress, to
verb	kudhuru	1. faire du mal 2. blesser	1. to harm 2. to injure
verb	kudondoka	dégoutter	drip, to

parts of speech	swahili	french	english
verb	kudukiza	écouter en cachette	eavesdrop, to
verb	kudumu	continuer	continue, to
verb	kudumu, kuvumilia	supporter	endure, to
verb	kudunda	percuter contre	crash into, to
verb	kuegemea, kutegemea	s'appuyer contre	lean on, to
verb	kuelea	intelligible, être	clear, to be
verb	kuelea	1. flotter 2. nager	1. to float 2. to swim
verb	kueleka	porter sur la hanche	carry on one's hip, to
adv.	kuelekeana	en face de	opposite
verb	kuelemea	accabler	weighed down, to be
verb	kueleza	expliquer	explain, to
verb	kuelimisha	instruire	educate, to
verb	kuenda au kuendesha mbele	avancer	advance, to
phrase	Kuenda chooni.	Va à la selle.	stool., Go to
verb	kuenda upande	dévier	deviate, to
verb	kuendelea	1. continuer 2. s'avancer	1. to carry on 2. to keep on 3. to progress
verb	kuendesha	1. conduire 2. interroger avec insistance	1. to drive 2. to prosecute
verb	kuenea	1. tendre 2. espacer	1. to extend 2. to spread out
verb	kuepuka	éviter	1. to avoid 2. to evade
n.	kuezeka	paille (pour couvrir un toit de paille)	straw (to cover a roof)
verb	kufa	mourir	die, to
n.	kufa (pl. kufa), mauti	mort (f)	death
phrase	kufa ganzi	engourdi, être	numb, to be
verb	kufa maji	noyer	drown, to
verb	kufa, kuisha	1. expirer 2. décéder	1. to expire 2. to die
verb	kufaa	suffire	suffice, to
verb	kufadhili	1. donner son amitié à 2. traiter avec condescendance	1. to befriend 2. to patronize
verb	kufagia	balayer	sweep, to
verb	kufahamisha	instruire, notifier	inform, to
verb	kufahamu	1. comprendre 2. être conscient 3. concevoir	1. to comprehend 2. to be aware 3. to conceive
verb	kufahamu {Unaelewa?} [Sielewi.]	comprendre {Comprends-tu?} [Je n'ai pas compris.]	understand, to {Do you understand?} [I did not understand.]
verb	kufanana	1. s'entendre avec (quelqu'un) 2. se ressembler	1. to correspond with 2. to resemble
verb	kufanana na	ressembler à	like, to be

146

parts of speech	swahili	french	english
verb	kufanya	1. faire 2. fabriquer	1. to do 2. to make
verb	kufanya -eupe	blanchir	whiten, to
verb	kufanya adui	provoquer	antagonize
verb	kufanya biashara	faire du commerce	trade, to
verb	kufanya bidii	s'efforcer	work with zeal, to
verb	kufanya dhambi	pécher	sin, to
verb	kufanya haraka	marcher vite	hurry, to
verb	kufanya huru	libérer	1. to liberate 2. to release
verb	kufanya mzaha	se moquer de	ridicule, to
verb	kufanya rahisi	faciliter	facilitate, to
verb	kufanya vifinyo	rider	wrinkle, to
verb	kufanya, kutenda	faire	do, to
verb	kufanyika	avoir lieu	take place, to
verb	kufanyiza	1. être cause de 2. construire 3. fabriquer	1. to cause 2. to construct 3. to make
verb	kufarakisha	aliéner	alienate, to
verb	kufariji	1. réconforter 2. consoler	1. to comfort 2. to console
verb	kufasiri	demander des explications	interpret, to ask to
verb	kufasiri, kutafsiri	traduire	translate, to
verb	kufaulu	1. achever 2. se tirer d'affaire 3. passer	1. to achieve 2. to finish 3. to make good 4. to pass
verb	kufazaika	troubler, se	troubled, to be
verb	kuficha	1. dissimuler 2. cacher	1. to conceal 2. to hide
verb	kufifia	1. se faner 2. flétrir	1. to fade 2. to wilt
verb	kufika	1. arriver 2. parvenir à 3. surgir	1. to arrive 2. reach 3. to spring up
verb	kufikia	atteindre	attain, to
verb	kufikicha	s'ébouler	crumble, to
verb	kufikili	considérer	consider, to
verb	kufikiri	1. méditer 2. réfléchir	1. to cogitate 2. to ponder 3. to reflect 4. to think about
verb	kufikiri yasivyo	mal calculer	miscalculate, to
verb	kufingirisha	rouler	roll along, to
verb	kufitini	se révolter contra	revolt against, to
verb	kufua	laver les vêtements	wash, to (clothes)
verb	kufuahisha	réjouir	rejoice, to
verb	kufuasa nyuma	rebrousser chemin	retrace the path
verb	kufuata	suivre	follow, to
verb	kufuatana na	escorter	escort, to
verb	kufuatana na, kusindikiza	accompagner	accompany, to
verb	kufuatisha	transcrire	transcribe, to

parts of speech	swahili	french	english
verb	**kufudikiza**	reverser	turn upside down, to
verb	**kufufua**	1. revivre 2. remettre en état	revive, to
verb	**kufukua**	exhumer	exhume, to
verb	**kufukuza**	1. chasser 2. repousser	1. to drive away 2. to repel
n.	**kufuli**	cadenas (m)	padlock
verb	**kufumbua, kuvumbua**	découvrir	discover, to
verb	**kufundisha**	1. inculquer 2. instruire 3. enseigner	1. to inculcate 2. to instruct 3. to teach
verb	**kufundishwa, kujifunza**	apprendre	learn, to
verb	**kufunga**	1. lier 2. fermer à clef 3. fermer 4. attacher	1. to bind 2. to lock 3. to shut 4. to close 5. to tie or tie up
verb	**kufunga chakula**	jeûner	fast, to
verb	**kufunga, kufumba**	fermer	close, to
verb	**kufunganya**	emballer	pack, to
verb	**kufungua**	1. ouvrir 2. dénouer	1. to unlock 2. to untie
verb	**kufungua (Fungua mlango.)**	ouvrir {Ouvre la porte.}	open, to {Open the door.}
verb	**kufunika**	envelopper	wrap, to
verb	**kufunika, kutamani**	couvrir	cover, to
verb	**kufunua**	dévoiler	1. to reveal 2. to unveil
verb	**kufupisha**	1. abréger 2. raccourcir	1. to abbreviate 2. to abridge 3. to shorten
verb	**kufurahi**	heureux, être	1. to be happy 2. to be glad
verb	**kufurahia**	aimer, trouver agréable	enjoy, to
verb	**kufurahisha**	1. égayer 2. faire heureux	1. to entertain 2. to make happy
verb	**kufurika**	déborder	overflow, to
verb	**kufuta**	effacer	1. to erase 2. to wipe away
verb	**kuganda**	coaguler, se	coagulate, to
verb	**kugawa**	diviser	divide, to
verb	**kugawanyia**	1. allouer 2. assigner	1. to allocate 2. to assign
verb	**kugeuka**	se retourner	turn around, to
verb	**kugeuka rangi**	rougir	blush, to
verb	**kugeuza kidogo**	faire changer de forme	modify, to
verb	**kugeuza kwa uongo**	falsifier	falsify, to
verb	**kugeuza, kujifanya**	affecter	affect
verb	**kughairi**	changer d'avis	change one's mind, to
verb	**kugomba**	quereller	quarrel, to
verb	**kugombeza**	1. réprimander 2. gronder (orage)	1. to rebuke 2. to roar (like a storm)
verb	**kugonga**	frapper	knock, to

parts of speech	swahili	french	english
verb	kugua	malade, être	sick, to be
verb	kugugumiza	balbutier	stutter, to
verb	kugusa	1. palper 2. toucher	1. to palpate 2. to touch
verb	kuhadisi	raconter	recount, to
verb	kuhakiki	1. assurer 2. affirmer 3. contrôler	1. to monitor 2. to testify 3. to verify
verb	kuhakikisha	certifier	make sure, to
verb	kuhalalisha	légaliser	legalize, to
verb	kuhama	déménager	move, to (dwelling)
verb	kuhamakia	réprimander	1. to reprimand 2. to scold
verb	kuhamisha	1. exiler 2. fuir à	1. to banish 2. to be in exile
verb	kuhara	avoir la diarrhée	diarrhea, to have
verb	kuhara damu	dysenterie, avoir la	dysentery, to have
verb	kuharibika	périr	perish, to
n.	kuharibika mimba	échec (m)	miscarriage
verb	kuharibu	1. abîmer 2. gaspiller	1. to spoil 2. to squander 3. to waste
verb	kuharimisha	excommunier	excommunicate, to
verb	kuhasi	châtrer	castrate, to
verb	kuhesabu	1. compter 2. sous-estimer	1. to count 2. to underestimate
verb	kuheshimu	1. honorer 2. respecter	1. to honor 2. to respect
verb	kuhifadhi	conserver	preserve, to
verb	kuhimiza	1. accélérer 2. faire exécuter rapidement	1. to accelerate 2. expedite
verb	kuhitaji	avoir besoin de	need, to
verb	kuhitilafiana	différent, être	different, to be
verb	kuhofu, kufadhaika	être anxieux	anxious, to be
verb	kuhubiri	prêcher	preach, to
verb	kuhukumu	rendre un jugement	judge, to
verb	kuhukumu au pima	critiquer	talk against, to
verb	kuhuzunika	triste, être	sad, to be
verb	kuiba	voler	steal, to
verb	kuiga	imiter	1. imitate 2. to mimic
verb	kuimarisha	stabiliser	stabilize, to
verb	kuimba	chanter	sing, to
verb	kuinama	se pencher	1. to stoop down 2. to bend over
verb	kuingia	entrer	enter, to
verb	kuingia mwezini	avoir ses règles	menstruate, to

parts of speech	swahili	french	english
verb	**kuingiza**	1. permettre (admit) 2. faire entrer 3. faire escale 4. introduire	1. to admit (into a place) 2. to bring in 3. to introduce (something new) 4. to put in
verb	**kuingiza ndani**	insérer	insert, to
verb	**kuinua**	1. lever 2. soulever	1. to lift 2. to raise
verb	**kuinuka**	s'élever	arise, to
verb	**kuishi**	vivre	live to
verb	**kuishi baada ya kufiwa**	survivre à	survive, to
verb	**kuita**	appeler	call, to
phrase	**kuiva**	cuit, être	cooked, to be well (to be done)
verb	**kuja**	venir	come, to
verb	**kujaa**	ne plus avoir faim; s'emplir	full, to be (not hungry)
verb	**kujadiliana**	débattre	debate, to
verb	**kujalia**	accorder	grant, to
verb	**kujaribu**	1. essayer 2. dissuader 3. s'efforcer d'obtenir 4. tenter	1. to attempt 2. to dissuade 3. to strive for 4. to tempt 5. to try
verb	**kujaza**	remplir	fill, to
verb	**kujenga**	bâtir	build, to
verb	**kujiangalia**	indépendant, être	independent, to be
verb	**kujiba**	répondre	answer, to
verb	**kujifanya**	faire semblant	make believe, to
verb	**kujifunza**	1. faire des études 2. étudier	study, to
verb	**kujifunza kwa moyo**	retenir	memorize, to
verb	**kujigamba**	se vanter	brag, to
verb	**kujihadhari**	prendre garde à	beware, to
verb	**kujinyata**	s'accroupir	crouch, to
verb	**kujinyima**	s'abstenir de,	abstain, to
verb	**kujipatia**	acquérir	acquire, to
verb	**kujipatia tena**	retrouver	recover, to (find again)
phrase	**kujipenda nafsi**	aimer-se	self-love
verb	**kujipigapiga**	se débattre	thrash around, to
verb	**kujishikia yote**	monopoliser	monopolize, to
n.	**kujistahi nafsi**	amour-propre (m)	self-respect
verb	**kujisumbua bure**	faire des histoires	fuss, to
verb	**Kujitafutiya kuingiya.**	défendre à d'entrer	forbid entry, to
verb	**kujitahidi**	s'efforcer	effort, to make an
verb	**kujitatiza**	s'enchevêtrer	tangled up, to get
verb	**kujivuna**	se vanter de	boast, to
verb	**kujizuia**	se retenir de	refrain from, to

150

parts of speech	swahili	french	english
verb	kujongea	déplacer; s'avancer	move, to
verb	kujua	1. savoir 2. connaître	know, to
verb	kujuana	connaître	acquainted, to be
verb	kujukuna	gratter, se	scratch oneself, to
verb	kujulisha	signaler	notify, to
verb	kujumlisha	1. additionner 2. résumer	1. to add up 2. to sum up
verb	kukaa	1. demeurer 2. rester 3. habiter	1. to dwell 2. to stay 3. to remain 4. to inhabit
verb	kukaa, kuketi	s'asseoir	sit, to
verb	kukaanga	frire	fry, to
verb	kukaba au kukabwa roho	étouffer	choke, to
verb	kukabidhi	mettre de côté	save, to
verb	kukabili	1 .se mesurer à 2. se tenir l'un face de l'autre	1. confront 2. to face (someone)
verb	kukagua hesabu	vérifier	audit, to
verb	kukalia	occuper	occupy, to
verb	kukama	traire	milk, to
verb	kukamata	capturer	capture, to
verb	kukamata	1. attraper 2. saisir	1. to catch 2. to seize
verb	kukamatisha	coller à	stick to, to
verb	kukamua	essorer	wring out to
verb	kukana	1. nier 2. démentir	deny, to
verb	kukanda	malaxer, pétrir	knead (as in bread), to
verb	kukandika	plâtre	plaster, to
verb	kukanyaga	1. piétiner 2. marcher	1. to stamp one's feet 2. to trample on 3. to tread on
verb	kukaribia	1. s'approcher de 2. tirer	1. to approach 2. to draw near
verb	kukaribisha	accueillir	welcome, to
verb	kukaripia	gronder	chide, to
verb	kukasirika	fâcher, se	angry, to get
verb	kukata	1. couper 2. séparer 3. amputer 4. inciser	1. to cut 2. to sever 3. to amputate 4. to incise
verb	kukata majani	faucher	mow, to
verb	kukata tamaa	désespérer	despair, to
verb	kukataa	1. décliner 2. exclure 3. refuser 4. rejeter	1. to decline 2. to exclude 3. to refuse 4. to reject
verb	kukataza	défendre	1. to forbid 2. to prohibit
verb	kukausha	sécher	dry, to
verb	kukawa	tarder	delay, to
verb	kukaza	1. serrer 2. fixer	1. to tighten 2. to clench 3. to fix

151

parts of speech	swahili	french	english
verb	kukaza nia	déterminer	determine, to
verb	kukaza ukweli	affirmer	assert, to
verb	kukeua	redresser ce qui est courbé	straighten that which is bent, to
verb	kukiasi	estimer	estimate, to
verb	kukimbia	fuir/s'enfuir	flee, to
verb	kukimbiza	poursuivre	chase, to
verb	kukiri	1. reconnaître 2. confesser 3. admettre 4. avouer	1. to acknowledge 2. to confess 3. to admit
verb	kukisi	deviner	guess, to
verb	kukiuka	enjamber	step over, to
verb	kukodoa	écarquiller les yeux	stare wide-eyed, to
verb	kukodolea	regarder fixement	stare at, to; to gaze at
verb	kukohoa	tousser	cough, to
verb	kukojoa, kunya	uriner	urinate, to
verb	kukokota	traîner	drag, to
phrase	kukolea	assaisonné, être	seasoned, to be well
verb	kukoleza	donner du goût à	flavor, to
verb	kukoma	cesser	cease, to
verb	kukomba	évider	hollow out, to
verb	kukomboa	racheter	redeem, to
verb	kukomea	boulonner	bolt, to
verb	kukomesha	1. terminer 2. mettre fin à	1. to end 2. to put an end to
verb	kukomesha kabisa	exterminer	exterminate, to
verb	kukonda	maigrir	1. to become thin 2. to lose weight
verb	kukondesha	faire maigrir	lose weight, to
verb	kukopa	emprunter	borrow, to (money)
verb	kukopesha	prêter	1. to lend 2. to loan
verb	kukoroga	agiter (un liquide)	stir, to; shake, to
verb	kukoroma	ronfler	snore, to
verb	kukosa	1. commettre une faute 2. échouer 3. négliger 4. manquer	1. to commit an error 2. to fail 3. to miss
verb	kukosa adabu	conduire mal, se	misbehave, to
verb	kukosa kutia	omettre	omit, to
n.	kuku	1. volaille (f) 2. poule (f)	1. fowl 2. hen
verb	kukubali	1. convenir de 2. concéder 3. consentir	1. to agree on 2. to concede 3. to consent
verb	kukubali, kupokea	d'accord, être	approve, to
verb	kukubalia, kupokea	accepter	accept, to

parts of speech	swahili	french	english
verb	**kukumbatia**	1. entourer de ses bras 2. serrer dans ses bras	1. to embrace 2. to hug
verb	**kukumbatia kwa upendo**	caresser	caress, to
phrase	**kukumbuka**	1. se rappeler 2. se souvenir de	1. to bear in mind 2. to remember
verb	**kukumbusha**	rappeler	remind, to
verb	**kukunguta**	secouer	shake, to (as rug)
verb	**kukunja**	plier	1. to bend 2. to fold
verb	**kukunja uso**	froncer les sourcils	frown, to
verb	**kukusanya**	1. amasser 2. assembler	1. to amass 2. to assemble
verb	**kukusudi**	avoir l'intention	intend, to
verb	**kukuta**	1. traverser 2. trouver	1. to come across 2. to find
verb	**kukutana**	rencontrer	meet, to
verb	**kukuza**	grossir	magnify, to
verb	**kukuza hali**	améliorer	improve, to
verb	**kukwaa**	trébucher	stumble, to
verb	**kukwama**	bloqué, être	stuck, to be
verb	**kula**	manger	eat, to
verb	**kula rushwa**	accepter soudoyer	bribe, to take
verb	**kulaani, kutukana**	maudire	curse, to
verb	**kulala**	s'étendre dormir	1. to sleep 2. to lie down
verb	**kulamba**	lécher	lick, to
verb	**kulaumu**	rejeter la responsabilité	blame, to
adv.	**kule**	là-bas	there
verb	**kulegea**	se détendre	relax, to
verb	**kuleta**	amener	bring to
verb	**kuleta hoja**	plaider	plead, to (court)
verb	**kuleta msaada**	renforcer	reinforce, to
verb	**kulewa**	1. être ivre 2. s'enivrer	1. to be drunk 2. to be intoxicated
verb	**kulia**	1. pleurer 2. hurler	1. to cry 2. to weep 3. to yell or howl in sorrow
verb	**kulima**	1. cultiver 2. biner 3. labourer	1. to cultivate 2. to hoe 3. to plow
verb	**kulinda**	défendre protéger	1. to defend 2. to protect 3. to shield
verb	**kulingana**	coïncider	coincide, to
verb	**kulinganisha**	comparer	compare, to
n.	**kulinganisha, kusawazisha**	rajustement (m)	adjustment
verb	**kulipa**	1. payer 2. rembourser	1. to pay 2. to reimburse
verb	**kulipiza kisasi**	venger	avenge, to
verb	**kulisha**	1. nourrir 2. brouter	1. to feed 2. to graze

parts of speech	swahili	french	english
verb	kulisha vema	nourrir	nourish, to
verb	kuloga	ensorceler	bewitch, to
verb	kuloweka	mouiller	wet, to
n.	kuma	vagin (m)	vagina
verb	kumaliza	1. conclure 2. épuiser 3. finir	1. to conclude 2. to exhaust 3. to finish
phrase	Kumbe!	Quoi!	What!
verb	kumbwaga	répandre	spill, to
verb	kumega	grignoter	nibble, to
verb	kumenya	1. peler 2. éplucher	peel, to
verb	kumeza	avaler	swallow, to
n. & adj.	kumi	dix (m)	ten
n.	kumi na mbili	douze	twelve
n.	kumi na moja	onze	eleven
n.	kumi na nane	dix-huit	eighteen
n.	kumi na nne	quatorze	fourteen
n.	kumi na saba	dix-sept	seventeen
n.	kumi na sita	seize	sixteen
n.	kumi na tano	quinze	fifteen
n.	kumi na tatu	treize	thirteen
n.	kumi na tisa	dix-neuf	nineteen
verb	kumiliki	posséder	own, to
verb	kumimina	verser	pour, to
verb	kumulika ghafula	clignoter	flash, to
verb	kumumunya maneno	marmotter	mumble, to
verb	kumwaga	vider	empty, to
verb	kumwanga	renverser	spill, to
verb	kumwangika	se répandre	spill, to
phrase	Kuna shida gani?	De quoi souffres-tu?	suffering from?, What are you
phrase	Kuna...	Il y a...	There is...
pronoun	Kuna...	ce sont, ils sont, elles sont	they are
verb	kunajisi	violer d'un objet sacré	defile, to
verb	kunasa, kutega	piéger	trap, to
verb	kunawa	laver mains ou pieds, se	wash hands and feet, to
verb	kunawa	laver se	wash, to (body-self)
n.	kundi (pl. makundi)	1. troupeau (m) 2. groupe (m) de personnes 3. essaim (m) 4. troupeau (m)	1. flock (of sheep) 2. group 3. swarm 4. herd
verb	kunenepa	devenir obèse	obese, to become
verb	kungaa, kuwaka	briller, faire reluire	shine, to
verb	kungariza	miroiter	sparkle, to

parts of speech	swahili	french	english
verb	kungoa	arracher	take out, to; pull out, to
verb	kungoja	1. attendre 2. patienter	wait for, to
n.	kunguni	insecte (m)	bug
verb	kunguruma	1. gronder 2. mugir 3. tonner	1. to growl 2. to roar 3. to thunder
verb	kung'arisha	polir	polish, to
verb	kung'uta chuja	passer	strain, to (filter)
n.	kuni	bois (m)	wood (for fire)
n.	kunjo (pl. makunjo)	ride (m)	wrinkle
verb	kunjua	déplier	unfold, to
verb	kunoa	aiguiser	sharpen, to
verb	kunongona	ne parler pas clairement	speak indistinctly, to
verb	kunuka	puer, sentir mauvais	stink, to
verb	kununa	bouder	sulk, to
verb	kunungunika	bougonner	grumble, to
verb	kunung'unika	se plaindre	complain, to
verb	kununua	acheter	buy, to
verb	kunusa	sentir	smell, to
verb	kunya; kuenda choo	déféquer	have a stool (bowel movement), to
verb	kunyakua	empoigner	grab, to
verb	kunyamaa	taire, se	stop talking, to
verb	kunyamaza	se taire	silent, to be
verb	kunyamazisha	1. faire tranquille 2. faire taire	1. to make quiet 2. to silence
verb	kunyanganya	piller	plunder, to
verb	kunyauka	faner, se	dry, to become; to wither
verb	kunyenyekea	humble, être	humble, to be
verb	kunyesha, kunya	pleuvoir	rain, to
verb	kunyima	1. priver 2. refuser	1. to deprive 2. to withhold
verb	kunyoa	raser	shave, to
verb	kunyoloka	droit, être	straight, to be (as in line)
verb	kunyolosha	redresser	straighten, to
verb	kunyonya	téter	suck, to
verb	kunyonyesha	allaiter	1. to breast-feed 2. to nurse (suckle)
verb	kunyosha	se tendre	strained, to become
verb	kunyunyizia	saupoudrer	sprinkle, to
verb	kunywa (Unataka kunywa nini?)	1. boire (Que voulez-vous boire?) 2. absorber	1. drink, to (What would you like to drink?) 2. to absorb
verb	kunywea	rétrécir	shrink, to

155

parts of speech	swahili	french	english
verb	**kuoa (man)**	marier, se	marry, to
verb	**kuoga**	se baigner	bathe, to (oneself)
verb	**kuogofya**	1. faire peur à 2. effrayer	1. to frighten 2. to startle
verb	**kuogolea**	nager	swim, to
verb	**kuogopa**	1. avoir peur de 2. appréhender 3. craindre	1. to be afraid 2. to dread 3. to fear
verb	**kuoka**	1. faire cuire 2. rôtir	1. to bake 2. to roast
verb	**kuokoa**	sauver	save, to
verb	**kuokota**	ramasser	pick up, to
verb	**kuolewa (woman)**	marier, se	marry, to
verb	**kuomba**	1. réclamer 2. faire appeler 3. demander 4. mendier	1. to reclaim 2. to appeal 3. to ask for 4. to beg
verb	**kuomba radhi**	s'excuser de	apologize, to
verb	**kuomboleza**	1. se lamenter 2. pleurer	mourn, to
verb	**kuona**	voir	see, to
verb	**kuona haya**	avoir honte	ashamed of, to be
verb	**kuondoa**	déranger	trouble, to
verb	**kuondoka**	1. partir 2. se tenir droit	1. to depart 2. to go away 3. to stand up straight
verb	**kuondosha**	ôter	remove, to
verb	**kuonekana**	1. apparaître 2. montrer se 3. être visible	1. to appear 2. to show oneself 3. to be visible
verb	**kuongeza**	augmenter	augment, to
verb	**kuongeza nguvu**	fortifier	fortify, to
verb	**kuongeza urefu**	allonger	lengthen, to
verb	**kuongezeka kwa kulimbikwa**	accumuler	accumulate, to
verb	**kuongoza**	mener	lead, to
verb	**kuonja**	goûter	taste, to
verb	**kuonya**	conseiller	counsel, to
verb	**kuonyesha**	1. exhiber 2. montrer	1. to exhibit 2. to show
verb	**kuosha**	1. rincer 2. laver	1. to rinse 2. to wash
verb	**kuota**	croître	grow, to
verb	**kuota jua**	se dorer	bask (in the sun), to
verb	**kuota ndoto**	rêver	dream, to
verb	**kuotea njiani**	tendre une embuscade à	ambush, to
verb	**kuoza**	1. se détériorer 2. pourrir 3. se gâter	1. to decay 2. to rot 3. to deteriorate 4. to spoil (food)
verb	**kupa**	donner	give, to
verb	**kupaka mafuta**	oindre	anoint, to
verb	**kupakaa**	1. peindre 2. salir	1. to paint 2. to smear

parts of speech	swahili	french	english
verb	kupakana na	contourner	skirt around, to
verb	kupakiza	charger	load, to
verb	kupalia magugu	sarcler	weed, to
verb	kupamba	1. décorer 2. embellir	1. to decorate 2. to embellish
verb	kupamba nyumba	fournir	furnish, to
verb	kupambanua	distinguer	distinguish between, to
verb	kupana mikono	serrer la main à	shake hands, to
verb	kupanda	1. monter 2. gravir 3. planter 4. ensemencer	1. to ascend 2. to climb 3. to plant 4. to sow
verb	kupanda na kushuka	fluctuer	fluctuate, to
verb	kupanga, kutandika	arranger (Arrangez toutes ces choses.)	arrange, to (Put all these things in order.)
verb	kupanganya	s'entasser	pile, to
verb	kupangusa	1. brosser 2. épousseter 3. essuyer	1. to brush 2. to dust 3. to wipe
verb	kupapasa	1. sentir 2. palper	1. to feel 2. to stroke
verb	kuparua	égratigner	scratch, to
verb	kuparuza	racler	scrape, to
verb	kupasha habari	annoncer les nouvelles	tell the news, to
verb	kupasha habari	prévenir	warn, to
verb	kupasha moto	chauffer	heat, to
verb	kupasua	1. fendre en long 2. déchirer	1. to cut lengthwise 2. to rip 3. to tear
verb	kupasua kwa msumeno	scier	saw, to
verb	kupasua mgonjwa	opérer	operate (medical), to
verb	kupasuka	fendre	split, to
verb	kupasuka ghafula	éclater	burst, to
verb	kupaswa	devoir	ought (to have to), must
verb	kupata	1. recevoir 2. obtenir	1. to get 2. to be given 3. to obtain
verb	kupata afya tena	se remettre	recover, to (from illness)
verb	kupata faida	gagner	gain, to
verb	kupata mali	se multiplier	thrive, to
verb	kupata nafuu, kuponya	guérir	better (after illness) to be; to be improved physically
verb	kupata tena	rentrer en possession de	regain, to
verb	kupatana	être d'accord	1. to agree 2. to concur
verb	kupatanisha	réconcilier	reconcile, to
verb	kupatiliza	condamner	condemn, to
phrase	kupatwa jua	éclipse de soleil	eclipse of the sun
verb	kupatwa na	éprouver	experience, to

parts of speech	swahili	french	english
verb	kupayuka	babiller	babble, to
verb	kupaza sauti	faire voix fort	raise voice, to
verb	kupeleka	expédier	speed, to
phrase	kupeleka maombi kwa	s'appliquer	apply oneself, to
n.	kupeleka simu	radio (f)	radio
verb	kupelekeana habari	communiquer	communicate, to
verb	kupeleleza	1. scruter 2. espionner	1. to investigate 2. to spy on
verb	kupembea	se balancer	swing, to
verb	kupembeza	bercer	rock, to
verb	kupenda	aimer	1. to love 2. to like 3. to be fond of
verb	kupendeza	plaire à	please, to
verb	kupendezwa	contenter	satisfy, to
verb	kupenya	pénétrer	penetrate, to
verb	kupepesa macho	cligner des yeux	blink, to
verb	kupfanya upatanisho	expier	atone, to
verb	kupiga	1. frapper 2. battre	1. to hit 2. to beat
verb	kupiga bei	marchander	bargain, to
verb	kupiga bunduki	tirer	shoot, to (gun)
verb	kupiga chafya	éternuer	sneeze, to
verb	kupiga filimbi	siffler avec un sifflet	blow a whistle, to
verb	kupiga fundo	nouer	knot, to tie a
verb	kupiga hodi	demande entrée	ask entrance, to
verb	kupiga kafi	pagayer	paddle, to
verb	kupiga kambi	camper	camp, to
verb	kupiga kelele	faire du bruit	noise, to make
verb	kupiga kengele	sonner à la porte	ring a bell, to
verb	kupiga kite	soupirer	sigh, to
verb	kupiga kiyowe	vociférer	scream, to
verb	kupiga kofi	gifler	slap, to
verb	kupiga kura	jouer un tour à, le tromper	cast lots, to
verb	kupiga mabawa	battre des ailes	flap wings, to
verb	kupiga magoti	s'agenouiller	kneel, to
verb	kupiga makofi	applaudir	1. to applaud 2. to clap
verb	kupiga mbio	courir	run, to
verb	kupiga miayo	bâiller	yawn, to
verb	kupiga mustari	fixer les limites	draw a line, to
verb	kupiga musumari	clouer	nail, to
phrase	kupiga ngumi	coup de poing	punch
verb	kupiga pagi	repasser	iron, to

parts of speech	swahili	french	english
verb	**kupiga sanamu**	photographier	photograph, to
verb	**kupiga shabaha**	braquer	aim, to take
verb	**kupiga teke**	donner un coup de pied	kick, to
verb	**kupiga, kugonga**	frapper	strike, to (hit)
verb	**kupigana**	combattre	fight, to
verb	**kupika**	cuire	cook, to
verb	**kupika pombe**	brasser de la bière	beer, to brew
verb	**kupima**	1. mesurer 2. mettre l'épreuve 3. peser 4. examiner	1. to measure 2. to test 3. to weigh 4. to examine
verb	**kupima kwa hatua**	poser le pied en marchant	step, to
verb	**kupima visivyo**	mal évaluer	misjudge, to
verb	**kupindua**	1. renverser 2. intervertir 3. peiner	1. to triumph 2. to turn over 3. to upset
verb	**kupinduka**	répandre	overturn, to
verb	**kupinga**	obstruer	obstruct, to
verb	**kupisha**	transmettre à	transmit, to
adv.	**kupita**	au delà	beyond
verb	**kupita**	1. passer avant 2. passer, se 3. surpasser	1. to happen 2. to go past 3. to surpass
adj.	**kupita yote**	le plus	most
verb	**kupitia**	se détacher	slip out, to
verb	**kupoa**	1. être froid 2. devenir frais	1. to be cold 2. to become cool
verb	**kupokea**	recevoir	receive, to
verb	**kupokea kama mwana**	adopter	adopt (child)
verb	**kupokea na kufuata**	choisir	adopt (habit)
verb	**kupona**	1. guérir 2. remets-toi	1. to heal 2. to cure 3. to get well
verb	**kuponda**	écraser	crush, to
verb	**kupongeza**	féliciter (en ce qui concerne obtention du diplôme)	congratulate, to (graduate)
verb	**kuponya**	1. guérir 2. délivrer	1. to cure 2. to rescue
verb	**kuponyoka**	échapper	escape, to
phrase	**kuposa**	1. demande en mariage 2. faire la cour à	1. marriage proposal 2. to woo
verb	**kupotea**	1. s'égarer 2. se perdre	1. to go astray 2. to be lost
verb	**kupotewa na uzuri**	dégrader, se	deteriorate, to
verb	**kupoteza**	perdre	lose, to
verb	**kupua**	écosser	shell, to
verb	**kupuliza**	gonfler avec l'air	swollen with air
verb	**kupumzika**	se reposer	rest, to
verb	**kupungua**	se détendre	slacken, to

parts of speech	swahili	french	english
verb	**kupungua thamani**	déprécier	depreciate, to
verb	**kupungua, kupunguza**	s'apaiser	abate, to
verb	**kupunguka**	diminuer	decrease, to
verb	**kupunguza**	diminuer quantité	1. to diminish the quantity 2. to reduce
verb	**kupunguza gharama**	économiser	economize, to
verb	**kupunja**	duper	trick, to
verb	**kupwesha**	dégonfler	deflate, to
verb	**kurehemu**	plaindre	pity, to
verb	**kuridhisha**	faire amende honorable	amends, make
verb	**kurisi**	hériter	inherit, to
verb	**kurudi**	1. revenir 2. retourner	1. to come back 2. to return
verb	**kurudi nyuma**	reculer (par peur)	recoil, to (through fear)
verb	**kurudisha**	1. rendre 2. remettre 3. ramener	1. to give back 2. to put back 3. to take back
verb	**kurudisha kitu**	rendre quelque chose	return something, to
verb	**kurudishia hali**	remplacer	replace, to
verb	**kurudufya**	doubler	double, to
verb	**kuruhusu**	permettre (admit)	allow, to
verb	**kuruhusu**	permettre	permit, to
verb	**kuruka**	1. voler 2. sauter 3. bondir	1. to fly 2. to jump 3. to leap
verb	**kuruka kama mpira**	rebondir	bounce, to
verb	**kusadiki**	croire	believe, to
verb	**kusadikisha**	convaincre	convince, to
z	**kusafiri**	voyager	travel, to
n.	**kusafiri**	voyageur (m)	traveller
verb	**kusafisha**	nettoyer	1. to clean 2. to scour
verb	**kusaga**	1. moudre 2. grincer	1. to grind 2. to squeak
verb	**kusahau**	oublier	forget, to
verb	**kusahihisha**	1. corriger 2. rectifier	1. to correct 2. to rectify
verb	**kusaidia**	aider à	1. to aid 2. to assist 3. to help
verb	**kusaidiana**	coopérer	cooperate, to
verb	**kusali**	prier	pray, to
phrase	**kusalimisha**	se rendre à	surrender to, to
verb	**kusalimu**	accueillir	greet, to
verb	**kusaliti**	trahir	betray, to
verb	**kusambaa, kutawanya**	se disperser	1. to scatter 2. to disperse
verb	**kusamehe**	pardonner	1. to forgive 2. to pardon
verb	**kusawazisha**	tenir en équilibre	balance, to

parts of speech	swahili	french	english
verb	**kusema**	1. dire 2. parler	1. to say 2. to speak 3. to talk
verb	**kusema na**	1. dire à 2. parler à	1. to say to 2. to speak to
verb	**kusema uongo**	mentir	lie, to
phrase	**kusema uwongo**	dire de mensonge	tell a lie, to
verb	**kusemezana, kuzungumza**	converser	converse with, to
verb	**kusengenya**	diffamer	defame, to
verb	**kuseta**	faire de la purée	mash, to
verb	**kushambulia**	1. attaquer 2. envahir	1. to attack 2. to invade
n.	**kushambuliwa na maradhi**	crise cardiaque (f)	heart attack
phrase	**kushangaa**	stupéfier, être	astounded, to be
verb	**kushangaza**	1. étonner 2. émerveiller 3. surprendre	1. to amaze 2. to astonish 3. to surprise
verb	**kushangilia**	célébrer	celebrate, to
verb	**kushariki**	participer	1. to compete 2. to take part in
verb	**kushauri**	consulter	consult, to
verb	**kushawishi**	persuader	persuade, to
verb	**kushibisha**	rassasier	satisfy, to
verb	**kushika**	1. se conformer à 2. tenir 3. maintenir 4. saisir	1. to abide by 2. to hold 3. to maintain 4. to take hold of
adj.	**kushikwa na fadhaa**	atterré	aghast, to be
verb	**kushinda**	1. conquérir 2. vaincre 3. dominer 4. maîtriser 5. surmonter 6. gagner	1. to conquer 2. to defeat 3. to dominate 4. to master 5. to overcome 6. to succeed 7. to vanquish 8. to win
verb	**kushindilia**	tasser	cram, to
verb	**kushindwa**	renoncer	give in, to
verb	**kushiriki**	1. partager entre plusieurs 2. participer	1. to share with others 2. to participate
verb	**kushirikiana katika kazi**	collaborer	collaborate, to
verb	**kushona**	coudre	sew, to
verb	**kushtaki**	accuser	accuse, to
verb	**kushtua**	se désarticuler (ie. bras)	dislocate, to (one's joint)
verb	**kushuhuda**	témoin de, être	witness, to
verb	**kushuhudia**	attester	attest, to
verb	**kushuka**	débarquer	get off, to
verb	**kushuka, kutelemuka**	descendre	descend, to; go down, to
verb	**kushuku**	1. douter (de) 2. soupçonner 3. se méfier de	1. to doubt 2. to suspect 3. to mistrust
verb	**kushukuru**	remercier	thank, to

161

parts of speech	swahili	french	english
verb	kushurutisha	1. contraindre 2. forcer 3. insister	1. to coerce 2. to force 3. to insist
verb	kushusha	abaisser	lower, to
verb	kushusha	décharger	unload, to
verb	kusifu	louer	praise, to
verb	kusihi	1. supplier 2. implorer	1. to beseech 2. to implore
verb	kusihi sana	urgent, être	urgent, to be
verb	kusikia	entendre	hear, to
verb	kusikiliza	écouter	listen, to
verb	kusikitika	peiner	grieve, to
verb	kusimama	1. se tenir debout 2. se lever 3. se redresser	1. to stand up 2. to get up 3. to recover 4. to arise (from lying position)
verb	kusimamia	1. surveiller 2. résister à	1. to withstand 2. to supervise
verb	kusimamisha	1. arrêter 2. ériger 3. cesser	1. to arrest 2. to erect 3. to stop
verb	kusimulia	raconter	narrate, to
verb	kusindikiza	accompagner	accompany, to (part of the way)
verb	kusingizia	1. calomnier 2. proférer des imprécations	1. to malign 2. to slander
n.	kusini	sud (m)	south
verb	kusita	hésiter	hesitate, to
n.	kusita moyoni	indécision (f)	indecision
verb	kusitawi	prospérer	flourish, to
verb	kusokota	1. tresser 2. tordre	1. to braid 2. to twist
verb	kusoma	lire	read, to
phrase	kustaajabu	étonné, être	surprised, to be
verb	kustahili	mériter	1. to deserve 2. to mert
verb	kustarehe	à l'aise, être	ease, to be at
verb	kustawi	réussir	successful, to be
n.	kusudi	1. intention (f) 2. motif (m) 3. but (m) 4. résolution (f) 5. volonté (f)	1. intention 2. motive 3. purpose 4. resolution 5. will
verb	kusugua	frotter	scrub, to
verb	kusuka	tricoter	knit, to
verb	kusukasuka	ballotter	roll around, to
verb	kusukula meno	se laver les dents	brush teeth, to
verb	kusukuma	1. mouvoir 2. pousser	1. to move 2. to push
verb	kusukumana	bousculer	jostle, to
verb	kusukusuka	secouer	shake, to
verb	kusukutua kooni	gargariser	gargle, to

parts of speech	swahili	french	english
verb	kusulibi	crucifier	crucify, to
verb	kusuta	se moquer	taunt, to
verb	kutabiri	1. prédire 2. prophétiser	1. to foretell 2. to predict 3. to prophesy
verb	kutafakari	1. contempler 2. méditer	1. to contemplate 2. to meditate
verb	kutafuna	1. mâcher 2. mastiquer	chew, to
verb	kutafuta	chercher	1. to look for 2. to seek 3. to search
verb	kutaharuki	s'affairer	bustle about, to
verb	kutahayarisha	embarrasser	embarrass, to
verb	kutahiri	circoncire	circumcise, to
verb	kutaja	1. faire allusion 2. mentionner 3. nommer 4. citer	1. to allude 2. to mention 3. to quote or cite 4. to name
verb	kutajirisha	enrichir	enrich, to
verb	kutaka	1. désirer 2. vouloir	1. to desire 2. to want
n.	kutaka thibitisho	défi (m)	challenge
verb	kutakasa	nettoyer, purifier	cleanse, to
verb	kutamani	1. convoiter 2. désirer ardemment	1. to covet 2. to long for
verb	kutambaa	ramper	creep, to
verb	kutambua	1. reconnaître 2. discerner	1. to recognize 2. to discern
verb	kutambua maana	déduire	deduce, to
phrase	kutambusha	en plus	what is more
verb	kutandika kitanda	faire un lit (de l'herbe)	bed, to make a (with grass)
verb	kutangatanga	flâner	dawdle, to
verb	kutangatanga	vagabonder	stray, to
verb	kutangaza	1. communiquer 2. publier	1. to announce 2. to publish
verb	kutangua	annuler	annul, to
verb	kutangua	se défaire	undo, to
verb	kutangulia	précéder	1. to go before 2. to precede
verb	kutanisha	réunir	reunite, to
verb	kutanua	dilater	expand, to
verb	kutapika {Ninatapita minyoo.)	vomir {Je vomis des vers.}	vomit, to {I am vomiting worms.}
verb	kutatiza	1. déconcerter 2. enchevêtrer	1. to baffle 2. to tangle (ensnare)
verb	kutawala	1. contrôler 2. gouverner	1. to control 2. to govern 3. to rule
verb	kutayarisha	apprêter	prepare, to
verb	kutayarisha	préparer	prepare, to

parts of speech	swahili	french	english
verb	**kutazama**	1. apercevoir 2. regarder 3. observer	1. to behold 2. to notice 3. to look 4. to observe
verb	**kutazama mbele**	prévoir	foresee, to
verb	**kutazamia**	s'attendre à	expect, to
verb	**kutazamia mbele**	prévoir	anticipate, to
n.	**kutega kwa hila**	compère (m)	decoy
verb	**kutegemea**	1. dépendre de 2. compter sur	1. to depend on 2. to rely on
verb	**kutegemeza**	soutenir	support, to
verb	**kutekenya**	chatouiller	tickle, to
verb	**kutelemka**	descendre (l'arbre)	climb down, (tree), to
n.	**kuteleza**	glissade (f)	slide
verb	**kuteleza**	se glisser	slide, to
verb	**kutema mate**	cracher	1. to expectorate 2. to spit
verb	**kutembea**	1. divaguer 2. se promener	1. to ramble 2. to go for a walk
phrase	**kutembea parini**	faire une randonnée	hiking, to go
verb	**kutenda**	se conduire	behave, to
verb	**kutenda, kuigiza hadithi**	agir	act, to
verb	**kutendea**	traiter	treat (medical), to
verb	**kutenga**	1. détacher 2. se désunir 3. séparer	1. to detach 2. to disconnect 3. to separate
verb	**kutengeneza**	améliorer raccommoder organiser réparer	1. to ameliorate 2. to mend 3. to organize 4. repair
verb	**kutengeneza ifae zaidi**	amender	amend, to
verb	**kutesa**	1. harceler 2. persécuter 3. affliger	1. to harass 2. to persecute 3. to torture
verb	**kutetemeka**	1. grelotter 2. trembler	1. to shiver 2. to tremble
verb	**kutetisha**	asseoir	seat, to
verb	**kuthamini**	se rendre compte de	appreciate, to
verb	**kuthibitisha**	confirmer	confirm, to
verb	**kuthubutu**	oser	dare, to
verb	**kutia alama**	marquer	mark, to
verb	**kutia chumvi**	exagérer	exaggerate, to
verb	**kutia hasara**	endommager	damage, to
verb	**kutia hewa ya**	aérer une plantation	aerate, to
n.	**kutia kiwi**	éblouissement (m)	dazzle
phrase	**kutia mapaa**	couvrir un toit	roof, to put on
verb	**kutia moyo**	encourager	encourage, to
verb	**kutia moyoni**	inspirer	inspire, to
verb	**kutia nguvu**	fortifier	invigorate, to
n.	**kutia pua**	souder	solder, to

parts of speech	swahili	french	english
verb	**kutia sumu**	empoisonner	poison, to
verb	**kutia wasiwasi**	ahurir	bewilder, to
verb	**kutia, kuweka**	poser	set, to
verb	**kutii**	obéir à	obey, to
verb	**kutikisa**	secouer/agiter	shake (object) hard, to
verb	**kutimia**	raisonner	reason, to
verb	**kutimiza**	accomplir	1. to accomplish 2. to fulfill
verb	**kutirika**	dégouliner	trickle, to
verb	**kutiririka**	couler	flow, to
verb	**kutisha**	intimider	intimidate, to
verb	**kutoa**	1. donner 2. produire 3. dépenser 4. soustraire	1. to give 2. to produce 3. to (fruit) spend 4. to subtract
n.	**kutoa damu**	hémorragie (f)	hemorrhage
verb	**kutoa fedha au msaada**	contribuer	contribute, to
verb	**kutoa rushwa**	soudoyer	bribe, to
verb	**kutoa sadaka**	sacrifier	sacrifice, to
verb	**kutoa shauri, kuonya**	conseiller	advise, to
verb	**kutoangalia**	négliger	1. to ignore someone 2. to neglect
verb	**kutoboa**	percer	drill, to (a hole)
verb	**kutoka**	1. reprendre 2. verser 3. sortir	1. to shed 2. to take out 3. to go out 4. to exit
verb	**kutoka damu**	saigner	bleed, to
verb	**kutoka jasho**	transpirer	sweat, to
verb	**kutoka kamasi**	pleurnicher	snivel, to
verb	**kutokea**	paraître	appear, to
verb	**kutokea wazi**	sortir de	come out of, to
verb	**kutokuwapo**	s'absenter	absent, to be
verb	**kutolea**	offrir	offer, to
verb	**kutomoa**	défoncer	smash up, to
verb	**kutopatana**	ne pas être d'accord	disagree, to
verb	**kutopitika**	se trouver dans une impasse	impasse, to be at an
verb	**kutoridhia**	désapprouver	disapprove, to
verb	**kutorosha**	enlever	abduct, to
verb	**kutosha**	suffire	sufficient, to be
n.	**kutotaka**	réticence (f)	reluctance
verb	**kutoweka**	disparaître	disappear, to
verb	**kutowezekana**	impossible à faire, être	impossible to do, to be
verb	**kutoza kwa nguvu**	extorquer	extort, to
n.	**kutu**	rouille (f)	rust

parts of speech	swahili	french	english
verb	kutua	hésiter	pause, to
verb	kutubu	repentir, se	repent, to
verb	kutufata	fouiller	search, to
verb	kutukia	lieu, avoir	occur, to
verb	kutukuza	exalter	exalt, to
verb	kutulia	calme, se	calm down, to
verb	kutuma	envoyer	send, to
verb	kutumaini	espérer	hope, to
verb	kutumia	se servir de	use, to
verb	kutumia vibaya, kutukana	s'insulter	abuse, to (verbal)
verb	kutumika	travailler	work, to
verb	kutumikia	servir	serve, to (food)
verb	kutundika	1. raccrocher 2. suspendre	1. to hang up 2. to suspend
verb	kutunga	composer	compose, to
verb	kutungika	suspendre, être pendant	hang, to
verb	kutunza	1. soigner 2. s'occuper de	1. to care for (the sick) 2. to look after
verb	kutupa	1. jeter 2. lancer	1. to cast 2. to fling 3. to discard 4. to sling 4. to throw
n.	kutupa jicho	coup d'oeil	glance
verb	kutuza	récompenser	reward, to
verb	kutwaa	1. reprendre 2. emporter	1. to resume 2. to take
verb	kutwaa; kushika	prendre	take, to
verb	kutwalia	emporter	take from, to
n.	kutwaliwa	privation (f)	deprivation
verb	kutwanga	piler, broyer	pound, to; to crush
verb	kutweta	1. avoir le souffle coupé 2. haleter	1. to gasp 2. to pant
phrase	kutwetatweta	essoufflé, être	breathless, to be
verb	kutweza	mépriser	despise, to
verb	kuua	tuer	kill, to
verb	kuudhi	1. ennuyer 2. irriter 3. importuner	1. to annoy 2. to irritate 3. to pester
verb	kuudhi, kuongeza ubaya	aggraver	aggravate, to
verb	kuugua	1. gémir 2. être malade	1. to groan 2. to wail 3. to be ill 4. to moan
phrase	kuuguza	soigner	sick, to care for the
verb	kuuliza	demander à	ask (question), to
verb	kuulizauliza	interroger	interrogate, to
verb	kuuma	1. faire mal 2. mordre 3. souffrir	1. to ache 2. to bite 3. to have pain 4. to suffer

parts of speech	swahili	french	english
adj.	**kuuma**	douloureux	sore (painful)
verb	**kuumba**	créer	create, to
verb	**kuumwa**	être blesser	wounded, to be
verb	**kuunga**	1. relier 2. se joindre 3. unir	1. to connect 2. to join (things) 3. to unite
verb	**kuupepo**	enrouler	wind, to
verb	**kuuza**	vendre	sell, to
verb	**kuuzi**	1. taquiner 2. tracasser	1. to tease 2. to be worried
verb	**kuvaa nguo**	couvrir, se	cover oneself, to
verb	**kuvaa; kuchukua**	porter	wear, to
verb	**kuvalia**	vêtir	dress, to
verb	**kuvika**	1. vêtir 2. mettre à (quelqu'un) un vêtement	1. to clothe 2. to dress another
verb	**kuvimba**	1. gonfler 2. enfler	swell, to
verb	**kuvimbisha**	grossir	weight, to gain
verb	**kuvua**	pêcher	fish, to
verb	**kuvuja**	fuir	leak, to
verb	**kuvuka**	1. croiser 2. traverser	1. to cross 2. to traverse
verb	**kuvuma**	souffler	blow, to
verb	**kuvumbua**	1. explorer 2. inventer	1. to explore 2. to invent
verb	**kuvuna**	récolter	harvest, to
verb	**kuvunga**	changer de l'argent	change money, to
verb	**kuvunja**	casser	break, to
verb	**kuvunja moyo**	décourager	discourage, to
verb	**kuvunja ndoa**	divorcer	divorce, to
n.	**kuvunjika meli**	navire (m) naufragé	shipwreck
verb	**kuvuta**	1. attirer 2. tirer 3. entraîner	1. to attract 2. to pull 3. to train (child)
verb	**kuvuta kwa werevu**	amadouer	entice, to
verb	**kuvuta makasia**	ramer	row, to (boat)
verb	**kuvuta mawazo pengine**	distraire	distract, to
verb	**kuvuta pumzi**	respirer	breathe
verb	**kuvuta tumbako**	fumer du tabac	smoke, to
verb	**kuwa**	être	be, to
verb	**kuwa macho**	alerte, être	alert, to be
verb	**kuwa mali yake**	appartenir à	belong to, to
verb	**kuwa mgonjwa**	malade, être	ill, to be
verb	**kuwa mwangilizi**	s'occuper de	charge, to be in
verb	**kuwa na**	1. avoir 2. posséder	1. to have 2. to possess
verb	**kuwa na kigugumizi**	bredouiller	stammer, to
verb	**kuwa na lazima**	devoir	should; to be obligated
verb	**kuwa na mimba**	enceinte, être	pregnant, to be

parts of speech	swahili	french	english
verb	kuwa na upogo	loucher	squint, to
verb	kuwa, kufaa	devenir	become, to
phrase	kuwahi	à l'heure	time, on
verb	kuwaka	prendre feu	catch fire, to
verb	kuwako	exister	exist, to
verb	kuwasha	1. démanger 2. allumer 3. se ranimer	1. to itch 2. to light (kindle) 3. to rekindle
n.	kuwasho	irritation (f)	irritation
verb	kuwasifu	décrire	describe, to
verb	kuwasili	atteindre	reach, to
verb	kuwaza	penser	think, to
verb	kuwaza; kufikiri	penser à	think of, to
verb	kuweka	1. mettre 2. déposer 3. garder	1. to put 2. to deposit 3. to keep
verb	kuweka ahadi	s'engager	commit oneself, to
verb	kuweka akiba	épargner	save, to
verb	kuweka imara	instaurer	establish, to
verb	kuweka mpaka	limiter	limit, to
verb	kuweka nadhiri	jurer	vow, to, to swear (oath)
verb	kuweka, kulaza	poser	lay, to
verb	kuweza	pouvoir	1. can 2. to be able
verb	kuwezekana	1. être faisable 2. être possible	1. to be feasible 2. to be possible
verb	kuwezesha	permettre	enable, to
verb	kuwika	chanter	crow, to
n.	kuwika jogoo	chant (m) du coq	cock-crowing
verb	kuwinda	chasser	hunt, to
verb	kuyeyuka	dissoudre	dissolve, to
verb	kuyeyusha	fondre	melt, to (sugar)
verb	kuyumbayumba	vaciller	sway, to
verb	kuzaa	1. donner naissance à 2. accoucher 3. enfanter	1. to bear (child) 2. to give birth
verb	kuzalisha	se propager	propagate, to
verb	kuzaliwa	naître	born, to be
verb	kuzama	enfoncer	sink, to
verb	kuzamisha	submerger	submerge, to
verb	kuzani	supposer, imaginer	suppose, to
verb	kuzarau	1. calomnier 2. insulter	insult, to
verb	kuziba	boucher	stop up, to
verb	kuziba njia	boucher	block, to
verb	kuzidi	1. dépasser 2. augmenter	1. to exceed 2. to increase
verb	kuzidisha	multiplier	multiply, to

parts of speech	swahili	french	english
verb	kuzika	1. enterrer 2. enfouir	bury, to
verb	kuzima	éteindre	extinguish, to
verb	kuzimia	s'évanouir	faint, to
phrase	kuzimika	s'éteindre	go out (fire) , to
verb	kuzingira	entourer	encircle, to
verb	kuzini	commettre l'adultère	adultery, to commit
verb	kuzoea	1. être accoutumé 2. exercer 3. pratiquer	1. to be accustomed 2. exercise 3. to practice
verb	kuzomea	huer	boo, to
verb	kuzuia	1. gêner 2. empêcher	1. to hinder 2. to prevent
verb	kuzunguka	1. contourner 2. circuler 3. entourer	1. to go around 2. circulate 3. to surround
verb	kuzungumza	causer	chat, to
verb	kuzungumzia habari	discuter	discuss, to
verb	kuzungusha	cerner (Avoir les yeux cernés.)	surround, to (To have rings under one's eyes.)
verb	kuzuru	visiter	visit, to
prep.	kwa	1. pour 2. pendant 3. depuis 4. à	1. for 2. to
adv.	kwa ajilini gani	pourquoi	why?
adv.	kwa dhahiri	clairement	clearly
n.	kwa heri	bonsoir (m)	good-night
phrase	Kwa heri.	Au revoir.	Good-bye.
adv.	kwa hiyo	en conséquence	accordingly
adv.	kwa kawaida	généralement	1. generally 2. normally
adv.	kwa kusudi	intentionnellement	intentionally
conj.	kwa kuwa, kwa maana, kwa sababu	parce que	because
conj.	kwa maana	tandis que	whereas
adv.	kwa maana gani	pourquoi	why
prep.	kwa mbele	le long de	along
phrase	kwa mfano	exemple, par	instance, for
phrase	kwa muda gani	combien de temps	how long
adv.	kwa nini, mbona	pourquoi	why
adv.	kwa nusu	en partie	partly
conj.	kwa sababu hii	à cause de	because of
adv.	kwa saburi	patiemment	patiently
adv.	kwa shida	1. à peine 2. de justesse	1. barely 2. narrowly
phrase	kwa upande wa kuume	à droit	right, on the
prep.	kwa, na	par / près de	by (through)/ (near)
prep.	kwa, na, pamoja na	avec, de	with

parts of speech	swahili	french	english
conj.	**kwani, maana, kwa sababu**	car	because
adv.	**kwanza**	d'abord	1. at first 2. to begin with
n.	**kwapa**	aisselle (f)	armpit
adv.	**kweli**	1. en effet 2. vraiment	1. indeed 2. in fact 3. really
n.	**kweli**	vérité (f)	truth
adj.	**kweli {Kweli.}**	vrai {Tu dis vrai.}	true {You speak the truth.}
verb	**kwenda**	1. marcher 2. aller	1. to walk 2. to go
verb	**kwenda kuamkia**	rendre visite à	call on, to
verb	**kwenda; kuondoka**	partir	go, to; to leave
n.	**kwikwi**	hoquet (m)	hiccup
adv.	**labda**	1. peut-être 2. il est possible que	1. maybe 2. perhaps 3. possibly
n.	**ladha**	goût (m)	flavor
adj.	**laini**	1. lisse 2. uni 3. souple	1. smooth 2. soft
n. & adj.	**laki**	cent mille	hundred thousand
conj.	**lakini**	1. mais 2. au moindre	1. but 2. at least
n.	**lawama**	condamnation (f)	condemnation
verb	**lazima**	1. devoir 2. il faut que	must
n.	**lazimu**	nécessité (f)	necessity
adv.	**leo**	aujourd'hui	today
n.	**limau (pl. malimau)**	citron (m)	lemon
interj.	**Lino!**	Attention!	Look!
n.	**lugha**	langage (m)	language
n.	**lulu (pl. malulu)**	perle (f)	pearl
n.	**maafa**	calamité (f)	calamity
n	**maakuli mema**	nourriture (f)	nourishment
n.	**maamuzi**	décision (f)	decision (final)
n.	**maana**	1. importance (f) 2. sens (m)	1. importance 2. meaning 3. significance
n.	**maarifa**	1. science (f) 2. connaissance (f)	knowledge
n.	**maarifa ya vita**	tactiques (f)	tactics
n.	**maasi (pl.)**	révolte (f)	revolt
n.	**mabishano**	1. dispute (f) 2. controverse (f)	1. argument (dispute) 2. controversy
n.	**machafuko makubwa**	chaos (m)	chaos
n.	**machela**	brancard (m)	stretcher
n.	**Machi; mwezi wa tatu wa mwaka wa kizungu**	mars (m)	March
n.	**machila**	hamac (m)	hammock
n.	**machozi**	larmes (f)	tears

parts of speech	swahili	french	english
n.	machukio	aversion (f)	aversion
n.	madakizo	interruption (f)	interruption
n.	madaraka	responsabilité (f)	liability
n.	madhara	blessure (f)	injury
n.	madini	1. métal (m) 2. outil (m)	1. metal 2. tool
n.	maelekeo	tendance (f)	tendency
n.	maelezo	explication (f)	explanation
n.	maendeleo	progrès (m)	progress
n.	maendeleo mazuri	amélioration (f)	improvement
n.	mafundisho; somo (pl. masomo)	leçon (f)	teaching, (lesson)
n.	mafunzo	éducation (f)	education
n.	mafuriko	inondation (f)	flood
n.	mafuta	1. gras (m) 2. graisse (f) 3. lubrifiant (m) 4. huile (f)	1. fat 2. grease 3. lubricant 4. oil
n.	mafuta ya motakaa	pétrole (m)	petroleum
phrase	Magalibi imefika.	La nuit tombe.	dark., It is getting
phrase	Magalibi mzuli.	Ayez la bonne soirée.	Have a good evening.
n.	maganda (pl.)	épluchures (f)	peelings
n.	magharibi	coucher du soleil (m)	sunset
n. & adj.	magharibi	ouest (m)	west
n.	magombezi	réprimande (f)	reprimand
n.	mahali fulani	localité (f)	locality
n.	mahali nyumbani pa kukokea moto	cheminée (f)	fireplace
verb	mahali pa kukaa	loger	accommodate, to
n.	mahali pa kukaa	logement (m)	lodging place
adj.,adv.	mahali pengine	absent	away
n.	mahari	dot (f)	dowry
n.	maheshe	gorille (m)	gorilla
n.	maili	mile (m)	mile
n.	maini	foie (m)	liver
n.	maisha	existence (f)	existence
n.	maisha, udogo	vie (f)	life
n.	maishilio	moyens (m) d'existence	livelihood
n.	maiti	cadavre (m)	corpse
n.	majani (pl.)	herbe (f)	grass
n.	maji	eau (f)	water
adj.	majimaji	1. humide 2. mouillé	1. damp 2. wet
n.	majivu (pl.)	cendres (f)	ashes
n.	makaa ya miti	charbon de bois (m)	charcoal
n.	makaa ya moto	braise (f)	embers

parts of speech	swahili	french	english
n.	makaburini	cimetière (m)	cemetery
n.	makamasi	morve (f)	nasal mucous
n.	makasi	ciseaux (m)	scissors
n.	makelele	bruit (m)	noise
n.	makelele mengi	tohu-bohu (m)	pandemonium
interj.	Makelele!	Taisez-vous!	Silence!
n.	makokoto (pl.)	caillou (m)	pebble
n. & adj.	makumi mawili; ishirini	vingt (m)	twenty
n.	malaika	ange (m)	angel
n.	malalo ya mnyama wa mwitu	tanière (f)	lair
phrase	Malangapi?	Combien de fois?	How many times?
n.	malaya	prostituée (f)	prostitute
n.	mali	propriété (f)	property
n.	mali, utajiri	richesse (f)	wealth
n.	malipo	1. expiation 2. paiement (m)	1. atonement 2. payment
n.	malipo ya uzeeni	pension (f)	pension
n.	malisho	pâturage (m)	pasture
n.	malkia	reine (f)	queen
n.	mama mdogo	tante maternelle	aunt (mother's sister)
n.	mama mkuu; nyanya	grand-mère (f)	grandmother
n.	mama mzazi	mère (f)	1. mama 2. mother
n.	mamba	crocodile (m)	crocodile
n.	mamba wa (Amerika)	alligator (m)	alligator
phrase	Mambo?	Comment fait-tu?	How are you doing?
n.	mamena	aine (f)	groin
n.	mamlaka	1. pouvoir (m) 2. règle (f)	1. power (authority) 2. rule
n.	maneno	message (m)	message
n.	manukato	parfum (m)	perfume
n.	maombi	prière (f)	prayer
n.	maongezi	causerie (f)	chat
n.	maono	sentiment (m)	feelings
n.	mapatano	1. accord (m) 2. marché (m) 3. sympathie (f) 4. compassion (f)	1. agreement 2. bargain 3. sympathy
n.	mapatano ya kukutana	rendez-vous (m)	appointment
adv.	mapema	de bonne heure , tôt	early
n.	mapendo	amour (m)	love
n.	mapenzi	désir (m)	wish
n.	mapigano	conflit (m)	conflict
n.	mapokeo	tradition (f)	tradition
n.	mara	occasion (f)	occasion

172

parts of speech	swahili	french	english
adv.	**mara kwa mara**	1. maintes et maintes fois 2. fréquemment 3. de temps en temps	1. again and again 2. frequently 3. now and then 4. occasionally 5. from time to time
adv.	**mara mbili**	deux fois	twice
adv.	**mara moja**	immédiatement	1. immediately 2. right now 3. instantly
adv.	**mara moja tu**	une fois	once
adv.	**mara na mara**	quelquefois	sometimes
adv.	**mara nyingi**	souvent	often
adv., n.	**mara, wakati (pl. nyakati)**	fois, une fois	time
n.	**maradhi ya pukupuku**	épidémie (f)	epidemic
n.	**marhamu**	pommade (f)	ointment
n.	**marufuku**	défendu	forbidden
n.	**masamaha**	pardon (m)	forgiveness
n.	**mashaka**	1. épreuves (f) privations 2. perplexité (f)	1. hardship 2. perplexity
n.	**mashaka; taabu**	difficulté (f)	difficulty
n.	**mashambulio**	attaque (f)	attack
n.	**mashariki**	est (m)	east
n.	**mashini**	machine (f)	machine
n.	**mashtaka**	1. accusation (f) 2. procès (m)	1. accusation 2. trial
adj.	**mashuhuri**	célèbre	famous
adj.	**masikini**	pauvre	poor
phrase	**masikini**	mendiant (m)	poor person
n.	**masimulizi**	récit (m)	narrative
n.	**masingizio**	calomnie (f)	slander
n.	**masizi**	1. noir de fumée 2. suie (f)	soot
n.	**matamvua**	frange (f)	fringe
n.	**matata**	complication (f)	complication
n.	**matatizo?**	introduire une requête	problem?
n.	**mate**	1. salive (f) 2. crachat (m)	1. saliva 2. spit
n.	**matembezi ugenini**	excursion (f)	excursion
n.	**matengenezo**	1. amendement (m) 2. organisation (f) 3. préparation (f)	1. amendment 2. organization 3. preparation
n.	**mateso**	persécution (f)	persecution
n.	**matoke**	banane plantain	plantain
n.	**matope**	boue (f)	mud
n.	**matubwitubwi**	oreillons (m)	mumps
n.	**matukio**	événement (m)	occurrence
n.	**matumaini**	espérance (f), espoir (m)	hope

parts of speech	swahili	french	english
n., med	matumbo (pl.)	intestins	intestines
n.	matumizi	usage (m)	use
n.	matunda	dessert (m)	dessert
n.	matusi (pl.)	insulte (f)	insult
n.	maugomvi (pl.)	querelles (f)	quarrels
n.	mauguzi	gémissement (m)	groan
n.	maulana	seigneur (m)	lord
n.	maumbile	nature (f)	nature
n.	maumivu (pl.)	1. douleur (f) 2. souffrance (f)	1. pain 2. ache
n.	maumivu makali	angoisse (f)	agony
n.	maumivu ya kichwa	mal de tête (m)	headache
n., med	maumivu ya viunoni	lumbago	lumbago
n.	maungamo	confession (f)	confession
n.	mavi (pl.)	excréments	excrement
n.	mavumbi	poussière (f)	dust
n.	mavuno (pl.)	1. récolte (f) 2. moisson (f)	1. crop (farming) 2. harvest
n.	mawese	huile de palmier (m)	palm oil
n.	mawindo	gibier (m)	game, wild
n.	mazabahu	autel (m)	altar
n.	mazeru (pl.)	albinos (m,f)	albinos
n.	mazigazi	hallucination (f)	hallucination
n.	maziko	enterrement (m)	funeral
n.	mazingira	milieu (m)	environment
n.	maziwa (pl.)	lait (m)	milk
n.	maziwa ya mama	lait (m) de femme	breast milk
n.	maziwa ya mtindi	crème (f)	cream
phrase	maziwa ya unga	lait en poudre	powdered milk
n.	maziwa yaliyoenguliwa	lait (m) écrémé	skim milk
n.	mazungumzo	1. conversation (f) 2. causerie (f) 3. discussion (f)	1. conversation 2. dialogue 3. discussion 4. talk
n.	mbaazi (pl. mibaazi)	pois (m)	pea
adj.	mbali	1. distant 2. à part 3. loin	1. aloof 2. apart 3. far
adj.	mbali mbali	différent	different
prep.	mbali na	loin de	far from
adv.	mbali zaide	plus loin	farther
n.	mbegu	semence (f)	seed
adv.	mbele	devant	1. ahead 2. in front of
prep.	mbele ya	avant	before
adv.	mbele ya, kabla ya	avant de (place) avant (time)	before
adv.	mbele zaidi	plus	further

parts of speech	swahili	french	english
n.	Mbelgiji	Belgique (f)	Belgium
n. & adj.	mbili	deux (m)	two
n.	mbinguni	ciel (m)	heaven
adv.	mbio, upesi	rapidement	quickly
n.	mboga	1. courge (f) 2. légume (m)	1. squash (botanical) 2. vegetable
n.	mbolea	engrais (m)	fertilizer
n., med	mboni ya jicho	pupille (f) de l'oeil	pupil, (eye)
n.	mbu	moustique (m)	mosquito
n.	mbuni	caféier (m)	coffee plant
n.	mbuzi	chèvre (f)	goat
n.	mbwa	chien (m)	dog
n.	mbweha	renard (m)	fox
n.	mchaguo	élection (f)	election
n.	mchana	journée (f)	daytime
n.	mchana kutwa	toute la journée	day long, all
n.	mchanga (pl. michanga)	sable (m)	sand
n.	mchanganyiko (pl. michanganyiko)	mélange (m)	mixture
n.	mchawi (pl. wachawi)	sorcier (m)	witch
n.	mchele (pl. michele)	riz (m)	rice
n.	mchezo (pl. michezo)	jeu (f)	game
n.	mchirizi	caniveau (m)	gutter
n.	mchukuzi	porteur (m)	porter
n.	mchumba	fiancé (m)	fiancé
n.	mchungaji (pl. wachungaji)	berger (m)	shepherd
n.	mchungaji wa roho	pasteur (m)	pastor
n.	mchuzi (pl. michuzi)	jus (m) de viande 2. sauce (f) 3. soupe (f)	1. gravy 2. sauce 3. soup
n.	mchuzi wa nyanya	ketchup (m)	ketchup
n.	mdanganyifu (pl. wadanganyifu)	escroc (m)	cheater
n.	mdomo (pl. midomo)	lèvre (f)	lip
n.	mdudu (pl. wadudu)	insecte (m)	insect
phrase	mdukizi	touche-à-tout	meddler
n.	Mei; mwezi wa tano wa mwaka wa kizingu	mai (m)	May
adv.	melini, chomboni	a' bord de	aboard
n.	mende	cancrelat (m)	cockroach
n.	meta	compteur (m)	meter
n.	methali	proverbe (m)	proverb

parts of speech	swahili	french	english
n.	meza	1. table (f) 2. bureau (m)	1. table 2. desk
n.	mfalme (pl. wafalme)	roi (m)	king
n.	mfano (pl. mifano)	1. analogie (f) 2. comparaison (f) 3. exemple (m) 4. ressemblance (f) 5. symbole (m)	1. analogy 2. comparison 3. example 4. likeness 5. symbol
n.	mfano wenye mafundisho	parabole (f)	parable
n.	mfanya kazi	travailleur	worker
n.	mfanyi biashara	commerçant (m)	trader
n.	mfereji (pl. mifereji)	1. canal (m) 2. fossé (m)	1. channel 2. ditch
n.	mfu (pl. wafu)	les morts	dead person
n.	mfuko (pl. mifuko)	1. sac (m) 2. poche (f)	1. bag 2. pouch 3. pocket 4. sack
n. med	mfuko wa pumbu	scrotum	scrotum
n.	mfulizo	continuation (f)	continuation
n.	mfumu (pl. wafumu)	docteur (m) de sorcière	witch doctor
n.	mfungwa (pl. wafungwa)	prisonnier (m)	prisoner
n.	mfupa (pl. mifupa)	os (m)	bone
n., med	mfupa wa mkono katkati ya kiko na bega	humérus	humerus
x	mganga (pl. waganga)	docteur (m), médecin (m)	doctor (academic, medicine)
n.	mgawo	division (f)	division
n.	mgeni (pl. wageni)	1. étranger (m) 2. invité (m), invitée (f)	1. foreigner 2. guest 3. visitor
n., med	mgogoro	l'impasse	deadlock
n., med	mgongo	dos, (m)	back (of a person)
adj. & n.	mgonjwa (pl. wagonjwa)	1. infirme (m,f) 2. malade (f)	1. invalid 2. sick person
n.	mguu (pl. miguu)	1. pied (m) 2. jambe (f)	1. foot 2. leg
n.	mhalifu	criminel (m), criminelle (f)	criminal
n.	Mhindi	Indien (m)	Indian
n.	mhubiri (pl. wahubiri)	prédicateur (m)	preacher
n.	mhunzi	forgeron (m)	blacksmith
adj. & n.	mia	cent (m)	hundred (one hundred)
n.	mia kenda	neuf cents	nine hundred
n.	mia mbili	deux cents	two hundred
n.	mia nne	quatre cents	four hundred
n.	mia saba	sept cents	seven hundred
n.	mia sita	six cents	six hundred
n.	mia tano	cinq cents	five hundred
n.	mia tatu	trois cents	three hundred
n.	mifugo	bétail (m)	cattle

parts of speech	swahili	french	english
adv.	mikono bule	avoir les mains vides	empty-handed, (to be)
adv.	milele	pour toujours	forever
n.	mimba	1. embryon (m) 2. foetus 3. grossesse (f)	1. embryo 2. fetus 3. pregnancy
pronoun	mimi	1. Je 2. moi	1. I 2. me
pronoun	mimi mwenyewe	moi-même	myself
phrase	Mimi ni mgonjwa.	Je suis malade.	I am ill.
n., med	minyoo	vers (ascaris)	intestinal worms
n.	miwani	lunettes (f)	glasses (eye)
n.	mizigo	bagages (m pl.)	luggage
n.	mjane (pl. wajane)	veuf (m)	widower
n.	mjane (pl. wajane)	veuve (f)	widow
n.	mjengaji (pl. wajengaji)	constructeur (m)	builder
n.	Mjeremani, Kidachi	allemand (m)	German
n.	mji (pl. miji)	1. ville (f) 2. cité (f) 3. agglomération (f)	1. city 2. town
n.	mji mkuu	capitale (f)	capital (city)
n., med	mji wa mimba	utérus	uterus
n.	mjinga (pl. wajinga)	ignare (m,f)	ignoramus
n.	mjomba (pl. wajomba)	oncle (m) maternel	uncle, maternal
n.	mjukuu	petit-fils (m),petit-fille (f)	grandchild
n.	mjumbe	prédécesseur (m)	precursor
n	mjumbe (pl. wajumbe)	messager (m)	messenger
n.	mjusi	lézard (m)	lizard
n.	mkaguaji	examinateur (m)	examiner
n.	mkahawa (pl. mikahawa)	café (m) {endroit où l'on boit le café}	café
n.	mkale	ancêtre (m)	ancestor
n.	mkalimani	interprète (m,f)	interpreter
n.	mkana Mungu	athée (m,f)	atheist
n.	mkangazi	acajou (f)	mahogany
n.	mkate (pl. mikate)	pain (m)	bread
n.	mkato	section (f)	section
n.	mkeka (pl. mikeka)	paillasson (m), herbe	mat, grass woven
n.	mkia (pl. mikia)	queue (f)	tail
n.	mkichaa	fou (m), folle (f)	lunatic
n.	mkimbizi	réfugié (m)	refugee
n., med	mkojo	urine	urine
n.	mkombozi	racheterier	redeemer
n.	mkombozi (pl. wakombozi)	remplaçant (m,f)	replacement

parts of speech	swahili	french	english
n.	mkono (pl. mikono)	1. bras (m) 2. main (f) 3. trompe (de l'éléphant) (f)	1. arm 2. hand 3. trunk (of elephant)
n.	mkopo	fardeau (m)	loan (borrowing)
n.	Mkristo	Chrétien (m)	Christian
n.	mkuki (pl. mikuki)	lance (f)	spear
n.	mkulima	paysan (m), paysanne (f)	peasant
n.	mkulima (pl. wakulima)	cultivateur (m)	cultivator
n.	mkundu	anus (m)	anus
n.	mkunga	sage-femme (f)	midwife
n.	mkutano (pl. mikutano)	1. foule (f) 2. réunion (f) 3. rassemblement (m)	1. crowd 2. meeting 3. gathering
adj. & n.	mkuu wa jeshi	général (m)	general
n.	mlafi (pl. walafi)	goinfre (m)	glutton
n.	mlango (pl. milango)	1. entrée (f) 2. but (m) 3. porte (f)	1. door 2. goal (as in football) 3. entrance
n.	mlango wa nje	porte (f)/barrière (f)	gate
n.	mlevi (pl. walevi)	ivrogne (m)	drunkard
n.	mlima (pl. milima)	1. colline (f) 2. montagne (f)	1. hill 2 mountain
n.	mlima wa moto	volcan (m)	volcano
n.	mlimaji (pl. walimaji)	fermier (m)	farmer
n.	mlinzi (pl. walinzi), zamu	1. garde (f) 2. gardien (m)	guard
n.	mluzi	sifflet (m)	whistle
n.	mbuti (pl. wabuti)	batwa	pygmy
n.	mmea (pl. mimea)	plante (f)	plant
n.	mnara (pl. minara)	tour (f)	tower
n.	mngoje	gardien (m)	watchman
adv.	mno	extrêmement	extremely
n.	mnyama (pl. wanyama)	animal (m)	animal
n.	mnyanganyi (pl. wanyanganyi)	voleur (m)	1. robber 2. thief
n.	mnyororo (pl. minyororo)	chaîne (f)	chain
adj. & n.	moja	un, une	one
n.	momonyoko wa ardhi	érosion (f)	erosion
n.	moshi	fumée (f)	smoke
n.	motakaa	1. automobile (f) 2. voiture (f) 3. véhicule	1. automobile 2. car
n.	motakaa ya abiria	autobus (m)	bus
n.	moto (pl. mioto)	feu (m)	fire
n.	moyo (pl. mioyo)	cœur (m)	heart
n.	moyo nafsi	âme (f)	soul
n.	moyo, nafasi	moi (m), personne (f)	self
n.	mpaka	limitation (f)	limitation

parts of speech	swahili	french	english
n.	mpaka (pl. mipaka)	1 .frontière 2. borne (f)	1. frontier (border) 2. limit 3. boundary
phrase	mpaka sasa	ici et y là	hither and yon
n.	mpala	gazelle (f)	gazelle
n.	mpato	revenu (m)	income
n.	mpelelezi (pl. wapelelezi)	espion (m)	spy
n.	mpenzi	copain (m)	boyfriend
n.	mpenzi	copine (f)	girlfriend
n.	mpini, shikio	anse (f)	handle
n.	mpira	pneu (m)	tire
n.	mpira (pl. mipira)	1. balle (m) 2. ballon (m) 3. caoutchouc (m)	1. ball 2. football (U.S. soccer ball) 3. rubber
n.	mpishi (pl. wapishi)	cuisinier (m)	cook
n.	mpitaji	passant (m)	passerby
n.	mpumbavu (pl. wapumbavu)	bouffon (m)	fool
n.	mpwa	neveu (m)	nephew
n.	mpwa wa kike	nièce (f)	niece
n.	mrija	entonnoir (m)	funnel
n.	mrungula	chantage (m)	blackmail
n.	msaada	1. maintien (m) 2. soutien (m) 3. secours financier	1. maintenance 2. backing (support) 3. aid, financial
n.	msafa (pl. misafa)	1. alignement (m) 2. rang (m)	1. alignment 2. row
n.	msafiri (pl. wasafiri)	voyageur (m), voyageuse (f)	traveler
n.	msaidizi	assistant (m), assistante (f)	assistant
n.	msalaba (pl. misalaba)	croix (f)	cross
n.	mshahara (pl. mishahara)	1. salarie (m) 2. appointements (m)	1. wages 2. salary
n.	mshairi	poète (m)	poet
n.	mshale (pl. mishale)	flèche (f)	arrow
n.	mshangao (pl. mishangao)	merveille (f)	wonder
adj. & n.	mshenzi (pl. washenzi)	païen (m), païenne (f)	heathen
n.	mshinda (pl. washinda)	vainqueur (m)	winner
n.	mshipa (pl. mishipa)	1. nerf (m) 2. muscle (m)	1. nerve 2. muscle
n.	mshipa mkubwa wa damu	artère (f)	artery
n.	mshipi (pl. mishipi)	ceinture (f)	belt
n.	mshiriki katika kazi	associé (m), associée (f)	partner
n.	mshitaki (pl. washitaki)	plaignant (m,f)	plaintiff
n.	mshtuko, kamsa	alarme (f)	alarm
n.	mshuhuda (pl. washuhuda)	témoin (m)	witness

parts of speech	swahili	french	english
n.	**mshumaa**	bougie (f)	candle
n.	**msiba**	adversité (f)	adversity
n.	**msiba mkuu**	catastrophe (f)	catastrophe
n.	**msichana (pl. wasichana)**	jeune fille (f)	girl
n	**msikwao**	sans abri	homeless
n.	**msikwao**	proscrit (m), proscrite (f)	outcast
n.	**msimamizi (pl. wasimamizi)**	1. directeur (m) 2. steward (m) 3. patron (m), patronne (f)	1. director 2. steward 3. boss 4. manager
n.	**msimiko**	érection (f)	erection
n.	**msingi (pl. misingi)**	fondation (f)	foundation
n.	**mstadi, (pl. wastadi)**	artiste (m)	artist
n.	**mstari (pl. mistari)**	ligne (f)	line
n.	**msumari (pl. misumari)**	1. épingle (f) 2. clou (m)	1. pin 2. nail (metal)
n.	**msumeno**	scie (f)	saw
n.	**mswaki (pl. miswaki)**	brosse (f) à dents	toothbrush
n.	**mtai (pl. mitai)**	égratignure (f)	scratch
n.	**mtaka kazi au cheo fulani**	candidat (m)	candidate
n.	**mtama (pl. mitama)**	1. sorgho 2. grain (m)	1. sorghum 2. millet
n.	**mtangulizi (pl. watangulizi)**	précurseur	forerunner
adj. & n.	**mtawa (pl. watawa)**	célibataire (m, f)	unmarried person
n.	**mtawa mwanamume**	moine (m)	monk
n.	**mtawa wa kike**	bonne sœur (f)	nun
n.	**mtego (pl. mitego)**	piège (m)	trap, snare
n.	**mtenda (pl. watenda)**	acteur (m)	actor
n.	**mtesi (pl. watesi)**	persécuteur (m)	persecutor
n.	**mteteaji**	défenseur (m)	advocate
n.	**mti (pl. miti)**	arbre (m)	tree
n.	**mti wa jamii ya mnazi**	palmier	palm tree
n.	**mtindo**	type (m)	type
n.	**mtini**	figuier (m)	fig tree
n.	**mto (pl. mito)**	1. fleuve (m) 2. oreiller (m)	1. river 2. pillow
n.	**mtoto (pl. watoto); mwana (pl. wana)**	enfant (m,f); fils; fille	child
n.	**mtoto mdogo**	un nouveau-né	infant
n.	**mtoto muchanga**	nouveau né	baby (newborn)
n.	**mtoto wa bandia**	poupée (f)	doll
n.	**mtoto wa kipepeo**	chenille (f)	caterpillar
n.	**mtoto wa kiume**	garçon (m)	boy
n.	**mtu (pl. watu)**	personne (f)	person
adj. & n.	**mtu asiye Mkristo**	païen (m)	pagan

parts of speech	swahili	french	english
n.	mtu asiyeoa	célibataire (m)	bachelor
n.	mtu wa kazi	employé (m)	employee
n., med	mtulinga	1. clavicule 2. omoplate	1. clavicle 2. scapula
n.	mtumbwi (pl. mitumbwi)	pirogue (f)	canoe (dugout)
n.	mtume (pl. mitume)	apôtre (m)	apostle
n.	mtumishi (pl. watumishi)	domestique (m,f)	servant (male or female)
n.	mtumwa (pl. watumwa)	esclave (m,f)	slave
n.	mtungaji (pl. watungaji)	inventeur (m)	inventor
n.	mtungi (pl. mitungi)	1. cruche (f) 2. pot (m) de l'eau	1. jug 2. water pot
n.	mtunza bustani	jardinier (m)	gardener
n.	mubilingani (pl. mibilingani)	aubergine (f)	eggplant
phrase	Muchana muzuli.	Ayez la bonne journée	Have a good morning.
n.	muda	1. délai (m) 2. durée (f) 3. période (f)	1. deadline 2. duration 3. period (of time)
n.	muda wa kati	intérim (m)	interim
adj.	muhimu	important	important
n.	muhindi (pl. mihindi)	maïs (m)	1. corn 2. maize
n.	muhogo, (pl. mihogo)	manioc	cassava
n.	muhtasari	œuvre (f)	summary
n.	muhuri (pl. mihuri)	cachet (m)	seal
n.	mukono wa kushoto	main gauche	hand, left
n.	mukono wa kuume	main droit	hand, right
n.	mume (pl. waume)	mari (m)	husband
n.	Mungu	Dieu (m)	God
adv.	muno	1. extrêmement 2. avec excès 3. beaucoup	1. exceedingly 2. very much
n.	mupango, matengenezo	arrangement (m)	arrangement
n.	musaada	aide (f)	help
n., med	mushipa wa damu	vaisseau sanguin	blood vessel
n.	mutakatifu (pl. watakatifu)	saint (m), sainte (f)	saint
n.	mutawala (pl. watawala)	chef (m)	ruler (person)
n., med	muundi wa mguu	tibia (os de la jambe)	tibia
n.	muwa (pl. miwa)	canne à sucre	sugar cane
n.	muziki	musique (f)	music
n.	mviringo (pl. miviringo), duara	cercle (m)	circle
n.	mvivu (pl. wavivu)	fainéant (m), fainéante (f)	lazy person
n.	mvo	torrent (m)	torrent
n.	mvua	pluie (f)	rain

parts of speech	swahili	french	english
n.	mvua ya mawe	grêle (f)	hail
n.	mvuke (pl. mivuke)	vapeur (f)	1. steam 2. vapor
n.	mvuke kama hewa	gaz (m)	gas
n.	mvulana (pl. wavulana)	jeune homme pubère	young man, (unmarried)
n.	mvunjo	fracture (f)	fracture
n.	mvuto	influence (f)	influence
n.	mvuvi (pl. wavuvi)	pêcheur (m)	fisherman
n.	mwadhimisho	célébration (f)	celebration
phrase	mwahdishi ovyo	texte rédigé	scribe
phrase	mwaka huu	cette an	this year
adv.	mwaka kwa mwaka	an après an	year after year
phrase	mwaka wa jana	an passé	last year
phrase	mwaka wa kesho	an prochain	next year
n.	mwaka, (pl. miaka)	an (m), année (f)	year
n.	mwali; kibibi (pl. vibibi)	mademoiselle (f)	1. young lady (unmarried) 2. Miss
n.	mwalimu (pl. walimu)	1. enseignant (m) 2. instituteur (m) 3. maître (m)	1. teacher 2. master
n.	mwalimu mkuu	professeur (m)	professor
n.	mwamba (pl. miamba)	roche (f)	rock
n.	mwamuzi (pl. waamuzi)	juge (m)	judge
n.	mwana (pl. wana)	fils (m)	son
n.	mwana sheria	juriste (m)	lawyer
n.	mwana wa mfalme	prince (m)	prince
n.	mwanadamu (pl. wanadamu)	homme (m)	man
n.	mwanafunzi (pl. wanafunzi)	1. élève (m,f) 2. étudiant (m)	1. pupil 2. student
n.	mwanafunzi wa kazi	apprenti (m,f)	apprentice
n.	mwanamke (pl. wanawake)	genre féminin	female
adj. & n.	mwanamume (pl. wanaume)	mâle (m)	male
n.	mwanamwali	bonne (f)	maid
n.	mwanaume (pl. wanaume)	homme (m)	man
n.	mwandishi (pl. wandishi)	secrétaire (m,f)	secretary
n.	mwangalizi	gardien (m), gardienne (f)	caretaker
n.	mwanya	ouverture (f)	gap
n.	mwanzi (pl. mianzi)	bambou (m)	bamboo
n.	mwanzo (pl. mianzo)	1. début (m) 2. commencement (m)	1. beginning 2. inception
n.	Mwarabu	Arabe (m, f)	Arab

parts of speech	swahili	french	english
n.	**mwashi**	maçon (m)	mason
n.	**mwashi aakaye kwa matofali**	ouvrier-maçon (m)	bricklayer
adj. & n.	**mwasi (pl. wawasi)**	1. rebelle (m,f) 2. insurgé (m)	1. rebel 2. insurgent
n.	**mwavuli (pl. miavuli)**	parapluie (m)	umbrella
n.	**mwendo (pl. miwendo)**	1. voyage (m) 2. rythme (m) 3. mouvement (m)	1. trip 2. journey 3. rhythm 4. movement
n.	**mwenendo (pl. mienendo)**	1. conduite (f) 2. comportement (m)	1. behavior 2. conduct
n.	**mwenge (pl. miwenge)**	torche (f)	torch
n.	**mwenye akili maalum**	génie (m)	genius
n.	**mwenye amri**	chef (m)	commander
n.	**mwenye kuwapo**	spectateur (m), spectatrice (f)	bystander
n.	**mwenye ukoma**	lépreux (m)	leper
n.	**mwenye-kiti**	président (m)	chairman
n.	**mwenyeji (pl. wenyeji)**	indigène (m,f)	native
n.	**mwenyeji wa Canada**	Canadien (m)	Canadian
n.	**mwenzi**	1. compagnon (m), compagne (f) 2. camarade (m,f)	1. mate (a pair of things) 2. companion 3. associate
n. & adj.	**mweusi**	Noir (m), Noire (f)	black (for person)
n.	**mwezi (pl. miezi)**	1. mois (m) 2. lune (f)	1. month 2. moon
phrase	**mwezi kesho**	mois prochain	next month
n.	**mwiba (pl. miiba)**	épine (f)	thorn
n.	**mwigo sawasawa**	fac-similé (m)	facsimile
n.	**mwiko (pl. miiko)**	1. truelle (f) 2. tabou (m)	1. trowel 2. taboo
n.	**mwili (pl. miili)**	corps (m)	body
n.	**mwindaji (pl. waindaji)**	chausseur (m)	hunter
adv.	**mwisho**	1. enfin 2. finalement	1. at last 2. finally
n.	**mwisho (pl. miisho)**	1. conclusion (f) 2. terme (m) 3. fin (f)	1. conclusion 2. end
n.	**mwito (pl. miito)**	appel (m)	call
n.	**mwito wa kuku kwa watoto wake**	bruit (m)	cluck
n.	**mwitu**	1. forêt (f) 2. jungle (f) 3. brousse (f)	1. forest 2. jungle
adj.	**mwivi**	voleur	thieving
n.	**mwoga**	lâche (m,f)	coward
n.	**mwokozi**	1. libérateur (m) 2. sauveur (m)	1. rescuer 2. savior
n.	**mwombaji (pl. waombaji)**	mendiant (m)	beggar

parts of speech	swahili	french	english
n.	mwongo	menteur (m), menteuse (f)	liar
n.	mwuaji (pl. waji)	assassin (m)	murderer
n.	mwuguzi	infirmière (f), infirmier (m); garde malade	nurse
n.	mwujiza	miracle (m)	miracle
n.	mwungano	alliance (f)	alliance
n.	mwungwana	monsieur (m)	gentleman
n.	mwuza (pl. wauza)	vendeur (m), vendeuse (f)	vendor
n.	mwuza nyama	boucher (m)	butcher
n.	mzabibu (pl. mizabibu)	vigne (f)	vine
n.	mzao (pl. wazao)	progéniture (f)	offspring
n.	mzazi (pl. wazazi)	père (m), mère (f)	parent
n.	mzee (pl. wazee)	vieillard (m)	old man
n.	mzigo (pl. mizigo)	1. fardeau (m) 2. charge (f)	1. burden 2. load
n.	mzinga	ruche (f)	beehive (empty)
n.	mzingo	circonférence (f)	circumference
n.	mzio	allergie (f)	allergy
n.	mzizi (pl. mizizi)	racine (f)	root
adj.	Mzungu (pl. Wazungu)	européen	European
n.	mzungu (pl. wazungu)	le blanc	white person
conj.	na	et	and
n.	nabii (pl. manabii)	prophète (m)	prophet, seer
phrase	Naelewa.	Je ne comprends pas.	I don't understand.
n.	nafaka	grain (m)	grain
n.	nafasi	1. occasion (f) 2. relâche (m) 3. espace (m)	1. opportunity 2. respite 3. space
phrase	Nafikiri...	Je pense que...	think that..., I
phrase	Nafurahi kukufahamu.	Enchanté de rencontrer avec toi.	Nice to meet you. (one person)
phrase	Nahitaji mwuguzi sasa.	J'ai besoin une infirmière tout de suite.	I need a nurse right away.
phrase	Nahitaji...	J'ai besoin...	I need...
interj.	Nakubali.	D'accord.	O.K.
n.	namna	1. genre (m) 2. sorte (f)	1. kind (species) 2. sort
adv.	namna gani	comment	how
n.	namna ya fulana nzito	pull-over (m)	sweater
n.	nanasi (pl. mananasi)	ananas (m)	pineapple
adj. & n.	nane	huit (m)	eight
n.	nanga	ancre (f)	anchor
phrase	nani (Unatafuta nani?)	qui (Qu'est-ce qui tu cherches?)	who (Who are you looking for?)
phrase	Nasema kidogo Kiswahili.	Je parle un peu le kiswahili.	I speak a little Swahili.

parts of speech	swahili	french	english
phrase	**Nasikia hafifu.**	Je suis fatigué.	I am tired.
phrase	**Nasikia kiu.**	J'ai soif.	I am thirsty.
phrase	**Nataka dawa kwa kuhara.**	J'ai besoin de quelque chose contre la diarrhée.	I want something to treat diarrhea.
phrase	**Nataka...**	Je voudrais..., Je veux...	1. I want... 2. I am looking for
n.	**nauli**	prix (m)	fare, price
n.	**ncha**	pointe (f)	point
adj.	**nchi**	1. campagnard 2. terre (f)	1. country 2. land
n.	**nchi ya Africa**	continent africain (m)	African continent
n.	**nchi ya Amerika**	États-Unis du Amérique (f)	America, US of
n.	**ndama {shavu la mguu}**	veau (m) {mollet}	calf {calf - lower leg}
adv. prep.	**ndani ya**	dedans (m)	inside
n.	**ndege**	1. avion (m) 2. oiseau (m)	1. airplane 2. bird (small)
n.	**ndege mbaya**	augure (m), mauvais	omen, bad
n.	**ndege njema**	augure (m), bon	omen, good
n.	**ndevu (poil de barbe = udevu)**	barbe (f)	beard
adv.	**ndi**	voici	here is
n.	**ndimu**	citron (m) vert	lime (fruit)
adv.	**ndiyo; ndivyo; naam**	oui	yes
n	**ndizi**	banane (f)	banana
n.	**ndoa**	mariage (m)	marriage
n.	**ndoana**	hameçon (m)	fish-hook
n.	**ndobani, kulabu**	hameçon (m)	hook
n.	**ndoo**	seau (m)	1. bucket 2. pail
n.	**ndoto**	rêve (m)	dream
n.	**ndugu**	relatif (m)	relative
n.	**ndugu, kaka**	frère (m)	brother
n.	**neema**	grâce (f)	grace
n.	**neno (pl. maneno)**	mot (m)	word
n.	**neno la kuchekesha**	plaisanterie (f)	joke
phrase	**Neno...lina maana gani?**	Que signifie ce mot?	word mean?, What does this
n.	**ngabo**	bouclier (m)	shield
adv.	**ngambo**	de l'autre côté	other side
n.	**ngamia**	chameau (m)	camel
n.	**ngano**	blé (m)	wheat
n.	**ngazi**	1. échelle (f) 2. escalier (m)	1. ladder 2. staircase
phrase	**Ngo jasaa kidogo.**	Attends une minute.	minute., Just a
interj.	**Ngoja!**	Attends!	Wait!
n.	**ngoma**	tambour (m)	drum

parts of speech	swahili	french	english
n.	ngombe	vache (f)	cow
n.	ngome	château (m)	castle
n.	ngozi	peau (f)	1. skin 2. pelt
n.	ngozi laini ya manyoya	fourrure (f)	fur
n.	ngumi	poing (m)	fist
n.	nguo	vêtements (m)	1. clothes 2. garment
n.	nguo ya kimia	lacet (m)	lace
n.	nguo ya kutandika kitandani	drap (m) de lit	sheet
n.	nguruwe	cochon (m)	pig
n.	nguvu; bidii	1. force (f) 2. vertu (f) 3. vigueur (f)	1. strength 2. virtue 3. energy
n.	nguvu ya kushika	ténacité (f)	tenacity
n.	nguzo	pilier (m)	pillar
n.	ng'ombe dume	taureau (m)	bull
verb	ni	être	is (to be)
phrase	Ni bei gani?	Combien est ceci?	How much does this cost?
phrase	Ni ghali mno.	C'est trop cher.	That's too expensive. (thing)
phrase	Ni karibu?	C'est près?	Is it close?
phrase	Ni mamoja kwangu.	Pas de problème.	I don't mind.
phrase	Ni mbali?	C'est loin?	Is it far?
x	Nibeyisana.	C'est trop cher.	That is too expensive. (service)
n.	nidhamu	discipline (f)	discipline
phrase	Nimeshiba.	Je suis rassasié.	I am full.
phrase	Nina agizo la daktari.	Voici une ordonnance de mon médecin.	Here is my prescription for medicine.
phrase	Nina maumiva ya kichwa.	J'ai mal à la tête.	I've got a headache.
phrase	Nina njaa.	J'ai faim.	I am hungry.
phrase	Ninajua.	Je sais (or) Je connais.	I know.
phrase	Ninakwenda uwanja wa ndege.	Je vais à l'aéroport.	I am going to the airport.
phrase	Ninakwenda...	Je vais à...	I am going to...
phrase	Ninapenda...	J'aime...	I like...
pronoun	ninyi	vous	you (plural)
phrase	Nisikia furaha.	Je suis heureux.	I am happy.
phrase	Niwie radhi.	Je m'excuse. Pardon!	Excuse me.
n.	njaa	faim (f)	hunger
n.	njaa kuu	famine (f)	famine
adv.	nje	dehors	1. out 2. outside
prep.	nje ya	en dehors de	outside of

parts of speech	swahili	french	english
n.	njia	1. moyen (m) 2. rue (f) 3. chemin (m)	1. means (of doing something) 2. street 3. road
n.	njia panda	carrefour (m)	crossroads
n.	njia ya kufikia	accès (m)	access
n.	njia ya kufikia	sentier (m)	path
n.	njia ya kukatiliza	raccourci (m)	short cut
n. & adj.	njia ya pili	choix (m); autre	alternative
n.	njiwa	pigeon (m)	pigeon
n.	njuga	grelot (m)	bell
adj. & n.	nne	quatre (m)	four
n.	nondo	papillon (m) de nuit	moth
verb	nong'ona	chuchoter	whisper, to
n.	Novemba	novembre (m)	November
n.	nta	cire (f)	wax
n.	nukta	moment (m)	moment
n.	nuru	lumière (f)	light
n.	nusu	moitié (f)	half
adv.	nusu	demi	half
n.	nyama	viande (f)	meat
n.	nyama (kimbibi)	chair (f) (avoir la chair de poule)	flesh (to have goose bumps)
n.	nyama ya nguruwe	porc (m)	pork, hog
n.	nyani	singe (m)	ape
n.	nyanya	tomate (f)	tomato
n.	nyati	buffle (m)	buffalo
n.	nyoka	1. cobra (m) 2. serpent (m)	1. cobra 2. snake
n., med	nyongo	1. bile (f) 2. vésicule biliaire	1. bile 2. gallbladder
n.	nyota	étoile (f)	star
n.	nyoya	plume (f)	feather
n.	nyuki	abeille (f)	bee
adv.	nyuma	en arrière	backwards
adv, n. prep.	nyuma ya	derrière (m)	behind
n.	nyumba	maison (f)	dwelling place, house
prep.	nyumba	chez	home
n.	nyumba ndogo	gîte (m)	cottage
n.	nyumba ya mfaime	cour (f)	court
n.	nyumba ya sayansi	laboratoire (m)	laboratory
n.	nyundo	marteau (m)	hammer
n.	nyushi	sourcil (m)	eyebrow
n.	nzige	sauterelle (f)	locust
phrase	Nzuri kabisa.	C'est bien.	It is good.

parts of speech	swahili	french	english
n.	**Ogusti, mwezi wa nane wa mwaka wa kizungu**	août	August
n.	**Oktoba**	octobre (m)	October
n.	**orodha ya vyakula**	menu (m)	menu
n.	**oteo**	embuscade (f)	ambush
n.	**paa**	1. antilope (f) 2. gazelle (f)	1. antelope 2. gazelle
adj. & n.	**pacha**	jumeau (m), jumelle (f)	twin
n.	**pafu**	poumon (m)	lung
n.	**pahali (pl. pahali)**	endroit (m)	place
n.	**paja (pl. mapaja)**	cuisse (f)	thigh
n.	**paji la uso**	front (m)	forehead
n.	**paka**	chat (m), chatte (f)	cat
adv.	**pale**	là-bas	over there
adj.	**pale pale**	instantané	instantaneous
n.	**palipo katikati hasa**	centre (f)	center, in the
n.	**pamba**	coton (m)	cotton
n.	**pambazuko**	aube (f)	dawn
adv.	**pamoja**	ensemble	together
n.	**panga (pl. mapanga)**	machette	machete
n.	**pango (pl. mapango)**	galerie souterraine	cave
n.	**pango la mnyama**	antre (m)	den
n.	**panja**	temple (m)	temple
n.	**panya**	rat (m)	rat
n.	**panya mdogo**	souris (f)	mouse
n.	**panzi (pl. mapanzi)**	sauterelle (f)	grasshopper
n.	**papai**	papaye	papaya
n.	**papo la moyo**	palpitation (f)	palpitation
n.	**Pasaka**	Pâques (m)	Easter
n.	**pasi**	fer (m) à repasser	iron (for clothes)
adj.	**pasipo maana**	frivole	frivolous
adj.	**pasipo nguvu**	impotent	impotent
n.	**pata (pl. mapata)**	gond (m)	hinge
adj.	**peke yake**	seul	alone
n.	**pembe (pl. mapembe)**	1. corne (f) 2. coin (m)	1. horn (of animal) 2. corner
n.	**pembea**	balançoire (f)	swing (for child to use)
adv.	**pengine**	1. ailleurs 2. parfois	1. elsewhere 2. sometimes 3. somewhere else
prep.	**penye, kwa**	à	at
phrase	**pepo**	toute poésie moderne	spirit, harmful
n.	**pepo mbaya**	démon (m)	demon
n.	**pera**	goyave	guava

parts of speech	swahili	french	english
n.	pete	anneau (m)	ring
adv.	pia	1. aussi 2. complètement 3. tout à fait	1. as well 2. completely 3. totally
n.	pia ya goti	rotule (du genou)	knee cap
n.	picha iliyopigwa kwa kamera	photographie (f)	photograph
n.	picha ya mtu	portrait (m)	portrait
n.	picha, sanamu	tableau (m)	picture
verb	piga kikumbo	pousser pour déplacer	push away, to
n.	pigano (pl. mapigano)	bataille (f)	battle
adv.	pikipiki	motocyclette (f)	motorcycle
n.	pilipili manga	poivre (m)	pepper
n.	pinga ya mikono	menotte (f)	handcuffs
n.	pingamizi	objection (f)	objection
phrase	po pote	1. n'importe où 2. quelque part	1. anywhere 2. somewhere
adv.	po pote; kila mahali	partout	everywhere, throughout
adv.	polepole	1. facilement 2. tout doucement 3. lentement	1. easily 2. gently 3. slowly
n.	polisi (pl. mapolisi)	agent (m) de police	police agent
n.	pombe	bière (f)	beer
n.	porojo	bavardage (m)	gossip
n.	posta	poste (f)	1. mail 2. post
n.	povu	1. bulle (f) 2. mousse (f) 3. écume (f)	1. bubble 2. foam 3. froth
n.	pua	1. nez (m) 2. acier	1. nose 2. steel
n., med	pumbu (pl. mapumbu)	testicule (m)	testicle
n.	pumzi	haleine (f)	breath
n.	punda	âne (m)	donkey
n.	punda milia	zèbre (m)	zebra
n.	pwani	plage (f)	1. beach 2. coast (of river)
n.	pweza	pieuvre (f)	octopus
n.	radi	tonnerre (m)	thunder
n.	rafiki	ami (m), amie (f)	friend
n.	raha	aise (f)	ease
n.	rahani	garantie (f)	guarantee
adj.	rahisi	bon marché	cheap
n.	rai	opinion (f)	opinion
n.	raia	citoyen (m)	citizen
n.	ramani	carte (f) géographique	map
n.	rangi	1. couleur (f) 2. peinture (f)	1. color 2. peinture (f)
adj.	rangi ya kunde	brun	brown

parts of speech	swahili	french	english
adj. & n.	rangi ya zambarau bivu	violet (m)	purple
n.	rehema	miséricorde (f)	mercy
n.	risasi ya bunduki	balle (f)	bullet
n.	roho	esprit (m)	spirit
n.	Roho Mtakatifu	Saint-Esprit (m)	Holy Spirit
n.	roho, kizuka	fantôme (m)	ghost
n.	ruhusa	1. permission (f) 2. vacances (m)	1. permission 2. time off
n.	ruhusa ya kupita	passeport (m)	passport
n.	ruhusu	patente (f)	license
n.	rushwa	pot-de-vin	bribe
n.	rutuba	humidité (f)	moisture
n.	saa	1. horloge (f) 2. heure (f) 3. montre (f)	1. clock 2. hour 3. watch
phrase	Saa ngapi?	Que est-ce que temps?	time?, At what
n.	saa sita usika	minuit (m)	midnight
adj. & n.	saba	sept (m)	seven
n.	sababu	cause (f)	cause
adj. & n.	sabini	soixante-dix (m)	seventy
n.	sabini na kenda	soixante-dix-neuf	seventy-nine
n.	sabini na mbili	soixante-douze	seventy-two
n.	sabini na moja	soixante et onze	seventy-one
n.	sabini na nane	soixante-dix-huit	seventy-eight
n.	sabini na nne	soixante-quatorze	seventy-four
n.	sabini na saba	soixante-dix-sept	seventy-seven
n.	sabini na sita	soixante-seize	seventy-six
n.	sabini na tano	soixante-quinze	seventy-five
n.	sabini na tatu	soixante-treize	seventy-three
n.	sabuni	savon (m)	soap
n.	saburi	patience (f)	patience
phrase	Safari njema.	Ayez la bon voyage.	Have a good trip.
adj.	safi	1. propre 2. exact	1. clean 2. correct
n.	safura	jaunisse (f)	jaundice
n.	sahani	1. plat (m) 2. assiette (f)	1. dish 2. plate
adj.	sahihi	exact	accurate
n.	sahihi	approbation (f)	endorsement
n.	sakafu ya chini	plancher (m)	floor
n.	saladi	laitue (f)	lettuce
n.	salamu	salutation (f)	greetings
n.	samaki	poisson (m)	fish
n.	sambamba	parallèle (m)	parallel

parts of speech	swahili	french	english
adv.	**sana**	1. fortement 2. très	1. strongly 2. very
adv.	**sana kidogo**	honnêtement	fairly
adj.	**sana, tele**	abondant	abundant
n.	**sanamu ya kuabudiwa**	idole (f)	idol
n.	**sanduku (pl. masanduku)**	1. caisse (f) 2. boîte (f)	1. chest (crate) 2. box
n.	**sanduku la maiti**	cercueil (m)	coffin
n.	**sarafu**	pièce (f) de monnaie	coin
n.	**sarafu ya kifaransa**	franc (m)	franc
adv.	**sasa**	maintenant	now
adv.	**sasa hivi**	1. en ce moment 2. tout de suite	1. right now 2. right away
n.	**sauti**	voix (f)	voice
adj.	**sawa**	1. égal 2. plat 3. droit	1. equal 2. level 3. straight
adv.	**sawa**	également	equally
n.	**sawa; badala**	équivalent (m)	equivalent
adv.	**sawasawa**	naturellement	precisely
n.	**sehemu**	portion (f)	portion
n., med	**sehemu ya chini ya tumbo kubwa**	gros intestin	colon
n., med	**sekeneko**	syphilis	syphilis
n.	**seluji**	neige (f)	snow
n.	**semeki**	beaux-parents (m)	in-laws
n.	**senti**	monnaie (f)	change (coins)
n.	**Septemba**	septembre (m)	September
n.	**seremala (pl. maseremala)**	menuisier (m)	carpenter
n.	**serkali**	1. gouvernement (m) 2. administration (f)	1. government 2. administration
n.	**shaba**	1. cuivre jaune (m) 2. cuivre (m)	1. brass 2. copper
n.	**shaba nyeusi**	bronze (m)	bronze
n.	**shabaha**	cible (f)	target
n.	**shahidi**	martyr (m), martyre (f)	martyr
n.	**shaka**	1. doute (m) 2. appréhension	1. doubt 2. misgiving
n.	**shamba (pl. mashamba)**	1. champ (m) 2. jardin (m) 3. plantation (f) 4. campagne (f)	1. field 2. garden 3. plantation 4. rural
n.	**shamba la mizabibu**	vigne (f)	vineyard
n.	**shambilio**	agression (f)	aggression
n.	**shambulio**	charge (f)	charge (in battle)
n.	**shangazi (pl. mashangzi)**	tante paternelle	aunt (father's sister)
n.	**shati**	chemise (f)	shirt

191

parts of speech	swahili	french	english
n.	shauri	délibération (f)	deliberation
n.	shauri (pl. mashauri)	conseil (m)	advice
n.	shavu la uso	joue (f)	cheek
n.	shayiri	orge (f)	barley
n.	sheria	loi (f)	law
n.	sheria ya serkali	constitution (f)	constitution
n.	sherizi	résine (f)	glue
n.	shimo (pl. mashimo)	1. cavité (f) 2. fosse (f) 3. tunnel (m)	1. cavity 2. pit 3. tunnel
n.	shindano (pl. mashindano)	compétition (f)	competition
n.	shingo (mashingo)	cou (m)	neck
n.	shirika	1. coopération (f) 2. association (f)	1. cooperation 2. partnership
n.	shoka	hache (f)	ax
n.	shughuli	1. inquiétude (f) 2. affaire (f)	1. concern 2. business
n.	shujaa	héros (m)	hero
n.	shwari	calme (m)	calm, quiet
adv.	si	pas, non	not
adj.	si -a shari	inoffensif	harmless
pronoun	si kitu	rien	nothing
adv.	si mahali po pote	nulle part	nowhere
adj.	si mara nyingi	peu fréquent	infrequent
pronoun	si mtu	personne, ne...personne	no one
adv.	si sana	avec modération	moderately
adj.	si ya kawaida	irrégulier	irregular
n.	siagi	beurre (m)	butter
n.	sidiria	soutien-gorge (m)	bra
n.	sifa	1. renommée (f) 2. éloge (m) 3. réputation (f)	1. fame 2. praise 3. reputation
phrase	sifa mbaya	avoir mauvaise réputation	reputation, to have a bad
n.	sifongo	éponge (f)	sponge
n.	sifuri	zéro (m)	zero
n.	sigara	cigare (m)	cigar
n.	sigareti	cigarette (f)	cigarette
phrase	Sijambo	Ça va bien.	I'm fine.
phrase	Sijui.	Je ne connais pas (ou) Je ne sais pas.	I don't know.
n.	siki	vinaigre (m)	vinegar
n.	sikio (pl. masikio)	oreille (f)	ear
n.	sikitiko	chagrin (m)	sorrow, deep
n.	siku	jour (m)	day

parts of speech	swahili	french	english
adv.	siku hizi	dernièrement	lately
n.	siku ya nne; alhamisi	jeudi (m)	Thursday
n.	siku yo yote ya juma isipokuwa Jumapili	jour (m) de semaine	weekday
adv.	siku zote	tout le temps	all the time
n.	sikukuu ya kuzaliza	anniversaire (m)	birthday
phrase	sikupata	ne pas trouver	unable to find
verb	sikuya vyombo vya nyimbo	jouer d'un instrument	play an instrument, to
adv.	sikuzote	toujours	always
n.	silaha	arme (f)	weapon
n.	simba	lion (m)	lion
phrase	Sina pesa.	Je n'ai pas de l'argent.	I don't have money.
phrase	Sina...	Je n'ai pas...	I don't have...
n.	sindano	aiguille (f)	needle
phrase	Sipenda...	Je n'aime pas...	I do not like...
n.	siri	secret (m)	secret
n.	siri, fumbo	mystère (m)	mystery
pronoun	sisi wenyewe	elles-même	ourselves
pronoun	sisi, siye	nous	we, us
phrase	Sisikii njaa.	J'ai ne pas faim.	I am not hungry.
adj. & n.	sita	six (m)	six
phrase	Sitaki...	Je ne veux pas...	I do not want...
adj. & n.	sitini	soixante (m)	sixty
adv.	sivyo	ça n'est pas le cas	not so; (that is not so)
phrase	Siwezi.	Je ne puis pas.	I cannot.
n.	soko (pl. masoko)	marché (m)	market
n.	sokwe	chimpanzé (m)	chimpanzee
phrase	Starehe.	Faites comme chez vous.	Feel at home.
n.	sufuria (pl. masufuria)	casserole (f)	pan, cooking
n.	sukari	1. glucose (f) 2. sucre (m)	1. glucose 2. sugar
n.	suke	épi (m)	ear (of sorghum)
n.	sultani	chef (m)	chief
n.	sumu	poison (m)	poison
n.	sungura	1. lièvre (m) 2. lapin (m)	1. hare 2. rabbit
n.	sura	1. chapitre (m) 2. image (f)	1. chapter 2. image
n.	surua	rougeole (f)	measles
n.	suruali	pantalon (m)	pants
n.	swali (pl. maswali)	1. enquête (f) 2. question (f)	1. inquiry 2. question
n.	taa	lampe (f)	lamp
n.	taabu	1. problème (m) 2. souci (m)	1. trouble 2. problem 3. worry

parts of speech	swahili	french	english
n.	taarifa ya gharama	budget (m)	budget
n.	tabia	1. caractère (m) 2. qualité (f) 3. tempérament (m)	1. character 2. quality 3. temperament
phrase	Tafadhali.	S'il vous plaît.	Please.
n.	tai (pl. matai)	1. vautour (m) 2. aigle (m)	1. vulture 2. eagle
n	taifa (pl. mataifa)	nation (f)	nation
n.	taifa la mtu fulani	nationalité (f)	nationality
n.	taji	couronne (f)	crown
adj.	tajiri (pl. matajiri)	riche	rich
verb	taka bei kubwa kuliko haki	demander un prix exagéré	overcharge, to
n.	takataka	1. ordures (m) 2. saleté (f)	1. garbage 2. dirt
n.	takia (pl. matakia)	coussin (m)	cushion
n.	tako (pl. matako)	fesse (f)	buttock
n.	takwimu	calendrier (m)	calendar
n.	tamaa	1. luxure (f) 2. aspirée (f)	1. lust 2. aspiration
n.	tamaa ya chakula	appétit (m)	appetite
n.	tambarare	plaine (f)	plain (near river)
n.	tamutamu	bonbon (m)	candy
n.	tangawizi	gingembre (m)	ginger
n.	tangazo (pl. matangazo)	1. avis (m) 2. annonce (f)	1. notice 2. announcement
adv.	tangu	depuis	since
phrase	Tangu lini?	Il y a combien de temps?	ago?, How long
adv.	tangu sasa	dorénavant	henceforth
prep.	tangu...hata	de...à	from...to (time)
adj. & n.	tano	cinq (m)	five
n.	tanuu	four (m)	kiln
adv.	taratibu	1. soigneusement 2. méthodique	1. carefully 2. orderly
n.	tarehe	date (f)	date (in month)
n.	tasbihi	chapelet (f)	rosary
n.	tatu	trois	three
n.	tawi (pl. matawi)	branche (f)	branch
n.	taya (pl. mataya)	mâchoire (f)	jaw
adv.	tayari	1. être sur le point de 2. déjà	1. to be about to 2. already
adj.	tayari	prêt	ready
phrase	teke (pl. mateke)	coup de pied	kick
adj.	teketeke, zaifu	faible	weak
adj.	tele	copieux	copious
n.	tembo	éléphant (m)	elephant
adv.	tena	1. de nouveau 2. aussi 3. encore	1. again 2. also 3. too

parts of speech	swahili	french	english
n.	tende	datte	date (fruit)
n.	tendo (pl. matendo)	action (f)	action
n.	tendo bora, utimizo	exploit (m)	achievement
n.	tendo la kukamatwa	appréhension (f)	apprehension
n.	tendo la kutia	application (f)	application
n.	tetemeko	tremblement (m) de terre	tremble (earthquake)
n.	tetemeko la nchi	grande tremblement (m) (de terre)	earthquake
n.	tetewanga	varicelle (f)	chicken pox
n., med	tezi la nyuma ya pua	ganglion engorgé	adenoids
adj.	thabiti madhubuti	sain et sauf	safe and sound
n.	thamani	valeur (f)	1. value 2. worth
adj. & n.	thelathini (makumi matatu)	trente (m)	thirty
n.	thelathini na moja	trente et un	thirty-one
n.	themanini; makumi manane	quatre-vingts	eighty
n.	tiara	cerf-volant (m)	kite
n.	tini	figue (f)	fig
adj.	tisa; kenda	neuf	nine
n.	tisini	quatre-vingt-dix (m)	ninety
n.	tisini na mbili	quatre-vingt-douze	ninety-two
n.	tisini na moja	quatre-vingt-onze	ninety-one
n.	tofali	brique (f)	brick
n.	tofauti	1. différence (f) 2. divergence 3. trait (m)	1. difference 2. divergence 3. trait
n.	tohara	circoncision (f)	circumcision
prep.	toka	de, (depuis)	from, (time)
prep.	toka upande mmoja mpaka upande wa pili	à travers	across (valley)
interj.	Toka!	Va-t'en!	Off with you!
prep.	toka...hata	de...à	from...to (place)
n.	tokeo (pl. matokeo)	1. effet (m) 2. issue (f) 3. apparence (f)	1. effect 2. outcome 3. appearance
adv.	tu	1. simplement 2. seulement	1. merely 2. only
n.	tufani, zoruba	déluge (m)	storm
n.	tukio (pl. matukio)	1. incident (m) 2. accident (m)	1. incident 2. accident
n.	tumaini	confiance (f) (J'ai confiance en lui.)	trust (I trust him.)
n.	tumbako	tabac (m)	tobacco
n.	tumbo (pl. matumbo)	1. abdomen (m) 2. estomac (m)	1. abdomen 2. stomach

195

parts of speech	swahili	french	english
n.	tumbo linanyonga	crampe (f) d'estomac	stomach cramp
phrase	Tumbo yangu inauma.	J'ai mal au ventre.	I've have a stomach ache.
n.	tunda (pl. matunda)	fruit (m)	fruit
n.	tunda a kizungu	pomme (f)	apple
n.	tunda la pua	narine (f)	nostril
n.	tundu (pl. matundu)	1. trou (m) 2. cage (f)	1. hole 2. cage
n.	turubali	bâche (f)	tarpaulin
phrase	Tutaonana baadaye.	À bientôt.	See you next time/soon.
phrase	Tutaonana kesho.	À demain.	See you tomorrow.
phrase	Tutaonana...	Au revoir...	See you...
n.	twiga	girafe (f)	giraffe
n.	ua (pl. maua)	fleur (f)	flower
n.	uadui	hostilité	1. feud 2. hostility
n.	uaminifu	1. fidélité (f) 2. honnêteté (f)	1. faithfulness 2. honesty
n.	uangalifu	considération (f)	consideration
n.	uasherati	adultère (m)	adultery
n.	ubaba	lame (f)	blade (knife)
n.	ubainisho	définition (f)	definition
n.	ubao (pl. mbao)	planche (f)	board (plank)
n.	ubao wa kukalia	banc (m)	bench
n.	ubao wa skuli	tableau noir (m)	blackboard
n.	ubatizo	baptême (m)	baptism
n.	ubavu	côte (f) (côte à côte)	rib, shore (side by side)
n.	ubaya	méchanceté (f)	badness
n., med	uboho	moelle (des os)	bone marrow
n.	ubongo	cerveau (m)	brain
n.	uchafu	1. saleté (f) 2. pollution (f)	1. filth 2. pollution
phrase	uchawi	métier de sorcière	witchcraft
n.	uchi	nudité (f)	nakedness
n	uchokozi	1. provocation (f) 2. sarcasme (m)	1. provocation 2. sarcasm
n.	uchovu	1. ennui (m) 2. fatigue (f)	1. boredom 2. fatigue
n.	uchungu	1. amertume (f) 2. ressentiment (m)	1. bitterness 2. resentment
n.	udaktari, kazi ya surgeon	chirurgie (f)	surgery
n.	udanganyifu	tromperie (f)	deceit
n.	udhia	ennui (m)	nuisance
n.	udhuru	excuse (f)	excuse
n.	udongo	1. argile (f) 2. glaise (f) 3. sol (m) 4. terroir (m)	1. clay 2. earth (ground) 3. soil
n.	udongo ulaya	ciment (m)	cement

196

parts of speech	swahili	french	english
n.	udumu	persévérance (f)	perseverance
n.	ufa (pl. nyufa)	1. fente (f) 2. fissure (f)	1. crack (fissure) 2. crevice
n.	ufagio (pl. fagio)	balai (m)	1. brush 2. broom
n.	ufahamu	compréhension (f)	1. understanding 2. comprehension
n.	ufalme	royaume (m)	kingdom
phrase	ufananaji wa mtoto na wazazi wake	caractère héréditaire	hereditary trait
n.	ufidhuli	insolence (f)	insolence
n.	ufilisi	faillite (f)	bankruptcy
n.	ufisadi	dépravation (f)	depravity
n.	ufufuko	résurrection (f)	resurrection
n.	ufukara	destitution (f)	destitution
n.	ufundi	technique (f)	technique
n.	ufungu	rapport (m)	relationship
n.	ufunguo (pl. funguo) {Nilipoteza funguo.)	clé (f) {J'ai perdu mes clefs.}	key {I lost my keys.}
n.	ufunuo	manifestation (f)	manifestation
n.	ufunuo	révélation (f)	revelation
n., med	ugagazi	nausée	nausea
n.	uganga	1. magie (f) 2. l'art de guérir 3. remède (m)	1. magic 2. practice of medicine 3. remedy
n.	ughaibu	absence (f)	absence
n.	ugo (pl. nyugo)	1. clôture (f) 2. haie (f)	1. fence 2. hedge
n.	ugomvi	dispute (f)	dispute
n.	ugonjwa (pl. maogonjwa)	maladie (f)	1. illness 2. disease 3. sickness 4. malady
n.	ugonjwa fulani	tuberculose (f)	tuberculosis
n.	ugonjwa mmojawapo wa tumbo	gastrite (f)	gastritis
n.	ugonjwa wa akili	hystérie (f)	hysteria
n., med	ugonjwa wa kifua	bronchite	bronchitis
n., med	ugonjwa wa kuumia kikoromeo	laryngite (f)	laryngitis
n., med	ugonjwa wa matende	éléphantiasis des jambes	elephantiasis of legs
n., med	ugonjwa wa ngozi inayufunika ubongo	méningite	meningitis
n.	ugonjwa wa pumu	asthme (m)	asthma
n., med	ugonjwa wa umio	angine (f)	tonsillitis
n.	ugumu	dureté (f)	hardness, severity
n.	ugwe (pl. nyugwe)	ficelle (f)	string
n.	uharibifu	destruction (f)	destruction
n.	uhodari	courage (m)	courage

parts of speech	swahili	french	english
n.	uhuru	liberté (f)	1. liberty 2. freedom
n.	ujamaa	race (f)	race (people)
n.	ujana	jeunesse (f)	youth
n.	ujasiri	1. hardiesse (f) 2. courage (m)	1. boldness 2. bravery
n.	ujazi, wingi	abondance (f)	abundance
n.	ujazo, nafasi	capacité (f)	capacity
interj.	Uje hapa!	Viens ici!	Come here!
n.	uji mzito	bouillie (f)	porridge
n.	ujinga	1. folie (f) 2. ignorance (f)	1. folly 2. ignorance
n.	ujira	récompense (f)	pay (noun)
n.	ujirani	voisinage (m)	1. neighborhood 2. vicinity
n.	ujuvi	présomption (f)	presumption
n.	ujuzi maarifa, mtu umjuaye	connaissance (f)	acquaintance
n.	ukaguzi	examen (m)	examination
n.	ukaidi	désobéissance (f)	disobedience
n.	ukali	sévérité (f)	severity
n.	ukamilifu	perfection (f)	perfection
n.	ukarimu	générosité (f)	generosity
n.	ukatili	cruauté (f)	cruelty
n., med	ukimwi	sida (m)	AIDS
n.	ukingo	bord (m) (d'un pot en argile)	1. brim 2. edge
n.	ukini (pl. kuni)	bois (m) de chauffage	firewood
phrase	Uko nafanya nini?	Qu'est-ce que vous faites?	What are you doing?
phrase	Uko nasema nini?	Qu'est-ce que vous dites?	What are you saying?
n.	ukoma	lèpre (f)	leprosy
n.	ukombozi	1. rançon (f) 2. rédemption (f)	1. ransom 2. redemption
n.	ukomo	cessation (f)	cessation
phrase	Ukonayo...	Avez-vous...	Do you have...
n.	ukoo	clan (m)	clan
n.	ukope	1. cil (m) 2. paupière (f)	1. eyelash 2. eyelid
n.	ukosefu wa chakula chema	sous-alimentation (f)	malnutrition
n.	ukosefu wa mvua	sécheresse (f)	drought
n.	ukubwa	grandeur (f)	1. greatness 2. magnitude 3. size
n.	ukucha (pl. kucha)	ongle (m)	1. fingernail 2. toenail
n.	ukumbuko	souvenir (m)	souvenir

parts of speech	swahili	french	english
n.	ukumbusho wa kila mwaka	anniversaire (m)	anniversary
n.	ukungu	brume (f)	mist
n.	ukungu wa ijioni	crépuscule (m)	twilight
phrase	ukuni	le feu de bois	stick of firewood
n.	ukurasa (pl. kurasa)	1. page (f) 2. feuille de papier	1. page 2. sheet of paper
n.	ukwato (pl. kwato)	sabot (m)	hoof
n.	Ulaya	Europe (f)	Europe
n.	ulimi (pl. ndimi)	langue (f)	tongue
n.	ulimwengu	monde (m)	world
n.	ulinzi	défense	defense
n.	uma (pl. nyuma)	fourchette (f)	fork
n.	umande	1. rosée(f) 2. brouillard (m)	1. dew 2. fog
n.	umasikini	pauvreté (f)	poverty
n.	umbali	distance (f)	distance
n.	umbo	forme (f)	shape, form
phrase	Umekuwa hivyo kwa muda gani?	Il y a combien de temps que tu es malade?	How long have you been ill?
n.	umeme	1. électricité (f) 2. éclair (m)	1. electricity 2. lightning
phrase	Umeyok wapi?	Où viens-tu?	Where are you coming from?
n., med	umio wa pumzi	trachée	trachea
n	umizo la moto	brûlure (f)	burn
n.	umoja	unité (f)	unity
n.	umri, maisha, miaka (Una miaka mingapi?)	âge (m) (Quel âge avez-vous?)	age (How old are you?)
phrase	Una watoto?	Est-ce que tu as des enfants?	Do you have children?
phrase	Unafanya kazi gani?	Quelle est ton (votre) profession?	What is your profession?
n.	unafiki	hypocrisie (f)	hypocrisy
phrase	Unajua.	Vous savez, vous connaissez.	You know.
phrase	Unakaa hapa?	Habitez-vous ici?	Do you live here?
phrase	Unakwenda wapi?	Où allez-vous?	Where are you going?
phrase	Unasikia furaha?	Êtes-vous heureux?	Are you happy?
phrase	Unasikia njaa?	Avez-vous faim?	Are you hungry?
phrase	Unatafuta nini?	Qu'est-ce que tu-veux?	What are you looking for?
n.	unene	embonpoint (m)	stoutness
n.	unga	1. farine (f) 2. poudre (f)	1. flour 2. powder
n.	unga wa mbao	sciure (f)	sawdust
n.	unyasi (pl. nyasi)	rousseau	reeds

parts of speech	swahili	french	english
n.	unyenyekevu	humilité (f)	humility
n.	unyenyezi	brume (f)	haze
n.	unywele (pl. nywele) {Nataka kutaka nywele.}	cheveu(m) {J'ai besoin me faire couper les cheveux.}	hair (of human) {I want a haircut.}
n.	uongo	fabrication (f)	fabrication
n.	upaa	calvitie (f)	baldness
n.	upana	largeur (f)	width
n.	upande (karibu na)	côté (m) (à côté de)	side (next to)
n.	upande (pl. pande)	1. région (f) 2. direction (f)	1. region 2. direction
n.	upande wa chini	fond (m)	bottom
n.	upande wa juu wa chumba	plafond (m)	ceiling
n.	upande wa kushuto	gauche (f)	left
n.	upande wa ndani	intérieur (m)	interior
n.	upanga (pl. panga)	épée (f)	sword
n	upele	1. démangeaison (f) 2. éruption (f)	1. itch 2. rash
n.	upele wa mbwa	gale (f)	mange
n.	upendeleo	préférence (f)	preference
n.	upeo wa macho	horizon (m)	horizon
n.	upepo (pl. pepo)	vent (m)	wind
adj.	upesi	rapide	fast
n.	upesi	vitesse (f)	speed
n.	upigano (pl. maupigano)	lutte (f)	strife
n.	upinde (pl. pinde)	arc (m)	bow (as in arrow)
n.	upindi wa mvua	arc-en-ciel (m)	rainbow
n.	upofu	cécité (f)	blindness
n.	upujufu	obscénité (f)	obscenity
n.	upumbavu	stupidité (f)	stupidity
n.	upungufu wa damu	anémie (f)	anemia
n.	upunguo	diminution (f)	decrease
n.	upuzi	bêtises (f)	nonsense
n.	upweke	solitude (f)	loneliness
n.	urafiki	amitié (f)	friendship
n.	urefu	1. profondeur 2. longueur (f)/durée (f) 3. haut (m)	1. depth 2. length (dimension, time) 3. top (on the top)
n.	urithi	patrimoine (m)	patrimony
n.	uriti	héritage (m)	inheritance
n.	usafi	1. propreté 2. innocence (f) 3. pureté (f)	1. cleanliness 2. innocence 3. purity
n., med	usaha	pus (m)	pus

parts of speech	swahili	french	english
n.	usamehe	pardon (m)	pardon, forgiveness
n.	usawa	correct	right (correct)
n.	usemi	manière de parler	speech
n.	usermala	menuiserie (f)	carpentry
n.	ushahidi	preuve (f)	proof
n.	ushirika	1. union (f) 2. participation (f)	1. fellowship 2. participation
n.	ushuhuda	allégation (f)	allegation
n.	usiku	nuit (f)	night
adv.	usiku huu	cette nuit	tonight
n.	usiku kucha	tout la nuit	night, all
phrase	Usiku muzuli.	Ayez la bonne nuit.	Have a good night.
adv.	usiku wa leo	nuit dernière, la	night, last
n.	usingizi	sommeil (m)	sleep
n.	usingizi mfupi	petit somme (m)	nap
n.	usitawi	prospérité (f)	prosperity
n.	uso (pl. nyuso)	visage (m)	face
n.	ustahimilivu	endurance (f)	endurance
n.	utabibu wa kupasua	opérer	operation (surgery)
n.	utaji	voile (m)	veil
n.	utambi	mèche de lampe	wick
n.	utando wa buibui	toile d'araignée (f)	cobweb
n.	utaratibu	système (m)	system
n.	utawala	règne (m)	reign
n.	utawala wa raia	démocratie (f)	democracy
n.	utepe	tresse (f)	braid
n.	uthabiti	entêtement (m)	stubbornness
n.	uti wa mgongo	épine (f) dorsal	spine
n.	utongozi	débauche (f)	debauchery
n.	utoto	1. enfance (f) 2. toute petite enfance (f)	1. childhood 2. infancy
n.	utumwa	1. captivité (f) 2. esclavage (m)	1. captivity 2. slavery
n.	uuaji	meurtre (m)	murder
n.	uume	pénis (m)	penis
n., med	uvimbe wa mboni	conjonctivite	conjunctivitis
n.	uvimbi wa ini	hépatite (f)	hepatitis
n.	uvivu	1. oisiveté (f) 2. paresse (f)	1. idleness 2. laziness
adj.	uvuguvugu	tiède	lukewarm
n.	uvumbuzi	exploration (f)	exploration
n.	uvumi	rumeur (f)	rumor
n.	uwezo	puissance (f)	power (strength)

parts of speech	swahili	french	english
n.	uwezo wa kukumbuka	mémoire (f)	memory
n.	uwongo	1. malhonnêteté (f) 2. mensonge (m)	1. dishonesty 2. lie 3. falsehood
n.	uzaifu	faiblesse (f)	weakness
n.	uzazi	naissance (f)	birth
n.	uzee	vieillesse (f)	age, old
n.	uzembe	négligence	negligence
n.	uzi (pl. nyuzi)	fil (m)	thread
n.	uzingo	auréole (f)	halo
n.	uzito	1. pesanteur (f) 2. poids (m)	1. gravity 2. weight
n.	uzuri	beauté (f)	beauty
n.	vazi la kike	robe (f)	robe, dress
adv.	vema	1. convenablement 2. bien 3. correctement	1. properly 2. well
phrase	Vema.	C'est bien.	All right.
adv.	vibaya	méchamment	badly
adv.	vile vile	idem	ditto
adv., conj.	vile, vivyo, basi	alors, ainsi	so
phrase	Vipi?	Qu'est-ce qu'il y a?	What's up? (familiar person)
n.	vita	guerre (f)	war
n.	vituo	ponctuation (f)	punctuation
adj., adv.	vizuri	bien	well, very
n.	vyakula	provisions (f)	groceries
phrase	vyo vyote	n'importe comment	anyhow
adj & pr	vyote viwili	tous (les) deux (m); toutes (les) deux (f)	both
n.	Wafaransa (people, Kifaransa (language)	français (m)	French
n.	Waingereza	Anglais (m)	English (people)
n.	wajibu	devoir (m)	1. duty 2. obligation
phrase	Wakaligani.	C'est ça.	That's right.
n.	wakati	temps (m)	time
conj.	Wakati gani?	Quand est-ce que?	When?
n.	wakati ujao	avenir (m)	future
prep.	wakati wa	pendant	during
n., med	wakati wa mwanamke kuingia ugumba	ménopause	menopause
phrase	wakati wo wote	n'importe quelle heure	any time
phrase	wala	pas même	not the same
conj.	wala...wala	ni...ni	neither...nor

parts of speech	swahili	french	english
adv.	walakini	1. pourtant 2. cependant 3. néanmoins	1. however 2. nevertheless
adj & pr	wale (pl. person); zile (pl. thing)	ces, ceux-là (m), celles-là (f)	those
pronoun	wao	ils (m), elles (f) (et eux)	they (and they)
pronoun	wao, hao, wale	eux (m), elles (f)	them
conj.	wapi	où	where
phrase	Wapi ni...?	Où est...?	Where is...?
interj.	Wapi!	De grâce!	For pity's sake!
n.	wavu (pl. nyavu)	filet (m)	net
n.	wazao	progéniture (f)	progeny
adj.	wazi	1. clair 2. évident 3. ouvert	1. clear 2. evident 3. open
adv.	waziwazi	ouvertement	openly
adj.	waziwazi	public (m); publique (f)	public
n.	wazo	1. idée (f) 2. pensée (f)	1. idea 2. thought
phrase	wazungu	les blancs	white people
n.	wema	bonté (f)	goodness
n.	wembamba	tendresse (f)	tenderness
n.	wembe (pl. nyembe)	rasoir (m)	razor
adj.	werevu	astucieux	trickery
phrase	weupe	blancheur éclatante	whiteness, dazzling
n.	weusi	noir (m) {couleur}	black {color}
pronoun	wewe	tu, vous	you (singular)
phrase	wiki hii	cette semaine	this week
adv.	wima	position debout	upright
n.	wimbi (pl. mawimbe)	vague (f)	wave (of water)
n.	wimbo (pl. nyimbo)	1. hymne (m) 2. chanson (f) 3. chant (m)	1. hymn 2. song
n.	wingi	1. abondance (f) 2. majorité (f)	1. plenty 2. majority
n.	wingi kupita kiasi	excédent (m)	excess, surplus
n.	wingu (mawingu)	nuage (m)	cloud
n.	wino	encre (f)	ink
n.	wivu	1. envie (f) 2. jalousie (f)	1. envy 2. jealousy
n.	wizi	vol (m)	theft
n.	woga	crainte (f)	fear
n.	woga mkuu	panique (f)	panic
n.	wokovu	salut (m)	salvation
n.	yai (pl. mayai)	œuf (m)	egg
n.	yatima	orphelin (m)	orphan
pronoun	ye yote	quelqu'un	anybody (somebody)
n.	Yesu	Jésus (m)	Jesus

parts of speech	swahili	french	english
pronoun	yeye	1. il 2. le, lui 3. elle	1. he 2. him 3. she
pronoun	yeye mwenyewe	elle-même	herself
adj & pr	yeye, -ake	son (m), sa (f), ses (pl)	her
adj.,pro.	yule (sing. person); ile (sing. thing)	ce, cet, cette	that
n.	zabibu (pl.)	du raisin (m)	grape
n.	zabihu	sacrifice (m)	sacrifice
n.	zaburi	psaume (m)	psalm
adj.	zaidi	de plus	extra
adv.	zaidi	1. plus 2. pour la plupart 3. en outre	1. more 2. mostly 3. furthermore
adv.	zaidi ya hayo	de plus, d'ailleurs	moreover
n.	zaka	offrande	tithe
adv.	zamani	jadis	formerly
adv.	zamani sana	il y a longtemps	long ago
n.	zambi	péché (m)	sin
n.	zana	soupçon (m)	suspicion
n.	zawabu	récompense (f)	reward
n.	zawadi	1. don (m) 2. cadeau (m) 3. pourboire (m)	1. gift 2. present 3. tip (gratuity)
n.	ziada	prime (f)	bonus
n.	ziwa (pl. maziwa)	lac (m)	lake
n.	zoruba	1. ouragan (m) 2. orage (m)	1. hurricane 2. storm on lake
n.	zuio (pl. mazuio)	obstacle (m)	obstruction
n.	zulia (pl. mazulia)	tapis (m)	rug

parts of speech	french	swahili	english
prep.	à	1. hadi 2. kwenye 2. penye 4. kwa	1. to 2. at
verb	abaisser	kushusha	lower, to
verb	abandonner	kuacha	1. to abandon 2. to forsake
n.	abcès (m)	jipu (pl. majipu)	abscess
n.	abdomen (m)	tumbo (pl. matumbo)	abdomen
n.	abeille (f)	nyuki	bee
phrase	À bientôt.	Tutaonana baadaye.	See you next time/soon.
verb	abîmer	kuharibu	spoil, to
n.	abondance (f)	1. ujazi 2. wingi	1. abundance 2. plenty
adj.	abondant	sana, tele	abundant
adv.	a' bord de	melini, chomboni	aboard
verb	aboyer	kubweka	bark, to
verb	abréger	kufupisha	1. to abbreviate 2. to abridge
n.	absence (f)	ughaibu	absence
adj.,adv.	absent	mahali pengine	away
adv.	absolument, tout à fait	kabisa	absolutely
verb	absorber	kunywa	absorb, to
n.	acajou (f)	mkangazi	mahogany
conj.	à cause de	kwa sababu hii	because of
n.	accablement (m)	état de faiblesse	exhaustion
verb	accabler	kuelemea	weighed down, to be
verb	accélérer	kuhimiza	accelerate, to
verb	accepter	kukubalia, kupokea	accept, to
verb	accepter soudoyer	kula rushwa	bribe, to take
n.	accès (m)	njia ya kufikia	access
n.	accident (m)	tukio (pl.matukio), ajali	accident
verb	accompagner	1. kufuatana na 2. kusindikiza	accompany, to
verb	accomplir	kutimiza	1. to accomplish 2. to fulfill
n.	accord (m)	mapatano	agreement
verb	accorder	kujalia	grant, to
verb	accoucher	kuzaa	birth, to give
verb	accoutumé, être	kuzoea	accustomed, to be
verb	accueillir	1. kukaribisha 2. kusalimu	1. to welcome 2. to greet
verb	accumuler	kuongezeka kwa kulimbikwa	accumulate, to
n.	accusation (f)	mashtaka	accusation
verb	accuser	kushtaki	accuse, to

parts of speech	french	swahili	english
verb	acheter	kununua	buy, to
verb	achever	kufaulu	achieve, to; finish, to
adj.	acide	-chungu, -kali	acid
n.	acier	pua	steel
adv.	à côté de	1. kando 2. karibu na 3. kando ya	1. alongside 2. beside 3. next to 4. on the side of
verb	acquérir	kujipatia	acquire, to
n.	acteur (m)	mtenda (pl. watenda)	actor
n.	action (f)	tendo (pl. matendo)	action
verb	additionner	kujumlisha	add up, to
phrase	À demain.	Tutaonana kesho.	See you tomorrow.
verb	adhérer à	kuambatana, kushika	adhere, to
verb	admettre	kukiri	admit, to (confess)
n.	administration (f)	serkali, usimamizi	administration
verb	adopter	kupokea kama mwana	adopt (child)
n.	adoption (f)	kibali	approval
verb	adorer	kuabudu	adore, to
verb	adresser	kuandika anwani, (2) kuhutubu	address, to 1. letter 2. speech
phrase	à droit	kwa upande wa kuume	right, on the
n.	adultère (m)	uasherati	adultery
n.	adversité (f)	msiba	adversity
verb	aérer une plantation	kutia hewa ya	aerate, to
n.	affaire (f)	1. shughuli 2. kazi 3. jambo	1. business 2. affair
adj.	affamé	-enye njaa	hungry
verb	affecter	kugeuza, kujifanya	affect
verb	affirmer	1. kukaza ukweli 2. kuhakiki	1. to assert 2. to testify
verb	affliger	kutesa	torture, to
adj.	affreux	-baya sana	awful
conj.	afin que	ili, kusudi	so that, in order to
n.	âge (m) (Quel âge avez-vous?)	umri, maisha, miaka (Una miaka mingapi?)	age (How old are you?)
n.	agent (m) de police	polisi (pl. mapolisi)	police agent
n.	agglomération (f)	mji (pl. miji)	town
verb	agglutiner	kuambatanisha	stick together, to
verb	aggraver	kuudhi, kuongeza ubaya	aggravate, to
verb	agir	kutenda, kuigiza hadithi	act, to
verb	agiter (un liquide)	kukoroga	stir, to; shake, to
n.	agression (f)	shambilio	aggression
adj.	agréable	-tamu	sweet
n.	agriculture (f)	kilimo, ukulima	agriculture

parts of speech	french	swahili	english
verb	ahurir	kutia wasiwasi	bewilder, to
n.	aide (f)	musaada	help
verb	aider à	kusaidia	1. to aid 2. to assist 3. to help
n.	aigle (m)	tai	eagle
adj.	aigre	-kali	sour
n.	aiguille (f)	sindano	needle
adj.	aiguise	-a kali	sharp
verb	aiguiser	kunoa	sharpen, to
n.	ail (m)	kitunguu saumu	garlic
n.	aile (f)	bawa	wing
adv.	ailleurs	pengine	1. somewhere else 2. elsewhere
verb	aimer	kupenda	1. to love 2. to like
verb	aimer beaucoup	kupenda	fond of, to be
verb	aimer, trouver agréable	kufurahia	enjoy, to
phrase	aimer-se	kujipenda nafsi	self-love
n.	aine (f)	mamena	groin
adv.	ainsi (et ainsi de suite)	hivi, vile (na vingine vivyo hivyo)	thus (and so on)
adv.	ainsi que	kama vile	as well as
n.	air (m)	hewa	air
n.	aise (f)	raha	ease
n.	aisselle (f)	kwapa	armpit
verb	à l'aise, être	kustarehe	ease, to be at
n.	alarme (f)	mshtuko, kamsa	alarm
n.	albinos (m,f)	mazeru (pl.)	albinos
n.	alcool (m)	kileo	alcohol
verb	alerte, être	kuwa macho	alert, to be
phrase	à l'heure	kuwahi	time, on
adv.	alias	jina la pili la kificho	alias
n.	alibi (m)	dai la kuwapo mahali pengine	alibi
verb	aliéner	kufarakisha	alienate, to
n.	alignement (m)	msafa (pl. misafa)	alignment
phrase	Aliment, repas est bon.	Chakula kitamu sana.	The food is good.
verb	allaiter	kunyonyesha	1. to nurse (suckle) 2. to breast-feed
n.	allégation (f)	ushuhuda	allegation
n.	allemand (m)	Mjeremani, Kidachi	German
verb	aller	kwenda	go, to
n.	allergie (f)	mzio	allergy

parts of speech	french	swahili	english
n.	**alliance (f)**	mwungano	alliance
n.	**alligator (m)**	mamba wa (Amerika)	alligator
verb	**allonger**	kuongeza urefu	lengthen, to
interj.	**Allô.**	Jambo.	Hello.
phrase	**Allons donc!**	Haiwezekani!	You don't really mean that!
phrase	**Allons-y!**	Basi, safari!	Let's go!
verb	**allouer**	kugawanyia	allocate, to
verb	**allumer**	kuwasha	light (kindle), to
n.	**allumette (f)**	kiberiti (pl. viberiti)	match
adv.	**alors**	kisha	then
adv., conj.	**alors, ainsi**	vile, vivyo, basi	so
verb	**amadouer**	1. kuvuta kwa werevu 2. kubembeleza	1. to entice 2. to coax
verb	**amasser**	kukusanya	amass, to
n.	**ambassade (f)**	jumba la balozi	embassy
n.	**ambassadeur (m)**	balozi (pl. malozi)	ambassador
n.	**âme (f)**	moyo nafsi	soul
n.	**amélioration (f)**	maendeleo mazuri	improvement
verb	**améliorer**	1. kukuza hali 2. kutengeneza	1. to improve 2. to ameliorate
adj.	**ambigu**	-enye maana mbili	ambiguous
adj.	**ambitieux**	-enye kutaka makuu	ambitious
n.	**ambulance (f)**	gari au namna ya machela ya kuchukulia wagonjwa	ambulance
n.	**amende (f)**	faini	fine (i.e. to pay a)
n.	**amendement (m)**	matengenezo	amendment
verb	**amender**	kutengeneza ifae zaidi	amend, to
verb	**amener**	kuleta	bring to
adj.	**amer**	-chungu	bitter
n.	**amertume (f)**	uchungu	bitterness
n.	**ami (m), amie (f)**	rafiki	friend
n.	**amitié (f)**	urafiki	friendship
n.	**amour (m)**	mapendo	love
n.	**amour-propre (m)**	kujistahi nafsi	self-respect
verb	**amputer**	kukata	amputate, to
n.	**amusement (m)**	furaha	amusement
verb	**amuser**	kuchekesha	amuse, to
n.	**an (m), année (f)**	mwaka, (pl. miaka)	year
adv.	**an après an**	mwaka kwa mwaka	year after year
phrase	**an passé**	mwaka wa jana	last year
phrase	**an prochain**	mwaka wa kesho	next year

208

parts of speech	french	swahili	english
n.	analogie (f)	mfano (pl. mifano)	analogy
n.	ananas (m)	nanasi (pl. mananasi)	pineapple
n.	ancêtre (m)	mkale	ancestor
adj.	ancien	-a kale	ancient
n.	Ancien Testament	Agano la Kale	Testament, Old
n.	ancre (f)	nanga	anchor
n.	âne (m)	punda	donkey
verb	anéantir	kuangamiza kabisa	annihilate, to
n.	anecdote (f)	hekaya	anecdote
n.	anémie (f)	upungufu wa damu	anemia
n.	ange (m)	malaika	angel
n., med	angine (f)	ugonjwa wa umio	tonsillitis
n.	Anglais (m)	Waingereza	English (people)
n.	anglais (Parlez-vous anglais?)	Kiingereza (Umasema Kiingereza?)	English {language} (Do you speak English?)
n.	angoisse (f)	1. maumivu makali 2. huzuni kuu	1. agony 2. anguish
n.	animal (m)	mnyama (pl. wanyama)	animal
n.	anneau (m)	pete	ring
n.	anniversaire (m)	ukumbusho wa kila mwaka	anniversary
n.	anniversaire (m)	sikukuu ya kuzaliza	birthday
n.	annonce (f)	tangazo	announcement
verb	annoncer les nouvelles	kupasha habari	tell the news, to
verb	annuler	kutangua	annul, to
n.	anse (f)	mpini, shikio	handle
adj.	antérieur	-a kabla	anterior
adj.	antérieur	-a kwanza	prior to
n.	antilope (f)	paa	antelope
n.	antre (m)	pango la mnyama	den
n.	anus (m)	mkundu	anus
n.	anxiété (f)	hofu, fadhaa	anxiety
verb	être anxieux	kuhofu, kufadhaika	anxious, to be
n.	août	Ogusti, mwezi wa nane wa mwaka wa kizungu	August
adv.	à part	mbali	apart
adv.	à peine	kwa shida	barely
verb	apercevoir	kutazama	behold, to; notice, to
adv.	à peu près, environ	habari za, yapata	about (approximately)
n.	apôtre (m)	mtume (pl. mitume)	apostle
verb	apparaître	kuonekana	appear, to
n.	apparence (f)	tokeo	appearance
adj.	apparent	dhahiri	apparent

parts of speech	french	swahili	english
verb	appartenir à	kuwa mali yake	belong to, to
n.	appel (m)	mwito (pl. miito)	call
verb	appeler	kuita	call, to
n.	appentis (m)	kibanda cha nje	outhouse
n.	appétit (m)	tamaa ya chakula	appetite
verb	applaudir	kupiga makofi	1. to applaud 2. to clap
n.	application (f)	tendo la kutia	application
n.	appointements (m)	mshahara	salary
verb	appréhender	kuogopa	dread, to
adj.	appréhensif	-enye akili	apprehensive
n.	appréhension (f)	1. tendo la kukamatwa 2. shaka	1. apprehension 2. misgiving
verb	apprendre	kufundishwa, kujifunza	learn, to
n.	apprenti (m,f)	mwanafunzi wa kazi	apprentice
verb	apprêter	kutayarisha	prepare, to
n.	approbation (f)	sahihi	endorsement
n.	approximation (f)	kisio	approximation
verb	appuyer	kubana, kusonga	press, to
adv.	après	baada ya, nyuma ya	after
adv.	après cela	baadaye	hereafter
phrase	après-demain	kesho kutwa	tomorrow, day after
n.	après-midi (m or f)	alasiri, mangaribi	afternoon
n.	après-semaine (f); semaine (f) dernière	juma jana	week, last
n.	Arabe (m, f)	Mwarabu	Arab
n.	arachide (f)	karanga	1. ground nut 2. peanut
n.	araignée (f)	buibui	spider
adj.	arbitraire	-geugeu	arbitrary
n.	arbre (m)	mti (pl. miti)	tree
n.	arc (m)	upinde (pl. pinde)	bow (as in arrow)
n.	arc-en-ciel (m)	upindi wa mvua	rainbow
n.	ardoise (f)	kibao cha jiwe	slate (to write on)
n.	argent (m)	1. fedha taslimu 2. feza	1. cash 2. money 3. silver
n.	argile (f), glaise (f)	udongo	clay
n.	arme (f)	silaha	weapon
n.	arme à feu (f)	bunduki	gun
n.	armée (f)	jeshi	army
n.	armée en marche, tyrannie	jeuri	assault
n.	armoire (f)	kabati	cupboard
verb	arracher	kungoa	take out, to; pull out, to
n.	arrangement (m)	mupango, matengenezo	arrangement

parts of speech	french	swahili	english
verb	arranger (Arrangez toutes ces choses.)	kupanga, kutandika	arrange, to (Put all these things in order.)
n.	arrêt	kituo	stop
verb	arrêter	kusimamisha	arrest, to
interj.	Arrêtez!	Basi!	Stop!
verb	arriver	kufika	arrive, to
n.	artère (f)	mshipa mkubwa wa damu	artery
n.	articulation (f)	kiungo (pl. viungo)	joint (anatomy), articulation
n.	articulation (f) du doigt	konzi	knuckles
n.	artisan (m)	fundi (pl. mafundi)	craftsman
n.	artiste (m)	mstadi, (pl. wastadi)	artist
n.	asile (m)	kimbilio	refuge
n.	aspirée (f)	tamaa	aspiration
phrase	assaisonné, être	kukolea	seasoned, to be well
n.	assassin (m)	mwuaji (pl. waji)	murderer
verb	assembler	kukusanya	assemble, to
verb	asseoir	kutetisha	seat, to
adj.	assez de	-a kutosha	enough
interj.	Assez!	Basi!	Enough!
n.	assiette (f)	sahani	plate
verb	assigner	kugawanyia	assign, to
n.	assistant (m), assistante (f)	msaidizi	assistant
n.	association (f)	shirika	partnership
n.	associé (m), associée (f)	mshiriki katika kazi	partner
verb	assurer	kuhakiki	monitor, to
n.	asthme (m)	ugonjwa wa pumu	asthma
adj.	astucieux	werevu	trickery
n.	atelier (m)	kibanda (pl. vibanda)	workshop
phrase	À tes souhaits.	Akuweke.	Bless you.
n.	athée (m,f)	mkana Mungu	atheist
n.	atmosphère (f)	hewa	atmosphere
prep.	à travers	toka upande mmoja mpaka upande wa pili	across (valley)
verb	attacher	kufunga	tie, to
n.	attaque (f)	mashambulio	attack
verb	attaquer	kushambulia	attack, to
verb	atteindre	1. kufikia 2. kuwasili	1. to attain 2. to reach
verb	attendre	kungoja	wait, to
phrase	Attends une minute.	Ngo jasaa kidogo.	minute., Just a
interj.	Attends!	Ngoja!	Wait!
interj.	Attention!	Lino!	Look!

parts of speech	french	swahili	english
adj.	atterré	kushikwa na fadhaa	aghast, to be
verb	attester	kushuhudia	attest, to
verb	attirer	kuvuta	attract, to
verb	attraper	kukamata	catch, to
adj.	au bord de	hali moja na	side, on this
adv.	au delà	kupita	beyond
adv.	au lieu de	badala ya	place of, in
adv.	au lieu de cela	badalya ya	instead
phrase	au moindre	lakini	least, at
phrase	Au revoir.	Kwa heri.	Good-bye.
phrase	Au revoir...	Tutaonana...	See you...
adv.	au-dessus de, sur	juu ya	above; on top of
n.	aube (f)	pambazuko	dawn
n.	aubergine (f)	mubilingani (pl. mibilingani)	eggplant
pronoun	aucun	hata moja	none
adj.	audacieux	-jasiri	audacious
verb	augmenter	1. kuongeza 2. kuzidi	1. to augment 2. to increase
n.	augure (m), bon	ndege njema	omen, good
n.	augure (m), mauvais	ndege mbaya	omen, bad
adv.	aujourd'hui	leo	today
n.	auréole (f)	uzingo	halo
adv.	aussi	1. pia 2. tena	1. as well 2. also 3. too 4. again
n.	autel (m)	mazabahu	altar
n.	autobus (m)	motakaa ya abiria	bus
n.	automobile (f)	motakaa	automobile
n.	autorité (f)	amri, mamlaka	authority
adj & pr	autre	-ingine	other
phrase	autrefois	kale	time ago, long
verb	avaler	kumeza	swallow, to
verb	avancer	kuenda au kuendesha mbele	advance, to
adv.prep	avant de (place) avant (time)	mbele ya, kabla ya	before
adv.	avant-hier	juzi	day before yesterday
n.	avare (m,f)	bahili	miser
adv.	avec excès	muno	excessively
adv.	avec modération	si sana	moderately
prep.	avec, de	kwa, na, pamoja na	with
n.	avenir (m)	wakati ujao	future
n.	aversion (f)	machukio	aversion

parts of speech	french	swahili	english
adj.	aveugle	-pofu	blind
adv.	aveuglément	kipofu	blindly
phrase	Avez-vous faim?	Unasikia njaa?	Are you hungry?
phrase	Avez-vous...	Ukonayo...	Do you have...
n.	avidité (f)	choyo	greed
n.	avion (m)	ndege	airplane
n.	avis (m)	tangazo (pl. matangazo)	notice
verb	avoir	kuwa na	have, to
verb	avoir besoin de	kuhitaji	need, to
adj.	avoir de la chance	-a heri	fortunate
verb	avoir des haut-le-cœur	kokomoka	retch, to
verb	avoir fatigué	kuchoka	tired, to be
verb	avoir honte	kuona haya	ashamed of, to be
verb	avoir la diarrhée	kuhara	diarrhea, to have
verb	avoir le souffle coupé	kutweta	gasp, to
adv.	avoir les mains vides	mikono bule	empty-handed, (to be)
verb	avoir lieu	kufanyika	take place, to
verb	avoir l'intention	kukusudi	intend, to
phrase	avoir mauvaise réputation	sifa mbaya	reputation, to have a bad
verb	avoir peur de	kuogopa	afraid, to be
verb	avoir ses règles	kuingia mwezini	menstruate, to
phrase	avoir soif	-a enye kiu	thirsty, to be
phrase	avoir un lien de famille	-wa ndugu ya	related, to be
verb	avouer	kukiri	confess, to
n.	avril (m)	Aprili, mwezi wa nne wa mwaka wa kizungu	April
phrase	Ayez la bon voyage.	Safari njema.	Have a good trip.
phrase	Ayez la bonne journée	Muchana muzuli.	Have a good morning.
phrase	Ayez la bonne nuit.	Usiku muzuli.	Have a good night.
phrase	Ayez la bonne soirée.	Magalibi mzuli.	Have a good evening.
verb	babiller	kupayuka	babble, to
n.	bâche (f)	turubali	tarpaulin
verb	badiner	kucheka	joke, to
n.	bagages (m pl.)	mizigo	luggage
n.	baie (f)	ghuba	bay
verb	bâiller	kupiga miayo	yawn, to
n.	bain (m)	chombo cha kuogea	bath
verb	baisser	kushusha	lower, to
n.	balai (m)	ufagio (pl. fagio)	1. broom 2. brush
n.	balançoire (f)	pembea	swing (for child to use)
verb	balayer	kufagia	sweep, to

parts of speech	french	swahili	english
verb	**balbutier**	kugugumiza	stutter, to
n.	**balle (f)**	risasi ya bunduki	bullet
n.	**balle (m)**	mpira (pl. mipira)	ball
n.	**ballon (m)**	mpira (pl. mipira)	football (U.S. soccer ball)
verb	**ballotter**	kusukasuka	roll around, to
n.	**bambou (m)**	mwanzi (pl. mianzi)	bamboo
n	**banane (f)**	ndizi	banana
n.	**banane plantain**	matoke	plantain
n.	**banc (m)**	ubao wa kukalia	bench
n.	**banque (f)**	benki ya fedha	bank (for money)
n.	**baptême (m)**	ubatizo	baptism
verb	**baptiser**	kuabatiza	baptize, to
n.	**barbe (f)**	ndevu (poil de barbe = udevu)	beard
n.	**barbier (m)**	kinyozi	barber
adj.	**bas (f. basse)**	-fupi	low
n.	**bataille (f)**	pigano (pl. mapigano)	battle
n.	**bateau (m)**	chombo (pl. vyombo)	boat
n.	**bâtiment (m)**	jengo (pl. majengo)	building (construction)
verb	**bâtir**	kujenga	build, to
n.	**bâton (m)**	fimbo	stick
verb	**battre**	kupiga	beat, to
verb	**battre des ailes**	kupiga mabawa	flap wings, to
n.	**batwa**	mmbuti (pl. wabuti)	pygmy
adj.	**bavard**	-a maneno mengi	talkative
n.	**bavardage (m)**	porojo	gossip
adj.	**beau**	-zuri	handsome
adj.	**beau (m), belle (f)**	-zuri	beautiful
adj & pr	**beaucoup**	-ingi	1. much 2. a lot 3. many
adv.	**beaucoup**	muno	very much
n.	**beauté (f)**	uzuri	beauty
n.	**beaux-parents (m)**	semeki	in-laws
n.	**bêche (f)**	jembe (pl. majembe)	spade
verb	**bégayer**	kubabaika	1. to stammer 2. to stutter
n.	**beignet**	kitumbua, (pl. vitumbua)	donut
n.	**Belgique (f)**	Mbelgiji	Belgium
n.	**bénédiction (f)**	baraka	blessing
verb	**bénir**	kubariki	bless, to
verb	**bercer**	kupembeza	rock, to
n.	**berceuse (f)**	kitumbuizo	lullaby
n.	**berger (m)**	mchungaji (pl. wachungaji)	shepherd

parts of speech	french	swahili	english
n.	**besoin (m)**	haja	need
n.	**bétail (m)**	mifugo	cattle
adj.	**bête**	-jinga	foolish
n.	**bêtises (f)**	upuzi	nonsense
n.	**beurre (m)**	siagi	butter
n.	**Bible (f)**	Biblia	Bible
n.	**bibliothèque (f)**	jamii ya vitabu	library
n.	**bicyclette (f)**	baisikeli	bicycle
adj., adv.	**bien**	1. vizuri 2. -ema 3. vema	1. well 2. good
adj.	**bien portant**	-zima	whole (good healthy)
conj.	**bien que**	1. ingawa 2. ijapo	1. although 2. even though
n.	**bienfait (m)**	fadhili	kindness
adv.	**bientôt**	bado kidogo	soon
phrase	**Bienvenu.**	Karibu.	Welcome.
n.	**bière (f)**	pombe	beer
n.	**bijou (m)**	johari	jewel
n., med	**bile (f)**	nyongo	bile
n., med	**bilharzia**	kichocho	bilharzia (schistosomiasis)
n.	**billet (m)**	cheti (pl. vyeti)	ticket
verb	**biner**	kulima	hoe, to
n.	**biscuit (m)**	biskuti	cracker
adj.	**blanc**	-eupe	white
phrase	**blancheur éclatante**	weupe	whiteness, dazzling
verb	**blanchir**	kufanya -eupe	whiten, to
n.	**blé (m)**	ngano	wheat
n. med	**blennorragie (f)**	kisonono	gonorrhea
verb	**blesser**	kudhuru	injure, to
verb	**être blesser**	kuumwa	wounded, to be
n.	**blessure (f)**	1. madhara 2. jeraha	1. injury 2. ulcer 3. wound 4. injury
adj.	**bleu, couleur**	buluu, samawati	blue
verb	**bloqué, être**	kukwama	stuck, to be
n.	**bobine (f) de fil à coudre**	kijiti cha kukunjia uzi	reel
verb	**boire (Que voulez-vous boire?)**	kunywa (Unataka kunywa nini?)	drink, to (What would you like to drink?)
n.	**bois (m)**	kuni	wood (for fire)
n.	**bois (m) de chauffage**	ukini (pl. kuni)	firewood
n.	**boisson (f)**	kinyweo (pl. vinyweo)	drink
n.	**boîte (f)**	1. sanduku 2. kopo	1. box 2. tin can
n.	**bol (m)**	bakuli	bowl
n.	**bombe (f)**	kombora	bomb

parts of speech	french	swahili	english
adj.	**bon (m), bonne (f)**	-ema	good
phrase	**bon appétit.**	karibu chakula	enjoy your meal
adj.	**bon marché**	rahisi	cheap
n.	**bonbon (m)**	tamutamu	candy
verb	**bondir**	kuruka	leap, to
n.	**bonheur (m)**	1. heri 2. furaha	1. happiness 2. fun
n.	**bonne (f)**	mwanamwali	maid
n.	**bonne sœur (f)**	mtawa wa kike	nun
n.	**bonnes manières (f)**	adabu	manners, good
n.	**bonsoir (m)**	kwa heri	good-night
n.	**bonté (f)**	wema	goodness
n.	**bord (m)**	ukingo	edge
n.	**bord (m) (d'un pot en argile)**	ukingo	brim
n.	**bord relevé**	kando	bank of river
n.	**borne (f)**	mpaka (pl. mipaka)	limit, boundary
n.	**botte (f)**	1. kiatu kirefu 2. kichala (pl. vichala)	1. boot 2. bunch (of fruit)
n.	**bouche (f)**	kinywa (pl. vinywa)	mouth
verb	**boucher**	1. kuziba njia 2. kuziba	1. to block 2. to stop up
n.	**boucher (m)**	mwuza nyama	butcher
n.	**bouchon (m)**	kizibo (pl. vizibo)	stopper (in bottle), cork
n.	**bouclier (m)**	ngabo	shield
verb	**bouder**	kununa	sulk, to
n.	**boue (f)**	matope	mud
n.	**bouffon (m)**	mpumbavu (pl. wapumbavu)	fool
n.	**bougeoir (m)**	kinara (pl. vinara)	candlestick
n.	**bougie (f)**	mshumaa	candle
verb	**bougonner**	kunungunika	grumble, to
n.	**bouillie (f)**	uji mzito	porridge
verb	**bouillir**	kuchmuka, kutokosa	boil, to
verb	**boulonner**	kukomea	bolt, to
n.	**bourse (f)**	kifuko cha kutilia fedha	purse
verb	**bousculer**	kusukumana	jostle, to
n.	**bouteille (f)**	chupa (pl. machupa)	bottle
n.	**boutique (f)**	duka (pl. maduka)	shop
n.	**bouton (m)**	kipele (pl. vipele)	pimple
n.	**bouton (m)**	kifungo (pl. vifungo)	button
n.	**bracelet (m)**	kikuku	bracelet
n.	**braise (f)**	makaa ya moto	embers
n.	**brancard (m)**	machela	stretcher

216

parts of speech	french	swahili	english
n.	branche (f)	tawi (pl. matawi)	branch
verb	braquer	kupiga shabaha	aim, to take
n.	bras (m)	mkono (pl. mikono)	arm
verb	brasser de la bière	kupika pombe	beer, to brew
adj.	brave	hodari	brave
verb	bredouiller	kuwa na kigugumizi	stammer, to
adj.	bref	-fupi	brief
verb	briller	kuangaza	reflect light, to
verb	briller, faire reluire	kungaa, kuwaka	shine, to
n.	brin (m)	jani	blade (grass)
n.	brique (f)	tofali	brick
n., med	bronchite	ugonjwa wa kifua	bronchitis
n.	bronze (m)	shaba nyeusi	bronze
n.	brosse (f) (la brosse due peintre) {la brosse à cheveux}	burashi (hair or paint brush)	brush (paintbrush) {hair brush}
n.	brosse (f) à dents	mswaki (pl. miswaki)	toothbrush
n.	brosse à cheveux (f)	burashi ya nywele	hairbrush
verb	brosser	kupangusa	brush, to
n.	brouillard (m)	umande	fog
n.	brousse (f)	kichaka (pl. vichaka)	bush
verb	brouter	kulisha	graze, to
n.	bruit (m)	1. kishindo 2. mwito wa kuku kwa watoto wake 3. makelele	1. clatter (of voices) 2. cluck 3. noise
verb	brûler	kuchoma, kuwaka	burn, to
n	brûlure (f)	umizo la moto	burn
n.	brume (f)	1. unyenyezi 2. ukungu	1. haze 2. mist
adj.	brun	rangi ya kunde	brown
adj.	brusque	-a ghafula	sudden, abrupt
adv.	brusquement	gafula	suddenly
adj.	bruyant	-enye makelele	noisy
n.	bûche (f)	gogo (pl. magogo)	log
n.	budget (m)	taarifa ya gharama	budget
n.	buffle (m)	nyati	buffalo
n.	bulle (f)	povu	bubble
n.	bureau (m)	meza	desk
n.	bureau (m) de poste	barua za posta	post office
n.	but (m)	1. mlango 2. kusudi	1. goal (as in football) 2. purpose
n.	cabane (f)	kijumba melini	cabin
n.	cabinet (m)	choo (pl. vyoo)	toilet

217

parts of speech	french	swahili	english
verb	**cacher**	kuficha	hide, to
n.	**cachet (m)**	muhuri (pl. mihuri)	seal
n.	**cachot (m)**	kifungo	dungeon
n.	**cadavre (m)**	maiti	corpse
n.	**cadeau (m)**	zawadi	present (gift)
n.	**cadenas (m)**	kufuli	padlock
n.	**café (m)**	kahawa	coffee
n.	**café (m) {endroit où l'on boit le café}**	mkahawa (pl. mikahawa)	café
n.	**caféier (m)**	mbuni	coffee plant
n.	**cage (f)**	tundu (pl. matundu), kizimba (pl. vizimba)	cage
n.	**caillou (m)**	makokoto (pl.)	pebble
n.	**caisse (f)**	sanduku (pl. masanduku)	chest (crate)
n.	**calamité (f)**	maafa	calamity
n.	**caleçon (m)**	chupi	boxer shorts (or slip)
n.	**calendrier (m)**	takwimu	calendar
n.	**calme (m)**	shwari	calm, quiet
verb	**calme, se**	kutulia	calm down, to
n.	**calomnie (f)**	masingizio	slander
verb	**calomnier**	1. kusingizia 2. kuzarau	1. to malign 2. to slander 2. to insult
n.	**calvitie (f)**	upaa	baldness
n.	**camarade (m,f)**	mwenzi	associate
n.	**caméléon (m)**	kinyonga (pl. vinyonga)	chameleon
n.	**camion (m)**	gari doga	truck
adj.	**campagnard**	nchi	country
n.	**campagne (f)**	shamba (pl. mashamba)	rural
n.	**campement (m)**	kambi (pl. makambi)	camp
verb	**camper**	kupiga kambi	camp, to
n.	**Canadien (m)**	mwenyeji wa Canada	Canadian
n.	**canal (m)**	mfereji (pl. mifereji)	channel
n.	**canard (m)**	bata (pl. mabata)	duck
n.	**cancer (m)**	jamii moja ya nyota	cancer
n.	**cancrelat (m)**	mende	cockroach
n.	**candidat (m)**	mtaka kazi au cheo fulani	candidate
phrase	**ça ne fait rien**	haidhuru	never mind
phrase	**Ça ne fait rien.**	Hamna shida. Hapana maneno.	It does not matter.
adv.	**ça n'est pas le cas**	sivyo	not so; (that is not so)
phrase	**Ça va bien.**	Sijambo	I'm fine.
n.	**caniveau (m)**	mchirizi	gutter

parts of speech	french	swahili	english
n.	canne (f)	fimbo	1. cane 2. walking stick
n.	canne à sucre	muwa (pl. miwa)	sugar cane
n.	caoutchouc (m)	mpira (pl. mipira)	rubber
n.	capable	akili, ustadi, uwezo	ability, (to have)
adj.	capable	-enye kuweza	1. capable 2. able
n.	capacité (f)	ujazo, nafasi	capacity
n.	capitale (f)	mji mkuu	capital (city)
n.	capitale (f)	herufi kubwa	capital (letter)
n.	captivité (f)	utumwa	captivity
verb	capturer	kukamata	capture, to
conj.	car	kwani, maana, kwa sababu	because
n.	caractère (m)	tabia	character
phrase	caractère héréditaire	ufananaji wa mtoto na wazazi wake	hereditary trait
verb	caresser	kukumbatia kwa upendo	caress, to
n.	carotte (f)	karoti	carrot
n.	carrefour (m)	njia panda	crossroads
n.	carte (f) géographique	ramani	map
n.	cas (m)	jambo, kesi	case
n.	cascade (f)	anguko la maji	waterfall
verb	casser	1. kuvunja 2. kualika	1. to break 2. to crack
n.	casserole (f)	sufuria (pl. masufuria)	pan, cooking
n.	cassier (m)	karani wa fedha	cashier
n.	catastrophe (f)	msiba mkuu	catastrophe
n.	catégorie (f)	aina, jamii	category
n.	catholique (m,f)	katoliko	catholic
n.	cause (f)	sababu	cause
verb	être cause de	kufanyiza	cause, to
verb	causer	kuzungumza	chat, to
n.	causerie (f)	1. maongezi 2. mazungumzo	1. chat 2. dialogue
n.	cave (f)	ghala ya chini	cellar
n.	cavité (f)	shimo (pl. mashimo)	cavity
pronoun	ce sont, ils sont, elles sont	Kuna...	they are
adj.,pro.	ce, cet, cette	yule (sing. person); ile (sing. thing)	that
adj.,pro.	ce, cet, cette	huyu (person, sing.); hii (thing, sing.)	this
n.	cécité (f)	upofu	blindness
n.	ceinture (f)	mshipi (pl. mishipi)	belt
pronoun	cela (C'est cela.)	ile, kile, vile (Ndivyo.)	it, that (That is right.)
adj.	célèbre	mashuhuri	famous

219

parts of speech	french	swahili	english
n.	célébration (f)	mwadhimisho	celebration
verb	célébrer	kushangilia	celebrate, to
n.	célibataire (m)	mtu asiyeoa	bachelor
adj. & n.	célibataire (m, f)	mtawa (pl. watawa)	unmarried person
pronoun	celui-là, celle-là	hiyo	that one
n.	cendres (f)	majivu (pl.)	ashes
adj. & n.	cent (m)	mia	hundred (one hundred)
n. & adj.	cent mille	laki	hundred thousand
n.	centre (f)	palipo katikati hasa	center, in the
n.	centre de santé (f)	kituo cha afya	health center
adv.	cependant	walakini	however
n.	cercle (m)	mviringo (pl. miviringo), duara	circle
n.	cercueil (m)	sanduku la maiti	coffin
n.	cérémonie (f)	ibada au sherehe ya heshima	ceremony
n.	cerf-volant (m)	tiara	kite
verb	cerner (Avoir les yeux cernés.)	kuzungusha	surround, to (To have rings under one's eyes.)
adj.	certain	fulani	certain
adv.	certainement	hakika	certainly
verb	certifier	kuhakikisha	make sure, to
adv.	certitude	hakika	surely
n.	cerveau (m)	ubongo	brain
adj & pr	ces, ceux-ci (m), celles-ci (f)	hawa (pl. person); hizi (pl. things)	these
adj & pr	ces, ceux-là (m), celles-là (f)	wale (pl. person); zile (pl. thing)	those
n.	cessation (f)	ukomo	cessation
verb	cesser	1. kukoma 2. kusimamisha	1. to cease 2. to stop
phrase	C'est bien.	Nzuri kabisa.	It is good.
phrase	C'est bien.	Vema.	All right.
phrase	C'est ça.	Wakaligani.	That's right.
phrase	C'est loin?	Ni mbali?	Is it far?
phrase	C'est près?	Ni karibu?	Is it close?
phrase	C'est trop cher.	Nibeyisana.	That is too expensive. (service)
phrase	C'est trop cher.	Ni ghali mno.	That's too expensive. (thing)
phrase	cette an	mwaka huu	this year
adv.	cette nuit	usiku huu	tonight
phrase	cette semaine	wiki hii	this week

parts of speech	french	swahili	english
pronoun	chacun	kila	each
n.	chagrin (m)	1. sikitiko 2. huzuni	1. deep sorrow 2. grief
n.	chaîne (f)	mnyororo (pl. minyororo)	chain
n.	chair (f) (avoir la chair de poule)	nyama (kimbibi)	flesh (to have goose bumps)
n.	chaise (f)	kiti (pl. viti)	chair
n.	chaleur (f)	joto, moto	heat
n.	chambre (f)	chumba	room (in house)
n.	chambre d'amis (f)	chomba cha mgeni	guest room
n.	chameau (m)	ngamia	camel
n.	champ (m)	shamba (pl. mashamba)	field
n.	champignon (m)	kiyoga (pl. viyoga)	mushroom
n.	chance (f)	bahati	fortune, luck
adj.	chance, avoir de la	-a bahati njema	lucky
verb	changer de	kubadilisha	change, to
verb	changer de l'argent	kuvunga	change money, to
verb	changer d'avis	kughairi	change one's mind, to
n.	chanson (f), chant (m)	wimbo (pl. nyimbo)	song
n.	chant (m) du coq	kuwika jogoo	cock-crowing
n.	chantage (m)	mrungula	blackmail
verb	chanter	kuwika	crow, to
verb	chanter	kuimba	sing, to
n.	chaos (m)	machafuko makubwa	chaos
n.	chapeau (m)	kofia	hat
n.	chapelet (f)	tasbihi	rosary
n.	chapitre (m)	sura	chapter
adj.	chaque	kila	each
adj.	chaque, entier (toujours)	kila (daima)	every, whole (always)
n.	charbon de bois (m)	makaa ya miti	charcoal
n.	charge (f)	shambulio	charge (in battle)
n.	charge (f)	mzigo (pl. mizigo)	load
adj.	charge supplémentaire	-a kuongeza	supplementary
verb	charger	kupakiza	load, to
adj.	charmant	-a kupendeza	delightful
n.	charme (m) (amulette)	hirizi	charm
verb	chasser	1. kufukuza 2. kuwinda	1. to drive away 2. to hunt
n.	chat (m), chatte (f)	paka	cat
verb	chatouiller	kutekenya	tickle, to
adj.	chaud	-a moto	hot
adj.	chaud	-a moto	warm
verb	chauffer	kupasha moto	heat, to

221

parts of speech	french	swahili	english
n.	chauffeur (m)	1. dreva wa motakaa 2. dereva	1. chauffeur 2. driver
n.	chaussette (f)	kama mfuko wa kuvaa mguuni	sock
n.	chausseur (m)	mwindaji (pl. waindaji)	hunter
n.	chaussure (f)	kiatu (pl. viatu)	shoe
n.	château (m)	ngome	castle
verb	châtier	kuadhibu	castigate, to
verb	châtrer	kuhasi	castrate, to
n.	chef (m)	1. sultani 2. mwenye amri 3. kiongozi (pl. viongozi) 4. mutawala (pl. watawala)	1. chief 2. commander 3. leader 4. ruler (person)
n.	chemin (m)	njia	way (road)
n.	cheminée (f)	mahali nyumbani pa kukokea moto	fireplace
n.	chemise (f)	shati	shirt
n.	chenille (f)	mtoto wa kipepeo	caterpillar
adj.	cher (m), chère (f)	1. -penzi 2. ghali	1. dear 2. expensive
n.	cher (m,f)	ghali	dear
verb	chercher	kutafuta	1. to seek 2. to search 3. to look for
adj.	chétif	-dogo	puny
n.	cheval (m)	farasi	horse
n.	cheveu(m) {J'ai besoin me faire couper les cheveux.}	unywele (pl. nywele) {Nataka kutaka nywele.}	hair (of human) {I want a haircut.}
n., med	cheville (f)	kifundo cha muguu (pl, vifundo cha muguu)	ankle
n.	chèvre (f)	mbuzi	goat
prep.	chez	nyumba	home
n.	chien (m)	mbwa	dog
n.	chiffon (m)	kitambaa (pl. vitambaa)	rag
n.	chimpanzé (m)	sokwe	chimpanzee
n.	chirurgie (f)	udaktari, kazi ya surgeon	surgery
n.	chœur (m)	jamii ya waimbaji	choir
verb	choisir	1. kupokea na kufuata 2. kuchagua	1. to adopt (habit) 2. to choose
n.	choix (m)	hiari	choice
n. & adj.	choix (m); autre	njia ya pili	alternative
n., med	choléra	kipindupindu	cholera
n.	chose (f)	kitu (pl. vitu)	thing
n.	Chrétien (m)	Mkristo	Christian
adj.	chronique	-a kusedeka	chronic
verb	chuchoter	nong'ona	whisper, to

parts of speech	french	swahili	english
adv.	ci (Par ci, part là.)	hapa, huko (huko na huko)	here (Here and there.)
adv.	ci-dessous	chini ya	below
adv.	ci-dessus, sur	juu (ya)	above
n.	cible (f)	shabaha	target
n.	cicatrice (f)	kovu (pl. makovu)	scar
n.	ciel (m)	1. mbinguni 2. anga	1. heaven 2. sky
n.	cigare (m)	sigara	cigar
n.	cigarette (f)	sigareti	cigarette
n.	cil (m)	ukope	eyelash
n.	ciment (m)	udongo ulaya	cement
n.	cimetière (m)	makaburini	cemetery
n.	cinéma (m)	filamu	movie theater
adj. & n.	cinq (m)	tano	five
n.	cinq cents	mia tano	five hundred
n.	cinq mille	elfu tano	five thousand
adj. & n.	cinquante (m)	hamsini	fifty
adj.	cinquième	-a tano	fifth
verb	circoncire	kutahiri	circumcise, to
n.	circoncision (f)	tohara	circumcision
n.	circonférence (f)	mzingo	circumference
n.	circonstance (f)	jambo, maneno	circumstance
verb	circuler	kuzunguka	circulate, to
n.	cire (f)	nta	wax
n.	ciseaux (m)	makasi	scissors
verb	citer	kutaja	quote or cite, to
n.	citoyen (m)	raia	citizen
n.	citron (m)	limau (pl. malimau)	lemon
n.	citron (m) vert	ndimu	lime (fruit)
adj.	civilisé	-staarabu	civilized
adj.	clair	wazi	clear
adv.	clairement	kwa dhahiri	clearly
n.	clan (m)	ukoo	clan
n.	claque (f)	kofi	slap
verb	clarifier	kubainisha	clarify, to
n.	classe (f)	darasa	class (students)
n., med	clavicule	mtulinga	clavicle
n.	clé (f) {J'ai perdu mes clefs.}	ufunguo (pl. funguo) {Nilipoteza funguo.)	key {I lost my keys.}
n.	clémence (f)	huruma	clemency
verb	cligner des yeux	kupepesa macho	blink, to
verb	clignoter	kumulika ghafula	flash, to

parts of speech	french	swahili	english
n.	**cloche (m)**	kengele	bell
n.	**clou (m)**	msumari (pl. misumari)	nail (metal)
verb	**clouer**	kupiga musumari	nail, to
n.	**clôture (f)**	ugo (pl. nyugo)	fence
verb	**coaguler, se**	kuganda	coagulate, to
n.	**cobra (m)**	nyoka	cobra
n., med	**coccyx (os du bassin)**	kifandugu	coccyx
n.	**cochon (m)**	nguruwe	pig
n.	**cœur (m)**	moyo (pl. mioyo)	heart
n.	**coffre-fort (m)**	kilindo (pl. vilindo)	safe (to hold valuables)
n.	**coin (m)**	pembe	corner
verb	**coïncider**	kulingana	coincide, to
n	**colère (f)**	gazabu, kasirani	anger
verb	**collaborer**	kushirikiana katika kazi	collaborate, to
verb	**coller à**	kukamatisha	stick to, to
n.	**colline (f)**	mlima (pl. milima)	hill
n.	**colombe (f)**	hua	dove
verb	**combattre**	kupigana	fight, to
adv.	**combien**	-ngapi	how much
phrase	**Combien de fois?**	Malangapi?	How many times?
phrase	**combien de temps**	kwa muda gani	how long
phrase	**Combien est ceci?**	Ni bei gani?	How much does this cost?
n.	**comité (m)**	halmashauri	committee
n.	**commandement (m)**	amri (pl. amri)	command
verb	**commander**	kuamuru	command, to
adv.	**comme**	kama, -vyo, kwa sababu	as
n.	**commencement (m)**	mwanzo (pl. mianzo)	1. beginning 2. inception
verb	**commencer**	kuanza	commence, to
adv.	**comment**	namna gani	how
phrase	**Comment ça va?**	Hujambo? (singular); Hamjambo? (plural)	How are you?
phrase	**Comment est votre famille?**	Habari za nyumbani?	How is your family?
phrase	**Comment fait-tu?**	Mambo?	How are you doing?
n.	**commerçant (m)**	mfanyi biashara	trader
verb	**commettre l'adultère**	kuzini	adultery, to commit
verb	**commettre une faute**	kukosa	commit an error, to
n.	**commode (f)**	kabati	dresser
adj.	**commun**	-a kawaida	common
verb	**communiquer**	1. kupelekeana habari 2. kutangaza	1. to communicate 2. to announce

224

parts of speech	french	swahili	english
n.	compagnon (m), compagne (f)	mwenzi	1. companion 2. mate (a pair of things)
n.	comparaison (f)	mfano (pl. mifano)	comparison
verb	comparer	kulinganisha	compare, to
n.	compassion (f)	mapatano	sympathy
n.	compère (m)	kutega kwa hila	decoy
n.	compétition (f)	shindano (pl. mashindano)	competition
adj.	complet	-timilifu	complete
adv.	complètement, tout à fait	pia	completely, totally
n.	complication (f)	matata	complication
verb	composer	kutunga	compose, to
n.	compréhension (f)	ufahamu	1. comprehension 2. understanding
verb	comprendre	kufahamu	comprehend, to
verb	comprendre {Comprends-tu?} [Je n'ai pas compris.]	kufahamu {Unaelewa?} [Sielewi.]	understand, to {Do you understand?} [I did not understand.]
n.	comprimé (m)	kibonge	tablet (pill)
n.	compte (m)	hesabu, masimulizi	account (finance)
verb	compter	kuhesabu	count, to
verb	compter sur	kutegemea	rely on, to
n.	compteur (m)	meta	meter
verb	concéder	kukubali	concede, to
verb	concevoir	kufahamu	conceive, to
verb	conclure	kumaliza	conclude, to
n.	conclusion (f)	mwisho	conclusion
n.	condamnation (f)	lawama	condemnation
verb	condamner	kupatiliza	condemn, to
n.	condition (f)	hali	condition
verb	conduire	kuendesha	drive, to
verb	conduire mal, se	kukosa adabu	misbehave, to
n.	conduite (f)	mwenendo (pl. mienendo)	1. behavior 2. conduct
verb	confesser	kukiri	confess, to
n.	confession (f)	maungamo	confession
n.	confiance (f)	imani	beliefs (confidence)
n.	confiance (f) (J'ai confiance en lui.)	tumaini	trust (I trust him.)
verb	confirmer	kuthibitisha	confirm, to
n.	conflit (m)	mapigano	conflict
verb	confondre	kuchafua	confuse, to
n.	confort (m)	faraja	comfort
adj.	confortable	-enye raha	comfortable

225

parts of speech	french	swahili	english
n.	confusion (f)	chafuko	confusion
n.	congé (m)	kuacha	vacation
verb	conjecturer	kudhani tu	conjecture about, to
n., med	conjonctivite	uvimbe wa mboni	conjunctivitis
n.	connaissance (f)	1. ujuzi maarifa 2. mtu umjuaye 3. maarifa	1. acquaintance 2. knowledge
verb	connaître	1. kujua 2. kujuana	1. to know 2. to be acquainted
verb	conquérir	kushinda	conquer, to
n.	conscience (f)	dhamiri	conscience
phrase	conscient, être	kufahamu	aware, to be
n.	conseil (m)	1. shauri (pl. mashauri) 2. baraza	1. advice 2. council
verb	conseiller	1. kutoa shauri 2. kuonya	1. to advise 2. to counsel
verb	consentir	kukubali	consent, to
n.	conséquence (sans conséquence)	jambo litokealo kwa sababu fulani	consequence (without repercussions)
verb	conserver	kuhifadhi	preserve, to
n.	considération (f)	uangalifu	consideration
verb	considérer	kufikili	consider, to
verb	consoler	kufariji	console, to
adv.	constamment	daima	constantly
n.	constitution (f)	sheria ya serkali	constitution
n.	constructeur (m)	mjengaji (pl. wajengaji)	builder
verb	construire	kufanyiza	construct, to
verb	consulter	kushauri	consult, to
adj.	contagieux	-a kuambukiza	contagious
verb	contempler	kutafakari	contemplate, to
verb	contenter	kupendezwa	satisfy, to
n.	continent africain (m)	nchi ya Africa	African continent
adj.	continu	bila kukoma	continuous
n.	continuation (f)	mfulizo	continuation
verb	continuer	1. kudumu 2. kuendelea	1. to continue 2. to carry on 3. to keep on
verb	contourner	1. kuzunguka 2. kupakana na	1. to go around 1. to skirt around
verb	contraindre	kushurutisha	coerce, to
verb	contredire	kubisha	contradict, to
verb	contribuer	kutoa fedha au msaada	contribute, to
n.	contribution (f)	kitu kilichotolewa	contribution
n.	controverse (f)	mabishano	controversy

parts of speech	french	swahili	english
verb	contrôler	1. kuhakiki 2. kutawala	1. to verify 2. to control (govern)
n.	contusion (f)	chubuo	contusion
verb	convaincre	kusadikisha	convince, to
adj.	convenable	-ema	suitable
adv.	convenablement, correctement	vema	properly
verb	convenir de	kukubali	agree on, to
n.	conversation (f)	mazungumzo	1. conversation 2. talk
verb	converser	kusemezana, kuzungumza	converse with, to
verb	convoiter	kutamani	covet, to
n.	convulsion (f)	kifafa	convulsion
n.	coopération (f)	shirika	cooperation
verb	coopérer	kusaidiana	cooperate, to
n.	copain (m)	mpenzi	boyfriend
adj.	copieux	tele	copious
n.	copine (f)	mpenzi	girlfriend
n.	coq (m)	jogoo	rooster, cock (fowl)
n.	coquille (f)	ganda la yai	eggshell
n.	corde (f)	kamba	1. cord 2. rope
n., med	cordon ombilical	kitovu (pl. vitovu)	umbilical cord
n.	corne (f)	pembe (pl. mapembe)	horn (of animal)
n.	corps (m)	mwili (pl. miili)	body
n.	correct	usawa	right (correct)
verb	corriger	kusahihisha	correct, to
n.	côte (f) (côte à côte)	ubavu (sawasawa)	1. rib 2. shore (side by side)
n.	côté (m) (à côté de)	upande (karibu na)	side (next to)
n.	coton (m)	pamba	cotton
n.	cou (m)	shingo (mashingo)	neck
n.	coucher du soleil (m)	magharibi	sunset
verb	coucher, se	kuchwa	set, to (sun)
n.	coude (m)	kiko cha mkono; kivi	elbow
verb	coudre	kushona	sew, to
verb	couler	kutiririka	flow, to
verb	couler goutte à goutte	kutiririka	trickle, to
n.	couleur (f)	rangi	color
phrase	coup de pied	teke (pl. mateke)	kick
phrase	coup de poing	kupiga ngumi	punch
n.	coup d'oeil	kutupa jicho	glance
verb	couper	kukata	cut, to
n.	couple (m)	jozi	couple

parts of speech	french	swahili	english
n.	cour (f)	nyumba ya mfaime	court
n.	courage (m)	1. ujasiri 2. uhodari	1. bravery 2. courage
adj.	courageux	-jasiri	courageous
adj.	courbé	-a kupotoka	crooked
n.	courge (f)	mboga	squash (botanical)
verb	courir	kupiga mbio	run, to
n.	couronne (f)	taji	crown
adj.	court	-fupi	short
n.	courtoisie (f)	jamala	courtesy
n.	coussin (m)	takia (pl. matakia)	cushion
n.	coût (m)	bei, gharama	cost
n.	couteau (m)	kisu (pl. visu)	knife
n.	coutume (f)	desturi	custom
n.	couvercle (m)	kifuniko (pl. vifuniko)	1. cover 2. lid
n.	couverture (f)	balangiti	blanket
verb	couvrir	kufunika, kutamani	cover, to
phrase	couvrir un toit	kutia mapaa	roof, to put on
verb	couvrir, se	kuvaa nguo	cover oneself, to
n.	crachat (m)	mate	spit
verb	cracher	kutema mate	1. to expectorate 2. to spit
n.	craie (f)	chaki	chalk
verb	craindre	kuogopa	fear, to
n.	crainte (f)	woga	fear
adj.	craintif	-oga	timid
n.	crampe (f) d'estomac	tumbo linanyonga	stomach cramp
n.	crapaud (m)	chura (pl. vyura)	toad
n.	crayon (m)	kalamu	pencil
n.	créature (f)	kiumbe (pl. viumbe)	creature
adj.	crédule	-jinga	gullible
verb	créer	kuumba	create, to
n.	crème (f)	maziwa ya mtindi	cream
n.	crépuscule (m)	1. giza la jioni 2. ukungu wa ijioni	1. dusk 2. twilight
n.	crible (m)	kitandawili (pl. vitandawili)	riddle
n.	crime (m)	hatia	crime
n.	criminel (m), criminelle (f)	mhalifu	criminal
n.	crise cardiaque (f)	kushambuliwa na maradhi	heart attack
verb	critiquer	kuhukumu au pima	talk against, to
n.	crocodile (m)	mamba	crocodile
verb	croire	1. kusadiki 2. kuamini	believe, to
verb	croiser	kuvuka	cross, to

228

parts of speech	french	swahili	english
n.	croix (f)	msalaba (pl. misalaba)	cross
verb	croître	kuota	grow, to
adj.	cru	-bichi	raw
n.	cruauté (f)	ukatili	cruelty
n.	cruche (f)	1. mtungi (pl. mitungi) 2. gudulia	1. jug 2. pitcher
verb	crucifier	kusulibi	crucify, to
verb	cueillir	kuchuma	pick, to
n.	cuiller (f)	kijiko (pl. vijiko)	spoon
verb	cuire	kupika	cook, to
n.	cuisine (f)	jiko	kitchen
n.	cuisinier (m)	mpishi (pl. wapishi)	cook
n.	cuisse (f)	paja (pl. mapaja)	thigh
phrase	cuit, être	kuiva	cooked, to be well (to be done)
n.	cuivre (m)	shaba	copper
n.	cuivre jaune (m)	shaba	brass
n.	culpabilité (f)	hatia	guilt
n.	cultivateur (m)	mkulima (pl. wakulima)	cultivator
verb	cultiver	kulima	cultivate, to
adj.	cupide	-lafi	greedy
n.	curiosité (f)	kitu cha shani	curiosity
n.	cuvette (f)	bakuli	basin (wash)
n.	cyclone (m)	kimbunga; tufani	cyclone
adv.	d'abord	kwanza	1. at first 2. to begin with
verb	d'accord, être	kupatana	1. to agree 2. to approve 3. to concur
interj.	D'accord.	Nakubali.	O.K.
n.	dame (f)	bibi	lady
n.	danger (m)	hatari	danger
adj.	dangereux	-a hatari	dangerous
n.	danse (f)	dansi	dance
verb	danser	kucheza ngoma	dance, to
n.	date (f)	tarehe	date (in month)
n.	datte	tende	date (fruit)
prep.	de, (depuis)	toka	from, (time)
prep.	de...à	toka...hata	from...to (place)
prep.	de...à	tangu...hata	from...to (time)
verb	débarquer	kushuka	get off, to
n.	débat (m)	jadiliano	debate
verb	débattre	kujadiliana	debate, to
n.	débauche (f)	utongozi	debauchery

parts of speech	french	swahili	english
verb	**déboîter**	kuchopoa	pull out, to
adv.	**de bonne heure , tôt**	mapema	early
verb	**déborder**	kufurika	overflow, to
n.	**débris (m)**	kifusi	debris
n.	**début (m)**	mwanzo (pl. mianzo)	beginning
verb	**débuter, commencer**	kuanza	begin, to
n.	**décembre (m)**	Desemba; mwezi wa kumi na mbili wa mwaka wa kizungu	December
verb	**décevoir**	kudanganya	deceive, to
verb	**décharger**	kushusha	unload, to
verb	**déchirer**	kupasua	tear, to
verb	**décider**	kuamua	decide, to
n.	**décision (f)**	maamuzi	decision (final)
verb	**décliner**	kukataa	decline, to
verb	**déconcerter**	kutatiza	baffle, to
verb	**décorer**	kupamba	decorate, to
verb	**découper**	kuchora	carve, to
verb	**décourager**	kuvunja moyo	discourage, to
verb	**découvrir**	kufumbua, kuvumbua	discover, to
verb	**décrire**	kuwasifu	describe, to
n.	**dédain (m)**	dharau	disdain
adv. prep.	**dedans (m)**	ndani ya	inside
n.	**dédommagement (m)**	fidia	compensation
verb	**déduire**	kutambua maana	deduce, to
n.	**défaut (m)**	kombo	flaw
verb	**défendre**	1. kulinda 2. kukataza	1. to defend 2. to forbid 3. to prohibit
verb	**défendre à d'entrer**	kujitafutiya kuingiya	forbid entry, to
n.	**défendu**	marufuku	forbidden
n.	**défense**	ulinzi	defense
n.	**défenseur (m)**	mteteaji	advocate
verb	**déféquer**	kunya; kuenda choo	have a stool (bowel movement), to
n.	**défi (m)**	kutaka thibitisho	challenge
verb	**définir**	kubainisha	define, to
n.	**définition (f)**	ubainisho	definition
adv.	**définitivement**	-a mwisho	final
verb	**défoncer**	kutomoa	smash up, to
verb	**défroisser**	adoucir	smooth out, to
verb	**dégonfler**	kupwesha	deflate, to
verb	**dégouliner**	kutirika	trickle, to

parts of speech	french	swahili	english
verb	dégoutter	kudondoka	drip, to
n.	dégoût (m)	karaha	disgust
interj.	De grâce!	Wapi!	For pity's sake!
verb	dégrader, se	kupotewa na uzuri	deteriorate, to
adv.	dehors	nje	1. out 2. outside
adv.	de justesse	kwa shida	narrowly
adv.	déjà	tayari	already
n.	déjeuner (f)	chakula cha mchana	lunch
n.	déjeuner (f)	chakula kikubwa cha kutwa	dinner (noon)
n.	délai (m)	muda	deadline
n.	délibération (f)	shauri	deliberation
adv.	délicat	-enye matata	awkward
adj.	délicieux	-tamu	delicious
verb	délivrer	kuponya	rescue, to
adv.	de long en large	huko na huko	to and fro
n.	déluge (m)	tufani, zoruba	storm
adv.	de l'autre côté	ngambo	other side
adv.	demain	kesho	tomorrow
phrase	demande en mariage	kuposa	marriage proposal
verb	demande entrée	kupiga hodi	ask entrance, to
verb	demander	kuomba	ask for, to
verb	demander à	kuuliza	ask (question), to
verb	demander des explications	kufasiri	interpret, to ask to
verb	demander un prix exagéré	taka bei kubwa kuliko haki	overcharge, to
n.	démangeaison (f)	1. kiwasho 2. upele	1. pruritus 2. itch
verb	démanger	kuwasha	itch, to
verb	démentir	kukana	deny, to
verb	déménager	kuhama	move, to (dwelling)
verb	demeurer	1. kukaa 2. kubaki	1. to dwell 2. to remain
adv.	demi	nusu	half
n.	démocratie (f)	utawala wa raia	democracy
verb	démolir	kubomoa	1. to demolish 2. to tear down
verb	dénigrer	kuchongea	denigrate, to
verb	dénouer	kufungua	untie, to
adv.	de nouveau	tena	again
n.	dentiste (m,f)	daktari wa meno	dentist
adj.	dénué de sens	bila maana	meaningless
verb	dépasser	kuzidi	exceed, to
verb	dépendre de	kutegemea	depend on, to

parts of speech	french	swahili	english
verb	dépenser	kutoa	spend, to
verb	déplacer; s'avancer	kujongea	move, to
verb	déplier	kunjua	unfold, to
adj.	de plus	zaidi	extra
adv.	de plus, d'ailleurs	zaidi ya hayo	moreover
verb	déposer	kuweka	deposit, to
phrase	dépourvue de dents	-siye na meno	teeth, lacking
n.	dépravation (f)	ufisadi	depravity
verb	déprécier	kupungua thamani	depreciate, to
adv.	depuis	tangu	since
phrase	De quoi souffres-tu?	Kuna shida gani?	suffering from?, What are you
n.	dent (f) {J'ai mal aux dents.}	jino (pl. meno) {Nina maumivu ya jino.}	tooth {I have a toothache.}
adj.	déraisonnable	isiyo na maana	irrational
verb	déranger	kuondoa	trouble, to
adj.	dernier	-a mwisho	last
adv.	dernièrement	siku hizi	lately
adv, n. prep.	derrière (m)	nyuma ya	behind
adj.	désagréable	-a kuchukiza	nasty
verb	désapprouver	kutoridhia	disapprove, to
n.	désastre (m)	baa, msiba	disaster
verb	descendre	kushuka, kutelemuka	descend, to; go down, to
verb	descendre (l'arbre)	kutelemka	climb down, (tree), to
n.	désert	jangwa	desert (ie. Sahara desert)
n.	désert (m)	jangwa	wilderness
verb	désespérer	kukata tamaa	despair, to
n.	désir (m)	1. mapenzi 2. hamu	1. wish 2. desire
verb	désirer	kutaka	desire, to
verb	désirer ardemment	kutamani	long for, to
adj.	désireux	-enye bidii	eager
verb	désobéir	kuasi	disobey, to
n.	désobéissance (f)	ukaidi	disobedience
n.	désordre (m)	fujo (pl. mafujo)	disorder
phrase	de sorte que	hata	so, so that
n.	dessein (m)	kielelezo	design (sketch)
n.	dessert (m)	matunda	dessert
verb	dessiner	kuandika sanamu	draw, to
adv.	dessous	chini ya	under
n.	destin (m)	ajali	destiny
n.	destitution (f)	ufukara	destitution

parts of speech	french	swahili	english
n.	**destruction (f)**	uharibifu	destruction
verb	**détacher**	kutenga	detach, to
adv.	**de temps en temps**	mara kwa mara	1. from time to time 2. occasionally 3. now and then
verb	**déterminer**	kukaza nia	determine, to
verb	**détester**	kuchukia sana	detest, to
n.	**détresse (f)**	huzuni, dhiki	distress
verb	**détruire**	kuangamiza, kuharibu	destroy, to
n.	**dette (f)**	deni	debt
n.	**deuil (m)**	kilio	mourning
n. & adj.	**deux (m)**	mbili	two
n.	**deux cents**	mia mbili	two hundred
adv.	**deux fois**	mara mbili	twice
n.	**deux mille**	elfu mbili	two thousand
adj.	**deuxième**	-a pili	second
adj.	**de valeur**	-a thamani	valuable
adv.	**devant**	mbele	1. ahead 2. in front of
verb	**dévier**	kuenda upande	deviate, to
verb	**devenir**	kuwa, kufaa	become, to
verb	**devenir obèse**	kunenepa	obese, to become
verb	**deviner**	kukisi	guess, to
verb	**dévoiler**	kufunua	1. to reveal 2. to unveil
verb	**devoir**	kupaswa	1. must 2. ought to
n.	**devoir (m)**	wajibu	1. obligation 2. duty
n., med	**diabète**	kisukari	diabetes
n.	**diable (m)**	ibilisi	devil
n., med	**diaphragme (m)**	kiwambo	diaphragm
n.	**dictionnaire (m)**	kamusi	dictionary
n.	**Dieu (m)**	Mungu	God
verb	**diffamer**	kusengenya	defame, to
n.	**différence (f)**	tofauti	difference
adj.	**différent**	mbali mbali	different
verb	**différent, être**	kuhitilafiana	different, to be
adj.	**difficile**	-gumu	difficult
n.	**difficulté (f)**	mashaka, taabu	difficulty
n.	**dignité (f)**	heshima na upendo	dignity
n.	**digue (f)**	boma la kuzuia maji	dam
verb	**dilater**	kutanua	expand, to
n.	**dimanche (m)**	Jumapili	Sunday
verb	**diminuer**	kupunguka	decrease, to

parts of speech	french	swahili	english
verb	**diminuer**	kupunguza	reduce, to
verb	**diminuer quantité**	kupunguza	diminish the quantity, to
n.	**diminution (f)**	upunguo	decrease
n.	**dindon (m)**	bata mzinga	turkey
n.	**diplôme (m)**	hati ya sifa	diploma
verb	**dire**	kusema	say, to
verb	**dire à**	1. kusema na 2. kuambia	1. to say to 2. to tell
phrase	**dire de mensonge**	kusema uwongo	tell a lie, to
verb	**dire franchement**	-a kwenda sawa, être	speak frankly, to
n.	**directeur (m)**	msimamizi (pl. wasimamizi)	1. director 2. manager
n.	**direction (f)**	upande	direction
verb	**diriger**	kuagiza, kuongoza	direct, to
interj.	**Dis donc...**	Ati...	I say... (look here)
verb	**discerner**	kutambua	discern, to
n.	**discipline (f)**	nidhamu	discipline
n.	**discussion (f)**	mazungumzo	discussion
verb	**discuter**	kuzungumzia habari	discuss, to
verb	**disparaître**	kutoweka	disappear, to
n.	**dispute (f)**	1. ugomvi 2. mabishano	1. dispute 2. argument
n.	**dissension (f)**	faraka	dissension
verb	**dissimuler**	kuficha	conceal, to
verb	**dissoudre**	kuyeyuka	dissolve, to
verb	**dissuader**	kujaribu	dissuade, to
n.	**distance (f)**	umbali	distance
adj.	**distant**	mbali	aloof
adj.	**distinct**	dhahiri	distinct
verb	**distinguer**	kupambanua	distinguish between, to
verb	**distraire**	kuvuta mawazo pengine	distract, to
adj.	**distrait**	-sahaulifu	absent-minded
verb	**divaguer**	kutembea	ramble, to
n.	**divergence**	tofauti	divergence
verb	**diverger**	kuachana	diverge, to
adj.	**divers**	-a namna nyingi	miscellaneous
verb	**diviser**	kugawa	divide, to
n.	**division (f)**	mgawo	division
verb	**divorcer**	kuvunja ndoa	divorce, to
n. & adj.	**dix (m)**	kumi	ten
n.	**dix-huit**	kumi na nane	eighteen
n.	**dix-neuf**	kumi na tisa	nineteen
n.	**dix-sept**	kumi na saba	seventeen

parts of speech	french	swahili	english
adj.	**dixième**	-a kumi	tenth
n.	**dîner (m)**	chakula kikuu cha siku	dinner (night)
n.	**docteur (m) de sorcière**	mfumu (pl. wafumu)	witch doctor
n.	**docteur (m), médecin (m)**	mganga (pl. waganga)	doctor (academic, medicine)
n.	**document (m)**	hati	document
n.	**doigt (m)**	kidole (pl. vidole)	finger
n.	**doigt (m) anneau**	kidole cha pete	finger, ring
n.	**doigt (m) du milieu**	kidole cha kati	finger, middle
n.	**doigt (m) index**	kidole cha shahada	finger, index
n.	**domestique (m,f)**	mtumishi (pl. watumishi)	servant (male or female)
verb	**dominer**	kushinda	dominate, to
n.	**don (m)**	zawadi	gift
verb	**donner**	1. kutoa 2. kupa	give, to
verb	**donner du goût à**	kukoleza	flavor, to
verb	**donner naissance à**	kuzaa	bear, to (child)
verb	**donner son amitié à**	kufadhili	befriend, to
verb	**donner un coup de pied**	kupiga teke	kick, to
adv.	**d'ordinaire**	desturi	usually
adv.	**dorénavant**	tangu sasa	henceforth
verb	**dormir**	kulala	sleep, to
n., med	**dos, (m)**	mgongo	back (of a person)
n.	**dose (f)**	kipimo cha dawa	dose
n.	**dot (f)**	mahari	dowry
verb	**doubler**	kurudufya	double, to
n.	**douleur (f)**	maumivu (pl.)	pain
adj.	**douloureux**	kuuma	sore (painful)
n.	**doute (m)**	shaka	doubt
verb	**douter (de)**	kushuku	doubt, to
adj.	**doux**	-pole	1. gentle 2. mild 3. meek
n.	**douze**	kumi na mbili	twelve
n.	**drap (m) de lit**	nguo ya kutandika kitandani	sheet
n.	**drapeau (m)**	bendera	flag
n.	**drogue (f)**	dawa	drug (medication)
adj.	**droit**	-a upande wa kuume	right
adj.	**droit**	sawa	straight
n.	**droit (m)**	haki	right (civil, legal)
verb	**droit, être**	kunyoloka	straight, to be (as in line)
adj.	**drôle**	-a kuchekesha	funny
n.	**du raisin (m)**	zabibu (pl.)	grape
verb	**duper**	1. kudanganya 2. kupunja	1. to fool 2. to trick

parts of speech	french	swahili	english
adj.	**dur**	-gumu	hard
n.	**dureté (f)**	ugumu	hardness, severity
n.	**durée (f)**	muda	duration
n	**dynamite (f)**	baruti ya kupasulia mwamba	dynamite
verb	**dysenterie, avoir la**	kuhara damu	dysentery, to have
n.	**eau (f)**	maji	water
n.	**éblouissement (m)**	kutia kiwi	dazzle
n.	**écailles (f)**	gamba (pl. magamba)	scales (fish)
verb	**écarquiller les yeux**	kukodoa	stare wide-eyed, to
verb	**échanger**	kubadilisha	exchange, to
verb	**échapper**	kuponyoka	escape, to
n.	**échec (m)**	kuharibika mimba	miscarriage
n.	**échelle (f)**	ngazi	ladder
verb	**échouer; négliger**	kukosa	fail, to
n., med	**ecchymose**	chubuko (pl. machubuko)	ecchymosis
n.	**éclair (m)**	umeme	lightning
verb	**éclater**	kupasuka ghafula	burst, to
phrase	**éclipse de soleil**	kupatwa jua	eclipse of the sun
n.	**école (f)**	chuo (pl. vyuo)	school
adj.	**économique**	-wekevu	economical
verb	**économiser**	kupunguza gharama	economize, to
n.	**écorce (f)**	gome	bark (tree)
n.	**écorchure (f)**	chubuko (pl. machubuko)	abrasion
verb	**écosser**	kupua	shell, to
verb	**écouter**	kusikiliza	listen, to
verb	**écouter en cachette**	kudukiza	eavesdrop, to
interj.	**Écouter!**	Ange!	Attention!
verb	**écraser**	kuponda	crush, to
verb	**écrire**	kuandika	write, to
n.	**écume (f)**	povu	froth, foam
n.	**éducation (f)**	mafunzo	education
verb	**effacer**	kufuta	1. to erase 2. to wipe away
n.	**effet (m)**	tokeo (pl. matokeo)	effect
verb	**effrayer**	kuogofya	startle, to
adj.	**égal**	sawa	equal
adv.	**également**	sawa	equally
verb	**égayer**	kufurahisha	entertain, to
n.	**église (f)**	kanisa	church (building)
n.	**égoïsme (m)**	choyo	selfishness
adj.	**égoïste**	-a choyo	selfish

parts of speech	french	swahili	english
verb	égratigner	kuparua	scratch, to
n.	égratignure (f)	mtai (pl. mitai)	scratch
n.	élection (f)	mchaguo	election
n.	électricité (f)	umeme	electricity
n.	éléphant (m)	tembo	elephant
n., med	éléphantiasis des jambes	ugonjwa wa matende	elephantiasis of legs
verb	élever la voix	kupaza sauti	raise the voice, to
n.	élève (m,f)	mwanafunzi (pl. wanafunzi)	pupil (student)
pronoun	elle	yeye	she
pronoun	elle-même	yeye mwenyewe	herself
pronoun	elles-même	sisi wenyewe	ourselves
n.	éloge (m)	sifa	praise
verb	emballer	kufunganya	pack, to
verb	embarrasser	kutahayarisha	embarrass, to
verb	embellir	kupamba	embellish, to
n.	embonpoint (m)	unene	stoutness
verb	embrasser	kubusu	kiss, to
n.	embryon (m)	mimba	embryo
n.	embuscade (f)	oteo	ambush
verb	émerveiller	kushangaza	astonish, to
n.	émeute (f)	ghasia	riot
n.	empêchement (m)	kizuio (pl. vizuio)	hinderance
verb	empêcher	kuzuia	prevent, to
n.	employé (m)	mtu wa kazi	employee
n.	employé(e) {m,(f)}	karani	clerk
verb	empoigner	kunyakua	grab, to
verb	empoisonner	kutia sumu	poison, to
verb	emporter	1. kutwalia 2. kuchukua 3. kutwaa	1. to take from 2. to take away 3. to take
verb	emprunter	kukopa	borrow, to (money)
adv.	en arrière	nyuma	backwards
adv.	en bas	chini	down
adv. prep.	en bas (adv), au-dessous de (prep)	chini ya	below
adv.	en ce moment	sasa hivi	now, right
adv.	en conséquence	kwa hiyo	accordingly
prep.	en dehors de	nje ya	outside of
adv.	en effet	kweli	indeed; in fact
adv.	en face de	kuelekeana	opposite
adv.	en outre	zaidi	furthermore
adv.	en partie	kwa nusu	partly

parts of speech	french	swahili	english
phrase	en plus	kutambusha	what is more
adv.	en tout	kabisa	altogether
adv.	en travers	-a kukingama	crosswise
prep.	en, dans	katika	in, into
adv.	en-dessous	china	underneath
verb	enceinte, être	kuwa na mimba	pregnant, to be
n.	encensoir (m)	chetezo	censer
phrase	Enchanté de rencontrer avec toi.	Nafurahi kukufahamu.	Nice to meet you. (one person)
verb	enchevêtrer	kutatiza	tangle, to (ensnare)
n.	enclos (m)	kitalu	enclosure
adv.	encore	bado; hata sasa	yet
verb	encourager	kutia moyo	encourage, to
n.	encre (f)	wino	ink
verb	endommager	kutia hasara	damage, to
n.	endroit (m)	pahali (pl. pahali)	place
n.	endurance (f)	ustahimilivu	endurance
n.	enfance (f)	utoto	childhood
n.	enfant (m,f); fils; fille	mtoto (pl. watoto); mwana (pl. wana)	child
n.	enfant, entre 10 et 12 ans	kijana (pl. vijana) (boy or girl)	youth
verb	enfanter	kuzaa	give birth, to
n.	enfer (m)	gehena	hell
adv.	enfin	mwisho	at last
verb	enfler	kuvimba	swell, to
n.	enflure (f)	kivimbe (pl. vivimbe)	swelling
verb	enfoncer	kuzama	sink, to
verb	enfouir	kuzika	bury, to
phrase	engourdi, être	kufa ganzi	numb, to be
n.	engourdissement (m)	ganzi	numbness
n.	engrais (m)	mbolea	fertilizer
verb	enjamber	kukiuka	step over, to
verb	enlever	kutorosha	abduct, to
adj. & n.	ennemi (m)	adui	enemy
n.	ennui (m)	1. uchovu 2. udhia	1. boredom 2. nuisance
n.	ennuis (m)	hoja	problems
verb	ennuyer	kuudhi	annoy, to
n.	enquête (f)	swali (pl. maswali)	inquiry
verb	enregistrer	kuandika	record, to
verb	être en retard	kuchelewa	late, to be
verb	enrichir	kutajirisha	enrich, to

238

parts of speech	french	swahili	english
verb	enrouler	kuupepo	wind, to
n.	enseignant (m)	mwalimu (pl. walimu)	teacher
verb	enseigner	kufundisha	teach, to
adv.	ensemble	pamoja	together
verb	ensemencer	kupanda	sow, to
adj.	ensoleillé	-a jua	sunny
verb	ensorceler	kuloga	bewitch, to
adv.	ensuite	1. baadaye 2. halafu 3. kisha	1. afterward 2. then
verb	entamer	kuanza	start, to
verb	entendre	kusikia	hear, to
n.	enterrement (m)	maziko	funeral
verb	enterrer	kuzika	bury, to
n.	entêtement (m)	uthabiti	stubbornness
adj.	entêtée	-kaidi	stubborn
adj.	entier, tout	-zima, -ote	entire
adv.	entièrement	kabisa	entirely
n.	entonnoir (m)	mrija	funnel
verb	entourer	1. kuzingira 2. kuzunguka	1. to encircle 2. to surround
verb	entourer de ses bras	kukumbatia	embrace, to
verb	entraîner	kuvuta	train, to (child)
n.	entrave (f)	kizuio (pl. vizuio)	obstacle
prep.	entre	katikati ya	between
n.	entrepôt (m)	gala	storehouse
verb	entrer	kuingia	enter, to
phrase	Entrez!	Karibu!	Come in!
n.	entrée (f)	mlango (pl. milango)	entrance
verb	envahir	kushambulia	invade, to
n.	enveloppe (f)	bahasha	envelope
verb	envelopper	kufunika	wrap, to
n.	envie (f)	wivu	envy
verb	envoyer	kutuma	send, to
verb	éplucher	kumenya	peel, to
n.	épluchures (f)	maganda (pl.)	peelings
n.	éponge (f)	sifongo	sponge
verb	épousseter	kupangusa	dust, to
n.	épouvantail (m)	kuamia shamba	scarecrow
n.	épreuve (f)	1. jaribio kali 2. jaribu	1. ordeal 2. test
n.	épreuves (f) privations	mashaka	hardship
verb	éprouver	kupatwa na	experience, to
verb	épuiser	kumaliza	exhaust, to

parts of speech	french	swahili	english
verb	épuisé, être	kuchoka kabisa	exhausted, to be
n.	équivalent (m)	sawa; badala	equivalent
n.	érection (f)	msimiko	erection
verb	ériger	kusimamisha	erect, to
n.	érosion (f)	momonyoko wa ardhi	erosion
n.	éruption (f)	upele	rash
n.	erreur (f)	kosa (pl. makosa)	error
n.	escalier (m)	ngazi	staircase
n.	esclavage (m)	utumwa	slavery
n.	esclave (m,f)	mtumwa (pl. watumwa)	slave
verb	escorter	kufuatana na	escort, to
n.	escroc (m)	mdanganyifu (pl. wadanganyifu)	cheater
n	espace (m)	nafasi	space
verb	espacer	kuenea	spread out, to
adj.	épais	-zito	dense
adj.	épanoui	-a angavu	radiant
verb	épargner	kuweka akiba	save, to
n.	épaule (f)	bega (pl. mabega)	shoulder
n.	épée (f)	upanga (pl. panga)	sword
n.	espérance (f), espoir (m)	matumaini	hope
verb	espérer	kutumaini	hope, to
n.	épi (m)	suke	ear (of sorghum)
n.	épidémie (f)	maradhi ya pukupuku	epidemic
n.	espièglerie (f)	fitina	mischief
n., med	épilepsie (f)	kifafa	epilepsy
n.	épine (f)	mwiba (pl. miiba)	thorn
n.	épine (f) dorsal	uti wa mgongo	spine
n.	épingle (f)	msumari (pl. misumari)	pin
n.	espion (m)	mpelelezi (pl. wapelelezi)	spy
verb	espionner	kupeleleza	spy on, to
n.	esprit (m)	1. akili 2. roho	1. mind 2. spirit
n.	essaim (m)	kundi	swarm
verb	essayer	kujaribu	1. to try 2. to attempt
adj.	essentiel	-a asili	essential
verb	essorer	kukamua	wring out to
phrase	essoufflé, être	kutwetatweta	breathless, to be
verb	essuyer	kupangusa	wipe, to
n.	est (m)	mashariki	east
phrase	Est-ce que tu as des enfants?	Una watoto?	Do you have children?

240

parts of speech	french	swahili	english
n.	estime (f)	heshima	esteem
verb	estimer	kukiasi	estimate, to
n., med	estomac (m)	tumbo (pl. matumbo)	stomach
n.	estropié (m)	kiwete	cripple
conj.	et	na	and
n	étage (m)	dari	story (floor)
n.	États-Unis du Amérique (f)	nchi ya Amerika	America, US of
verb	éteindre	kuzima	extinguish, to
prep.	éteint, annulé	katika	off
adv.	étendu face contre terre	kifudifudi	prone position
verb	éternuer	kupiga chafya	sneeze, to
phrase	Êtes-vous heureux?	Unasikia furaha?	Are you happy?
n.	étoile (f)	nyota	star
verb	étonner	kushangaza	amaze, to
phrase	étonné, être	kustaajabu	surprised, to be
verb	étouffer	kukaba au kukabwa roho	choke, to
adj.	étourdi	-a si ahgalifu	thoughtless
adj.	étranger	-geni	strange
n.	étranger (m)	mgeni (pl. wageni)	foreigner
verb	être	kuwa	be, to
adj.	étroit	-embamba	narrow
n.	étudiant (m)	mwanafunzi (pl. wanafunzi)	student
verb	étudier	kujifunza	study, to
n.	Europe (f)	Ulaya	Europe
adj.	européen	Mzungu (pl. Wazungu)	European
pronoun	eux (m), elles (f)	wao, hao, wale	them
n.	évaluation (f)	kadiri ipasayo	assessment
n.	évangile (m)	Injili	Gospel
n.	événement (m)	1. jambo 2. matukio	1. event 2. occurrence
adj.	évident	1. wazi 2. dhahiri	1. evident 2. obvious
verb	évider	kukomba	hollow out, to
verb	éviter	kuepuka	1. to avoid 2. to evade
adj.	exact	1. sahihi 2. safi	1. accurate 2. correct
verb	exagérer	kutia chumvi	exaggerate, to
verb	exalter	kutukuza	exalt, to
n.	examen (m)	ukaguzi	examination
n.	examinateur (m)	mkaguaji	examiner
verb	examiner	kupima	examine, to
adj.	excellent	1. bora 2. -zuri	1. excellent 2. fine
conj.	excepté	ila	except

241

parts of speech	french	swahili	english
adj.	excessif	-a kupita kiasi	excessive
n.	excédent (m)	wingi kupita kiasi	excess, surplus
verb	exclure	kukataa	exclude, to
verb	excommunier	kuharimisha	excommunicate, to
n.	excréments (m)	mavi (pl.)	excrement
n.	excursion (f)	matembezi ugenini	excursion
n.	excuse (f)	udhuru	excuse
n.	exemple (m)	mfano (pl. mifano)	example
phrase	exemple, par	kwa mfano	instance, for
verb	exercer	kuzoea	exercise, to
verb	exhiber	kuonyesha	exhibit, to
verb	exhumer	kufukua	exhume, to
verb	exiger	kudai	demand, to
verb	exiler	kuhamisha	banish, to
n.	existence (f)	maisha	existence
verb	exister	kuwako	exist, to
verb	expédier	kupeleka	speed, to
n.	expiation	malipo	atonement
verb	expier	kupfanya upatanisho	atone, to
verb	expirer, décéder	kufa, kuisha	expire, to; to die
n.	explication (f)	maelezo	explanation
verb	expliquer	kueleza	explain, to
n.	exploit (m)	tendo bora, utimizo	achievement
n.	exploration (f)	uvumbuzi	exploration
verb	explorer	kuvumbua	explore, to
n.	explosif (m)	baruti	explosive
n.	expression (f)	fungu la maneno machache	phrase
verb	exterminer	kukomesha kabisa	exterminate, to
adj.	extérieur	-nje	exterior
verb	extorquer	kutoza kwa nguvu	extort, to
adj.	extraordinaire	-a ajabu	extraordinary
adv.	extrêmement	mno	1. exceedingly 2. extremely
n.	évangile (m)	Injili	Gospel
n.	événement (m)	1. jambo 2. matukio	1. event 2. occurrence
adj.	évident	1. wazi 2. dhahiri	1. evident 2. obvious
verb	évider	kukomba	hollow out, to
verb	éviter	kuepuka	1. to avoid 2. to evade
n.	fable (f)	hadithi fupi	fable
n.	fabrication (f)	uongo	fabrication
verb	fabriquer	1. kufanyiza 2. kufanya	make, to

parts of speech	french	swahili	english
verb	fâcher, se	kukasirika	angry, to get
n.	fac-similé (m)	mwigo sawasawa	facsimile
adj.	facile	-epesi	easy
adv.	facilement	polepole	easily
verb	faciliter	kufanya rahisi	facilitate, to
n.	facture (f)	hesabu ya fedha	bill
adj.	faible	1. dhaifu 2. teketeke 3. zaifu 4. -regevu	1. feeble 2. weak
n.	faiblesse (f)	uzaifu	weakness
n.	faillite (f)	ufilisi	bankruptcy
n.	faim (f)	njaa	hunger
adj.	fainéant	-vivu	idle
n.	fainéant (m), fainéante (f)	mvivu (pl. wavivu)	lazy person
verb	faire	kufanya, kutenda	do, to
verb	faire allusion	kutaja	allude, to
verb	faire amende honorable	kuridhisha	amends, make
verb	faire appeler	kuomba	appeal, to
verb	faire attention à	kuangalia	pay attention, to
verb	faire changer de forme	kugeuza kidogo	modify, to
verb	faire cuire	kuoka	bake, to
verb	faire de la purée	kuseta	mash, to
verb	faire des études	kujifunza	study, to
verb	faire des histoires	kujisumbua bure	fuss, to
verb	faire du bruit	kupiga kelele	noise, to make
verb	faire du commerce	kufanya biashara	trade, to
verb	faire du mal	kudhuru	harm, to
verb	faire entrer	kuingiza	bring in, to
verb	faire escale	kuingiza	put in, to
verb	faire exécuter rapidement	kuhimiza	expedite, to
verb	faire heureux	kufurahisha	happy, to make
verb	faire la cour à	kuposa	woo, to
verb	faire le berger	kuchunga	shepherd, to
verb	faire maigrir	kukondesha	lose weight, to
verb	faire mal	kuuma	ache, to
verb	faire peur à	kuogofya	frighten, to
verb	faire semblant	kujifanya	make believe, to
verb	faire ses adieux à	kuaga	bid farewell, to
verb	faire taire	kunyamazisha	silence, to
verb	faire tranquille	kunyamazisha	quiet, to make
verb	faire un lit (de l'herbe)	kutandika kitanda	bed, to make a (with grass)
phrase	faire une randonnée	kutembea parini	hiking, to go

parts of speech	french	swahili	english
verb	faire voix fort	kupaza sauti	raise voice, to
verb	faisable, être	kuwezekana	feasible, to be
n.	fait (m)	jambo la hakika	fact
phrase	Faites comme chez vous.	Starehe.	Feel at home.
n.	falaise (f)	jabali	cliff
verb	falsifier	kugeuza kwa uongo	falsify, to
n.	famille (f)	jamaa	1. family 2. kin
n.	famine (f)	njaa kuu	famine
verb	faner, se	kunyauka	dry, to become; to wither
n.	fantôme (m)	roho, kizuka	ghost
n.	fardeau (m)	1. mzigo (pl. mizigo) 2. mkopo	1. burden 2. loan
n.	farine (f)	unga	flour
n.	fatigue (f)	uchovu	fatigue
verb	fatigué, être	kuchoka	tired, to be
verb	faucher	kukata majani	mow, to
n.	faute (f)	1. hatia 2. kosa (pl. makosa)	1. fault 2. mistake
adj.	faux (m), fausse (f)	-a uongo	FALSE
n.	favori (m), favorite (f)	kipenzi	favorite
interj.	Félicitations.	Hongera.	Congratulations.
verb	féliciter (en ce qui concerne obtention du diplôme)	kupongeza	congratulate, to (graduate)
adj.	féminin	-a kike	feminine
n.	femme (f), épouse	bibi; mke (pl. wake)	wife
verb	fendre	kupasuka	1. to split 2. to rip
verb	fendre en long	kupasua	cut lengthwise, to
n.	fenêtre (f)	dirisha (pl. madirisha)	window
n.	fente (f)	ufa (pl. nyufa)	crack (fissure)
n.	fer (m)	chuma	iron (ore)
n.	fer (m) à repasser	pasi	iron (for clothes)
adv.	fermement	imara	firmly
verb	fermer	1. kufunga 2. kufumba	1. to close 2. to shut
verb	fermer à clef	kufunga	lock, to
verb	fermer les yeux	fumba macho	close the eyes, to
n.	fermier (m)	mlimaji (pl. walimaji)	farmer
adj.	féroce	-kali	sharp (fierce)
adj.	fertile	-enye rutuba	fertile
n.	fesse (f)	tako (pl. matako)	buttock
n.	festin (m)	karamu	feast
n.	fête (f)	karamu	party (entertainment)
n.	feu (m)	moto (pl. mioto)	fire

parts of speech	french	swahili	english
n.	**feuille (f)**	jani	leaf
phrase	**feuille de papier**	ukurasa	sheet of paper
n.	**février (m)**	Februari; mwezi wa pili wa mwaka wa kizungu	February
n.	**fiancé (m)**	mchumba	fiancé
n.	**ficelle (f)**	ugwe (pl. nyugwe)	string
adj.	**fidèle**	-aminifu	faithful
n.	**fidélité (f)**	uaminifu	faithfulness
adj.	**fier**	-enye kiburi	proud
n.	**fierté (f)**	kiburi, majivuno	pride
n.	**fièvre (f) {Il a beaucoup de fièvre.}**	homa {Ana homa.}	fever {He has a high fever.}
n.	**figue (f)**	tini	fig
n.	**figuier (m)**	mtini	fig tree
n.	**fil (m)**	uzi (pl. nyuzi)	thread
n.	**filet (m)**	wavu (pl. nyavu)	net
n.	**fille (f)**	binti	daughter
n.	**fils (m)**	mwana (pl. wana)	son
verb	**filtrer**	kuchuja	filter, to
n.	**fin (f)**	mwisho (pl. miisho)	end
adv.	**finalement, enfin**	mwisho	finally
verb	**finir**	kumaliza	finish, to
n.	**fissure (f)**	ufa (pl. nyufa)	crevice
verb	**fixer**	kukaza	fix, to
verb	**fixer les limites**	kupiga mustari	draw a line, to
phrase	**flambant neuf**	-pya kabisa	brand new
n.	**flanc (m)**	kiuno (pl. viuno)	flank
verb	**flâner**	kutangatanga	dawdle, to
adj.	**flasque**	-tepetevu	flabby
verb	**flatter**	kubembeleza	flatter, to
n.	**flèche (f)**	mshale (pl. mishale)	arrow
verb	**flétrir**	kufifia	wilt, to
n.	**fleur (f)**	ua (pl. maua)	flower
n.	**fleuve (m)**	mto (pl. mito)	river
verb	**flotter**	kuelea	float, to
verb	**fluctuer**	kupanda na kushuka	fluctuate, to
n.	**foetus**	mimba	fetus
n.	**foi (f)**	imani	faith
n.	**foie (m)**	maini	liver
adv., n.	**fois, une fois**	mara, wakati (pl. nyakati)	time
n.	**folie (f)**	ujinga	folly

parts of speech	french	swahili	english
n., med	**folie, rage**	gazabu	rage
adj.	**foncé**	-eusi	dark
n.	**fond (m)**	upande wa chini	bottom
n.	**fondation (f)**	msingi (pl. misingi)	foundation
verb	**fondre**	kuyeyusha	melt, to (sugar)
n.	**fontaine (f)**	bomba la kurushia maji juu	fountain
n.	**force (f)**	nguvu	strength
verb	**forcer**	kushurutisha	force, to
n.	**forces, vigueur (f)**	nguvu; bidii	energy (strength)
n.	**forêt (f)**	mwitu	forest
n.	**forgeron (m)**	mhunzi	blacksmith
n.	**forme (f)**	umbo	shape, form
adj.	**fort**	hodari, -enye nguvu	strong
adv.	**fortement**	sana	strongly
verb	**fortifier**	1. kuongeza nguvu 2. kutia nguvu	1. to fortify 2. to invigorate
n.	**fortune (f) bien**	bahati	fortune, good
n.	**fosse (f)**	shimo (pl. mashimo)	pit
n.	**fossé (m)**	mfereji (pl. mifereji)	ditch
adj.	**fou**	-enye kichaa	crazy
adj.	**fou (f. folle)**	-enye wazimu	mad (insane)
n.	**fou (m), folle (f)**	mkichaa	lunatic
n.	**fouet (m)**	fimbo	whip
verb	**fouetter**	kuchapa	whip, to
verb	**fouiller**	1. kuchimba 2. kutufata	1. to dig 2. to search
n.	**foulard (m)**	kitambaa (pl. vitambaa)	scarf
n.	**foule (f)**	mkutano (pl. mikutano)	crowd
n.	**four (m)**	tanuu	kiln
n.	**fourchette (f)**	uma (pl. nyuma)	fork
n.	**fourmi (f)**	chungu	ant
verb	**fournir**	kupamba nyumba	furnish, to
n.	**fourrure (f)**	ngozi laini ya manyoya	fur
n.	**fracture (f)**	mvunjo	fracture
adj.	**fragile**	dhaifu	fragile
adj.	**frais (m), fraîche (f)**	1. -a baridi 2. -bichi	1. cool 2. fresh
verb	**frais, devenir**	kupoa	cool, to become
n.	**franc (m)**	sarafu ya kifaransa	franc
n.	**français (m)**	Wafaransa (people, Kifaransa (language)	French
n.	**frange (f)**	matamvua	fringe
verb	**frapper**	1. kupiga 2. kukonga	1. to hit 2. to strike 3. to knock

parts of speech	french	swahili	english
adv.	fréquemment	mara kwa mara	frequently
adj.	fréquent	-a mara nyingi	frequent
n.	frère (m)	ndugu, kaka	brother
verb	frire	kukaanga	fry, to
n.	frisson (m)	kitapo	shiver
adj.	frivole	pasipo maana	frivolous
adj.	froid	-a baridi	cold
verb	froid, être	kupoa	cold, to be
n.	fromage (m)	jibini	cheese
verb	froncer les sourcils	kukunja uso	frown, to
n.	fronde (f)	kombeo (pl. makombeo)	sling
n.	front (m)	paji la uso	forehead
n.	frontière	mpaka (pl. mipaka)	frontier (border)
verb	frotter	kusugua	scrub, to
adj.	frugal	-wekevu	frugal
n.	fruit (m)	tunda (pl. matunda)	fruit
verb	fuir	kuvuja	leak, to
verb	fuir à	kuhamisha	exile, to be in
verb	fuir/s'enfuir	kukimbia	flee, to
verb	fumer du tabac	kuvuta tumbako	smoke, to
n.	fumée (f)	moshi	smoke
adj.	furieux	-enye hasira nyingi	furious
n., med	furoncle (m)	jipu (pl. majipu)	boil (medical)
adj.	futile	bure	futile
verb	gagner	kupata faida	gain, to
verb	gagner	kuchuma kwa kazi	earn, to; to gain
verb	gagner	kushinda	win, to
n.	gain (m)	faida	gain
n.	gale (f)	upele wa mbwa	mange
n.	galerie souterraine	pango (pl. mapango)	cave
n., med	ganglion engorgé	tezi la nyuma ya pua	adenoids
n.	garantie (f)	rahani	guarantee
n.	garçon (m)	mtoto wa kiume	boy
n.	garde (f)	mlinzi (pl. walinzi), zamu	guard
verb	garder	kuchunga, kulinda	guard, to
verb	garder	kuweka	keep, to
n.	gardes du corps (m)	askari wafuasi	bodyguard
n.	gardien (m)	1. mlinzi (pl. walinzi) 2. zamu 3. mngoje	1. guard 2. watchman
n.	gardien (m), gardienne (f)	mwangalizi	caretaker
verb	gargariser	kusukutua kooni	gargle, to

parts of speech	french	swahili	english
verb	gaspiller	kuharibu	1. to waste 2. to squander
n.	gastrite (f)	ugonjwa mmojawapo wa tumbo	gastritis
verb	gâter, se	kuoza	spoil, to (food)
adj.	gauche	-a kushoto	left
n.	gauche (f)	upande wa kushuto	left
n.	gaz (m)	mvuke kama hewa	gas
n.	gazelle (f)	1. mpala 2. paa	gazelle
n.	géant (m)	jitu (pl. majitu)	giant
verb	gémir	kuugua	1. to groan 2. to wail 3. to moan
n.	gémissement (m)	mauguzi	groan
verb	gêner	kuzuia	hinder, to
adj. & n.	général (m)	mkuu wa jeshi	general
adv.	généralement	kwa kawaida	1. generally 2. normally
n.	génération (f)	kizazi (pl. vizazi)	generation
adj.	généreux	-karimu	generous
n.	générosité (f)	ukarimu	generosity
n.	génie (m)	mwenye akili maalum	genius
n	genou (m)	goti (pl. magoti)	knee
n.	genre (m)	namna	kind (species)
n.	genre féminin	mwanamke (pl. wanawake)	female
adj.	gentil (m), gentille (f)	1. -ema 2. -zuri	1. nice 2. friendly
verb	germer	kuchipuka	germinate, to
n.	gibier (m)	mawindo	game, wild
verb	gifler	kupiga kofi	slap, to
n.	gingembre (m)	tangawizi	ginger
n.	girafe (f)	twiga	giraffe
n.	gîte (m)	nyumba ndogo	cottage
n.	glace (f)	barafu	ice
n.	glissade (f)	kuteleza	slide
n.	glucose (f)	sukari	glucose
n.	goinfre (m)	mlafi (pl. walafi)	glutton
n.	gond (m)	pata (pl. mapata)	hinge
verb	gonfler	kuvimba	swell, to
verb	gonfler avec l'air	kupuliza	swollen with air
n.	gorge (f)	koo (pl. makoo)	throat
n.	gorille (m)	maheshe	gorilla
n.	gourde (f)	buyu (pl. mabuyu)	gourd
n.	goût (m)	ladha	flavor
verb	goûter	kuonja	taste, to

parts of speech	french	swahili	english
n.	gouvernement (m)	serkali	government
verb	gouverner	kutawala	1. to govern 2. to rule
n.	goyave	pera	guava
n.	grâce (f)	neema	grace
n.	grain (m)	1. nafaka 2. mtama	1. grain 2. millet
n.	grain (m) de café	buni	coffee bean
n.	graisse (f)	mafuta	grease
adj.	grand	-kubwa	1. big 2. great
adj.	grand	-refu	tall
n.	grand-mère (f)	mama mkuu; nyanya	grandmother
n.	grand-père (m)	babu	grandfather
n.	grande tremblement (m) (de terre)	tetemeko la nchi	earthquake
adj.	grande, gros	-kubwa	large
n.	grandeur (f)	ukubwa	1. greatness 2. magnitude 3. size
n.	grange (f)	banda	barn
n.	grappe (f)	kichala (pl. vichala)	cluster
n.	gras (m)	mafuta	fat
n. & adj.	gras (m), grasse (f)	-nene	fat
verb	gratter, se	kujukuna	scratch oneself, to
adj.	gratuit	bure	free (no charge)
n.	gravier (m)	changarawe	gravel
verb	gravir	kupanda	climb, to
n.	grêle (f)	mvua ya mawe	hail
n.	grelot (m)	njuga	bell
verb	grelotter	kutetemeka	shiver, to
n.	grenier (m)	chumba cha juu	attic
n.	grenouille (f)	chura (pl. vyura)	frog
n.	griffe (f)	kucha	claw
verb	grignoter	kumega	nibble, to
verb	griller	kuchoma	broil, to
verb	grincer	kusaga	squeak, to
n.	grippe (f)	fluu	flu
adj.	gris	kijivu	grey
verb	gronder	1. kukaripia 2. kunguruma	1. to chide 2. to growl
verb	gronder (orage)	kugombeza	roar, to (like a storm)
n.	gros canevas (m)	gunia (pl. magunia)	burlap
n., med	gros intestin	sehemu ya chini ya tumbo kubwa	colon
n.	grossesse (f)	mimba	pregnancy

249

parts of speech	french	swahili	english
verb	**grossir**	1. kukuza 2. kuvimbisha	1. to magnify 2. to gain weight
n.	**groupe (m) de personnes**	kundi	group
n.	**gué (m)**	kivuko (pl. vivuko)	ford
verb	**guérir**	1. kupata nafuu 2. kuponya 3. kupona	1. to be better (after illness) 2. to be improved physically 3. to heal 4. to cure
n.	**guerre (f)**	vita	war
n.	**guide (m)**	kiongozi (pl. viongozi)	guide
verb	**habiter**	kukaa	inhabit, to
phrase	**Habitez-vous ici?**	Unakaa hapa?	Do you live here?
n.	**habitude (f)**	desturi, mazoea	habit
n.	**hache (f)**	shoka	ax
n.	**haie (f)**	ugo (pl. nyugo)	hedge
verb	**haïr**	kuchukia	hate, to
n.	**haleine (f)**	pumzi	breath
verb	**haleter**	kutweta	pant, to
n.	**hallucination (f)**	mazigazi	hallucination
n.	**hamac (m)**	machila	hammock
n.	**hameçon (m)**	1. ndoana 2. ndobani 3. kulabu	1. fish-hook 2. hook
verb	**harceler**	kutesa	harass, to
n.	**hardiesse (f)**	ujasiri	boldness
n.	**haricot (m)**	haragwe (pl. maharagwe)	bean
n.	**harpe (f)**	kinubi (pl. vinubi)	harp
adj.	**hasardeux**	-a hatari	hazardous
n.	**hâte (f)**	haraka	hurry, haste
adj.	**haut**	-refu, -kuu	high
n.	**haut (m)**	urefu	top (on the top)
n.	**hémorragie (f)**	kutoa damu	hemorrhage
n.	**hépatite (f)**	uvimbi wa ini	hepatitis
n.	**herbe (f)**	majani (pl.)	grass
n.	**héritage (m)**	uriti	inheritance
verb	**hériter**	kurisi	inherit, to
n.	**héros (m)**	shujaa	hero
verb	**hésiter**	1. kusita 2. kutua	1. to hesitate 2. to pause
n.	**heure (f)**	saa	hour
adj.	**heureux**	-a furaha	happy
verb	**heureux, être**	kufurahi	1. to be glad 2. to be happy
n.	**hibou (m)**	bundi	owl
adj.	**hideux**	-enye sura ya kuchukiza	hideous

250

parts of speech	french	swahili	english
adv.	**hier**	jana	yesterday
n.	**Hindou (m)**	hindi	Hindu
n.	**hippopotame (m)**	kiboko (pl. viboko)	hippopotamus
n.	**histoire (f)**	1. hadisi 2. kisa (pl. visa)	1. history 2. story
n.	**homme (m)**	1. mwanadamu (pl. wanadamu) 2. mwanaume (pl. wanaume)	man
adj.	**honnête**	-nyofu	honest
adv.	**honnêtement**	sana kidogo	fairly
n.	**honnêteté (f)**	uaminifu	honesty
n.	**honneur (m)**	heshima	honor
verb	**honorer**	kuheshimu	honor, to
n.	**honte (f)**	1. aibu 2. haya	1. shame 2. disgrace
n.	**hôpital (m)**	hospitali	hospital
n.	**hoquet (m)**	kwikwi	hiccup
n.	**horizon (m)**	upeo wa macho	horizon
n.	**horloge (f)**	saa	clock
n.	**hostilité**	uadui	1. feud 2. hostility
n.	**houe (f)**	jembe (pl. majembe)	hoe
verb	**huer**	kuzomea	boo, to
n.	**huile (f)**	mafuta	oil
n.	**huile de palmier (m)**	mawese	palm oil
adj. & n.	**huit (m)**	nane	eight
adj.	**huitième**	-a nane	eighth
adj.	**humain**	-enye huruma	humane
adj.	**humain (m)**	-a mtu	human
verb	**humble, être**	kunyenyekea	humble, to be
n., med	**humérus**	mfupa wa mkono katkati ya kiko na bega	humerus
adj.	**humide**	majimaji	damp
n.	**humidité (f)**	rutuba	moisture
n.	**humilité (f)**	unyenyekevu	humility
verb	**hurler**	kulia	yell, to (pain, sorrow); to howl
n.	**hymne (m)**	wimbo (pl. nyimbo)	hymn
n.	**hypocrisie (f)**	unafiki	hypocrisy
n.	**hystérie (f)**	ugonjwa wa akili	hysteria
adv.	**ici**	hapa, huko	here
phrase	**ici et y là**	mpaka sasa	hither and yon
n.	**idée (f)**	wazo	idea
adv.	**idem**	vile vile	ditto
n.	**idiot (m)**	juha	idiot

251

parts of speech	french	swahili	english
n.	idole (f)	sanamu ya kuabudiwa	idol
n.	ignare (m,f)	mjinga (pl. wajinga)	ignoramus
n.	ignorance (f)	ujinga	ignorance
adj.	ignorant	-pumbavu	dull
pronoun	il	yeye	he
adv.	il est possible que, peut-être	labda	possibly
phrase	Il était une fois...	Hapo kale...	Once upon a time there was...
phrase	Il y a combien de temps que tu es malade?	Umekuwa hivyo kwa muda gani?	How long have you been ill?
phrase	Il y a combien de temps?	Tangu lini?	ago?, How long
adv.	il y a longtemps	zamani sana	ago, long
phrase	Il y a...	Kuna...	There is...
n.	île (f)	kisiwa (pl. visiwa)	island
adj.	illettré	asiyefundishwa	illiterate
pronoun	ils (m), elles (f) (et eux)	wao	they (and they)
n.	image (f)	sura	image
verb	imiter	kuiga	1. to imitate 2. to mimic
adv.	immédiatement	mara moja	1. immediately 2. right now 3. instantly
adj.	immobile	kimya	motionless
adj.	impartial	bila upendeleo	impartial
adj.	impatient	-enye haraka	impatient
verb	implorer	kusihi	implore, to
adj.	impoli	-sio adabu	impolite
n.	importance (f)	maana	1. importance 2. significance
adj.	important	muhimu	important
verb	importuner	kuudhi	pester, to
verb	impossible à faire, être	kutowezekana	impossible to do, to be
n.	impôt (m)	kodi	tax
adj.	impotent	1. hoi 2. pasipo nguvu	1. helpless 2. impotent
verb	imprimer	kuchapa, kupiga chapa	print, to
adj.	impulsif	-enye haraka	impulsive
adj.	incapable	-sioweza	incapable
n.	incident (m)	tukio (pl. matukio)	incident
verb	inciser	kukata	incise, to
adj.	inconscient	bila kufahamu	unconscious
verb	inculquer	kufundisha	inculcate, to
n.	indécision (f)	kusita moyoni	indecision
verb	indépendant, être	kujiangalia	independent, to be

parts of speech	french	swahili	english
n.	Indien (m)	Mhindi	Indian
n.	indigène (m,f)	mwenyeji (pl. wenyeji)	native
adj.	indiscret	-a kukosa busara	indiscreet
n.	indulgence (f)	huruma	leniency
adj.	inerte	-tepetevu	inert
n., med	infection (f)	ambukizo	infection
adj. & n.	inférieur (m)	1. duni 2. chini zaidi	1. inferior to 2. lower
adj. & n.	infirme (m,f)	mgonjwa (pl. wagonjwa)	invalid
n.	infirmière (f), infirmier (m); garde malade	mwuguzi	nurse
adj.	inflexible	-gumu	adamant
n.	influence (f)	mvuto	influence
n.	injection (f)	dawa ya sindano	injection
n.	innocence (f)	usafi	innocence
adj.	innocent	bila hatia	innocent
adj.	innombrable	bila idadi	countless
adj.	inoffensif	si -a shari	harmless
n.	inondation (f)	mafuriko	flood
n.	inquiétude (f)	shughuli	concern
adj.	insatiable	isiyotosheleka	insatiable
adj.	insatisfaisant	-sioridhisha	unsatisfactory
n.	insecte (m)	1. kunguni 2. mdudu (pl. wadudu)	1. bug 2. insect
verb	insérer	kuingiza ndani	insert, to
adj.	insignifiant	duni	insignificant
verb	insister	kushurutisha	insist, to
n.	insolence (f)	ufidhuli	insolence
verb	inspirer	kutia moyoni	inspire, to
adj.	instantané	pale pale	instantaneous
verb	instaurer	kuweka imara	establish, to
n.	instituteur (m)	mwalimu (pl. walimu)	teacher
verb	instruire	1. kuelimisha 2. kufundisha	1. to educate 2. to instruct
verb	instruire, notifier	kufahamisha	inform, to
adj.	insubordonné	-ate	insubordinate
adj.	insuffisant	haba	insufficient
n.	insulte (f)	matusi (pl.)	insult
verb	insulter	kuzarau	insult, to
n.	insurgé (m)	mwasi	insurgent
n.	intelligence (f)	akili	intelligence
adj.	intelligent	-enye akili	1. clever 2. intelligent
verb	intelligible, être	kuelea	clear, to be

parts of speech	french	swahili	english
n	intenter un procès	kesi	lawsuit
n.	intention (f)	kusudi	intention
adv.	intentionnellement	kwa kusudi	intentionally
n.	intérieur (m)	upande wa ndani	interior
n.	intérim (m)	muda wa kati	interim
adj.	intérimaire	-a wakati	temporary
adj.	interminable	-a daima	interminable
n.	interprète (m,f)	mkalimani	interpreter
verb	interroger	kuulizauliza	interrogate, to
verb	interroger avec insistance	kuendesha	prosecute, to
verb	interrompre	kudakiza	interrupt, to
n.	interruption (f)	madakizo	interruption
verb	intervertir	kupindua	turn over, to
n., med	intestins	matumbo (pl.)	intestines
n.	intimidation (f)	kitisho	intimidation
verb	intimider	kutisha	intimidate, to
adj.	intrépide	-a jasiri	fearless
verb	introduire	kuingiza	introduce (something new), to
n.	introduire une requête	matatizo?	problem?
adj.	inutile	-a bure	useless
verb	inventer	kuvumbua	invent, to
n.	inventeur (m)	mtungaji (pl. watungaji)	inventor
n.	investigation (f)	kuchungua	investigation
verb	inviter	kualika	invite, to
n.	invité (m), invitée (f)	mgeni (pl. wageni)	visitor (guest)
adj.	irrespectueux	-tovu wa heshima	disrespectful
adj.	irrégulier	si ya kawaida	irregular
n.	irritation (f)	kuwasho	irritation
verb	irriter	kuudhi	irritate, to
n.	issue (f)	tokeo	outcome
verb	ivre, être	kulewa	drunk, to be
n.	ivrogne (m)	mlevi (pl. walevi)	drunkard
adv.	jadis	zamani	formerly
phrase	J'ai besoin de quelque chose contre la diarrhée.	Nataka dawa kwa kuhara.	I want something to treat diarrhea.
phrase	J'ai besoin une infirmière tout de suite.	Nahitaji mwuguzi sasa.	I need a nurse right away.
phrase	J'ai besoin...	Nahitaji...	I need...
phrase	J'ai faim.	Nina njaa.	I am hungry.
phrase	J'ai mal au ventre.	Tumbo yangu inauma.	I've have a stomach ache.
phrase	J'ai mal à la tête.	Nina maumiva ya kichwa.	I've got a headache.

254

parts of speech	french	swahili	english
phrase	J'ai ne pas faim.	Sisikii njaa.	I am not hungry.
phrase	J'ai soif.	Nasikia kiu.	I am thirsty.
phrase	J'aime...	Ninapenda...	I like...
n.	jalousie (f)	wivu	jealousy
adj.	jaloux	-wivu	jealous
adv.	jamais	kamwe	never
interj.	Jamais!	Kamwe!	Never!
n.	jambe (f)	mguu (pl. miguu)	leg
n.	janvier (m)	Januari; mwezi wa kwanza wa mwaka wa kizungu	January
n.	jardin (m)	shamba (pl. mashamba)	garden
n.	jardinier (m)	mtunza bustani	gardener
adj. & n.	jaune (m)	-a kimanjano	yellow
n.	jaunisse (f)	safura	jaundice
pronoun	Je	mimi	I
phrase	Je m'appelle...	Jina langu ni...	My name is...
phrase	Je m'excuse. Pardon!	Niwie radhi.	Excuse me.
phrase	Je ne comprends pas.	Naelewa.	I don't understand.
phrase	Je ne connais pas (ou) Je ne sais pas.	Sijui.	I don't know.
phrase	Je ne puis pas.	Siwezi.	I cannot.
phrase	Je ne veux pas...	Sitaki...	I do not want...
phrase	Je n'ai pas de l'argent.	Sina pesa.	I don't have money.
phrase	Je n'ai pas...	Sina...	I don't have...
phrase	Je n'aime pas...	Sipenda...	I do not like...
phrase	Je parle un peu le kiswahili.	Nasema kidogo Kiswahili.	I speak a little Swahili.
phrase	Je pense que...	Nafikiri...	think that..., I
phrase	Je sais (or) Je connais.	Ninajua.	I know.
phrase	Je suis fatigué.	Nasikia hafifu.	I am tired.
phrase	Je suis heureux.	Nisikia furaha.	I am happy.
phrase	Je suis malade.	Mimi ni mgonjwa.	I am ill.
phrase	Je suis rassasié.	Nimeshiba.	I am full.
phrase	Je vais à l'aéroport.	Ninakwenda uwanja wa ndege.	I am going to the airport.
phrase	Je vais à...	Ninakwenda...	I am going to...
phrase	Je veux...	Nataka...	I am looking for...
phrase	Je voudrais..., Je veux...	Nataka...	I want...
n.	Jésus (m)	Yesu	Jesus
verb	jeter	kutupa	1. to cast 2. to fling 3. to discard 4. to throw away
n.	jeu (f)	mchezo (pl. michezo)	game

parts of speech	french	swahili	english
n.	jeudi (m)	siku ya nne; alhamisi	Thursday
n.	jeune fille (f)	msichana (pl. wasichana)	girl
n.	jeune homme	kijana mwanaume	young person
n.	jeune homme pubère	mvulana (pl. wavulana)	young man, (unmarried)
verb	jeûner	kufunga chakula	fast, to
n.	jeunesse (f)	ujana	youth
n.	joie (f)	furaha	joy
verb	joindre, se	kuunga	join, to (things, group)
adj.	joli	-zuri	pretty
n.	joue (f)	shavu la uso	cheek
verb	jouer	1. kucheza 2. kuchezea fedha	1. to play 2. to gamble
verb	jouer d'un instrument	sikuya vyombo vya nyimbo	play an instrument, to
verb	jouer un tour à, le tromper	kupiga kura	cast lots, to
n.	jour (m)	siku	day
n.	jour (m) de semaine	siku yo yote ya juma isipokuwa Jumapili	weekday
n.	journal (m)	gazeti	journal
n.	journée (f)	mchana	daytime
adj.	joyeux	-kunjufu	cheerful
phrase	Joyeux anniversaire.	Heri za siku kuu ya kuzaliwa.	Happy birthday.
n.	juge (m)	mwamuzi (pl. waamuzi)	judge
n.	jugement (m)	hukumu	judgement
n.	juillet (m)	Julai; mwezi wa saba wa mwaka wa kizungu	July
n.	juin (m)	Juni; mwezi wa sita wa mwaka kizungu	June
adj. & n.	jumeau (m), jumelle (f)	pacha	twin
n.	jungle (f), brousse (f)	mwitu	jungle
verb	jurer	kuweka nadhiri	vow, to, to swear (oath)
n.	juriste (m)	mwana sheria	lawyer
n.	jus (m) de viande	mchuzi (pl. michuzi)	gravy
prep.	jusqu'à	hata, mpaka	until
adj.	juste	-a haki	fair
n.	justice (f)	haki	justice
n.	ketchup (m)	mchuzi wa nyanya	ketchup
phrase	La nuit tombe.	Magalibi imefika.	dark., It is getting
adv.	là-bas	1. pale 2. kule	1. over there 2. there
n.	laboratoire (m)	nyumba ya sayansi	laboratory
verb	labourer	kulima	plow, to

parts of speech	french	swahili	english
n.	lac (m)	ziwa (pl. maziwa)	lake
n.	lacet (m)	nguo ya kimia	lace
n.	lâche (m,f)	mwoga	coward
verb	laisser	kuacha	1. to let 2. to leave
verb	laisser tomber	kuangusha	drop, to
n.	lait (m)	maziwa (pl.)	milk
n.	lait (m) écrémé	maziwa yaliyoenguliwa	skim milk
n.	lait (m) de femme	maziwa ya mama	breast milk
phrase	lait en poudre	maziwa ya unga	powdered milk
n.	laiterie (f)	duka la maziwa	dairy
n.	laitue (f)	saladi	lettuce
n.	lambeau (m)	kidogo	shred
n.	lame (f)	ubaba	blade (knife)
n.	lampe (f)	taa	lamp
n.	lance (f)	mkuki (pl. mikuki)	spear
verb	lancer	kutupa	sling, to; to throw
n.	langage (m)	lugha	language
n.	langue (f)	ulimi (pl. ndimi)	tongue
n.	lapin (m)	sungura	rabbit
adj.	large, spacieux	-pana	broad, wide, spacious
n.	largeur (f)	upana	width
n.	larmes (f)	machozi	tears
n., med	laryngite (f)	ugonjwa wa kuumia kikoromeo	laryngitis
n., med	larynx	kikoromeo	larynx
verb	laver	kuosha	wash, to
verb	laver les vêtements	kufua	wash, to (clothes)
verb	laver mains ou pieds, se	kunawa	wash hands and feet, to
verb	laver se	kunawa	wash, to (body-self)
n.	le blanc	mzungu (pl. wazungu)	white person
verb	lécher	kulamba	lick, to
n.	le Christ (m)	Kristo	Christ
n.	leçon (f)	mafundisho; somo (pl. masomo)	teaching, (lesson)
phrase	le feu de bois	ukuni	stick of firewood
adj.	légal	halali	lawful
verb	légaliser	kuhalalisha	legalize, to
n.	légende (f)	hekaya	legend
n.	léger	hafifu	flimsy
adj.	léger	-epesi	light
adv.	légèrement	kidogo	slightly

parts of speech	french	swahili	english
n.	**légume (m)**	mboga	vegetable
prep.	**le long de**	kwa mbele	along
pronoun	**le, lui**	yeye	him
n.	**le Nouveau Testament (m)**	Agano Jipya	New Testament
adv.	**lentement**	polepole	slowly
n.	**léopard (m)**	chui	leopard
adj.	**le plus**	kupita yote	most
n.	**lépreux (m)**	mwenye ukoma	leper
phrase	**les blancs**	wazungu	white people
n.	**les morts**	mfu (pl. wafu)	dead person
n.	**lèpre (f)**	ukoma	leprosy
n.	**le tribunal de la tribu**	baraza ya hukumu	tribunal
n.	**lettre (f)**	herufi	letter (of alphabet)
n.	**lettre (f)**	barua	letter (as in, I wrote a letter to a friend.)
adj.	**leur (sg), leurs (pl) (leurs enfants)**	-ao (wana wao)	their (their children)
n.	**leurre (m)**	chambo	bait
n.	**levain (m)**	chachu	leaven
verb	**lever**	kuinua	1. to lift 2. to raise
verb	**lever, se**	1. kusimama 2. kucha	1. to get up 2. to rise (sun)
n.	**lèvre (f)**	mdomo (pl. midomo)	lip
n.	**levure (f)**	chachu	yeast
n.	**lézard (m)**	mjusi	lizard
n.	**liasse (f)**	bunda	bundle
adv.	**libéralement**	bila sharti	freely
n.	**libérateur (m)**	mwokozi	rescuer
verb	**libérer**	kufanya huru	1. to liberate 2. to release
n.	**liberté (f)**	1. uhuru 2. ihtiari	1. liberty or freedom 2. autonomy
adj.	**libre**	huru	free
n	**lien (m)**	kifungo	bonds
verb	**lier**	kufunga	1. to bind 2. to tie up
verb	**lieu, avoir**	kutukia	occur, to
n.	**lièvre (m)**	sungura	hare
n.	**ligne (f)**	mstari (pl. mistari)	line
n.	**limitation (f)**	mpaka	limitation
verb	**limiter**	kuweka mpaka	limit, to
n.	**linge (m)**	kiwanda cha dobi	laundry
n.	**lion (m)**	simba	lion
verb	**lire**	kusoma	read, to
adj.	**lisse**	laini	smooth

parts of speech	french	swahili	english
n.	lit (m)	kitanda (pl. vitanda)	bed
n.	livre (m)	kitabu (pl. vitabu)	book
n.	localité (f)	mahali fulani	locality
n.	locomotive (f)	gari la moshe	train
n.	logement (m)	mahali pa kukaa	lodging place
verb	loger	mahali pa kukaa	accommodate, to
n.	loi (f)	sheria	law
adv.	loin	mbali	far
prep.	loin de	mbali na	far from
adj.	long (m), longue (f)	-refu	long
adv.	longtemps, il y a	zamani sana	long ago
n.	longueur (f)/durée (f)	urefu	length (dimension, time)
verb	loucher	kuwa na upogo	squint, to
verb	louer	1. kuajiri 2. kusifu	1. to hire 2. to praise
adj.	lourd	-zito	heavy
n.	lubrifiant (m)	mafuta	lubricant
pronoun	lui-même (m), elle-même (f)	-enyewe	itself
n., med	lumbago	maumivu ya viunoni	lumbago
n.	lumière (f)	nuru	light
n.	lundi (m)	Jamatatu	Monday
n.	lune (f)	mwezi (pl. miezi)	moon
n.	lunettes (f)	miwani	glasses (eye)
n.	lustre (m)	kondoo	sheep
n.	lutte (f)	upigano (pl. maupigano)	strife
n.	luxe (m)	anasa	luxury
n.	luxure (f)	tamaa	lust
phrase	l'art de guérir	uganga	medicine, practice of
phrase	l'assemblée nationale	halmashauri kuu	parliament
n., med	l'impasse	mgogoro	deadlock
n.	M. (m) (for Monsieur)	bwana	Mr.
verb	mâcher	kutafuna	chew, to
n.	machette	panga (pl. mapanga)	machete
n.	machine (f)	mashini	machine
n.	mâchoire (f)	taya (pl. mataya)	jaw
n.	maçon (m)	mwashi	mason
n.	madame (f)	bibi; mwanamke (pl. wanawake)	woman (married)
n.	madame (f) vieille	kizee	old woman
n.	mademoiselle (f)	1. mwali 2. kibibi (pl. vibibi)	1. Miss 2. young lady (unmarried)
n.	magasin (m)	duka	store (shop)

259

parts of speech	french	swahili	english
n.	**magie (f)**	uganga	magic
n.	**mai (m)**	Mei; mwezi wa tano wa mwaka wa kizingu	May
verb	**maigrir**	kukonda	1. to lose weight 2. to become thin
n.	**main (f)**	mkono (pl. mikono)	hand
n.	**main droit**	mukono wa kuume	hand, right
n.	**main gauche**	mukono wa kushoto	hand, left
adv.	**maintenant**	sasa	now
verb	**maintenir**	kushika	maintain, to
adv.	**maintes et maintes fois**	mara kwa mara	again and again
n.	**maintien (m)**	msaada	maintenance
conj.	**mais**	lakini	but
n.	**maïs (m)**	muhindi (pl. mihindi)	1. maize 2. corn
n.	**maison (f)**	nyumba	dwelling place, house
n.	**maison (f) (traditionnelle)**	nyumba	house (traditional)
n.	**maison (f) d'étudiants**	chumba cha kulala	dormitory
n.	**maître (m)**	mwalimu	master
verb	**maîtriser**	kushinda	master, to
n.	**majesté (f)**	enzi	majesty
n.	**majorité (f)**	wingi	majority
verb	**mal calculer**	kufikiri yasivyo	miscalculate, to
n.	**mal de tête (m)**	maumivu ya kichwa	headache
verb	**mal évaluer**	kupima visivyo	misjudge, to
n.	**malade (f)**	mgonjwa (wagonjwa)	sick person
verb	**malade, être**	1. kugua 2. kuugua 3. kuwa mgonjwa	1. to be sick 2. to be ill
n.	**maladie (f)**	ugonjwa (pl. maogonjwa)	1. illness 2. disease 3. sickness 4. malady
n.	**malaria (f)**	homa ya mbu	malaria
verb	**malaxer**	kuchanganya	mix, to
verb	**malaxer, pétrir**	kukanda	knead (as in bread), to
adj. & n.	**mâle (m)**	mwanamume (pl. wanaume)	male
n.	**malheur (m)**	bahati mbaya	misfortune
adj.	**malhonnête**	-danganyifu	dishonest
n.	**malhonnêteté (f)**	uwongo	dishonesty
verb	**manger**	kula	eat, to
n.	**mangue (f)**	embe (pl. maembe)	mango (fruit)
n.	**manière (f)**	jinsi	manner
n.	**manière de parler**	usemi	speech
n.	**manifestation (f)**	ufunuo	manifestation
n.	**manioc**	muhogo, (pl. mihogo)	cassava

parts of speech	french	swahili	english
verb	manquer	kukosa	miss, to
n.	manteau (m)	kifuniko	cloak
n.	manteau (m) {couche} (f)	koti {mpako}	coat (clothing), {of paint}
n.	marais (m)	bwawa	swamp, marsh
verb	marchander	kupiga bei	bargain, to
n.	marché (m)	mapatano	bargain
n.	marché (m)	soko (pl. masoko)	market
verb	marcher	1. kwenda 2. kukanyaga	1. to walk 2. to tread on
verb	marcher vite	kufanya haraka	hurry, to
n.	mardi (m)	Jumanne	Tuesday
n.	mare (f)	1. kiziwa (pl. viziwa) 2. kidimbwi	1. pond 2. pool
n.	mari (m)	mume (pl. waume)	husband
n.	mariage (m)	ndoa	marriage
n.	marié (m)	bwana arusi	bride-groom
n.	mariée (f)	bibi arusi	bride
verb	marier, se	1. kuoa (man) 2. kuolewa (woman)	marry, to
n.	marmite (f) de argile	chombo (pl. vyombo)	pot (clay)
verb	marmotter	kumumunya maneno	mumble, to
n.	marotte (f)	kinyongo	fad
n.	marque (f)	alama	mark
verb	marquer	kutia alama	mark, to
n.	mars (m)	Machi; mwezi wa tatu wa mwaka wa kizungu	March
n.	marteau (m)	nyundo	hammer
n.	martyr (m), martyre (f)	shahidi	martyr
n.	massue (f)	fimbo	club (stick)
verb	mastiquer	kutafuna	chew, to
n.	matelas (m)	godoro (pl. magodoro)	mattress
n.	mathématiques (f)	elimu ya hesabu	math
adv. n.	matin (m)	asubuhi	morning
verb	maudire	kulaani, kutukana	curse, to
adj.	mauvais	1. -baya 2. -bovu 3. -ovu	1. bad 2. evil
adj. & n.	maximum (m)	kipeo	maximum
n.	mécanicien (m)	fundi wa mashine	mechanic
adv.	méchamment	vibaya	badly
n.	méchanceté (f)	1. ubaya 2. kijicho	1. badness 2. malice
adj.	méchant	-ovu	wicked
n.	mèche de lampe	utambi	wick
n.	médicament (m)	dawa	medication
n.	médication (f)	dawa	medicine

261

parts of speech	french	swahili	english
verb	**méditer**	1. kufikiri 2. kutafakari	1. to cogitate 2. to meditate
adj.	**meilleur**	bora kabisa	best
n.	**mélange (m)**	mchanganyiko (pl. michanganyiko)	mixture
verb	**mélanger**	kuchanganya	1. to blend 2. to mix
n.	**membre (m)**	kiungo (pl. viungo)	member
adv.	**même**	hata, sawa	even
adj & pr	**même**	-moja, yule yule	same
adv.	**même si**	hata ikiwa	even if
n.	**mémoire (f)**	uwezo wa kukumbuka	memory
n.	**mendiant (m)**	mwombaji (pl. waombaji) 2. masikini	1. beggar 2. poor person
verb	**mendier**	kuomba	beg, to
verb	**mener**	kuongoza	lead, to
n., med	**méningite**	ugonjwa wa ngozi inayufunika ubongo	meningitis
n., med	**ménopause**	wakati wa mwanamke kuingia ugumba	menopause
n.	**menotte (f)**	pinga ya mikono	handcuffs
n.	**mensonge (m)**	uwongo	lie, falsehood
n.	**menstruation (f)**	hedhi	1. menstruation 2 to have period (female)
n.	**menteur (m), menteuse (f)**	mwongo	liar
verb	**mentionner**	kutaja	mention, to
verb	**mentir**	kusema uongo	lie, to
n.	**menton (m)**	kidevu	chin
n.	**menu (m)**	orodha ya vyakula	menu
n.	**menuiserie (f)**	usermala	carpentry
n.	**menuisier (m)**	seremala (pl. maseremala)	carpenter
n.	**mépris (m)**	dharau	contempt
verb	**mépriser**	1. kutweza 2. kuchukia	1. to despise 2. to scorn
n.	**mer (f)**	bahari	sea
adj. & n.	**mercenaire (m)**	askari mgeni wa mshahara	mercenary
phrase	**Merci beaucoup.**	Asante sana.	Thank you very much.
phrase	**Merci.**	Asante.	Thank you.
n.	**mercredi (m)**	Jumatano	Wednesday
n.	**mère (f)**	mama mzazi	1. mama 2. mother
verb	**mériter**	kustahili	1. to deserve 2. to merit
n.	**merveille (f)**	mshangao (pl. mishangao)	wonder
n.	**message (m)**	maneno	message
n	**messager (m)**	mjumbe (pl. wajumbe)	messenger

parts of speech	french	swahili	english
n.	mesure (f)	kipimo	measurement
verb	mesurer	kupima	measure, to
n.	métal (m)	madini	metal
n.	méthode (f)	kawaida	method
adv.	méthodique	taratibu	orderly
n.	métier (m)	biashara	trade
phrase	métier de sorcière	uchawi	witchcraft
verb	mettre	kuweka	put, to
verb	mettre à (quelqu'un) un vêtement	kuvika	dress another, to
verb	mettre de côté	kukabidhi	save, to
verb	mettre en vente	kuchuuza	peddle, to
verb	mettre fin à; terminer	kukomesha	put an end to, to
verb	mettre l'épreuve	kupima	test, to
n.	meurtre (m)	uuaji	murder
n.	midi (m)	adhuhuri	noon
n.	miel (m)	asali	honey
n.	miette (f)	kombo	crumb
adv.	mieux	afazali	better
n.	mile (m)	maili	mile
n.	milieu (m)	mazingira	environment
n.	milieu (m)	kati	middle
adj. & n.	mille (m)	elfu	thousand
n.	minuit (m)	saa sita usika	midnight
n.	minute (f)	dakika	minute
n.	miracle (m)	mwujiza	miracle
n.	miroir (m)	kioo (pl. vioo)	mirror
verb	miroiter	kungariza	sparkle, to
n.	misère	huzuni	misery
n.	miséricorde (f)	rehema	mercy
n.	Mme. (f) (for madame)	bibi	Mrs.
verb	modifier	kubadili	alter, to
n., med	moelle (des os)	uboho	bone marrow
pronoun	moi	mimi	me
n.	moi (m), personne (f)	moyo, nafasi	self
pronoun	moi-même	mimi mwenyewe	myself
adj.	moindre	-dogo kabisa	least
n.	moine (m)	mtawa mwanamume	monk
n.	mois (m)	mwezi (pl. miezi)	month
phrase	mois prochain	mwezi kesho	next month
n.	moisson (f)	mavuno (pl.)	harvest

parts of speech	french	swahili	english
n.	**moitié (f)**	nusu	half
n.	**moment (m)**	nukta	moment
adj.	**mon (m), ma (f), mes (pl) (mes enfants)**	-angu (wana wangu)	my (my children)
n.	**monceau (m)**	chungu	mound
n.	**monde (m)**	ulimwengu	world
n.	**monnaie (f)**	senti	change (coins)
verb	**monopoliser**	kujishikia yote	monopolize, to
n.	**monotonie (f)**	kuchosha	monotony
n.	**monsieur (m)**	1. mwungwana 2. bwana	1. gentleman 2. sir
n.	**montagne (f)**	mlima (pl. milima)	mountain
adj.	**montagneux**	-enye milima mingi	mountainous
verb	**monter**	kupanda	ascend, to
n.	**montre (f)**	saa	watch (clock)
verb	**montrer**	kuonyesha	show, to
phrase	**montrer se**	kuonekana	show oneself, to
n.	**morceau (m)**	1. bonge 2. kipande (pl. vipande)	1. lump 2. piece
verb	**mordre**	kuuma	bite, to
adj.	**moribond**	-a kufani	moribund
adj.	**mort**	amekufa	dead
n.	**mort (f)**	kufa (pl. kufa), mauti	death
n.	**morve (f)**	makamasi	nasal mucous
n.	**mot (m)**	neno (pl. maneno)	word
n.	**motif (m)**	1. kusudi 2. kilezo	1. motive 2. pattern
adv.	**motocyclette (f)**	pikipiki	motorcycle
n.	**mouche (f)**	inzi (pl. mainzi)	fly
n.	**mouchoir (m)**	kitambaa	handkerchief
verb	**moudre**	kusaga	grind, to
verb	**mouiller**	kuloweka	wet, to
adj.	**mouillé**	majimaji	wet
verb	**mourir**	kufa	die, to
n.	**mousse (f)**	povu	foam
n.	**moustiquaire (m)**	chandalua (pl. vyandalua)	mosquito net
n.	**moustique (m)**	mbu	mosquito
n.	**mouton (m)**	kondoo	sheep
n.	**mouvement (m)**	mwendo	movement
verb	**mouvoir**	kusukuma	move, to
adj.	**moyen**	-a kadiri	medium
n.	**moyen (m)**	njia	means (of doing something)
n.	**moyens (m) d'existence**	maishilio	livelihood

parts of speech	french	swahili	english
adj.	**muet**	bila sauti	mute (without speech)
verb	**mugir**	kunguruma	roar, to (bellow)
verb	**multiplier**	kuzidisha	multiply, to
n.	**mur (m)**	kiambaza (pl. viambaza)	wall
adj.	**mûr**	-bivu	ripe
n.	**muscle (m)**	mshipa	muscle
n.	**musique (f)**	muziki	music
n.	**mystère (m)**	siri, fumbo	mystery
verb	**nager**	kuogolea	swim, to
adj. & n.	**nain (m)**	kibeti	dwarf
n.	**naissance (f)**	uzazi	birth
verb	**naître**	kuzaliwa	born, to be
n.	**narine (f)**	tunda la pua	nostril
n	**nation (f)**	taifa (pl. mataifa)	nation
n.	**nationalité (f)**	taifa la mtu fulani	nationality
n.	**nature (f)**	maumbile	nature
adv.	**naturellement**	1. bila shaka 2. sawasawa	1. naturally 2. precisely
n., med	**nausée**	ugagazi	nausea
n.	**navire (m) naufragé**	kuvunjika meli	shipwreck
verb	**ne parler pas clairement**	kunongona	speak indistinctly, to
verb	**ne pas être d'accord**	kutopatana	disagree, to
verb	**ne pas tolérer**	kuchukia	dislike, to
phrase	**ne pas trouver**	sikupata	unable to find
verb	**ne plus avoir faim; s'emplir**	kujaa	full, to be (not hungry)
n.	**neige (f)**	seluji	snow
n.	**nerf (m)**	mshipa (pl. mishipa)	nerve
verb	**nettoyer**	kusafisha	1. to scour 2. to clean
verb	**nettoyer, purifier**	kutakasa	cleanse, to
adj.	**neuf**	tisa; kenda	nine
adj.	**neuf**	-pya	new
n.	**neuf cents**	mia kenda	nine hundred
verb	**neutraliser**	kubatilisha	counteract, to
adj.	**neuvième**	-a kenda	ninth
n.	**neveu (m)**	mpwa	nephew
n.	**nez (m)**	pua	nose
adv.	**néanmoins**	walakini	nevertheless
n.	**nécessité (f)**	lazimu	necessity
n.	**négligence**	uzembe	negligence
verb	**négliger**	kutoangalia	1. to ignore someone 2. to neglect

parts of speech	french	swahili	english
conj.	**ni...ni**	wala...wala	neither...nor
n.	**nid (m)**	kioto (pl. vioto)	nest
n.	**nièce (f)**	mpwa wa kike	niece
verb	**nier**	kukana	deny, to
phrase	**n'importe comment**	vyo vyote	anyhow
phrase	**n'importe où**	po pote	anywhere
phrase	**n'importe quelle heure**	wakati wo wote	any time
n.	**noces (f)**	arusi	wedding
n.	**nœud (m)**	fundo (pl. mafundo)	knot
n.	**Noël (m) {Bonne fête de Noël.}**	Krismas {Heri za Krismas.}	Christmas {Merry Christmas}
adj.	**noir**	-eusi, -a giza	black
n.	**noir (m)**	giza	dark
n.	**noir (m) {couleur}**	weusi	black {color}
n. & adj.	**Noir (m), Noire (f)**	mweusi	black (for person)
n.	**noir de fumée**	masizi	soot
n.	**noix (f) de coco**	dafu (pl. madafu)	coconut
n.	**noix de cajou**	korosho	cashew
n.	**nom (m)**	jina (pl. majina)	name
n.	**nombre (m)**	hesabu	number
adj.	**nombreux**	-ingi	numerous
n.	**nombril (m)**	kitovu (pl. vitovu)	umbilicus; navel
verb	**nommer**	kutaja	name, to
n.	**nord (m)**	kaskazini	north
adj.	**nostalgique**	hamu ya kwao	homesick
n.	**note (f)**	barua fupi	note
adj.	**notre (sg), nos (pl) (nos enfants)**	-etu (wana wetu)	our (our children)
verb	**nouer**	kupiga fundo	knot, to tie a
verb	**nourrir**	1. kulisha 2. kulisha vema	1. to feed 2. to nourish
n.	**nourriture (f)**	chakula (pl. vyakula)	1. food 2. nourishment
pronoun	**nous**	sisi, siye	we, us
n.	**nouveau né**	mtoto muchanga	baby (newborn)
n.	**nouvelles (f)**	habari	news
n.	**novembre (m)**	Novemba	November
verb	**noyer**	kufa maji	drown, to
adj.	**nu**	-tupu	nude
n.	**nuage (m)**	wingu (mawingu)	cloud
n.	**nudité (f)**	uchi	nakedness
n.	**nuit (f)**	usiku	night
adv.	**nuit dernière, la**	usiku wa leo	night, last

parts of speech	french	swahili	english
adv.	**nulle part**	si mahali po pote	nowhere
verb	**obéir à**	kutii	obey, to
adj.	**obéissant**	-sikivu	obedient
n.	**objectif (m)**	kikomo	goal
n.	**objection (f)**	pingamizi	objection
adj.	**obligeant**	-a kusaidia	helpful
n.	**obscénité (f)**	upujufu	obscenity
verb	**observer**	kutazama	observe, to
n.	**obstacle (m)**	zuio (pl. mazuio)	obstruction
adj.	**obstiné**	-kaidi	obstinate
verb	**obstruer**	kupinga	obstruct, to
verb	**obtenir**	kupata	obtain, to
n.	**occasion (f)**	1. mara 2. nafasi	1. occasion 2. opportunity
verb	**occuper**	kukalia	occupy, to
n.	**océan (m)**	bahari kuu	ocean
n.	**octobre (m)**	Oktoba	October
adj.	**odieux**	kuchukiza	obnoxious
n.	**œil (m)**	jicho (pl. macho)	eye
n.	**œuf (m)**	yai (pl. mayai)	egg
n.	**œuvre (f)**	muhtasari	summary
verb	**offenser**	kuchukiza	offend, to
n.	**office (m)**	afisi	office
n.	**offrande**	zaka	tithe
n.	**offre (f)**	kipaji	offering
verb	**offrir**	kutolea	offer, to
n.	**oignon (m)**	kitunguu (pl. vitunguu)	onion
verb	**oindre**	kupaka mafuta	anoint, to
n.	**oiseau (m)**	ndege	bird (small)
n.	**oisiveté (f)**	uvivu	idleness
n.	**ombre (f)**	kivuli (pl. vivuli)	shadow, shade
verb	**omettre**	kukosa kutia	omit, to
n.	**omission (f)**	jambo lililoachwa	omission
n., med	**omoplate**	mtulinga	scapula
n.	**oncle (m) maternel**	mjomba (pl. wajomba)	uncle, maternal
n.	**oncle paternel (aîné)**	baba mukubwa	uncle (father's older brother)
n.	**oncle paternel (plus jeune)**	baba mudogo	uncle (father's younger brother)
n.	**ongle (m)**	ukucha (pl. kucha)	1. fingernail 2. toenail
n.	**onze**	kumi na moja	eleven
verb	**opérer**	kupasua mgonjwa	operate (medical), to

parts of speech	french	swahili	english
n.	opérer	utabibu wa kupasua	operation (surgery)
n.	opinion (f)	rai	opinion
verb	opprimer	kudhulumu	oppress, to
n.	or (m)	dhahabu	gold
n.	orage (m)	zoruba	storm on lake
n.	orange (f)	chungwa (pl. machungwa)	orange (fruit)
adj.	ordinaire	-a kawaida	ordinary
verb	ordonner	1. kuagiza 2. kuamuru	1. to ordain 2. to order
n.	ordre (m)	amri (pl. amri)	order
n.	ordures (m)	takataka	garbage
n.	oreille (f)	sikio (pl. masikio)	ear
n.	oreiller (m)	mto (pl. mito)	pillow
n.	oreillons (m)	matubwitubwi	mumps
n	organisation (f)	matengenezo	organization
verb	organiser	kutengeneza	organize
n.	orge (f)	shayiri	barley
n.	origine (f)	asili	origin
n.	orphelin (m)	yatima	orphan
n.	orteil (m)	kidole cha mguu	toe
n.	os (m)	mfupa (pl. mifupa)	bone
verb	oser	kuthubutu	dare, to
verb	ôter	kuondosha	remove, to
prep.	ou	ama	or
conj.	où	wapi	where
phrase	Où allez-vous?	Unakwenda wapi?	Where are you going?
verb	oublier	kusahau	forget, to
adj.	oublieux	-sahaulifu	forgetful
n. & adj.	ouest (m)	magharibi	west
phrase	Où est...?	Wapi ni...?	Where is...?
phrase	Où est la salle de bain?	Choo kiko wapi?	Where is the bathroom?
adv.	oui	ndiyo; ndivyo; naam	yes
n.	ouragan (m)	zoruba	hurricane
n.	ours (m)	dubu	bear (animal)
n.	outil (m)	madini	tool (metal)
adj.	ouvert	wazi	open
adv.	ouvertement	waziwazi	openly
n.	ouverture (f)	mwanya	gap
phrase	Où viens-tu?	Umeyok wapi?	Where are you coming from?
n.	ouvre-bouteille (m)	kifungua chupa	bottle-opener

parts of speech	french	swahili	english
n.	ouvrier-maçon (m)	mwashi aakaye kwa matofali	bricklayer
verb	ouvrir {Ouvre la porte.}	kufungua (Fungua mlango.)	1. to open {Open the door.} 2. to unlock
n.	pagaie (f)	kafi	paddle
verb	pagayer	kupiga kafi	paddle, to
n.	page (f)	ukurasa (pl. kurasa)	page
adj. & n.	païen (m)	mtu asiye Mkristo	pagan
adj. & n.	païen (m), païenne (f)	mshenzi (pl. washenzi)	heathen
n.	paiement (m)	malipo	payment
n.	paillasson (m)	jamvi	mat
n.	paillasson (m), herbe	mkeka (pl. mikeka)	mat, grass woven
n.	paille (pour couvrir un toit de paille)	kuezeka	straw (to cover a roof)
n.	pain (m)	mkate (pl. mikate)	bread
n.	paire (f)	jozi	couple
n.	paix (f)	amani, salama	peace
n.	palmier	mti wa jamii ya mnazi	palm tree
verb	palper	1. kugusa 2. kupapasa	1. to palpate 2. to stroke
n.	palpitation (f)	papo la moyo	palpitation
n., med	pancréas (m)	kongosho	pancreas
n.	panier (m)	kitunga (pl. vitunga)	basket
n.	panique (f)	woga mkuu	panic
n.	pansement (m)	kitambaa cha kufungia dawa	bandage
n.	pantalon (m)	suruali	pants
n.	papaye	papai	papaya
n.	papier (m)	karatasi	paper
n.	papillon (m)	kipepeo (pl. vipepeo)	butterfly
n.	papillon (m) de nuit	nondo	moth
n.	Pâques (m)	Pasaka	Easter
n.	paquet (m)	bahasha	packet
prep.	par / près de	kwa, na	by (through)/ (near)
adv.	par-ci par-là	huko na huko	here and there
n.	parabole (f)	mfano wenye mafundisho	parable
verb	paraître	kutokea	appear, to
n.	parallèle (m)	sambamba	parallel
n.	paralysie (f)	kipooza	paralysis
n.	parapluie (m)	mwavuli (pl. miavuli)	umbrella
n.	parasite (m)	kimelea	parasite
conj.	parce que	kwa kuwa, kwa maana, kwa sababu	because

parts of speech	french	swahili	english
n.	**pardon (m)**	1. usamehe 2. masamaha	1. pardon 2. forgiveness
verb	**pardonner**	kusamehe	1. to pardon 2. to forgive
prep.	**pareil**	kama	like
n.	**paresse (f)**	uvivu	laziness
adj.	**paresseux**	-vivu	lazy
adj.	**parfait**	kamili	perfect
adv.	**parfois**	pengine	sometimes
n.	**parfum (m)**	1. harufu tamu 2. manukato	1. fragrance 2. perfume
verb	**parier**	kubahatisha fedha	bet, to
verb	**parler**	kusema	1. to talk 2. to speak
verb	**parler à**	kusema na	speak to, to
prep.	**parmi, entre**	katikati ya	among
verb	**partager entre plusieurs**	kushiriki	share with others, to
n.	**participation (f)**	ushirika	participation
verb	**participer**	kushariki	1. to compete 2. to participate
verb	**participer à**	kushariki	take part in, to
n.	**partie (f)**	kipande	part
verb	**partir**	1. kuondoka 2. kwenda	1. to depart 2. to go away 3. to go 4. to leave
adv.	**partout**	po pote, kila mahali	everywhere, throughout
verb	**parvenir à**	kufika	reach, to
interj.	**Pas possible!**	Haiwezekani!	Not possible!
n.	**pas (m)**	hatua	footstep
n.	**pas (m)**	hatua	pace
phrase	**Pas de problème.**	Ni mamoja kwangu.	I don't mind.
phrase	**Pas de problème.**	Hamna shida.	No problem.
adj., adv.	**pas de, non**	hapana, siyo	no
phrase	**Pas du tout!**	Hata kidogo!	Not at all!
adv.	**pas encore**	bado	not yet
phrase	**pas même**	wala	not the same
adj.	**pas mûr**	-bichi	green (unripe)
adv.	**pas, non**	si	not
n.	**passager (m), passagère (f)**	abiria	passenger
n.	**passant (m)**	mpitaji	passerby
n.	**passé (m)**	-a zamani	past
n.	**passeport (m)**	ruhusa ya kupita	passport
verb	**passer**	1. kufaulu 2. kung'uta chuja	1. to pass 2. to strain (filter)
verb	**passer avant**	kupita	past, to go
verb	**passer, se**	kupita	happen, to
n.	**pasteur (m)**	mchungaji wa roho	pastor

parts of speech	french	swahili	english
n.	pastille (f)	kidonge cha kufyonza	lozenge
n.	patates, douce	kiazi	sweet potatoes
n.	patente (f)	ruhusu	license
adv.	patiemment	kwa saburi	patiently
n.	patience (f)	saburi	patience
adj.	patient	-vumilivu	patient
verb	patienter	kungoja	wait, to
n.	patrimoine (m)	urithi	patrimony
n.	patron (m), patronne (f)	1. msimamizi 2. bwana wa kazi	1. boss 2. employer
n.	pâturage (m)	malisho	pasture
n.	paume (f)	kitanga cha mkono	palm of hand
n.	paupière (f)	ukope	eyelid
adj.	pauvre	masikini	poor
n.	pauvreté (f)	umasikini	poverty
verb	payer	kulipa	pay, to
n.	paysan (m), paysanne (f)	mkulima	peasant
n.	peau (f)	ngozi	1. skin 2. pelt
n.	péché (m)	zambi	sin
verb	pêcher	kuvua	fish, to
verb	pécher	kufanya dhambi	sin, to
n.	pêcheur (m)	mvuvi (pl. wavuvi)	fisherman
n.	peigne (m)	kitana	comb
verb	peigner	kuchana	comb, to
verb	peindre	kupakaa	paint, to
n.	peine (f)	azabu	punishment
verb	peiner	1. kusikitika 2. kupindua	1. to grieve 2. to upset
n.	peinture (f)	rangi	paint
verb	peler	kumenya	peel, to
adj.	pelé	-tupu	bare
n.	pellicules (f)	ganda (pl. maganda)	dry skin (dandruff)
prep.	pendant	wakati wa	during
verb	pénétrer	kupenya	penetrate, to
n.	pénis (m)	uume	penis
verb	penser	kuwaza	think, to
verb	penser à	kuwaza; kufikiri	think of, to
n.	pensée (f)	wazo	thought
n.	pension (f)	malipo ya uzeeni	pension
verb	percer	1. kutoboa 2. kuchoma	1. to drill (a hole) 2. to pierce
verb	percuter contre	kududnda	crash into, to

271

parts of speech	french	swahili	english
verb	perdre	kupoteza	lose, to
verb	perdre, se	kupotea	lost, to be
n.	père (m)	baba	1. father 2. papa
n.	père (m), mère (f)	mzazi (pl. wazazi)	parent
n.	père (m), mon	babangu	father (my)
n.	perfection (f)	ukamilifu	perfection
n.	période (f)	muda	period (of time)
verb	périr	kuharibika	perish, to
n.	perle (f)	lulu (pl. malulu)	pearl
verb	permettre	1. kuwezesha 2. kuruhusu	1. to enable 2. to permit 3. to allow
verb	permettre (admit)	kuingiza	admit, to (into a place)
n.	permission (f)	ruhusa	permission
n.	perplexité (f)	mashaka	perplexity
verb	persécuter	kutesa	persecute, to
n.	persécuteur (m)	mtesi (pl. watesi)	persecutor
n.	persécution (f)	mateso	persecution
n.	persévérance (f)	udumu	perseverance
n.	personne (f)	mtu (pl. watu)	person
n	personne aveugle	kipofu (pl. vipofu)	blind person
n.	personne sourd	kiziwi (pl. viziwi)	deaf person
pronoun	personne, ne...personne	si mtu	no one
verb	persuader	kushawishi	persuade, to
n.	pesanteur (f)	uzito	gravity
verb	peser	kupima	weigh, to
adj.	petit	-dogo	small
phrase	petit à petit	kidogo kwa kidogo	little by little
n.	petit déjeuner (m)	chakula cha asubuhi	breakfast
n.	petit doigt (m)	kidole cha mwisho	finger, little
n.	petit somme (m)	usingizi mfupi	nap
n.	petit-fils (m),petit-fille (f)	mjukuu	grandchild
n.	pétrole (m)	mafuta ya motakaa	petroleum
n. & adv	peu (m)	-dogo	little
adj.	peu de	-chache	few
adj.	peu fréquent	si mara nyingi	infrequent
adj.	peureux	-a hofu	fearful
adj.	peureux	-enye haya	shy
adv.	peut-être	labda	1. maybe 2. perhaps
n.	pharmacie (f)	duka la mwuza dawa	pharmacy
n.	photographie (f)	picha iliyopigwa kwa kamera	photograph

272

parts of speech	french	swahili	english
verb	**photographier**	kupiga sanamu	photograph, to
n.	**piano (m)**	kinanda (pl. vinanda)	piano
n.	**pied (m)**	mguu (pl. miguu)	foot
n.	**pièce (f)**	kiraka	patch
n.	**pièce (f) de monnaie**	sarafu	coin
verb	**piéger**	kunasa, kutega	trap, to
n.	**piège (m)**	mtego (pl. mitego)	trap, snare
n.	**pierre (f)**	jiwe (pl. mawe)	stone
verb	**piétiner**	kukanyaga	1. to stamp one's feet 2. to trample on
n.	**pieuvre (f)**	pweza	octopus
n.	**pigeon (m)**	njiwa	pigeon
verb	**piler, broyer**	kutwanga	pound, to; to crush
n.	**pilier (m)**	nguzo	pillar
verb	**piller**	kunyanganya	plunder, to
n.	**pilule (f)**	kidonge (pl. vidonge)	pill
n.	**pipe (f)**	kiko	pipe (tobacco)
verb	**piquer**	kuchoma	sting, to
n.	**pirogue (f)**	mtumbwi (pl. mitumbwi)	canoe (dugout)
n.	**pitié (f)**	huruma	pity
n.	**placard (m)**	kijumba	closet
n., med	**placenta**	kondo la nyuma	placenta
n.	**plafond (m)**	upande wa juu wa chumba	ceiling
n.	**plage (f)**	pwani	1. beach 2. coast of river
verb	**plaider**	kuleta hoja	plead, to (court)
n.	**plaignant (m,f)**	mshitaki (pl. washitaki)	plaintiff
verb	**plaindre**	kurehemu	pity, to
n.	**plaine (f)**	tambarare	plain (near river)
verb	**plaire à**	kupendeza	please, to
n.	**plaisanterie (f)**	neno la kuchekesha	joke
n.	**plaisir (m)**	anasa	pleasure
n.	**planche (f)**	ubao (pl. mbao)	board (plank)
n.	**plancher (m)**	sakafu ya chini	floor
n.	**plantation (f)**	shamba (pl. mashamba)	plantation
n.	**plante (f)**	mmea (pl. mimea)	plant
verb	**planter**	kupanda	plant, to
adj.	**plat**	-pana; sawa	1. flat 2. level
n.	**plat (m)**	sahani	dish
verb	**plâtre**	kukandika	plaster, to
adv.	**pleinement**	kabisa	fully

parts of speech	french	swahili	english
verb	**pleurer**	1. kulia 2. kuomboleza	1. to cry or weep 2. to mourn
verb	**pleurnicher**	kutoka kamasi	snivel, to
verb	**pleuvoir**	kunyesha, kunya	rain, to
verb	**plier**	kukunja	1. to bend 2. to fold
verb	**plonger**	kuchovya	immerse, to
n.	**pluie (f)**	mvua	rain
n.	**plume (f)**	nyoya	feather
adv.	**plus**	1. zaidi 2. mbele zaidi	1. more 2. further
adv.	**plus loin**	mbali zaide	farther
adv.	**plus retard**	baadaye	later
adv.	**plutôt**	afazali	rather (but rather)
n.	**pneu (m)**	mpira	tire
n.	**poche (f)**	mfuko (pl. mifuko)	pouch, pocket
n.	**poète (m)**	mshairi	poet
n.	**poids (m)**	uzito	weight
n.	**poignet (m)**	kiwiko (pl. viwiko)	wrist
n.	**poing (m)**	ngumi	fist
n.	**pointe (f)**	ncha	point
n.	**pois (m)**	mbaazi (pl. mibaazi)	pea
n.	**poison (m)**	sumu	poison
n.	**poisson (m)**	samaki	fish
n.	**poitrine (f)**	kifua (pl. vifua)	chest (body)
n.	**poivre (m)**	pilipili manga	pepper
verb	**polir**	kung'arisha	polish, to
n.	**politesse (f)**	adabu	politeness
n.	**pollution (f)**	uchafu	pollution
n.	**pommade (f)**	marhamu	ointment
n.	**pomme (f)**	tunda a kizungu	apple
n.	**ponctuation (f)**	vituo	punctuation
n.	**pont (m)**	daraja (pl. madaraja)	bridge
n.	**porc (m)**	nyama ya nguruwe	pork, hog
n.	**porche (m)**	baraza	porch
n.	**porte (f)**	mlango (pl. milango)	door
n.	**porte (f)/barrière (f)**	mlango wa nje	gate
verb	**porter**	1. kuchukua 2. kuvaa	1. to carry 2. to carry
verb	**porter sur la hanche**	kueleka	carry on one's hip, to
verb	**porter sur le dos**	kubeba	carry on one's back, to
n.	**porteur (m)**	mchukuzi	porter
n.	**portion (f)**	sehemu	portion
n.	**portrait (m)**	picha ya mtu	portrait

parts of speech	french	swahili	english
verb	**poser**	1. kuweka 2. kulaza	lay, to
verb	**poser**	1. kuweka 2. kutia	set, to
verb	**poser le pied en marchant**	kupima kwa hatua	step, to
adv.	**position debout**	wima	upright
verb	**posséder**	1. kumiliki 2. kuwa na	1. to own 2. to possess
verb	**possible, être**	kuwezekana	possible, to be
n.	**poste (f)**	posta	post (mail)
n.	**pot (m) de l'eau**	mtungi (pl. mitungi)	water pot
n.	**pot (m), petit**	chupa	jar (container/shock)
n.	**pot-de-vin**	rushwa	bribe
n.	**potiron (m)**	boga (pl. maboga)	pumpkin
n.	**pou (m)**	chawa	lice
n.	**pouce (m)**	1. inchi 2. kidole cha gumba	1. inch 2. thumb
n.	**poudre (f)**	unga	powder
n.	**poule (f)**	kuku	hen
n.	**poulet (m)**	kinda la kuku	chicken
n.	**poumon (m)**	pafu	lung
n.	**poupée (f)**	mtoto wa bandia	doll
adv.	**pour la plupart**	zaidi	mostly
phrase	**pour l'amour de**	ili kusaidia au kupendeza	sake of, for the
adv.	**pour toujours**	milele	forever
prep.	**pour, pendant, depuis**	kwa	for
n.	**pourboire (m)**	zawadi	tip (gratuity)
adv.	**pourquoi**	1. kwa ajilini gani 2. kwa maana gani 3. kwa nini 4. mbona	why?
adj.	**pourri**	-bovu	rotten
verb	**pourrir**	kuoza	rot, to; to deteriorate
verb	**poursuivre**	kukimbiza	chase, to
adv.	**pourtant**	walakini	however
verb	**pousser**	kusukuma	push, to
verb	**pousser pour déplacer**	piga kikumbo	push away, to
n.	**poussière (f)**	mavumbi	dust
verb	**pouvoir**	kuweza	1. can 2. to be able
n.	**pouvoir (m)**	mamlaka	power (authority)
verb	**pratiquer**	kuzoea	practice, to
adj.	**précaire**	-a hatari	precarious
verb	**précéder**	kutangulia	1. to go before 2. to precede
verb	**prêcher**	kuhubiri	preach, to
adv.	**précipitamment**	haraka	hurriedly
n.	**précurseur**	mtangulizi (pl. watangulizi)	forerunner

parts of speech	french	swahili	english
n.	prédécesseur (m)	mjumbe	precursor
n.	prédicateur (m)	mhubiri (pl. wahubiri)	preacher
verb	prédire	kutabiri	1. to foretell 2. to predict
n.	préférence (f)	upendeleo	preference
adj.	premier (m), première (f)	-a kwanza	first
verb	prendre	kutwaa; kushika	take, to
verb	prendre congé	kuaga	leave of, to take
verb	prendre feu	kuwaka	catch fire, to
verb	prendre garde à	kujihadhari	beware, to
n.	préparation (f)	matengenezo	preparation
verb	préparer	kutayarisha	prepare, to
adv. prep.	près	karibu na	near
adv.	près de	karibu na	close to
n.	président (m)	mwenye-kiti	chairman
n.	présomption (f)	ujuvi	presumption
adv.	presque	karibu	almost
adj.	prêt	tayari	ready
adj.	prétentieux	-a fahari	pretentious
verb	prêter	kukopesha	1. to lend 2. to loan
n.	prêtre (m)	kasisi (pl. makasisi)	priest
n.	preuve (f)	ushahidi	proof
verb	prévenir	kupasha habari	warn, to
verb	prévoir	1, kutazamia mbele 2. kuazimu 3. kutazama mbele	1. to anticipate 2. to plan 3. to foresee
verb	prier	kusali	pray, to
n.	prière (f)	maombi	prayer
n.	prime (f)	ziada	bonus
n.	prince (m)	mwana wa mfalme	prince
adj.	principal	-kuu	principal (important)
n.	priorité (f)	haki ya kutangulia	priority
n.	prison (f)	kifungo (pl. vifungo), gereza	1. jail 2. prison
n.	prisonnier (m)	mfungwa (pl. wafungwa)	prisoner
n.	privation (f)	kutwaliwa	deprivation
verb	priver	kunyima	deprive, to
n.	prix (m)	1. nauli 2. bei	1. fare 2. price
n.	problème (m)	taabu	trouble, problem
n.	procès (m)	mashtaka	trial
adj.	prochain, suivant	-a kufuata	next
adj.	proche	karibu	nearby
n.	procrastination (f)	kuahirisha	procrastination

parts of speech	french	swahili	english
adj.	**prodigue**	-a potevu wa mali	prodigal
verb	**produire**	kutoa	produce, to (fruit)
n.	**professeur (m)**	mwalimu mkuu	professor
n.	**profession (f)**	kazi ya elimu	profession
verb	**proférer des imprécations**	kusingizia	slander, to
n.	**profit (m)**	faida	profit (increase)
adj.	**profond**	-refu	profound
n.	**profondeur**	urefu	depth
n.	**progéniture (f)**	mzao (pl. wazao)	1. offspring 2. progeny
n.	**programme (m)**	azimio la mambo ya kufanyika	program
n.	**progrès (m)**	maendeleo	progress
n.	**projet (m)**	azimio (pl. mazimio)	project
n.	**promesse (f)**	ahandi	promise
verb	**promettre**	kuahidi	promise, to
n.	**prophète (m)**	nabii (pl. manabii)	prophet, seer
verb	**prophétiser**	kutabiri	prophesy
adj.	**propre**	safi	clean
n.	**propreté**	usafi	cleanliness
n.	**propriété (f)**	mali	property
n.	**proscrit (m), proscrite (f)**	msikwao	outcast
verb	**prospérer**	kusitawi	flourish, to
n.	**prospérité (f)**	usitawi	prosperity
n.	**prostituée (f)**	malaya	prostitute
verb	**protéger**	kulinda	1. to protect 2. to shield
n.	**proverbe (m)**	methali	proverb
n.	**provisions (f)**	vyakula	groceries
adj.	**provisoire**	-a kitambo	provisional
n	**provocation (f)**	uchokozi	provocation
verb	**provoquer**	1. kufanya adui 2. kuchokoza	1. to antagonize 2. to provoke
adj.	**prudent**	-angalifu	careful
adj.	**prudent**	-enye hadhari	cautious
n.	**psaume (m)**	zaburi	psalm
adj.	**public (m); publique (f)**	waziwazi	public
verb	**publier**	kutangaza	publish, to
n.	**puce (f)**	kiroboto (pl. viroboto)	flea
verb	**puer, sentir mauvais**	kunuka	stink, to
n.	**puissance (f)**	uwezo	power (strength)
n.	**puits (m)**	kisima (pl. visima)	well (ie. for water)
n.	**pull-over (m)**	namna ya fulana nzito	sweater

parts of speech	french	swahili	english
verb	**punir**	kuadhibu, kuazibu	punish, to
n., med	**pupille (f) de l'oeil**	mboni ya jicho	pupil, (eye)
n.	**pureté (f)**	usafi	purity
n., med	**pus (m)**	usaha	pus
n.	**pustule (f)**	kipele (pl. vipele)	pustule
n.	**python (m)**	chatu	python
n.	**qualité (f)**	tabia	quality
conj.	**quand**	wakati gani	when
conj.	**Quand est-ce que?**	Wakati gani?	When?
n.	**quantité (f)**	kiasi	quantity
adj. & n.	**quarante (m)**	arobaini	forty
adj.	**quatrième**	-a nne	fourth
n.	**quatorze**	kumi na nne	fourteen
adj. & n.	**quatre (m)**	nne	four
n.	**quatre cents**	mia nne	four hundred
n.	**quatre-vingt-dix (m)**	tisini	ninety
n.	**quatre-vingt-douze**	tisini na mbili	ninety-two
n.	**quatre-vingt-onze**	tisini na moja	ninety-one
n.	**quatre-vingts**	themanini; makumi manane	eighty
phrase	**Que est-ce que temps?**	Saa ngapi?	time?, At what
phrase	**Que signifie ce mot?**	Neno...lina maana gani?	word mean?, What does this
adj.	**quel (m), quelle (f)**	gani	which
phrase	**Quel est ton nom?**	Jina lako nani?	What is your name?
phrase	**Quelle est ton (votre) profession?**	Unafanya kazi gani?	What is your profession?
adj.	**quelque**	chache	some
pronoun	**quelque chose**	cho chote	anything (something)
adv.	**quelque part**	po pote	somewhere, anywhere
adv.	**quelquefois**	mara na mara	sometimes
pronoun	**quelqu'un**	ye yote	anybody (somebody)
verb	**quereller**	kugomba	quarrel, to
n.	**querelles (f)**	maugomvi (pl.)	quarrels
n.	**question (f)**	swali	question
n.	**queue (f)**	mkia (pl. mikia)	tail
pronoun	**qui**	nani	who
phrase	**qui (Qu'est-ce qui tu cherches?)**	nani (Unatafuta nani?)	who (Who are you looking for?)
adj.	**qui manque de soin**	-zembe	careless
n.	**quinze**	kumi na tano	fifteen
adj.	**quoi**	gani, nini	what
phrase	**Quoi!**	Kumbe!	What!

parts of speech	french	swahili	english
phrase	Qu'est-ce que vous faites?	Uko nafanya nini?	What are you doing?
phrase	Qu'est-ce que c'est?	Hapa ni gani?	What is this?
phrase	Qu'est-ce que tu-veux?	Unatafuta nini?	What are you looking for?
phrase	Qu'est-ce que vous dites?	Uko nasema nini?	What are you saying?
phrase	Qu'est-ce qu'il y a?	Vipi?	What's up? (familiar person)
verb	rabattre	kuangusha	pull down, to
verb	raccommoder	kutengeneza	mend, to
n.	raccourci (m)	njia ya kukatiliza	short cut
verb	raccourcir	kufupisha	shorten, to
verb	raccrocher	kutundika	hang up, to
n.	race (f)	ujamaa	race (people)
verb	racheter	kukomboa	redeem, to
n.	racheterier	mkombozi	redeemer
n.	racine (f)	mzizi (pl. mizizi)	root
verb	racler	kuparuza	scrape, to
verb	raconter	1. kuhadisi 2. kusimulia	1. to recount 2. to narrate
n.	radeau (m)	chelezo	raft
n.	radio (f)	kupeleka simu	radio
n.	rage (f)	kalab	rabies
n.	raillerie (f)	dhihaka	mockery
n.	raison (f)	akili	reason
verb	raisonner	kutimia	reason, to
n.	rajustement (m)	kulinganisha, kusawazisha	adjustment
verb	ramasser	1. kuchanga 2. kukusanya	collect, to
verb	ramasser	kuokota	pick up, to
n.	rame (f)	kasia (pl. makasia)	oar
verb	ramener	kurudisha	take back, to
verb	ramer	kuvuta makasia	row, to (boat)
verb	ramper	kutambaa	creep, to
n.	rancune (f)	husuda	ill-will
n.	rançon (f)	ukombozi	ransom
n.	rang (m)	msafa (pl. misafa)	row
adj.	rapide	upesi	fast
adv.	rapidement	mbio, upesi	quickly
verb	rappeler	kukumbusha	remind, to
n.	rapport (m)	1. kiungo (pl. viungo) 2. ufungu	1. joint 2. link 3. relationship
verb	raser	kunyoa	shave, to
n.	rasoir (m)	wembe (pl. nyembe)	razor
phrase	être rassasié	-enye kushiba	satisfied, to be (ate enough)

parts of speech	french	swahili	english
verb	**rassasier**	kushibisha	satisfy, to
n.	**rassemblement (m)**	mkutano	gathering
verb	**rassembler**	kuchuma	gather, to
n.	**rat (m)**	panya	rat
n.	**râteau (m)**	jembe la meno	rake
verb	**rattraper**	kubuni	make up, to
n.	**ravin (m)**	genge (pl. magenge)	ravine
adj. & n.	**rebelle (m,f)**	mwasi (pl. wawasi)	rebel
n	**rébellion (f)**	futina	rebellion
verb	**rebondir**	kuruka kama mpira	bounce, to
verb	**rebrousser chemin**	kufuasa nyuma	retrace the path
adv.	**récemment**	juzi juzi	recently
n.	**recensement (m)**	hesabu ya watu wa nchi	census
adj.	**récent**	-pya	recent
verb	**recevoir**	1. kupokea 2. kupata	1. to receive 2. to get or be given
n.	**récit (m)**	masimulizi	narrative
verb	**réclamer**	kuomba	reclaim, to
n.	**récolte (f)**	mavuno (pl.)	crop (farming)
verb	**récolter**	kuvuna	harvest, to
n.	**récompense (f)**	1. ujira 2. zawabu	1. pay 2. reward
verb	**récompenser**	kutuza	reward, to
verb	**réconcilier**	kupatanisha	reconcile, to
verb	**réconforter**	kufariji	comfort, to
verb	**reconnaître**	1. kukiri 2. kutambua	1 to acknowledge 2. to recognize
verb	**recracher**	kutema mate	spit out, to
verb	**rectifier**	kusahihisha	rectify, to
verb	**reculer (par peur)**	kurudi nyuma	recoil, to (through fear)
n.	**rédemption (f)**	ukombozi	redemption
verb	**redresser**	kunyolosha	straighten, to
verb	**redresser ce qui est courbé**	kukeua	straighten that which is bent, to
n.	**réflexion (f)**	fikira	reflection
verb	**réfléchir**	kufikiri	1. to ponder 2. to reflect 3. to think about
n.	**réfugié (m)**	mkimbizi	refugee
verb	**refuser**	1. kukataa 2. kunyima	1. to refuse 2. to withhold
verb	**regarder**	kutazama	look, to
verb	**regarder fixement**	kukodolea	stare at, to; to gaze at
n.	**région (f)**	1. upande (pl. pande) 2. jimbo (pl. majimbo)	1. region 2. area

parts of speech	french	swahili	english
n.	règle (f)	mamlaka	rule
n.	règne (m)	utawala	reign
n., med	rein (m)	figo (pl. mafigo)	kidney
n.	reine (f)	malkia	queen
verb	rejeter	kukataa	reject, to
verb	rejeter la responsabilité	kulaumu	blame, to
verb	réjouir	kufuahisha	rejoice, to
n.	relâche (m)	nafasi	respite
n.	relatif (m)	ndugu	relative
verb	relier	kuunga	connect, to
n	religion (f)	dini	religion
adj.	remarquable	-a ajabu	outstanding
verb	remarquer	kuangalia	1. to note 2. to notice
verb	rembourser	kulipa	reimburse, to
n.	remède (m)	1. dawa 2. uganga	1. cure 2. remedy
verb	remercier	kushukuru	thank, to
verb	remets-toi	kupona	well, to get
verb	remettre	kurudisha	put back, to
verb	remettre en état	kufufua	revive, to
n.	remplaçant (m,f)	mkombozi (pl. wakombozi)	replacement
verb	remplacer	kurudishia hali	replace, to
verb	remplir	kujaza	fill, to
n.	renard (m)	mbweha	fox
verb	rencontrer	kukutana	meet, to
n.	rendez-vous (m)	1. mapatano ya kukutana 2. kiagano	1. appointment 2. meeting place
verb	rendre	kurudisha	give back, to
verb	rendre quelque chose	kurudisha kitu	return something, to
verb	rendre un culte à Dieu	kuabudu	worship, to
verb	rendre un jugement	kuhukumu	judge, to
verb	rendre visite à	kwenda kuamkia	call on, to
verb	renforcer	kuleta msaada	reinforce, to
n.	renommée (f)	sifa	fame
verb	renoncer	kushindwa	give in, to
verb	rentrer en possession de	kupata tena	regain, to
verb	renverser	kumwanga	spill, to
verb	renverser	kupindua	triumph, to
verb	répandre	1. kupinduka 2. kumbwaga	1. to overturn 2. to spill
verb	réparer	kutengeneza	repair, to
n.	repas (m)	chakula (pl. vyakula)	meal
n.	repas du soir	chakula cha usika	supper

parts of speech	french	swahili	english
verb	**repasser**	kupiga pagi	iron, to
verb	**repentir, se**	kutubu	repent, to
verb	**répondre**	kujiba	answer, to
imper.	**Répondre!**	Jibu!	Answer!
n.	**réponse (f)**	jibu (pl. majibu)	1. answer 2. response
n.	**repos (m)**	kituo	pause
verb	**repousser**	kufukuza	repel, to
verb	**reprendre**	kutwaa	resume, to
verb	**reprendre, verser**	kutoka	shed, to
n.	**réprimande (f)**	magombezi	reprimand
verb	**réprimander**	1. kugombeza 2. kuhamakia	1. to rebuke 2. to reprimand 3. to scold
n.	**réputation (f)**	sifa	reputation
n.	**réserve (f)**	akiba	1. stock 2. reserve
n.	**résine (f)**	sherizi	glue
verb	**résister à**	kusimamia	withstand, to
n.	**résolution (f)**	kusudi	resolution
n.	**respect (m)**	heshima	respect
verb	**respecter**	kuheshimu	respect, to
verb	**respirer**	kuvuta pumzi	breathe
n.	**responsabilité (f)**	1. daraka (pl. madaraka) 2. hatia	1. liability 2. responsibility 3. blame
n.	**ressemblance (f)**	mfano (pl. mifano)	likeness
verb	**ressembler à**	kufanana na	like, to be
n.	**ressentiment (m)**	uchungu	resentment
verb	**rester**	kukaa	stay, to; to remain
verb	**résumer**	kujumlisha	sum up, to
n.	**résurrection (f)**	ufufuko	resurrection
verb	**retenir**	kujifunza kwa moyo	memorize, to
n.	**réticence (f)**	kutotaka	reluctance
verb	**retourner**	kurudi	return, to
verb	**rétrécir**	kunywea	shrink, to
verb	**retrouver**	kujipatia tena	recover, to (find again)
n.	**rêve (m)**	ndoto	dream
verb	**réveiller**	kuamsha	wake up, to
n.	**révélation (f)**	ufunuo	revelation
verb	**revendiquer**	kudai	claim, to
verb	**revenir**	kurudi	1. to come back 2. to return
n.	**revenu (m)**	mpato	income
verb	**rêver**	kuota ndoto	dream, to
verb	**reverser**	kufudikiza	turn upside down, to

parts of speech	french	swahili	english
verb	revivre	kufufua	revive, to
n.	révolte (f)	maasi (pl.)	revolt
n.	réunion (f)	mkutano (pl. mikutano)	meeting
verb	réunir	kutanisha	reunite, to
verb	réussir	kustawi	successful, to be
n.	rhinocéros (m)	kifaru (pl. vifaru)	rhinoceros
n.	rhume (m)	baridi	cold in head
adj.	riche	tajiri (pl. matajiri)	rich
adj.	riche	-enye mali	rich (person)
n.	richesse (f)	mali, utajiri	wealth
n.	ride (m)	kunjo (pl. makunjo)	wrinkle
verb	rider	kufanya vifinyo	wrinkle, to
pronoun	rien	si kitu	nothing
verb	rincer	kuosha	rinse, to
verb	rire	kucheka	laugh, to
n.	rires (m)	kicheko	laughter
n. & adj.	rituel	kawaida za dini	ritual
n.	riz (m)	mchele (pl. michele)	rice
n.	robe (f)	1. gauni 2. kanzu 3. vazi la kike	1. dress 2. gown
adj.	robuste	-a afya	robust
n.	roche (f)	mwamba (pl. miamba)	rock
n.	roi (m)	mfalme (pl. wafalme)	king
n.	romans (m)	hadithi tu	fiction
verb	ronfler	kukoroma	snore, to
n.	rosée(f)	umande	dew
verb	rôtir	kuoka	roast, to
n.	rotule (du genou)	pia ya goti	knee cap
adj.	roublard	-erevu	crafty
adj. & n.	rouge (f)	-ekundu	red
n.	rougeole (f)	surua	measles
verb	rougir	kugeuka rangi	blush, to
n.	rouille (f)	1. kawa 2. kutu	1. mildew 2. rust
verb	rouler	kufingirisha	roll along, to
n.	rousseau	unyasi (pl. nyasi)	reeds
n.	route (f)	barabara, njia	road
adj.	royal	-a kifalme	royal
n.	royaume (m)	ufalme	kingdom
n.	ruche (f)	mzinga	beehive (empty)
n.	rue (f)	njia	street
n.	ruisseau (m)	kijito (pl. vijito)	stream (small river)

283

parts of speech	french	swahili	english
n.	**rumeur (f)**	uvumi	rumor
n.	**ruse**	hila	cunning
adj.	**rustre**	-jinga	uncouth
n.	**rythme (m)**	mwendo	rhythm
n.	**sable (m)**	mchanga (pl. michanga)	sand
n.	**sabot (m)**	ukwato (pl. kwato)	hoof
verb	**s'absenter**	kutokuwapo	absent, to be
verb	**s'abstenir de,**	kujinyima	abstain, to
n.	**sac (m)**	mfuko (pl. mifuko)	1. sack 2. bag
verb	**s'accroupir**	kujinyata	crouch, to
n.	**sacrifice (m)**	zabihu	sacrifice
verb	**sacrifier**	kutoa sadaka	sacrifice, to
verb	**s'affairer**	kutaharuki	bustle about, to
adj.	**sage**	-a busara	wise
n.	**sage-femme (f)**	mkunga	midwife
verb	**s'agenouiller**	kupiga magoti	kneel, to
n.	**sagesse (f)**	akili	wisdom
verb	**saigner**	kutoka damu	bleed, to
adj.	**sain**	-enye afya	healthy
adj.	**sain et sauf**	thabiti madhubuti	safe and sound
adj.	**saint**	-takatifu	1. holy 2. saint
n.	**saint (m), sainte (f)**	mutakatifu (pl. watakatifu)	saint
n.	**Saint-Esprit (m)**	Roho Mtakatifu	Holy Spirit
verb	**saisir**	kukamata	seize, to
verb	**saisir**	kushika	take hold of, to
n.	**salarie (m)**	mshahara (pl. mishahara)	wages
adj.	**sale**	-chafu	dirty
n.	**saleté (f)**	1. takataka 2. uchafu	1. dirt 2. filth
verb	**saleur au départ**	kuaga	farewell, to bid
verb	**salir**	1. kuchafua 2. kupakaa	1. to soil 2. smear, to
n.	**salive (f)**	mate	saliva
n.	**salle de bain (f)**	choo	bathroom
n.	**salut (m)**	wokovu	salvation
adj.	**salutaire**	-enye manufaa	beneficial
n.	**salutation (f)**	salamu	greetings
n.	**samedi (m)**	Jumamosi	Saturday
n.	**sandale (f)**	kiatu (pl. viatu)	sandal
n.	**sang (m)**	damu	blood
prep.	**sans**	bila, pasipo	without
n	**sans abri**	msikwao	homeless
adj.	**sans mûr**	-bichi	unripe

284

parts of speech	french	swahili	english
adj.	sans rapport	isiyohusu	irrelevant
n.	santé (f)	afya	health
verb	s'apaiser	kupungua, kupunguza	abate, to
phrase	s'appliquer	kupeleka maombi kwa	apply oneself, to
verb	s'approcher de	kukaribia	approach, to
verb	s'appuyer contre	kuegemea, kutegemea	lean on, to
n.	sarcasme (m)	uchokozi	sarcasm
verb	sarcler	kupalia magugu	weed, to
verb	s'asseoir	kukaa, kuketi	sit, to
adj.	satisfaisant	-a kuridhisha	satisfactory
verb	s'attendre à	kutazamia	expect, to
n.	sauce (f)	mchuzi (pl. michuzi)	sauce
conj.	sauf	ila	unless
verb	saupoudrer	kunyunyizia	sprinkle, to
verb	sauter	kuruka	jump, to
n.	sauterelle (f)	panzi (pl. mapanzi)	grasshopper
n.	sauterelle (f)	nzige	locust
verb	sauver	kuokoa	save, to
n.	sauveur (m)	mwokozi	savior
verb	s'avancer	kuendelea	progress, to
adj.	savant	-enye elimu	learned
verb	savoir	kujua	know, to
n.	savon (m)	sabuni	soap
n.	scie (f)	msumeno	saw
n.	science (f)	maarifa	knowledge
verb	scier	kupasua kwa msumeno	saw, to
n.	sciure (f)	unga wa mbao	sawdust
n. med	scrotum	mfuko wa pumbu	scrotum
verb	scruter	kupeleleza	investigate, to
verb	scruter	kuchunguza	scrutinize, to
verb	se baigner	kuoga	bathe, to (oneself)
verb	se balancer	kupembea	swing, to
verb	se bichonner	kudekeza	pamper, to
verb	se conduire	kutenda	behave, to
verb	se conformer à	kushika	abide by, to
verb	se débattre	kujipigapiga	thrash around, to
verb	se défaire	kutangua	undo, to
verb	se désarticuler (ie. bras)	kushtua	dislocate, to (one's joint)
verb	se désunir	kutenga	disconnect, to
verb	se détacher	kupitia	slip out, to
verb	se détendre	kulegea	relax, to

parts of speech	french	swahili	english
verb	se détendre	kupungua	slacken, to
verb	se détériorer	kuoza	decay, to
verb	se disperser	1. kusambaa 2. kutawanya	1. to scatter 2. to disperse
verb	se disputer	kubishana	argue, to
verb	se dorer	kuota jua	bask (in the sun), to
verb	se faner	kufifia	fade, to
verb	se glisser	kuteleza	slide, to
verb	se lamenter	kuomboleza	mourn, to
verb	se laver les dents	kusukula meno	brush teeth, to
verb	se leurrer	kudanganya	delude oneself
verb	se lever	kusimama	rise (from lying position); to get up
verb	se mesurer à	kukabili	confront, to
verb	se méfier de	kushuku	mistrust, to
verb	se moquer de	1. kufanya mzaha 2. kudhihaki 3. kusuta	1. to ridicule 2. to mock 3. to taunt
verb	se multiplier	kupata mali	thrive, to
verb	se pencher	kuinama	1. to bend over 2. to stoop down
verb	se plaindre	kunung'unika	complain, to
verb	se précipiter	kuboromoka	rush, to
verb	se promener	kutembea	walk, to go for a
verb	se propager	kuzalisha	propagate, to
verb	se ranimer	kuwasha	rekindle, to
phrase	se rappeler	kukumbuka	1. to remember 2. to bear in mind
verb	se rebeller	kuasi	rebel, to
verb	se redresser	kusimama	recover, to
verb	se remettre	kupata afya tena	recover, to (from illness)
phrase	se rendre à	kusalimisha	surrender to, to
verb	se rendre compte de	kuthamini	appreciate, to
verb	se répandre	kumwangika	spill, to
verb	se reposer	kupumzika	rest, to
verb	se ressembler	kufanana	resemble, to
verb	se retenir de	kujizuia	refrain from, to
verb	se retourner	kugeuka	turn around, to
verb	se révolter contra	kufitini	revolt against, to
verb	se servir de	kutumia	use, to
verb	se souvenir de	kukumbuka	remember, to
verb	se taire	kunyamaza	silent, to be
verb	se tendre	kunyosha	strained, to become
verb	se tenir debout	kusimama	stand up, to

parts of speech	french	swahili	english
verb	se tenir droit	kuondoka	stand up straight, to
verb	se tenir l'un face de l'autre	kukabili	face (someone), to
verb	se tirer d'affaire	kufaulu	make good, to
verb	se trouver dans une impasse	kutopitika	impasse, to be at an
verb	se vanter	1. kujigamba 2. kujivuna	1. to brag 2. to boast
n.	seau (m)	ndoo	1. bucket 2. pail
verb	s'ébouler	kufikicha	crumble, to
adj.	sec	-kavu	dry
verb	sécher	kukausha	dry, to
n.	sécheresse (f)	ukosefu wa mvua	drought
n.	seconde (f)	dakika	second
verb	secouer	1. kusukusuka 2. kukunguta	shake, to
verb	secouer/agiter	kutikisa	shake (object) hard, to
phrase	secours financier	msaada	aid, financial
n.	secret (m)	siri	secret
n.	secrétaire (m,f)	mwandishi (pl. wandishi)	secretary
n.	section (f)	mkato	section
verb	s'effondrer	kuanguka	collapse, to
verb	s'efforcer	kufanya bidii	work with zeal, to
verb	s'efforcer	kujitahidi	effort, to make an
verb	s'efforcer d'obtenir	kujaribu	strive for, to
verb	s'égarer	kupotea	astray, to go
n.	seigneur (m)	maulana	lord
n.	sein (m)	kifua, maziwa	breast
n.	seize	kumi na sita	sixteen
n	sel (m)	chumvi	salt
verb	sélectionner	kuchagua	select, to
verb	s'élever	kuinuka	arise, to
n., med	selles	choo	stool (excrement)
adv.	selon	kadiri ya	according to
n.	semaine (f)	juma	week
phrase	semaine prochain	juma kesho	next week
adj.	semblable	-a kufanana	alike
n.	semence (f)	mbegu	seed
verb	s'enchevêtrer	kujitatiza	tangled up, to get
verb	s'engager	kuweka ahadi	commit oneself, to
verb	s'enivrer	kulewa	intoxicated, to be
n.	sens (m)	maana	meaning
verb	s'entasser	kupanganya	pile, to

287

parts of speech	french	swahili	english
verb	s'entendre avec (quelqu'un)	kufanana	correspond with, to
n.	sentier (m)	njia ya kufikia	path
n.	sentiment (m)	maono	feelings
verb	sentir	kunusa	smell, to
verb	sentir; palper	kupapasa	feel, to
verb	séparer	1. kutenga 2. kukata	1. to separate 2. to sever
adj. & n.	sept (m)	saba	seven
n.	sept cents	mia saba	seven hundred
n.	septembre (m)	Septemba	September
adj.	septième	-a saba	seventh
n., med	seringue	bomba ndogo	syringe
n.	serment (m)	kiapo (pl. viapo)	oath
n.	serpent (m)	nyoka	snake
verb	serrer	kukaza	1. to tighten 2. to clench
verb	serrer	1. kubana 2. kukamua	squeeze, to
verb	serrer dans ses bras	kukumbatia	hug, to
verb	serrer la main à	kupana mikono	shake hands, to
n.	serviette (de table)	kitambaa	napkin
verb	servir	kutumikia	serve, to (food)
n.	session (f)	baraza	session
phrase	s'éteindre	kuzimika	go out (fire) , to
verb	s'étendre	kulala	lie down, to
adj.	seul	peke yake	alone
adv.	seul (seulement)	tu	only
n.	sévérité (f)	ukali	severity
adj.	sévère	-kali	harsh
verb	s'excuser de	kuomba radhi	apologize, to
n.	sexe (m)	jinsi	sex (gender)
conj.	si	kama	if
n., med	sida (m)	ukimwi	AIDS
n.	siècle (m)	karne	century
n.	siège (m)	kiti (pl. viti)	seat
verb	siffler avec un sifflet	kupiga filimbi	blow a whistle, to
n.	sifflet (m)	mluzi	whistle
verb	signaler	kujulisha	notify, to
n.	signe (m)	alama	sign
adv.	silencieusement	1. kimya 2. polepole	1. quietly 2. silently
adj.	silencieux	-a nyamavu	silent
phrase	S'il vous plaît.	Tafadhali.	Please.
adv.	simplement	tu	merely

288

parts of speech	french	swahili	english
adj.	simplet	-tovu	lacking
n.	singe (m)	1. nyani 2. kima	1. ape 2. monkey
conj.	sinon	ama sivyo	otherwise
verb	s'insulter	kutumia vibaya, kutukana	abuse, to (verbal)
adj. & n.	six (m)	sita	six
n.	six cents	mia sita	six hundred
adj.	sixième	-a sita	sixth
verb	s'occuper de	1. kutunza 2. kuwa mwangilizi	1. to look after 2. to be in charge
n.	sœur (f)	dada; ndugu mke; (if spoken of by brother: umbu)	sister
phrase	Soie courage!	Bakia vizuri!	Be strong! (stay well)
n.	soif (f)	kiu	thirst
verb	soigner	1. kutunza 2. kuuguza	care for, to (the sick)
adv.	soigneusement	taratibu	carefully
adv. n.	soir (m)	jioni	evening
n.	soirée (f)	kikoa	together, a get
conj.	soit que	kama	whether
conj.	soit...soit	ama...ama	either...or
adj. & n.	soixante (m)	sitini	sixty
n.	soixante et onze	sabini na moja	seventy-one
adj. & n.	soixante-dix (m)	sabini	seventy
n.	soixante-dix-huit	sabini na nane	seventy-eight
n.	soixante-dix-neuf	sabini na kenda	seventy-nine
n.	soixante-dix-sept	sabini na saba	seventy-seven
n.	soixante-douze	sabini na mbili	seventy-two
n.	soixante-quatorze	sabini na nne	seventy-four
n.	soixante-quinze	sabini na tano	seventy-five
n.	soixante-seize	sabini na sita	seventy-six
n.	soixante-treize	sabini na tatu	seventy-three
n.	sol (m)	udongo	earth (ground)
n.	soldat (m)	askari	soldier
n.	soleil (m)	jua (pl. majua)	sun
adj.	solide	-nene	stout
n.	solitude (f)	upweke	loneliness
n.	sommeil (m)	usingizi	sleep
n.	sommet (m)	kilele (pl. vilele)	peak (mountain)
n.	son (m)	kapi (pl. makapi)	sound
adj & pr	son (m), sa (f), ses (pl)	yeye, -ake	her
adj.	son (m), sa (f), ses (pl)	-ake	his
verb	sonder	kuchungua	probe, to

parts of speech	french	swahili	english
verb	**sonner à la porte**	kupiga kengele	ring a bell, to
n.	**sorcier (m)**	mchawi (pl. wachawi)	witch
n.	**sorgho**	mtama (pl. mitama)	sorghum
n.	**sorte (f)**	namna	sort
verb	**sortir**	kutoka	1. to take out 2. to go out 3. to exit
verb	**sortir de**	kutokea wazi	come out of, to
n.	**souche (f)**	kisiki (pl. visiki)	stump
n.	**souci (m)**	taabu	worry
n.	**souder**	kutia pua	solder, to
verb	**soudoyer**	kutoa rushwa	bribe, to
verb	**souffler**	kuvuma	blow, to
n.	**souffrance (f)**	maumivu	ache
adj.	**souffrant**	-gonjwa	poorly
verb	**souffrir**	kuuma	pain, to have; to suffer
verb	**soulever**	kuinua	lift, to
n.	**soupçon (m)**	zana	suspicion
verb	**soupçonner**	kushuku	suspect, to
n.	**soupe (f)**	mchuzi (pl. michuzi)	soup
verb	**soupirer**	kupiga kite	sigh, to
n	**source (f)**	chemchemi	spring (of water)
n.	**sourcil (m)**	nyushi	eyebrow
verb	**sourire**	kucheka	smile, to
n.	**souris (f)**	panya mdogo	mouse
adv. prep.	**sous**	chini ya	beneath, under
n.	**sous-alimentation (f)**	ukosefu wa chakula chema	malnutrition
verb	**sous-estimer**	kuhesabu	underestimate, to
verb	**soustraire**	kutoa	subtract, to
verb	**soutenir**	kutegemeza	support, to
n	**soutien (m)**	msaada	backing (support)
n.	**soutien-gorge (m)**	sidiria	bra
n.	**souvenir (m)**	ukumbuko	souvenir
adv.	**souvent**	mara nyingi	often
adj.	**spacieux**	-pana	spacious
n.	**spatule (f)**	kisu kipana cha kufanyia dawa	spatula
n.	**spectateur (m), spectatrice (f)**	mwenye kuwapo	bystander
adj.	**spécial**	-a peke yake	special
verb	**stabiliser**	kuimarisha	stabilize, to
n.	**statistique (f)**	habari zinazoonyeshwa kwa hesabu	statistics

parts of speech	french	swahili	english
n.	steward (m)	msimamizi	steward
phrase	stupéfier, être	kushangaa	astounded, to be
n.	stupidité (f)	upumbavu	stupidity
verb	submerger	kuzamisha	submerge, to
n.	successeur (m)	halifa	successor
n.	sucre (m)	sukari	sugar
n.	sud (m)	kusini	south
n.	sueur (f)	jasho	sweat
verb	suffire	kufaa	suffice, to
verb	suffire	kutosha	sufficient, to be
adj.	suffisant	-a kutosha	adequate
n.	suie (f)	masizi	soot
verb	suivre	kufuata	follow, to
adj.	supérieur	-a juu	superior (chief)
verb	supplier	kusihi	beseech, to
verb	supporter	kudumu, kuvumilia	endure, to
verb	supposer, imaginer	kuzani	suppose, to
prep.	sur	juu ya	1. on 2. over
adv.	sur le dos	chalichali	supine position
adv.	être sur le point de	tayari	about to, to be
verb	surgir	kufika	spring up, to
verb	surmonter	kushinda	succeed, to
n.	surnom	jina la kupanga	name, first
n.	surnom (m)	jina la utani	nickname
verb	surpasser	kupita	surpass, to
n.	surplus (m)	baki	surplus
adj.	surprenant	-a kushtusha	startling
verb	surprendre	kushangaza	surprise, to
adj.	surtout	hasa	especially
verb	surveiller	kusimamia	supervise, to
verb	survivre à	kuishi baada ya kufiwa	survive, to
verb	suspendre	kutundika	suspend, to
verb	suspendre, être pendant	kutungika	hang, to
adj.	svelte	-embamba	thin
n.	symbole (m)	mfano (pl. mifano)	symbol
n.	sympathie (f)	mapatano	sympathy
n., med	syphilis	sekeneko	syphilis
n.	système (m)	utaratibu	system
n.	tabac (m)	tumbako	tobacco
n.	table (f)	meza	table
n.	tableau (m)	picha, sanamu	picture

parts of speech	french	swahili	english
n.	**tableau noir (m)**	ubao wa skuli	blackboard
n.	**tabou (m)**	mwiko	taboo
n.	**tâche (f)**	kazi	task
n.	**tactiques (f)**	maarifa ya vita	tactics
n.	**taille (f)**	kimo, urefu	height
verb	**taire, se**	kunyamaa	stop talking, to
interj.	**Taisez-vous!**	Makelele!	Silence!
n.	**talon (m)**	kisingino (pl. visingino)	heel
n.	**tambour (m)**	ngoma	drum
n.	**tamis (m)**	1. kiyongela (pl. viyongela) 2. kifumbu	1. sieve 2. strainer
verb	**tamiser**	kuchekecha	sift, to
conj.	**tandis que**	kwa maana	whereas
n.	**tanière (f)**	malalo ya mnyama wa mwitu	lair
n.	**tante maternelle**	mama mdogo	aunt (mother's sister)
n.	**tante paternelle**	shangazi (pl. mashangzi)	aunt (father's sister)
n.	**tapis (m)**	zulia (pl. mazulia)	rug
verb	**taquiner**	kuuzi	tease, to
verb	**tarder**	kukawa	delay, to
adj.	**tardif**	1. chelea 2. -zembe	1. belated 2. tardy
n.	**targette (f)**	komeo	bolt (of door)
n.	**tas (m)**	chungu	heap
n.	**tasse (f)**	kikombe (pl. vikombe)	cup
verb	**tasser**	kushindilia	cram, to
n.	**tatouage (m)**	chale	tattoo
n.	**taupe (f)**	fuko	mole
n.	**taureau (m)**	ng'ombe dume	bull
n.	**technique (f)**	ufundi	technique
n.	**teigne (f)**	baka	ringworm
adj.	**téméraire**	-jasiri	reckless
n.	**témoin (m)**	mshuhuda (pl. washuhuda)	witness
verb	**témoin de, être**	kushuhuda	witness, to
n.	**tempérament (m)**	tabia	temperament
n.	**tempérance (f)**	kiasi	temperance
n.	**temple (m)**	panja	temple
n.	**temps (m)**	wakati	time
n.	**ténacité (f)**	nguvu ya kushika	tenacity
n.	**tendance (f)**	maelekeo	tendency
verb	**tendre**	kuenea	extend, to
verb	**tendre une embuscade à**	kuotea njiani	ambush, to

parts of speech	french	swahili	english
n.	tendresse (f)	wembamba	tenderness
verb	tenir	kushika	hold, to
verb	tenir en équilibre	kusawazisha	balance, to
n.	tentation (f)	jaribu	temptation
n.	tente (f)	hema	tent
verb	tenter	kujaribu	tempt, to
n.	terme (m)	mwisho	end
verb	terminer	kukomesha	end, to
n.	terra blanche	chokaa	lime (substance)
n.	terrain (m) de jeu	kiwanja	playground
n.	terre (f)	1. ardhi 2. nchi	1. ground 2. land
n.	terre (f); univers	dunia	earth
n.	terreur (f)	hofu kuu	terror
n.	terroir (m)	udongo	soil
n.	tesson (m)	kipande kidogo	fragment
n., med	testicule (m)	pumbu (pl. mapumbu)	testicle
phrase	texte rédigé	mwahdishi ovyo	scribe
n.	tête (f)	kichwa (pl. vichwa)	head
verb	téter	kunyonya	suck, to
n	thé (m)	chai	tea
n., med	tibia (os de la jambe)	muundi wa mguu	tibia
adj.	tiède	uvuguvugu	lukewarm
n.	timbre-poste (m)	ada ya posta	postage stamp
adj.	timide	-enye haya	bashful
n.	tique	kimputu (pl. vimputu)	tick
n.	tire-bouchon (m)	kizibuo	corkscrew
verb	tirer	1. kuvuta 2. kupiga bunduki	1. to pull 2. to shoot (gun)
verb	tirer; s'approcher	kukaribia	draw near, to
n.	tohu-bohu (m)	makelele mengi	pandemonium
n.	toile d'araignée (f)	utando wa buibui	cobweb
n.	tomate (f)	nyanya	tomato
n.	tombe (f)	kaburi	grave
verb	tomber	kuanguka	fall, to
verb	tomber sur	kuangukia	fall on, to
verb	tonner	kunguruma	thunder, to
n.	tonnerre (m)	radi	thunder
n.	torche (f)	mwenge (pl. miwenge)	torch
verb	tordre	kusokota	twist, to
n.	torrent (m)	mvo	torrent
n.	tortue (f)	kobe (pl. makobe)	tortoise
phrase	touche-à-tout	mdukizi	meddler

293

parts of speech	french	swahili	english
verb	toucher	kugusa	touch, to
adv.	toujours	sikuzote	always
n.	tour (f)	mnara (pl. minara)	tower
n.	tourbillon (m)	kizingia cha maji	whirlpool
n.	tourment (m)	adhabu	torment
n.	tournure (f)	hali ya myo au mwili	attitudes
adj & pr	tous (les) deux (m); toutes (les) deux (f)	vyote viwili	both
adv.	tous les jours	kila siku	daily
adj.	tous les jours	-a kila siku	everyday
verb	tousser	kukohoa	cough, to
adj.	tout	1. -ote 2. kila kitu	1. all 2. everything
adv.	tout à fait	halisi	quite
phrase	tout de suite	sasa hivi	right now, right away
adv.	tout doucement	polepole	gently
n.	tout la nuit	usiku kucha	night, all
pronoun	tout le monde	kila mtu	everyone
adv.	tout le temps	siku zote	all the time
n.	toute la journée	mchana kutwa	day long, all
n.	toute petite enfance (f)	utoto	infancy
phrase	toute poésie moderne	pepo	spirit, harmful
conj.	toutes les fois que	kila mara	whenever
n.	toux (f)	kikohozi (pl. vikohozi)	cough
verb	tracasser	kuuzi	worried, to be
n., med	trachée	umio wa pumzi	trachea
n.	tradition (f)	mapokeo	tradition
verb	traduire	kufasiri, kutafsiri	translate, to
verb	trahir	kusaliti	betray, to
verb	traire	kukama	milk, to
n.	trait (m)	tofauti	trait
verb	traiter	kutendea	treat (medical), to
verb	traiter avec condescendance	kufadhili	patronize, to
verb	traîner	kukokota	drag, to
n.	tranche (f)	kipasu (pl. vipasu)	slice
adj.	tranquille	1. -pole 2. kimya	1. peaceful 2. still
verb	transcrire	kufuatisha	transcribe, to
verb	transmettre à	kupisha	transmit, to
n.	transpiration (f)	jasho	perspiration
verb	transpirer	kutoka jasho	sweat, to
n.	travail (m)	kazi	1. job 2. work

parts of speech	french	swahili	english
verb	**travailler**	kutumika	work, to
n.	**travailleur**	mfanya kazi	worker
verb	**traverser**	kukuta	1. to traverse 2. to come across
verb	**trébucher**	kukwaa	stumble, to
n.	**treize**	kumi na tatu	thirteen
n.	**tremblement (m)**	homa ya baridi	chills (tremor)
n.	**tremblement (m) de terre**	tetemeko	tremble (earthquake)
verb	**trembler**	kutetemeka	tremble, to
verb	**tremper, faire**	kubambika	soak, to
adj. & n.	**trente (m)**	thelathini (makumi matatu)	thirty
n.	**trente et un**	thelathini na moja	thirty-one
adv.	**très**	sana; kabisa	very
n.	**trésor (m)**	hazina	treasury
n.	**tresse (f)**	utepe	braid
verb	**tresser**	kusokota	braid, to
n.	**tribu (f)**	kabila (pl. mabila)	tribe
verb	**tricoter**	kusuka	knit, to
adj.	**triste**	-a huzuni	sad
verb	**triste, être**	kuhuzunika	sad, to be
n.	**tristesse (f)**	huzuni	1. sadness 2. sorrow
n.	**trois**	tatu	three
n.	**trois cents**	mia tatu	three hundred
adj.	**troisième**	-a tatu	third
n.	**trompe (de l'éléphant) (f)**	mkono (pl. mikono)	trunk (of elephant)
verb	**tromper**	kudanganya	1. to deceive 2. to cheat
n.	**tromperie (f)**	udanganyifu	deceit
n.	**tronc (m)**	kiwiliwili (pl. viwiliwili)	trunk (of body)
verb	**troquer**	1. kubadilishana 2. kubadili	1. to barter 2. to dicker
n.	**trou (m)**	tundu (pl. matundu)	hole
verb	**troubler, se**	kufazaika	troubled, to be
n.	**troubles (m)**	ghasia, fujo	disturbance
n.	**troupe (f)**	kikosi (pl. vikosi)	troop, company
n.	**troupeau (m)**	kundi (pl. makundi)	1. herd 2. flock (of sheep)
verb	**trouver**	kukuta	find, to
n.	**truelle (f)**	mwiko (pl. miiko)	trowel
pronoun	**tu, vous**	wewe	you (singular)
n.	**tuberculose (f)**	ugonjwa fulani	tuberculosis
n.	**tuer**	1. kuchinja 2. kuua	1. to slay 2. to kill
n.	**tuile (f)**	kigae (pl. vigae)	tile (roof)
n., med	**tumeur (f)**	kivimbe (pl. vivimbe)	tumor

parts of speech	french	swahili	english
n.	tumulte (m)	kelele (pl. makelele)	turmoil
n.	tunnel (m)	shimo (pl. mashimo)	tunnel
n.	tuyau (f)	bomba (pl. mabomba	pipe (hose)
n.	type (m)	mtindo	type
n., med	typhoïde fièvre	homa ya matumbo	typhoid fever
n., med	typhus	homa mbaya matumboni	typhoid
n.	ulcère (m)	jeraha, kidonda (pl. vidonda)	sore (ulcer)
adj.	un autre (m), une autre (f) (un autre homme)	-ingine	another (another man)
n.	un million	elfu mara elfu	one million
n.	un nouveau-né	mtoto mdogo	infant
adv.	un peu	kidogo	somewhat
adj. & n.	un, une	moja	one
adv.	une fois	mara moja tu	once
adj.	uni, souple	laini	soft
n.	union (f)	ushirika	fellowship
adj.	unique	1. -a peke 2. -a namna ya peke yake	1. sole 2. unique
verb	unir	kuunga	unite, to
n.	unité (f)	umoja	unity
verb	urgent, être	kusihi sana	urgent, to be
n., med	urine	mkojo	urine
verb	uriner	kukojoa, kunya	urinate, to
n.	usage (m)	matumizi	use
n., med	utérus	mji wa mimba	uterus
phrase	Va à la selle.	Kuenda chooni.	stool., Go to
interj.	Va-t'en!	Toka!	Off with you!
n.	vacances (m)	ruhusa .	time off
n.	vacarme (m)	ghasia	racket (noise)
n.	vache (f)	ngombe	cow
verb	vaciller	kuyumbayumba	sway, to
verb	vagabonder	kutangatanga	stray, to
n.	vagin (m)	kuma	vagina
n.	vague (f)	wimbi (pl. mawimbe)	wave (of water)
adj.	vain	-tupu	vain, in
verb	vaincre	kushinda	1. to defeat 2. to overcome 3. to vanquish
n.	vainqueur (m)	mshinda (pl. washinda)	winner
n., med	vaisseau sanguin	mushipa wa damu	blood vessel
n.	valeur (f)	thamani	1. worth 2. value
n.	vallée (f)	bonde	valley

parts of speech	french	swahili	english
n.	**vanité (f)**	kiburi	conceit
n.	**vapeur (f)**	mvuke (pl. mivuke)	1. steam 2. vapor
n.	**varicelle (f)**	tetewanga	chicken pox
adj.	**vaurien**	-a bure	good-for-nothing
n.	**vautour (m)**	tai (pl. matai)	vulture
n.	**veau (m) {mollet}**	ndama {shavu la mguu}	calf {calf - lower leg}
n.	**vendeur (m), vendeuse (f)**	mwuza (pl. wauza)	vendor
verb	**vendre**	kuuza	sell, to
n.	**vendredi (m)**	Ijumaa	Friday
n.	**vengeance (f)**	kisasi (pl. visasi)	revenge
verb	**venger**	kulipiza kisasi	avenge, to
verb	**venir**	kuja	come, to
n.	**vent (m)**	upepo (pl. pepo)	wind
n.	**ver (m)**	buu (pl. mabuu)	maggot
n.	**verbe (m)**	kiarifu	verb
verb	**vérifier**	kukagua hesabu	audit, to
adj.	**véritable**	hasilia	genuine
n.	**vérité (f)**	kweli	truth
n.	**verre (m)**	1. bilauri 2. kioo	1. drinking glass 2. glass
n., med	**vers (ascaris)**	minyoo	intestinal worms
n.	**vers (m)**	aya	verse
verb	**verser**	kumimina	pour, to
adj.	**vert**	-a rangi ya majani; kijani	green (color)
n.	**vertige (m)**	kizunguzungu	1. vertigo 2. dizziness
n.	**vertu (f)**	nguvu	virtue
n., med	**vésicule biliaire**	nyongo	gallbladder
n., med	**vessie (f)**	kibofu	bladder
n.	**veston (m), jaquette (f)**	koti	jacket
n.	**vêtement (m)**	nguo	1. garment 2. clothes
verb	**vêtir**	1. kuvika 2. kuvalia	1. to clothe 2. to dress
n.	**veuf (m)**	mjane	widower
n.	**veuve (f)**	mjane (pl. wajane)	widow
n.	**viande (f)**	nyama	meat
adj.	**vide**	-tupu	empty
verb	**vider**	kumwaga	empty, to
n.	**vie (f)**	maisha, udogo	life
n.	**vieillard (m)**	mzee (pl. wazee)	old man
n.	**vieillesse (f)**	uzee	age, old
interj.	**Viens ici!**	Uje hapa!	Come here!
adj.	**vieux**	-zee	old
adj.	**vif**	-enye kung'aa, -enye akili	bright

297

parts of speech	french	swahili	english
n.	**vigne (f)**	mzabibu (pl. mizabibu)	vine
n.	**vigne (f)**	shamba la mizabibu	vineyard
n.	**village (m)**	boma, kijiji, (pl. vijiji)	village
n.	**ville (f), cité (f)**	mji (pl. miji)	city
n.	**vin (m)**	divai	wine
n.	**vinaigre (m)**	siki	vinegar
n. & adj.	**vingt (m)**	makumi mawili; ishirini	twenty
n.	**vingt et un**	ishirini na moja	twenty-one
n.	**violence (f)**	jeuri	violence
verb	**violer**	kuanjisi mwanamke kwa jeuri	rape, to
verb	**violer d'un objet sacré**	kunajisi	defile, to
adj. & n.	**violet (m)**	rangi ya zambarau bivu	purple
n.	**visage (m)**	uso (pl. nyuso)	face
adj.	**visible**	-a kuonekana	visible
verb	**visible, être**	kuonekana	visible, to be
verb	**visiter**	kuzuru	visit, to
adv.	**vite**	bado kidogo	soon
n.	**vitesse (f)**	upesi	speed
adj.	**vivant**	hai, -zima	alive
verb	**vivre**	kuishi	live to
verb	**vociférer**	kupiga kiyowe	scream, to
adv.	**voici**	ndi	here is
phrase	**Voici une ordonnance de mon médecin.**	Nina agizo la daktari.	Here is my prescription for medicine.
n.	**voile (m)**	utaji	veil
verb	**voir**	kuona	see, to
adj.	**voisin**	-a kupakana	adjacent
n.	**voisin (m), voisine (f)**	jirani	neighbor
n.	**voisinage (m)**	ujirani	1. neighborhood 2. vicinity
n.	**voiture (f), véhicule**	motakaa	car
n.	**voix (f)**	sauti	voice
n.	**vol (m)**	wizi	theft
n.	**volaille (f)**	kuku	fowl
n.	**volcan (m)**	mlima wa moto	volcano
verb	**voler**	1. kuruka 2. kuiba	1. to fly 2. to steal
adj.	**voleur**	mwivi	thieving
n.	**voleur (m)**	mnyanganyi (pl. wanyanganyi)	1. robber 2. thief
n.	**volonté (f)**	kusudi	will
verb	**vomir {Je vomis des vers.}**	kutapika {Ninatapita minyoo.)	vomit, to {I am vomiting worms.}

parts of speech	french	swahili	english
adj.	**vos, votre (vos enfants)**	-enu (wana wenu)	your (plural) (your children)
adj.	**votre, ton, ta, tes (ton enfant)**	-ako (mwana wako)	your (singular) (your child)
verb	**vouloir**	kutaka	want, to
pronoun	**vous**	ninyi	you (plural)
phrase	**Vous savez, vous connaissez.**	Unajua.	You know.
n.	**voyage (m)**	mwendo (pl. miwendo)	trip, journey
verb	**voyager**	kusafiri	travel, to
n.	**voyageur (m), voyageuse (f)**	1. msafiri (pl. wasafiri) 2. kusafiri	traveler
adj.	**vrai {Tu dis vrai.}**	kweli {Kweli.}	true {You speak the truth.}
adv.	**vraiment**	1. kweli 2. hakika	1. really 2. truly
n.	**zèbre (m)**	punda milia	zebra
n.	**zèle (m)**	bidii	zeal
adj.	**zélé**	-enye bidii	zealous
n.	**zéro (m)**	sifuri	zero

Swahili pronunciation guide

A is pronounced as in father.

B is pronounced as it is in English.

C: ch is is pronounced as it is in English.

D: dh is pronounced as "th" as in that.

E is pronounced as "a" in lay.

F is pronounced as in fat.

G is pronounced as in got.

H is pronounced as it is in English.

I is pronounced as a long e as in bee.

J is pronounced like a soft g as in gentle.

K is pronounced as a k as in kite.

L is frequently interchanged for R.

M is pronounced as it is in English.

N, ng is pronounced as in bringing.

O is pronounced as in no.

P is pronounced as it is in English.

R is pronounced in a roll (as in French).

S is pronounced as in miss. Sometimes people add an "h"
sound between the s and the following consonant. S is never
pronounced as z.

T: th is pronounced as in thick.

U is pronounced as oo as in pool.

V is pronounced as it is in English.

W is pronounced as it is in English.

Y: yu is pronounced as in you.

Z: the z sound is often heard when a word starts with dh.

Swahili concordial prefixes

Listed below are the prefixes applied when adjectives are used with each of the eight classes of nouns.

Class	Singular	Plural	Example, singular	Example, plural	English meaning
1	m-, mw-	wa-, w-	mtoto mzuri	watoto wazuri	good child, good children
2	m-, mw-	mi-, m-	mlango mkubwa	milango mikubwa	big door, big doors
3	n-	n-	mbegu ndogo	mbegu ndogo	little seed, little seeds
4	ki-, ch-	vi-, vy-	kipepeo cheusi	vipepeo vyeusi	black butterfly, black butterflies
5	ji-, j-	ma-, m-	jengo jipya	majengo mapya	new building, new buildings
6	m-, mw-	n-, -	ukucha mufupi	kucha fupi	short fingernail, short fingernails
7	pa-	pa-	pahali pazuri	pahali pazuri	good place, good places
8	ku-	ku-	kusemezana kufupi	kusemezana kufupi	short conversation, short conversations.

Swahili Verb Conjugation Guide

In Swahili the infinitive of the verb starts with ku or kw, as in "kupiga or kwenda". Some dictionaries list all verbs with the stem only. For instance, kupiga would be listed as -piga. Listed below are commonly used verbs conjugated in the present, past, and future tense.

	English	1st person singular (infinitive)	2nd person singular	3rd person singular	1st person plural	2nd person plural	3rd person plural
present	to be	ni (kuwa)	ni	ni	ni	ni	ni
past		nilikuwa	ulikuwa	alikuwa	tulikuwa	mlikuwa	walikuwa
future		nitakuwa	utakuwa	atakuwa	tutakuwa	mtakuwa	watakuwa
present	to beat	ninapiga (kupiga)	unapiga	anapiga	tunapiga	mnapiga	wanapiga
past		nilipiga	ulipiga	alipiga	tulipiga	mlipiga	walipiga
future		nitapiga	utapiga	atapiga	tutapiga	mtapiga	watapiga
present	to believe	ninaamini (kuamini)	unaamini	anaamini	tunaamini	mnaamini	wanaamini
past		niliamini	uliamini	aliamini	tuliamini	mliamini	waliamini
future		nitaamini	utaamini	ataamini	tutaamini	mtaamini	wataamini
present	can	ninaweza (kuweza)	unaweza	anaweza	tunaweza	mnaweza	wanaweza
past		niliweza	uliweza	aliweza	tuliweza	mliweza	waliweza
future		nitaweza	utaweza	ataweza	tutaweza	mtaweza	wataweza
present	to come	ninakuja (kuja)	unakuja	anakuja	tunakuja	mnakuja	wanakuja
past		nilikuja	ulikuja	alikuja	tulikuja	mlikuja	walikuja
future		nitakuja	utakuja	atakuja	tutakuja	mtakuja	watakuja
present	to die	ninakufa (kufa)	unakufa	anakufa	tunakufa	mnakufa	wanakufa
past		nilikufa	ulikufa	alikufa	tulikufa	mlikufa	walikufa
future		nitakufa	utakufa	atakufa	tutakufa	mtakufa	watakufa
present	to drink	ninakunywa (kunywa)	unakunywa	anakunywa	tunakunywa	mnakunywa	wanakunywa
past		nilikunywa	ulikunywa	alikunywa	tulikunywa	mlikunywa	walikunywa
future		nitakunywa	utakunywa	atakunywa	tutakunywa	mtakunywa	watakunywa

	Eng-lish	1st person singular (infinitive)	2nd person singular	3rd person singular	1st person plural	2nd person plural	3rd person plural
present	to eat	ninakula (kula)	unakula	anakula	tunakula	mnakula	wanakula
past		nilikula	ulikula	alikula	tulikula	mlikula	walikula
future		nitakula	utakula	atakula	tutakula	mtakula	watakula
present	to go	ninakwenda (kwenda)	unakwenda	anakwenda	tunakwenda	mna-kwenda	wana-kwenda
past		nilikwenda	ulikwenda	alikwenda	tulikwenda	mlikwenda	walikwenda
future		nitakwenda	utakwenda	atakwenda	tutakwenda	mtakwenda	watakwenda
present	to have	nina (kuwa na)	una	ana	tuna	mna	wana
past		nilikuwa na	ulikuwa na	alikuwa na	tulikuwa na	mlikuwa na	walikuwa na
future		nitakuwa na	utakuwa na	atakuwa na	tutakuwa na	mtakuwa na	watakuwa na
present	to know	ninajua (kujua)	unajua	anajua	tunajua	mnajua	wanajua
past		nilijua	ulijua	alijua	tulijua	mlijua	walijua
future		nitajua	utajua	atajua	tutajua	mtajua	watajua
present	to live	ninaisha (kuisha)	unaisha	anaisha	tunaisha	mnaisha	wanaisha
past		niliisha	uliisha	aliisha	tuliisha	mliisha	waliisha
future		nitaisha	utaisha	ataisha	tutaisha	mtaisha	wataisha
present	to open	ninafungua (kufungua)	unafungua	anafungua	tunafungua	mna-fungua	wana-fungua
past		nilifungua	ulifungua	alifungua	tulifungua	mlifungua	walifungua
future		nitafungua	utafungua	atafungua	tutafungua	mtafungua	watafungua
present	to pray	ninasali (kusali)	unasali	anasali	tunasali	mnasali	wanasali
past		nilisali	ulisali	alisali	tulisali	mlisali	walisali
future		nitasali	utasali	atasali	tutasali	mtasali	watasali
present	to put	ninatia (kutia)	unatia	anatia	tunatia	mnatia	wanatia
past		nilitia	ulitia	alitia	tulitia	mlitia	walitia
future		nitatia	utatia	atatia	tutatia	mtatia	watatia
present	to read	ninasoma (kusoma)	unasoma	anasoma	tunasoma	mnasoma	wanasoma
past		nilisoma	ulisoma	alisoma	tulisoma	mlisoma	walisoma
future		nitasoma	utasoma	atasoma	tutasoma	mtasoma	watasoma
present	to say	ninasema (kusema)	unasema	anasema	tunasema	mnasema	wanasema
past		nilisema	ulisema	alisema	tulisema	mlisema	walisema
future		nitasema	utasema	atasema	tutasema	mtasema	watasema

	English	1st person singular (infinitive)	2nd person singular	3rd person singular	1st person plural	2nd person plural	3rd person plural
present	to see	ninaona (kuona)	unaona	anaona	tunaoma	mnaona	wanaona
past		niliona	uliona	aliona	tuliona	mliona	waliona
future		nitaona	utaona	ataona	tutaona	mtaona	wataona
present	to send	ninapeleka (kupeleka)	unapeleka	anapeleka	tunapeleka	mnapeleka	wanapeleka
past		nilipeleka	ulipeleka	alipeleka	tulipeleka	mlipeleka	walapeleka
future		nitapeleka	utapeleka	atapeleka	tutapeleka	mtapeleka	watapeleka
present	to sit down	ninakalisha (kukalisha)	unakalisha	anakalisha	tunakalisha	mna-kalisha	wana-kalisha
past		nilikalisha	ulikalisha	alikalisha	tulikalisha	mlikalisha	walikalisha
future		nitakalisha	utakalisha	atakalisha	tutakalisha	mtakalisha	watakalisha
present	to sleep	ninalala (kulala)	unalala	analala	tunalala	mnalala	wanalala
past		nililala	ulilala	alilala	tulilala	mlilala	walilala
future		nitalala	utalala	atalala	tutalala	mtalala	watalala
present	to take	ninatwaa (kutwaa)	unatwaa	anatwaa	tunatwaa	mnatwaa	wanatwaa
past		nilitwaa	ulitwaa	alitwaa	tulitwaa	mlitwaa	walitwaa
future		nitatwaa	utatwaa	atatwaa	tutatwaa	mtatwaa	watatwaa
present	to write	ninaandika (kuandika)	unaandika	anaandika	tunaandika	mna-andika	wana-andika
past		niliandika	uliandika	aliandika	tuliandika	mliandika	waliandika
future		nitaandika	utaandika	ataandika	tutaandika	mtaandika	wataandika

Swahili Proverbs

Swahili	English literal
Mtoto akililia	If a child asks for a razor-blade give it to him.
Mtoto wa nyoka ni nyoka.	The child of a snake is a snake.
Tabia ni ngozi.	Habit is like skin.
Hodi hodi naikome mwaka ujao naolewa.	Knock, knock should stop as I am getting married next year. (Used if a woman is engaged and wants no more suitors.)
Ulimi mauma kuliko meno.	The tongue hurts more than teeth.
Tonga si tuwi.	The juice of an immature coconut is not like that of a ripe coconut.
Penye wazee haliharibiki neno.	Where there are old people nothing goes wrong.
Painamapo ndipo painukapo.	Where it slopes down is where it slopes up.
Ngugu mwui afadhali kuwa naye.	A bad brother is better than no brother.
Mwekaji kisasi haambiwi mwerevu.	He who nurses vengeance is not wise.
Msitukane wakunga na uzazi ungalipo.	Do not abuse midwives while child-bearing continues.
Mbio za sakabuni huishia ukingoni.	Running on the roof finishes on the edge.
Kulea mimba si kazi kazi kulea mwana.	It is not hard to nurse a pregnancy but it is hard to bring up a child.
La kunvunda halina ubani.	There is no incense for something rotten.